HTML Quick Reference

Structure Tags

`<! ... >`	Creates a comment
`<HTML>...</HTML>`	Encloses the entire HTML document
`<HEAD>...</HEAD>`	Encloses the head of the HTML document
`<BODY>...</BODY>`	Encloses the body (text and tags) of the HTML document
`<ISINDEX>`	Indicates the document is a gateway script that allows searches

Headings and Titles

`<H1>...</H1>`	Headings 1 through 6
`<H2>...</H2>`	
`<H3>...</H3>`	
`<H4>...</H4>`	
`<H5>...</H5>`	
`<H6>...</H6>`	
`<TITLE>...</TITLE>`	The title of the document

Paragraphs

`<P>...</P>`	A plain paragraph. `</P>` is optional

Links

`<A>...</A>`	Creates a link or anchor
`HREF="..."`	The URL of the document to be linked to this one
`NAME=...`	The name of the anchor

Lists

`<OL>...</OL>`	An ordered (numbered) list
`<UL>...</UL>`	An unordered (bulleted) list
`<MENU>...</MENU>`	A menu list of items
`<DIR>...</DIR>`	A directory listing
`<LI>`	A list item
`<DL>...</DL>`	A definition or glossary list
`<DT>`	A definition term
`<DD>`	The corresponding definition to a definition term

Character Formatting

`<EM>...</EM>`	Emphasis (usually italic)
`<STRONG>...</STRONG>`	Stronger emphasis (usually bold)
`<CODE>...<`	Code (usually
`<KBD>...`	
`<VAR>...</VAR>`	
`<SAMP>...</SAMP>`	Samp.
`<DFN>...</DFN>`	(Proposed) A definition of a term
`<CITE>...</CITE>`	A citation
`<B>...</B>`	Boldface text
`<I>...</I>`	Italic text
`<TT>...</TT>`	Typewriter font

Other Elements

`<HR>`	A horizontal rule line
` `	A line break
`<BLOCKQUOTE>...</BLOCKQUOTE>`	Used for long quotes or citations
`<ADDRESS>...</ADDRESS>`	Signatures or general information about a document's author
`<FONT>...</FONT>`	Change the size of the font for the enclosed text
`SIZE="..."`	The size of the font, from 1 to 7
`<BASEFONT>`	Sets the default size of the font for the current page
`SIZE="..."`	The default size of the font, from 1 to 7

Images

`<IMG>`	Insert an inline image into the document
`ISMAP`	This image is a clickable image map
`SRC="..."`	The URL of the image
`ALT="..."`	A text string that will be displayed in browsers that cannot support images
`ALIGN="..."`	Determines the alignment of the given image
`VSPACE="..."`	The space between the image and the text above or below it
`HSPACE="..."`	The space between the image and the text to its left or right

continues

Forms

`<FORM>...</FORM>`	Indicates a form
`ACTION="..."`	The URL of the script to process this form input.
`METHOD="..."`	How the form input will be sent to the script on the server side. Possible values are `GET` and `POST`.
`ENCTYPE="..."`	Only one value right now: `application/x-www-form-urlencoded`.
`<INPUT>`	An input widget for a form
`TYPE="..."`	The type for this input widget. Possible values are `CHECKBOX`, `HIDDEN`, `RADIO`, `RESET`, `SUBMIT`, `TEXT`, or `IMAGE`.
`NAME="..."`	The name of this item, as passed to the gateway script as part of a name/value pair.
`VALUE="..."`	For a text or hidden widget, the default value; for a checkbox or radio button, the value to be submitted with the form; for Reset or Submit buttons, the label for the button itself.
`SRC="..."`	The source file for an image.
`CHECKED`	For checkboxes and radio buttons, indicates that the widget is checked.
`SIZE="..."`	The size, in characters, of a text widget.
`MAXLENGTH="..."`	The maximum number of characters that can be entered into a text widget.
`ALIGN="..."`	For images in forms, determines how the text and image will align (same as with the `<IMG>` tag).
`<TEXTAREA>...</TEXTAREA>`	Indicates a multiline text entry widget
`NAME="..."`	The name to be passed to the gateway script as part of the name/value pair.
`ROWS="..."`	The number of rows this text area displays.
`COLS="..."`	The number of columns (characters) this text area displays.
`<SELECT>...</SELECT>`	Creates a menu or scrolling list of possible items
`NAME="..."`	The name that is passed to the CGI script as part of the name/value pair.
`SIZE="..."`	The number of elements to display.
`MULTIPLE`	Allows multiple selections from the list.
`<OPTION>`	Indicates an item within a `<SELECT>` widget
`SELECTED`	With this attribute included, the `<OPTION>` will be selected by default in the list.
`VALUE="..."`	The value to submit if this `<OPTION>` is selected when the form is submitted.

Tables

`<TABLE>...</TABLE>`	Creates a table
`BORDER="..."`	Indicates whether the table should be drawn with or without a border.
`<CAPTION>...</CAPTION>`	The caption for the table
`ALIGN="..."`	The position of the caption. Possible values are `TOP` and `BOTTOM`.
`<TR>...</TR>`	A table row
`ALIGN="..."`	The horizontal alignment of the contents of the cells within this row. Possible values are `LEFT`, `RIGHT`, `CENTER`.
`VALIGN="..."`	The vertical alignment of the contents of the cells within this row. Possible values are `TOP`, `MIDDLE`, `BOTTOM`, and `BASELINE` (Netscape only).
`<TH>...</TH>`	A table heading cell
`ALIGN="..."`	The horizontal alignment of the contents of the cell.
`VALIGN="..."`	The vertical alignment of the contents of the cell.
`ROWSPAN="..."`	The number of rows this cell will span.
`COLSPAN="..."`	The number of columns this cell will span.
`NOWRAP`	Do not automatically wrap the contents of this cell.
`<TD>...</TD>`	Defines a table data cell
`ALIGN="..."`	The horizontal alignment of the contents of the cell.
`VALIGN="..."`	Vertical alignment of the contents of the cell
`ROWSPAN="..."`	The number of rows this cell will span.
`COLSPAN="..."`	The number of columns this cell will span.
`NOWRAP`	Do not automatically wrap the contents of this cell.

Here's what people are saying about Laura Lemay's *Teach Yourself Web Publishing with HTML*

"There are some good HTML primers on the Web itself, but it you're like me, you'll find it easier to learn by cracking a book. The best I've found is Laura Lemay's *Teach Yourself Web Publishing with HTML in a Week*."

—Marc Frons, *Business Week*

"Laura Lemay delivers on her title's promise. By following her clear sequence of explanations, examples and exercises, even the absolute Web novice can create serviceable documents within a few days. Better, she moves quickly beyond mechanics to techniques and tools for designing maximally effective and attractive presentations in spite of the medium's limitations."

—Michael K. Stone, *Whole Earth Review*

"Of all the HTML books out right now, I think Lemay's is the best, and I recommend it."

—Nancy McGough, Infinite Ink

"If you are looking for an easy-to-read introduction to HTML, this book is for you. Lemay has a clear understanding of what works and what doesn't and she conveys her thoughts in a concise, orderly fashion."

—Robert Stewart, *The Virtual Mirror*

"If you want to create a Web page, or even if you already have created one, and you want a *great* book to help you understand it all, check out Laura Lemay's *Teach Yourself Web Publishing with HTML in a Week*. I've used mine so much I practically know it by heart!"

—Camille Tillman, Book Stacks Unlimited

"All in all, this is a quality 'do-it-yourself' book for beginners of HTML publishing. The ABCs of HTML are explained clearly, and the exercises are instructive and easy to follow."

—Jim Duber, *Chorus*

"This is a very thorough book on HTML, and quite accurate. Laura Lemay is a good technical writer who explains things well. This is the book I wish I'd had when I started to learn HTML."

—Bob Cunningham, University of Hawaii

"My best recommendation goes to this book by **Laura Lemay**, entitled *Teach Yourself Web Publishing with HTML in a Week*. There is simply no better book available, and many that are much worse than this one. If you study it, you will know more than enough to create stunning Web pages of your own."

—Bob Bickford

"If you want a good book that will help you understand how everything is really working, take a look at Sams Publishing's *Teach Yourself Web Publishing with HTML in a Week*. It is a very well-written book, and it includes all the information in an easy to understand format."

—Ron Loewy, HyperAct, Inc.

"There's a superb new book about HTML called *Teach Yourself Web Publishing with HTML in a Week*...It is very thorough and well-laid out."

—Michael MacDonald

"I think Lemay's first book can take some degree of credit for the growth of the Web itself. I wonder how many of the tens of thousands of home pages created in the past six months have been done by folks with dog-eared copies of *Teach Yourself Web Publishing* within arm's reach.

—Dave Elliott, The Web Academy

About This Book

Here in one volume that you can keep by your desk and read, reference, and squish spiders with, is nearly all the information you need to create your own Web pages—everything from how to write them to how to link them together and how to set up your own Web server and use it to manage forms and create special programs to process them.

In addition, this book provides hints, suggestions, and examples of how to structure your overall presentation—not just the words within each page. This book won't just teach you how to create a Web presentation—it'll teach you how to create a good Web presentation.

Who Should Read This Book

You should read this book if

- ■ You've seen what's out on the Web, and you want to contribute your own content.
- ■ You're representing a company that wants to create an Internet presence, and you're not sure where to start.
- ■ You're an information developer, such as a technical writer, and you want to learn how the Web can help you present your information online.
- ■ You want to make your Web pages interactive with CGI scripts.

How This Book Is Structured

This book is intended to be read and absorbed over the course of a week (and that's a *real* week—seven days—not a business week). On each day, you'll read two chapters that present concepts related to Web presentation design. With this book in hand, you should be able to go from having a simple Web presentation to writing and putting up on the Web a more creative presentation—all this in a week, maybe even less.

Conventions

Note: A Note box presents interesting pieces of information related to the surrounding discussion.

Tip: A Tip box offers advice or teaches an easier way to do something.

Warning: A Warning box advises you about potential problems and helps you steer clear of disaster.

 Input: An Input icon identifies some new HTML code that you can type in yourself.

Output: An Output icon highlights what the same HTML code looks like when viewed by either Netscape or Mosaic.

Teach Yourself
Web Publishing
with HTML 3.0
in a Week

Laura Lemay

201 West 103rd Street
Indianapolis, Indiana 46290

Copyright © 1996 by Sams.net Publishing

SECOND EDITION

International Standard Book Number: 1-57521-064-9

Library of Congress Catalog Card Number: 95-72378

99 98 97 96   4 3 2 1

Interpretation of the printing code: the rightmost double-digit number is the year of the book's printing; the rightmost single-digit, the number of the book's printing. For example, a printing code of 96-1 shows that the first printing of the book occurred in 1996.

Composed in AGaramond and MCPdigital by Macmillan Computer Publishing

Printed in the United States of America

President, Sams Publishing	*Richard K. Swadley*
Publisher, Sams.net Publishing	*George Bond*
Marketing Manager	*John Pierce*
Publishing Manager	*Mark Taber*
Managing Editor	*Cindy Morrow*

Acquisitions Editor
Mark Taber

Development Editor
Fran Hatton

Technical Reviewers
Eric Garrison
George Hoh

Editorial Coordinator
Bill Whitmer

Technical Edit Coordinator
Lynette Quinn

Formatter
Frank Sinclair

Editorial Assistant
Carol Ackerman

Cover Designer
Tim Amrhein

Book Designer
Alyssa Yesh

Production Team Supervisor
Brad Chinn

Production
Carol Bowers
Mona Brown
Michael Brumitt
Charlotte Clapp
Jeanne Clark
George Hanlin
Jason Hand
Mike Henry
Kevin Laseau
Paula Lowell
Brian-Kent Proffitt
Bobbi Satterfield
SA Springer
Susan Van Ness
Mark Walchle
Colleen Williams

Overview

Contents

Appendixes

Acknowledgments

To Sams Publishing, for letting me write my first "real" book.

To the Coca-Cola company, for creating Diet Coke and selling so much of it to me.

To all the folks on the `comp.infosystems.www` newsgroups, the www-talk mailing list, and the Web conference on the WELL, for answering questions and putting up with my late night rants.

And to Eric, for moral support when I was sure I would never make my deadlines (and for encouraging me to go back to work), for accepting that I wasn't going to spend more than ten minutes outside the computer room for two months, and for setting up an enormous amount of UNIX and networking equipment for me to muck with.

About the Author

Laura Lemay

Laura Lemay is a technical writer and confirmed Web addict. Between spending 10 to 12 hours a day in front of a computer and consuming enormous amounts of Diet Coke, she sometimes manages to write a book. She was the author of *Teach Yourself Web Publishing in a Week* and *Teach Yourself More Web Publishing in a Week*, and now consults in just about anything related to Web page writing, design, programming, and Web-related publications systems. Her goal for the remainder of the year is to try to get one of her motorcycles to actually run.

You can send her mail at `lemay@lne.com` or visit her home page at `http://www.lne.com/lemay/`.

Introduction

So you've browsed the Web for a while, and you've seen the sort of stuff that people are putting up on the Net. And you're noticing that more and more stuff is going up all the time, and that more and more people are becoming interested in it. "I want to do that," you think. "How can I do that?" If you have the time and you know where to look, you could find out everything you need to know from the information out on the Web. It's all there; it's all available, and it's all free. Or, you could read this book instead. Here, in one volume that you can keep by your desk to read, reference, and squish spiders with, is nearly all the information you need to create your own Web pages—everything from how to write them to how to link them together to how to set up your own Web server and use it to manage forms and create special programs to process them.

But wait, there's more. This book goes beyond the scope of other books on how to create Web pages, which just teach you the basic technical details such as how to produce a boldface word. In this book, you'll learn why you should be producing a particular effect and when you should use it, as well as how. In addition, this book provides hints, suggestions, and examples of how to structure your overall presentation—not just the words within each page. This book won't just teach you how to create a Web presentation—it'll teach you how to create a good Web presentation.

Also, unlike many other books on this subject, this book doesn't focus on any one computer system. Regardless of whether you're using a PC running Windows, a Macintosh, or some dialect of UNIX (or any other computer system), the concepts in this book will be valuable to you, and you will be able to apply them to your Web pages regardless of your platform of choice.

Sound good? Glad you think so. I thought it was a good idea when I wrote it, and I hope you get as much out of this book reading it as I did writing it.

Who Should Read This Book

Is this book for you? That depends:

- If you've seen what's out on the Web, and you want to contribute your own content, this book is for you.

- If you represent a company that wants to create an Internet "presence" and you're not sure where to start, this book is for you.

- If you're an information developer, such as a technical writer, and you want to learn how the Web can help you present your information online, this book is for you.

- If you're doing research or polling and you're interested in creating a system that allows people to "register" comments or vote for particular suggestions or items, this book is for you.

- If you're just curious about how the Web works, some parts of this book are for you, although you might be able to find what you need on the Web itself.
- If you've never seen the Web before but you've heard that it's really nifty and want to get set up using it, this book isn't for you. You'll need a more general book about getting set up and browsing the Web before moving on to actually producing Web documents yourself.

What This Book Contains

This book is intended to be read and absorbed over the course of a week—and it's a real week, seven days (well, plus a bonus day). On each day you'll read two chapters, which describe one or two concepts related to Web presentation design.

- On Day 1, you get a general overview of the World Wide Web and what you can do with it and come up with a plan for your Web presentation.
- On Day 2, you learn about the basics of Web design and HTML, and how to write simple documents and link them together using hypertext links.
- On Day 3, you do more with HTML, including working with lists and character formatting. You also learn advanced tools that will help you hone your HTML skills.
- Day 4 you learn about the Netscape and Internet Explorer extensions to HTML and how to create tables.
- Day 5 tells you all about adding multimedia capabilities to your Web presentations: using images, sounds, and video to enhance your material.
- Day 6 provides some hints for creating a well-constructed Web presentation, and you explore some examples of Web presentations to get an idea of what sort of work you can do.
- Day 7 introduces more technical issues with coverage of servers and an introduction to CGI scripts.
- Finally, the Bonus Day delves into what it takes to work with forms and image maps, and what you need to know about the HTML 3.0 specifications.

With this book in hand you should be able to go from a simple idea for a Web presentation to writing that presentation and putting it up on the Web—and all this in a week, maybe even less!

What You Need Before You Start

There are seemingly hundreds of books on the market about how to get connected to the Internet, and lots of books about how to use the World Wide Web. This book isn't one of them. I'm assuming that if you're reading this book, you already have a working connection to the Internet, that you have a World Wide Web browser such as Netscape, Mosaic, or Lynx available

to you, and that you've used it at least a couple of times. You should also have at least a passing acquaintance with some other portions of the Internet such as electronic mail, Gopher, and Usenet news, as I may refer to them in general terms in this book. Although you won't need to explicitly use them to work through the content in this book, some parts of the Web may refer to these other concepts.

In other words, you need to have used the Web in order to provide content for the Web. If you have this one simple qualification, then read on!

This book has its own Web site. This site contains updated information about where to find tools and hints and source code for many Web tools you might be interested in incorporating into your own presentations. The site is at `http://www.lne.com/Web/`—check it out!

DAY

1

DAY

1

ONE

The World of
the World
Wide Web

The World of the World Wide Web

A journey of a thousand miles begins with a single step, and here you are at Day 1, Chapter 1, of a journey that will show you how to use HyperText Markup Language to produce documents on the World Wide Web. In this chapter, you learn the following basics:

- ☐ What the World Wide Web is and why it's terribly cool
- ☐ How to use a browser to explore the Web
- ☐ What a Web server is and why you need one
- ☐ What a Uniform Resource Locator is
- ☐ What home pages are used for

If you've already spent time exploring the Web, you may already be familiar with much of the content in this chapter, if not all of it. If so, by all means skip ahead to the next chapter, where you'll find an overview of things to think about when you design and organize your own Web documents.

What Is the World Wide Web?

I have a friend who likes to describe things with lots of meaningful words strung together in a chain, so that it takes several minutes to sort out what he's just said.

If I were he, I'd describe the World Wide Web as a global, interactive, dynamic, cross-platform, distributed, graphical hypertext information system that runs over the Internet. Whew! Unless you understand each of those words and how they fit together, that isn't going to make much sense. (My friend often doesn't make much sense, either.)

So let's take each one of those words and see what they mean in the context of how you'll be using the Web as a publishing medium.

The Web Is a Hypertext Information System

If you've used any sort of basic online help system, you're already familiar with the primary concept behind the World Wide Web: hypertext.

The idea behind hypertext is that instead of reading text in a rigid, linear structure (such as a book), you can easily skip from one point to another. You can get more information, go back, jump to other topics, and navigate through the text based on what interests you at the time.

Online help systems or help stacks such as those provided by Microsoft Windows Help or HyperCard on the Macintosh use hypertext to present information. To get more information

on a topic, just click on that topic. That topic might be a link that takes you to a new screen (or window, or dialog box) which contains that new information. Perhaps there are links on words or phrases that take you to still other screens, and links on those screens that take you even further away from your original topic. Figure 1.1 shows a simple diagram of how that kind of system works.

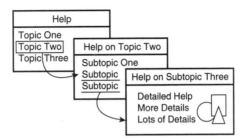

Figure 1.1. *A simple online help system.*

Now imagine that your online help system is linked to another online help system on another application related to yours; for example, your drawing program's help is linked to your word processor's help. Your word processor's help is then linked to an encyclopedia, where you can look up any other concepts that you don't understand. The encyclopedia is hooked into a global index of magazine articles that enables you to get the most recent information on the topics that the encyclopedia covers. The article index is then also linked into information about the writers of those articles, and some pictures of their children. (See Figure 1.2.)

If you had all these interlinked help systems available with every program you bought, you'd rapidly run out of disk space. You might also question whether you needed all this information when all you wanted to know was how to do one simple thing. All that information could be expensive, too.

But if the information didn't take up much disk space, and if it were freely available, and you could get it reasonably quickly anytime you wanted, then things would be more interesting. In fact, the information system might very well end up more interesting than the software you bought in the first place.

That's just what the World Wide Web is: more information than you could ever digest in a lifetime, linked together in various ways, out there on the Net, available for you to browse whenever you want. It's big, and deep, and easy to get lost in. But it's also an immense amount of fun.

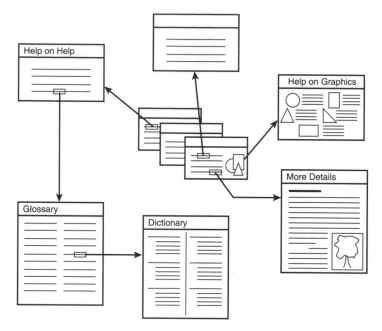

Figure 1.2. *A more complex online help system.*

The Web Is Graphical and Easy To Navigate

One of the best parts of the Web, and arguably the reason it has become so popular, is its ability to display both text and graphics in full color on the same page. Before the Web, using the Internet involved simple text-only connections. You had to navigate the Internet's various services using typed commands and arcane tools. Although there was lots of really exciting information on the Net, it wasn't necessarily pretty to look at.

The Web provides capabilities for graphics, sound, and video to be incorporated with the text Further, the interface is easily navigable—just jump from link to link, from page to page, across sites and servers.

Note: If the Web incorporates so much more than text, why do I keep calling the Web a Hyper*Text* system? Well, if you're going to be absolutely technically correct about it, the Web is not a hypertext system—it's a hyper*media* system. But, on the other hand, one could argue that the Web began as a text-only

system, and much of the content is still text-heavy, with extra bits of media added in as emphasis. There are many very educated people arguing these very points at this moment, and presenting their arguments in papers and discursive rants as educated people like to do. Whatever. I prefer the term hypertext, and it's my book, so I'm going to use it. You know what I mean.

The Web Is Cross-Platform

If you can access the Internet, you can access the World Wide Web. It doesn't matter what system you're running on or whether you think Windows widgets look better than Macintosh widgets or vice versa (or if you think both Mac and Windows people are weenies). The World Wide Web is not limited to any one kind of machine. The Web doesn't care about user-interface wars between companies with too much money, anyway.

You get access to the Web through an application called a *browser,* like Netscape's Navigator or NCSA's Mosaic. I explain more about what the browser actually does later in this chapter. There are lots of browsers out there, for most popular platforms. And once you've got a browser and a connection to the Internet, you've got it made. You're on the Web.

The Web Is Distributed

Information takes up an awful lot of space, particularly when you include images, sounds, and video. To store all the information that the Web provides, you'd need an untold amount of disk space, and managing it would be almost impossible. Imagine being prompted to insert CD-ROM #456 ALP through ALR into your drive when you looked something up in your online encyclopedia and wanted to find out more information about Alpacas.

The Web is successful in providing so much information because that information is distributed globally across thousands of sites, each of which contributes the space for the information it publishes. You, as a consumer of that information, go to that site to view the information. When you're done, you go somewhere else, and your system reclaims the disk space. You don't have to install it, or change disks, or do anything other than point your browser at that site.

The Web Is Dynamic

Because information on the Web is contained on the site that published it, the people who published it in the first place can update it at any time.

If you're browsing that information, you don't have to install a new version of the help system, buy another book, or call technical support to get updated information. Just bring up your browser and check out what's up there.

If you're publishing information on the Web, you can make sure the information you're publishing is up-to-date all the time. You don't have to spend a lot of time re-releasing updated documents. There is no cost of materials. You don't have to get bids on number of copies or quality of output. Color is free. And you won't get calls from hapless customers who have a version of the book that was obsolete four years ago.

An excellent example of how information can be dynamically updated on the Web is the "What's New on the Web" page at NCSA. If you have a Web browser, point it at `http://www.ncsa.uiuc.edu/SDG/Software/Mosaic/Docs/whats-new.html` or see Figure 1.3.

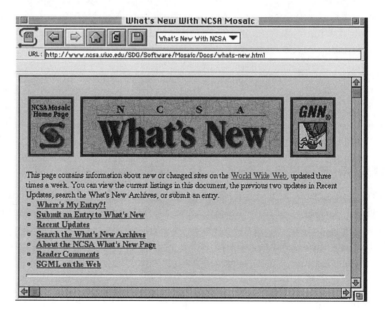

Figure 1.3. *What's New on the Web (from NCSA).*

The NCSA What's New page, which is updated every couple of days, contains descriptions of new Web servers that have appeared on the Net with links to those servers. What's New is often a good place to start browsing the Web because it contains much of the new stuff out there as it appears.

> **Note:** The pictures throughout this book are generally taken from a browser on the Macintosh (Netscape or Mosaic), or using the text-only browser Lynx. The only reason for this is because I'm writing this book on a Macintosh. If you're using Windows or a UNIX system, don't feel left out. As I noted earlier, the glory of the Web is that you see the same information regardless of the platform you're on (although that information might appear slightly differently depending on how the browser formats it). So ignore the buttons and window borders and focus on what's inside the window.

The Web Can Access Many Forms of Internet Information

When the World Wide Web was created, one of the new features it provided was a new Internet protocol for managing hypertext information across the Internet: HTTP, or HyperText Transfer Protocol. HTTP is a simple protocol that allows hypertext documents to be transferred quickly between Web browsers and servers. Unless you are writing your own server, or are overly curious about the innards of the Web, you won't really need to know much more about HTTP than that.

In addition to providing a new system for publishing and distributing information, the World Wide Web is also compatible with the older forms of information distribution.

And there are lots of them: FTP, Gopher, Usenet news, WAIS databases, Telnet, and e-mail. They all use different tools (that all need to be installed separately), and all those tools operate in different ways. It makes for a nice beefy book on How to Use the Internet, but remembering all the tools and how to use them makes exploring the Internet considerably more difficult.

The Web fixes that. Using just one Web browser you can read hypertext Web information, as well as get to files and information contained in these other information systems. And, even better, you can create links to information on those systems just as you would create links to other Web information. It's all seamless and all available through a single application.

To use a Gopher server from a Web browser, use a URL that looks something like this: `gopher://name_of_gopher_server`. For example, Figure 1.4 shows the Gopher server on the WELL, a popular Internet service in San Francisco.

To use FTP from the Web, use a URL that looks like this: `ftp://name_of_site/directory/filename`. You can also use just a directory and your Web server will show you a list of the files, as in Figure 1.5. The figure shows a listing of files from Simtel, a repository of Windows software at `ftp://oak.oakland.edu/SimTel/win3/winsock/`.

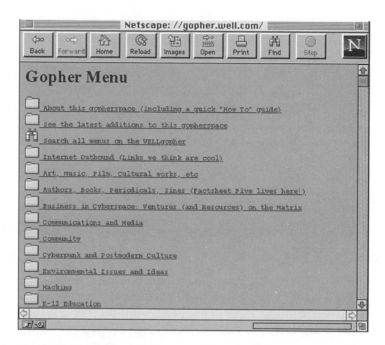

Figure 1.4. *The WELL's Gopher server.*

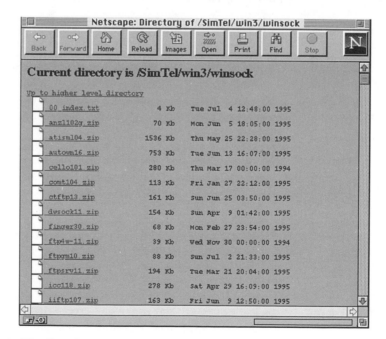

Figure 1.5. *The Simtel FTP Archive.*

You will learn how to use the World Wide Web to get access and to link to other forms of Internet information in Chapter 4, "Putting the Hype in Hypertext: All About Links and URLs."

The Web Is Interactive

The Web is interactive by nature; the act of selecting a link and retrieving another page of information is a form of interactivity. In addition to this simple interactivity, however, the Web enables you to design screens that look like forms. People browsing these screens can select from several choices (radio buttons), fill in information in slots, or select a button to perform a particular operation. You, as the publisher of the form, can then take the information and do whatever you want with it—build another page of information on the fly, add the current information to a database, or display a particular picture. Figure 1.6 shows an example of a simple form for the Surrealist Census (a form you'll create later on in the week):

Figure 1.6. *The Surrealist Census Form.*

In addition to forms, another popular way to interact on the Web is the imagemap. An imagemap is a picture on a page which has several different hot spots—where you click on the image determines what happens next. Imagemaps are commonly used for menus of different locations on a site, such as the one from Netscape's home page (shown in Figure 1.7), but can also be used for online games or other uses. You'll learn how to create imagemaps on the same day you learn how to create forms.

Figure 1.7. *An imagemap-based Menu.*

Who Owns the Web?

No single entity "owns" the World Wide Web. Given the enormous number of independent sites that supply information to the Web, it is impossible for any single organization to set rules or guidelines. There is, however, a World Wide Web (W3) Consortium, based at MIT in the U.S. and INRIA in Europe. The World Wide Web Consortium is an organization of individuals and organizations interested in supporting and defining the languages and protocols that make up the Web (HTTP, HTML, and so on). It also provides products (browsers, servers, and so on) that are freely available to anyone who wants to use them. The W3 Consortium is the closest anyone gets to setting the standards for and enforcing rules about the World Wide Web.

You can visit the Consortium's home page at `http://www.w3.org/`. Figure 1.8 shows that home page.

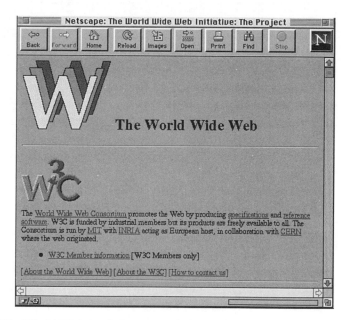

Figure 1.8. *The World Wide Web Consortium's home Page.*

Web Browsers

To access the World Wide Web, you use what is called a *Web browser*. Browsers are sometimes also called *Web clients*, since they get information from a *server*.

Currently the most popular browser for the World Wide Web is Netscape's Navigator, developed by Netscape Communications Corporation. Netscape has become so popular that using Netscape and using the Web have become synonymous to many people. However, despite the fact that Netscape has the lion's share of the market, it is not the only browser on the Web. It is important for you as a Web publisher to make a distinction between the information on the Web and the browser used to view it. (This will become very important later on in this book when you design your own Web pages.) Assuming Netscape is the only browser in use on the Web, and designing your pages accordingly, will limit the audience you can reach with the information you want to present.

A wide array of Web browsers is available for just about every platform you can imagine, including graphical user-interface based systems (Mac, Windows, X11), and text-only for dial-up UNIX connections. Most browsers are freeware or shareware (try before you buy) or, like Netscape, have a lenient licensing policy (Netscape allows you to use its browser for personal use for an evaluation time, after which you are expected to buy it). Usually all you have to do is download them from the Net.

If you get your Internet connection through a commercial online service such as America Online or CompuServe, there are usually Web browsers built into the software for that system as well.

What Does a Browser Do?

The browser's job is twofold: given a pointer to a piece of information on the Net (a URL), it has to be able to access that information or operate in some way based on the contents of that pointer. For hypertext Web documents, this means that the browser must be able to speak to the server using the HTTP protocol. Since the Web can also manage information contained on FTP and Gopher servers, in news postings, in mail, and so on, the browser has to speak the language of those tools as well.

What the browser does most often, however, is deal with Web documents. Each "page" that you load from the Web is a single document, written in a language called HTML (HyperText Markup Language), that includes the text of the document, its structure, and any links to other documents, images, and other media. (You'll learn all about HTML on Days Two and Three, since you need to know it in order to write your own Web pages.)

13

The browser talks to the Web server over the Net and retrieves a document from that server. If the document is an HTML file, it then interprets the HTML code contained in that document and formats and displays the document. If the document contains images or links to other documents, it manages those parts as well.

A Short Overview of Popular Browsers

This section describes a few of the more popular browsers that people are using to view Web documents. These are in no way all the browsers available, and if the browser you're using isn't here, don't feel that you have to use one of these. Whatever browser you have is fine as long as it works for you.

The browsers in this section can only be used if you have a direct Internet connection or a dial-up SLIP or PPP Internet connection. Getting your machine connected to the Internet is beyond the scope of this book, but there are plenty of books out there to help you do so.

If your connection to the Internet is through a commercial online service (AOL, CompuServe, or Prodigy), that system will have its own browsers for you to use and you may or may not be able to use the browsers in this section. Check with your provider.

Also, if the only connection you have to the Internet is through a dial-up text-only UNIX (or other) account, you are limited to using text-only browsers such as Lynx. You will not be able to view documents in color or view graphics online.

Netscape

By far the most popular browser in use on the Web today is Netscape Navigator, from Netscape Communications Corporation.

Netscape is available for Windows, Macintosh, and the X Window System, and if you employ it for personal use, it has a free evaluation period. After you're done evaluating it, you're expected to pay for it, but it's cheap ($40 at the time of this writing). Netscape is well supported and provides up-to-the-minute features. You can get the most recent version of Netscape at `ftp://ftp.netscape.com/`.

Figure 1.9 shows Netscape for the Macintosh.

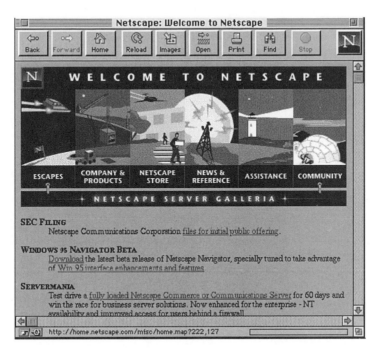

Figure 1.9. *Netscape (for Macintosh).*

NCSA Mosaic

A few scant months ago, Mosaic had Netscape's place on the Web as the most popular browser. Indeed, Mosaic was the first of the full-color graphical browsers and is usually credited with making the Web as popular as it is today.

Mosaic is provided by NCSA at the University of Illinois, with several supported commercial versions available from companies such as Spry and Spyglass. Mosaic comes in versions for X11 (UNIX), MS Windows, and Macintosh; each version is colloquially called XMosaic, WinMosaic, and MacMosaic, respectively. The development support for the X version tends to be somewhat ahead of the PC and Macintosh versions.

Figure 1.10 shows NCSA Mosaic for the Macintosh.

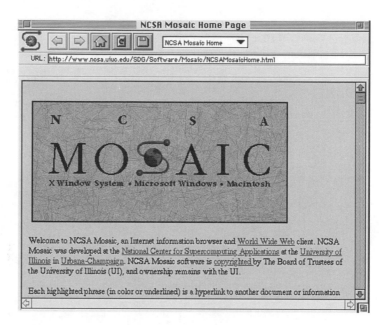

Figure 1.10. *Mosaic (for Macintosh).*

You can get all three versions of NCSA Mosaic via FTP at `ftp://ftp.ncsa.uiuc.edu/Mosaic`, although because the server is extremely busy, it may be difficult to connect. Try 5 p.m. and weekends.

Lynx

Lynx ("links," get it?), developed by the University of Kansas, is an excellent browser for text-only Internet connections such as dial-up UNIX accounts. It requires VT100 terminal emulation, which most terminal programs should support. Lynx enables you to use arrow keys to select and navigate links within Web documents.

A version of Lynx is also available for DOS systems. Lynx is available at `ftp://ftp2.cc.ukans.edu/pub/lynx`. Figure 1.11 shows Lynx running on a UNIX system.

Figure 1.11. *Lynx.*

MacWeb and WinWeb

TradeWare (formerly EINet) provides the browsers MacWeb and WinWeb for Macintosh and Windows, respectively. Both are in alpha release, but both provide many features (such as forms) and both tend to be smaller, faster, and more stable than their counterparts from Mosaic.

MacWeb is available from `ftp://ftp.einet.net/einet/mac/macweb`, and WinWeb from `ftp://ftp.einet.net/einet/pc/winweb`. Figure 1.12 shows MacWeb.

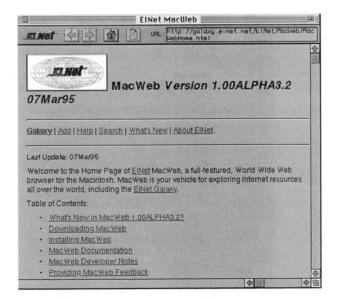

Figure 1.12. *MacWeb.*

Internet Explorer

Internet Explorer (Figure 1.13) appeared on the scene in August 1995 with Microsoft's introduction of Windows 95. Originally based on Mosaic technology, Internet Explorer—currently in version 2.0—has very rapidly evolved into a full-featured browser that may eventually challenge Netscape Navigator for world domination—at least the world of Windows 95. If you're running Windows 95, you can download Internet Explorer for free from The Microsoft Network or on the Web at `http://www.microsoft.com/windows/ie/iexlorer.htm`.

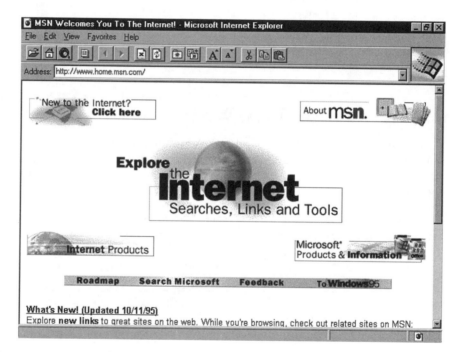

Figure 1.13. *Microsoft's Internet Explorer for Windows 95.*

Web Servers

To publish documents on the Web, you need some sort of server, which feeds documents and media to the browsers that request them. Whenever you point your browser at a Web document, the browser talks to the server to get at that document. Since the Web can read files from services such as FTP or Gopher, you can use those tools to serve Web documents. (Most browsers can figure out that they're reading a hypertext document even if it doesn't

come over the wire specifically using HTTP.) The best way to publish Web pages, however, is through the use of a dedicated Web server.

A Web server uses the HTTP protocol to listen for requests for files from browsers. It then delivers the files and any included images. Web servers can also be set up to handle commands sent back from the browser; for example, in the case of forms or other interactive Web pages. You can't do that with FTP or Gopher.

Many Web servers are available for whatever system you happen to be running. I describe more about the available servers on Day Seven.

Uniform Resource Locators

A URL is a pointer to some bit of data on the Web, be it a Web document, a file on FTP or Gopher, a posting on Usenet, or a data record in a database. When someone tells you to point your browser at a particular location on the Web, he or she will give you a URL that indicates where you're pointing. You've seen several URLs already in this chapter; you've been using them to get to the pages I've been pointing out along the way.

The URL provides a universal, consistent method for finding and accessing information, not necessarily for you, but mostly for your Web browser. (If they were for you they would be in a format that would make them easier to remember.) If someone tells you to check out a particular URL, you use the Open command (sometimes called Go or Open URL), then type in the URL (or copy and paste it if you can), and the browser goes to the document contained at that URL.

Besides this immediate use of URLs, you also use URLs when you create a hypertext link within a document to another document. So, any way you look at it, URLs are important to how you and your browser get around on the Web.

URLs contain information about how to get at the information (what protocol: FTP, gopher, HTTP), the Internet host name to look on (`www.ncsa.uiuc.edu`, or `ftp.apple.com`, or `netcom16.netcom.com`, and so on), and the directory or other location on that site to find the file. There are also special URLs for things like sending mail to people (called *mailto* URLs), and for using the Telnet program.

You'll learn all about URLs and what each part of them means as the book progresses.

Home Pages

You'll see the term *home page* a lot when you browse the Web, used in several different ways. If you are reading and browsing the Web, the home page is the Web page that loads when

you start your browser. Each browser has its own home page, which is often the same page for the site that developed the browser. (For example, the Mosaic home page is at NCSA, and the Lynx home page is at the University of Kansas.)

Within your browser you can change the default home page to start up any page you want—a common tactic I've seen many people use it to create a simple page of links to other interesting places or pages that they visit a lot. The procedure for changing your home page varies from browser to browser, so I won't explain it here. See the documentation that came with your browser for more information on changing your local home page.

The second use of a home page is more important to people publishing information on the Web—and since you bought this book, I assume you are one of those people. As a provider of information to the Web, your home page is the entry point to the pages you've provided. Your home page, therefore, will provide some information about what your server contains or what interrelated information it contains via links.

The home page you provide for your pages may contain a menu of items available deeper within your web, an index to the contents of the server, or some other general information. For example, Figure 1.14 shows a typical home page for a company, in this case, for Adobe Systems Incorporated.

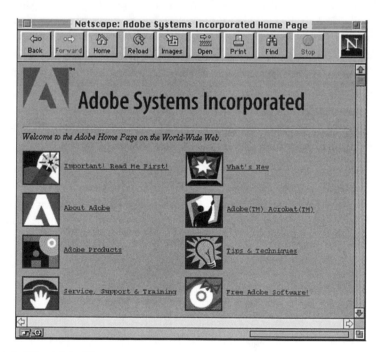

Figure 1.14. *The Adobe Home Page.*

Summary

In this chapter you've learned the basics of what the World Wide Web is, how it can be used, why it's useful, and the various features and terminology used to describe the Web and its tools. In particular, after reading this chapter, you should be able to use your browser to open any URL (and know what a URL is), know the difference between a browser and a server (and name several available browsers), and know what a home page is and how to recognize one in the wild.

Q&A

Q I use Gopher a lot. How is the Web different?

A Although Gopher and the Web are similar in the sense that they both distribute information to the Internet in a wide-spread and easily browsable fashion, they differ in their philosophy. Gopher provides information in a strict menu fashion: you either have an index or a document, so you search the indexes to find the information you want, and then read or download the document.

With the Web, everything is a page, and everything on that page can potentially be linked to other pages. There isn't any significant difference between indexes and documents on the Web; an index can be a document, and vice versa. Also, since you can get to Gopher on the Web, you can look at Gopher indexes and documents using the Web, too.

The Web also has the significant advantage of allowing mixed text and graphics on each page. Thus, the Web is less of a huge information kiosk, as Gopher tends to be, and more of a huge interactive hyperlinked magazine.

Q Why would anyone use a text-only browser like Lynx when there are graphical browsers available?

A You need a special Internet connection in order to use a graphical browser on the Web. If your machine isn't directly hooked up to the Internet (for example, on a network at work or school), you'll need to use a modem with a special account to make your system think it's on the Net, or an account with a commercial online service. These special accounts can be quite expensive, even in areas where there are a lot of Internet service providers. Even then, unless you have a very fast modem, Web pages can take a long time to load, particularly if there are lots of graphics on the page.

Lynx is the ideal solution for people who either don't have a direct Internet connection or don't want to take the time to use the Web graphically. It's fast and it enables you to get hold of just about everything on the Web; indirectly, yes, but it's there.

2

Get Organized

DAY

ONE

When you write a book, a paper, an article, or even a memo, you usually don't just jump right in with the first sentence and then write it through to the end. Same goes with the visual arts—you don't normally start from the top left corner of the canvas or page and work your way down to the bottom right.

A better way to write or draw or design a work is to do some planning beforehand—to know what it is you're going to do and what you're trying to accomplish, and to have a general idea or rough sketch of the structure of the piece before you jump in and work on it.

Just as with more traditional modes of communication, writing and designing Web pages takes some amount of planning and thought before you start flinging text and graphics around and linking them wildly to each other. Perhaps even more so, because trying to apply the rules of traditional writing or design to online hypertext often results in documents that are either difficult to understand and navigate online or that simply don't take advantage of the features that hypertext provides. Poorly organized Web documents are also difficult to revise or to expand.

In this chapter I describe some of the things you should think about before you jump in and start developing your Web pages. Specifically, you

- ☐ Learn the difference between a Web presentation, a Web page, and a Web document
- ☐ Think about the sort of information (content) you want to put on the Web
- ☐ Set your goals for the presentation
- ☐ Organize your content into main topics
- ☐ Come up with a general structure for pages and topics

After you have an overall idea of how you're going to construct your Web pages, you'll be ready to actually start writing and designing those pages tomorrow in Chapter 3, "Begin with the Basics."

Anatomy of a Web Presentation

First, let's look at some simple terminology that you'll be using throughout this book. You need to know what the following terms mean and how they apply to the body of work you're developing for the Web:

- ☐ Web presentations
- ☐ Web pages or documents
- ☐ Home pages

A Web *presentation* consists of one or more Web *pages* containing text and graphics, linked together in a meaningful way, which, as a whole, describe a body of information or create an overall consistent effect. (See Figure 2.1.)

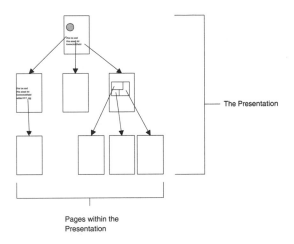

The Presentation

Pages within the
Presentation

Figure 2.1. *Web presentations and pages.*

Web pages are sometimes called Web *documents;* I refer to them as both pages and documents interchangeably in this book. Unlike in the hard copy world, where a document is a single body of work such as a book and a page is an element within that work, the terms *page* and *document* refer to the same thing on the Web: a single file on disk, retrieved and formatted by a Web browser.

The *home page*, as I mentioned briefly in the last chapter, is the "top" of your set of Web pages. It is the place where most people start exploring your Web presentation, and it is the URL of that home page you will give people when you tell them to check out your Web site. (See Figure 2.2.)

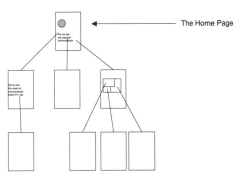

The Home Page

Figure 2.2. *The home page.*

The home page generally contains an overview of the content available from that starting point, often in the form of a table of contents. Although the home page usually contains a more general overview of specific information contained on other pages, if your content is small enough you may very well include everything on that single home page.

What Do You Want to Do on the Web?

This may seem like a silly question. You wouldn't have bought this book if you didn't have some idea of what you want to put online already. But maybe you don't really know what it is you want to put up on the Web, or you have a vague idea but nothing concrete. Maybe you just want to do something similar to some other Web page you've seen that you thought was particularly cool.

What you want to put on the Web is what I'll refer to throughout this book as your *content*. Content is a general term that can refer to text, or graphics, or media, or interactive forms, or anything. If you were to tell someone what your Web pages are "about," you would be describing your content.

What sort of content can you put on the Web? Just about anything you want to. Here are some of the kinds of content that are popular on the Web right now:

- ☐ **Personal Information.** You can communicate everything anyone could ever want to know about you and how incredibly marvelous you are—your hobbies, your resume, your picture, things you've done.

- ☐ **Hobbies or Special Interests.** A Web document could contain information about a particular topic or hobby or something you're interested in; for example, music, *Star Trek*, motorcycles, cult movies, hallucinogenic mushrooms, or upcoming concerts in your city.

- ☐ **Publications.** Newspapers, magazines, and other publications lend themselves particularly well to the Web, and they have the advantage of being more immediate and easier to update than their print counterparts.

- ☐ **Company Profiles.** This could offer information about what a company does, where it is located, job openings, data sheets, white papers, marketing collateral, who to contact; such a page might even present demonstration software, if that's what the company does.

- ☐ **Online Documentation.** The term *online documentation* can refer to everything from quick reference cards to full reference documentation to interactive tutorials or training modules. And it doesn't have to refer to product documentation; anything task-oriented (changing the oil in your car, making a soufflé, creating landscape portraits in oil) could be described as online documentation.

- **Shopping Catalogs.** If your company offers items for sale, making your lists available on the Web is a quick and easy way to let your customers know what you have available and your prices—and if prices change, you can just update your Web documents to reflect that. With interactive forms you can even let your readers order your product online.
- **Polling and Opinion Gathering.** Interactivity and forms on the Web allow you to get feedback on nearly any topic from your readers, including opinion polls, suggestion boxes, comments on your Web pages or your products, and so on.
- **Anything Else that Comes to Mind.** Hypertext fiction, online toys, media archives, collaborative art... anything!

The Web is limited only by what you want to do with it. In fact, if what you want to do with it isn't in this list, or seems especially wild or half-baked, then that's an excellent reason to try it. The most interesting Web pages out there are the ones that stretch the boundaries of what the Web is supposed to be capable of.

If you really have no idea of what to put up on the Web, don't feel that you have to stop here, put this book away, and come up with something before continuing. Maybe by reading through this book you'll get some ideas (and this book will be useful even if you don't have ideas). I've personally found that the best way to come up with ideas is to spend an afternoon browsing on the Web itself and exploring what other people have done.

Set Your Goals

What do you want people to be able to accomplish in your presentation? Are they looking for specific information on how to do something? Are they going to read through each page in turn, going on only when they're done with the page they're on? Are they just going to start at your home page and wander aimlessly around, exploring your "world" until they get bored and go somewhere else?

As an exercise, come up with a list of several goals that your readers might have for your Web pages. The clearer your goals, the better.

For example, say you were creating a Web presentation describing the company where you work. Some people reading that presentation may want to know about job openings. Others may want to know where you're actually located. Still others may have heard that your company makes technical white papers available over the Net and they want to download the most recent version of a particular one. Each of these is a valid goal, and you should list each one.

For a shopping catalog Web presentation, you might only have a few goals: to allow your readers to browse the items you have for sale by name or by price, and to order specific items once they're done browsing.

For a personal or special interest home page you may have only a single goal: to allow your reader to browse and explore the information you've provided.

The goals do not have to be lofty ("this Web presentation will bring about world peace") or even make much sense to anyone except you. Still, coming up with goals for your Web documents equips you to design, organize, and write your Web pages specifically to reach those goals. Goals also help you resist the urge to obscure your content with extra information.

Break Up Your Content into Main Topics

With your goals in mind, now try to organize your content into main topics or sections, chunking related information together under a single topic. Sometimes the goals you came up with in the previous section and your list of topics will be closely related. For example, if you're putting together a Web page for a bookstore, the goal of being able to order books fits nicely under a topic called, appropriately, "Ordering Books."

You don't have to be exact at this point in development; your goal here is just to try to come up with an idea of what, specifically, you'll be describing in your Web pages. You can organize things better later, as you write the actual pages.

For example, say you were designing a Web presentation about how to tune your car. This is a simple example, since tune-ups consist of a concrete set of steps that fit neatly into topic headings. In this example, your topics might be

- ☐ Change the oil and oil filter
- ☐ Check and adjust engine timing
- ☐ Check and adjust valve clearances
- ☐ Check and replace the spark plugs
- ☐ Check fluid levels, belts, and hoses

Don't worry about the order of the steps, or how you're going to get your reader to go from one section to another. Just list the things you want to describe in your presentation.

How about a less task-oriented example? Say you wanted to create a set of Web pages about a particular rock band because you're a big fan and you're sure there are other fans out there who would benefit from your extensive knowledge. Your topics might be

- ☐ The history of the band
- ☐ Biographies of each of the band members
- ☐ A "discography"—all the albums and singles the band has released

- ☐ Selected lyrics
- ☐ Images of album covers
- ☐ Information about upcoming shows and future products

You can come up with as many topics as you want, but try to keep each topic reasonably short. If a single topic seems too large, try to break it up into subtopics. If you have too many small topics, try to group them together into some sort of more general topic heading. For example, if you were creating an online encyclopedia of poisonous plants, having individual topics for each plant would be overkill; you could just as easily group each plant name under a letter of the alphabet (A, B, C, and so on) and use each letter as a topic. That's assuming, of course, that your readers will be looking up information in your encyclopedia alphabetically. If they want to look up poisonous plants using some other method, then you would have to come up with different topics.

Your goal is to have a set of topics that are roughly the same size and that group together related bits of the information you have to present.

Ideas for Organization and Navigation

At this point you should have a good idea about what you want to talk about, and a list of topics. The next step is to actually start structuring the information you have into a set of Web pages. But before you do that, consider some "standard" structures that have been used in other help systems and online tools. This section describes some of those structures, their various features, and some important considerations, including

- ☐ The kinds of information that work well for each structure
- ☐ How readers find their way through the content of each structure type to find what they need
- ☐ How to make sure readers can figure out where they are within your documents (context) and find their way back to a known position

Think, as you read this section, how your information might fit into one of these forms, or how you can combine these forms to create a new structure for your Web presentation.

Note: Many of the forms I describe in this section were drawn from a book called *Designing and Writing Online Documentation* by William K. Horton (John Wiley & Sons, 1990). Although Horton's book was written primarily for technical writers and developers working specifically with online help systems,

it's a great book for ideas on structuring documents and for dealing with hypertext information in general. If you start doing a lot of work with the Web, you might want to pick up this book; it provides a lot of insight beyond what I have to offer.

Hierarchies

Probably the easiest and most logical way to structure your Web documents is in a hierarchical or menu fashion, illustrated in Figure 2.3. Hierarchies and menus lend themselves especially well to online and hypertext documents. Most online help systems, for example, are hierarchical. You start with a list or menu of major topics; selecting one leads you to a list of subtopics, which then leads you to discussion about a particular topic. Different help systems have different levels, of course, but most follow this simple structure.

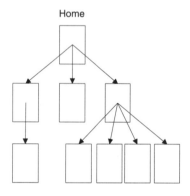

Figure 2.3. *Hierarchical organization.*

In a hierarchical organization, it is easy for readers to know their position in the structure; choices are to move up for more general information, or down for more specific information. Providing a link back to the top level enables your reader to get back to some known position quickly and easily.

In hierarchies, the home page provides the most general overview to the content below it. The home page also defines the main links for the pages further down in the hierarchy.

For example, a Web presentation about gardening might have a home page with the topics shown in Figure 2.4.

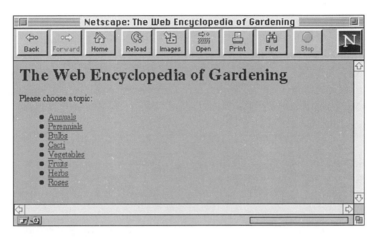

Figure 2.4. *Gardening home page*

If you selected Fruits, you would then be linked "down" to a page about fruits (Figure 2.5). From there you can go back to the home page or select another link and go further down into more specific information about particular fruits.

Figure 2.5. *Fruits.*

Selecting Soft Fruits takes you to yet another menu-like page, where you have still more categories to choose from (Figure 2.6). From there you can go up to Fruits, back to the home page, or down to one of the choices in this menu.

Note that each level has a consistent interface (up, down, back to index), and that each level has a limited set of choices for basic navigation. Hierarchies are structured enough that the chance of getting lost is minimal. (This is especially true if you provide clues about where "up" is; for example, a link that says "Up to Soft Fruits" as opposed to just "Up.") Additionally, if you organize each level of the hierarchy and avoid overlap between topics (and the content you have lends itself to a hierarchical organization), hierarchies can be an easy way to find particular bits of information. If that was one of your goals for your readers, using a hierarchy may work particularly well.

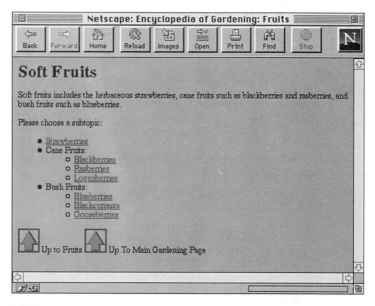

Figure 2.6. *Soft fruits.*

Avoid including too many levels and too many choices, however, as you can easily annoy your reader. Too many menu pages results in "voice mail syndrome." After having to choose from too many menus you forget what it was you originally wanted, and you're too annoyed to care. Try to keep your hierarchy two to three levels deep, combining information on the pages at the leaf nodes of the hierarchy if necessary.

Linear

Another way to organize your documents is to use a linear or sequential organization, much like printed documents are written. In a linear structure, illustrated in Figure 2.7, the home page is the title, or introduction, and each page follows sequentially from that structure. In a strict linear structure, there are links that move from one page to another, typically forward and back. You may also want to include a link to "Home" that takes you quickly back to the first page.

Context is generally easy to figure out in a linear structure simply because there are so few places to go.

A linear organization is very rigid and limits your readers' freedom to explore and your freedom to present information. Linear structures are good for putting material online when the information also has a very linear structure offline (such as short stories, step-by-step instructions, or computer-based training), or when you explicitly want to prevent your reader from skipping around.

For example, consider teaching someone how to make cheese using the Web. Cheese-making is a complex process that involves several steps that must be followed in a specific order.

Home

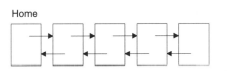

Figure 2.7. *Linear organization.*

Describing this process using Web pages lends itself to a linear structure rather well. When navigating a set of Web pages on this subject, you would start with the home page, which might have a summary or an overview of the steps to follow. Then, using the link for "forward," move on to the first step, "Choosing the Right Milk"; to the next step, "Setting and Curdling the Milk"; all the way through to the last step, "Curing and Ripening the Cheese." If you needed to review at any time, you could use the link for "back." Since the process is so linear, there would be little need for links that branch off from the main stem or links that join together different steps in the process.

Linear with Alternatives

You can soften the rigidity of a linear structure by allowing the reader to deviate from the main path. For example, you could have a linear structure with alternatives that branch out from a single point. (See Figure 2.8.) The off-shoots can then rejoin the main branch at some point further down, or they can continue down their separate tracks until they each come to an "end."

For example, say you had an installation procedure for a software package that was similar in most ways, regardless of the computer type, except for one step. At that point in the linear installation, you could branch out to cover each system, as shown in Figure 2.9.

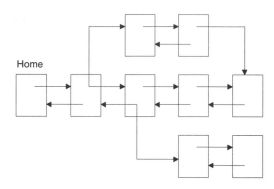

Home

Figure 2.8. *Linear with alternatives.*

Figure 2.9. *Different steps for different systems.*

After the system-specific part of the installation, you could then link back to the original branch and continue on with the generic installation.

In addition to branching from a linear structure, you could also provide links that allow readers to skip forward or back in the chain if they need to review a particular step or if they already understand some content. (See Figure 2.10.)

Combination of Linear and Hierarchical

A popular form of document organization on the Web is a combination of a linear structure and a hierarchical one, shown in Figure 2.11. This structure occurs most often when very structured but linear documents are put online; the popular FAQ (Frequently Asked Questions) files use this structure.

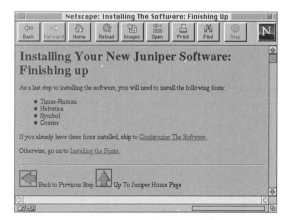

Figure 2.10. *Skip ahead or back.*

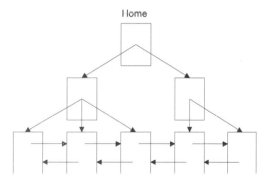

Figure 2.11. *Combination of linear and hierarchical.*

The combination of linear and hierarchical documents works well as long as there are appropriate clues regarding context. Because the reader can either move up and down OR forward and back, it's easy to lose one's mental positioning in the hierarchy when one crosses hierarchical boundaries by moving forward or back.

For example, say you were putting the Shakespearean play *Macbeth* online as a set of Web pages. In addition to the simple linear structure that the play provides, you could create a hierarchical table of contents and summary of each act linked to appropriate places within the text, something like that shown in Figure 2.12.

Because this is both a linear and hierarchical structure, on each page of the script you provide links to go forward, back, return to beginning, and up. But what is the context for going up?

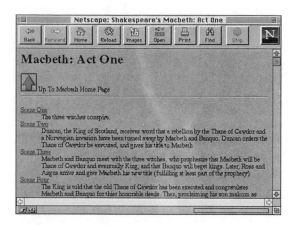

Figure 2.12. Macbeth *hierarchy.*

If you've just come down into this page from an Act summary, the context makes sense. "Up" means go back to the summary you just came from.

But say you went down from a summary, and then went forward, crossing an act boundary (say from Act 1 to Act 2). Now what does "up" mean? The fact that you're moving up to a page that you may not have seen before is disorienting given the nature of what you expect from a hierarchy. Up and down are supposed to be consistent.

Consider two possible solutions:

☐ Do not allow "forward" and "back" links across hierarchical boundaries. In this case, in order to read from Act 1 to Act 2 in *Macbeth*, you would have to move up in the hierarchy and then back down into Act 2.

☐ Provide more context in the link text. Instead of just "Up" or an icon for the link that moves up in the hierarchy, include a description as to where you're moving.

Web

A web is a set of documents with little or no actual overall structure; the only thing tying each page together is a link. (See Figure 2.13.) The reader drifts from document to document, following the links around.

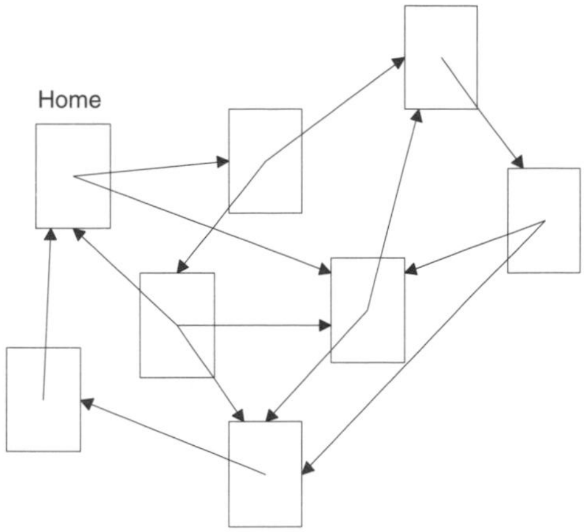

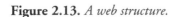

Figure 2.13. *A web structure.*

Web structures tend to be free-flowing and allow the reader to wander aimlessly through the content. Web structures are excellent for content that is intended to be meandering or unrelated, or when you want to encourage browsing. The World Wide Web itself is, of course, a giant web structure.

An example of content organized in a web structure might be a set of virtual "rooms" created using Web pages. If you've ever played an old text-adventure game like Zork or Dungeon, or if you've used a MUD (Multi-User Dungeon), you are familiar with this kind of environment.

In the context of a Web presentation, the environment is organized so that each page is a specific location (and usually contains a description of that location). From that location you can "move" in several different directions, exploring the environment much in the way you would move from room to room in a building in the real world (and getting lost just as easily). For example, the initial home page might look something like what's shown in Figure 2.14.

From that page you can then explore one of the links, say, to go into the building, which would take you to the page shown in Figure 2.15.

Each room has a set of links to each "adjacent" room in the environment. By following the links, you can explore the rooms in the environment.

The problem with web organizations is that it's too easy to get lost in them—just as you might in the "world" you were exploring in the example. Without any overall structure to the content, it's difficult to figure out the relationship between where you are and where you're going, and, often, where you've been. Context is difficult, and often the only way to find your way back out of a Web structure is to retrace your steps. Web structures can be extremely disorienting and immensely frustrating if you have a specific goal in mind.

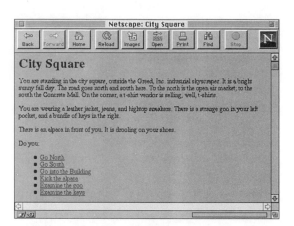

Figure 2.14. *The home page for a Web-based virtual environment.*

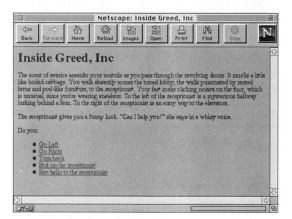

Figure 2.15. *Another page in the Web environment.*

To solve the problem of disorientation, you can use clues on each page. Two ideas:

☐ Provide a way out. "Return to home page" is an excellent link.

☐ Include a map of the overall structure on each page, with a "you are here" indication somewhere in the map. It doesn't have to be an actual visual map, but providing some sort of context will go a long way towards preventing your readers from getting lost.

Storyboarding Your Web Presentation

The next step in planning your Web presentation is to figure out what content goes on what page, and to come up with some simple links for navigation between those pages.

If you're using one of the structures described in the previous section, much of the organization may arise from that structure, in which case this section will be easy. If you want to combine different kinds of structures, however, or if you have a lot of content that needs to be linked together in sophisticated ways, sitting down and making a specific plan of what goes where will be incredibly useful later on as you develop and link each individual page.

What Is Storyboarding and Why Do I Need It?

Storyboarding a presentation is a concept borrowed from filmmaking in which each scene and each individual camera shot is sketched and roughed out in the order in which it occurs in the movie. Storyboarding provides an overall structure and plan to the film that allows the director and his staff to have a distinct idea of where each individual shot fits into the overall movie.

The storyboarding concept works quite well for developing Web pages as well. The storyboard provides an overall rough outline of what the presentation will look like when it's done, including which topics go on which pages, the primary links, maybe even some conceptual idea of what sort of graphics you'll be using and where they will go. With that representation in hand, you can develop each page in turn without trying to remember exactly where that page fits into the overall presentation and its often complex relationships among other pages.

In the case of really large sets of documents, a storyboard allows different people to develop different portions of the same Web presentation. With a clear storyboard, you can minimize duplication of work and reduce the amount of contextual information each individual person needs to remember.

For smaller or simpler Web presentations, or presentations with a simple logical structure, storyboarding may be unnecessary. But for larger and more complex projects, the existence of a storyboard can save enormous amounts of time and frustration. If you can't keep all the parts of your content and their relationships in your head, consider doing a storyboard.

So what does a storyboard for a Web presentation look like? It can be as simple as a couple of sheets of paper. Each sheet can represent a page, with a list of topics that each page will describe and some thoughts about the links that page will include. I've seen storyboards for

very complex hypertext systems that involved a really large bulletin board, index cards, and string. Each index card had a topic written on it, and the links were represented by string tied on pins from card to card. (See Figure 2.16.)

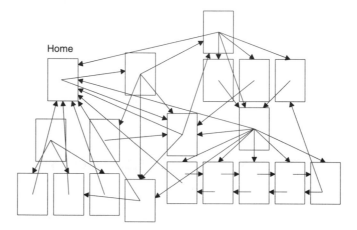

Home

Figure 2.16. *A complex storyboard.*

The point of a storyboard is that it organizes your Web pages in a way that works for you. If you like index cards and string, work with it. If a simple outline on paper or on the computer works better, use that instead.

Hints for Storyboarding

Some things to think about when developing your storyboard:

☐ Which topics will go on each page?

A simple rule of thumb is to have each topic represented by a single page. But if you have a large number of topics, maintaining and linking them can be a daunting task. Consider combining smaller, related topics onto a single page instead. But don't go overboard and put everything on one page; your reader still has to download your document over the Net. It's better to have several medium-sized pages (say, the size of two to ten pages in your word processor) than to have one monolithic page or hundreds of little tiny pages.

☐ What are the primary forms of navigation between pages?

What links will you need for your reader to navigate from page to page? These are the main links in your document that allow your reader to accomplish the goals you defined in the first section. Links for forward, back, up, down, or home all fall under the category of primary navigation.

- [ ] What alternative forms of navigation are you going to provide?

    In addition to the simple navigation links, some Web presentations contain extra information that is parallel to the main Web content, such as a glossary of terms, an alphabetical index of concepts, or a credits page. Consider these extra forms of information when designing your plan and think about how you are going to link them into the main content.

- [ ] What will you put on your home page?

    Since the home page is the starting point for the rest of the information in your presentation, consider what sort of information you're going to put on the home page. A general summary of what's to come? A list of links to other topics?

- [ ] Review your goals.

    As you design the framework for your Web presentation, keep your goals in mind, and make sure you are not obscuring your goals with extra information or content.

Summary

Designing a Web presentation, like designing a book outline, a building plan, or a painting, can sometimes be a complex and involved process. Having a plan before beginning can help you keep the details straight and help you develop the finished product with fewer false starts. In this chapter, you've learned how to put together a simple plan and structure for creating a set of Web pages, including

- [ ] Deciding what sort of content to present
- [ ] Coming up with a set of goals for that content
- [ ] Deciding on a set of topics
- [ ] Organizing and storyboarding the presentation

With that plan in place, you can now move on to the next few chapters and learn the specifics of how to write individual Web pages, create links between them, and add graphics and media to enhance the presentation for your audience.

Q&A

Q This all seems like an awful lot of work. All I want to do is make something simple, and you're telling me I have to have goals and topics and storyboards.

A If you are doing something simple, then no, you won't need to do much, if any, of the stuff I recommend in this chapter. But once you're talking about two or three interlinked pages or more, it really helps to have a plan before you start. If you just

dive in you may discover that keeping everything straight in your head is too difficult. And the result may not be what you expected, making it hard for people to get the information that they need out of your presentation, and difficult for you to reorganize it so that it makes sense. Having a plan before you start can't hurt, and it may save you time in the long run.

Q **You've talked a lot in this chapter about organizing topics and pages, but you've said nothing about the design and layout of individual pages.**

A I discuss that later in this book, after you've learned more about the sorts of layout HTML (the language used for Web pages) can do, and the stuff that it just can't do. There's a whole chapter and more about page layout and design on Day Six: Chapter 11, "Writing and Designing Web Pages: Do's and Don'ts."

Q **What if I don't like any of the basic structures you talked about in this chapter?**

A Then design your own. As long as your readers can find what they want or do what you want them to do, there are no rules that say you MUST use a hierarchy or a linear structure. I only presented those structures as potential ideas for organizing your Web pages.

DAY

2

3

Begin with the Basics

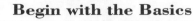

So after finishing up yesterday's discussion, with lots of text to read and concepts to digest, you're probably wondering when you're actually going to get to write an actual Web page. That is, after all, why you bought the book. Welcome to Day 2! Today you'll get to create Web pages, learn about HTML, the language for writing WWW hypertext documents, and specifically learn about the following things:

- ☐ What HTML is and why you have to use it
- ☐ What you can and cannot do when you design HTML documents
- ☐ HTML tags: what they are and how to use them
- ☐ Tags for overall document structure: `<HTML>`, `<HEAD>`, `<BODY>`
- ☐ Tags for titles and headings, and paragraphs: `<TITLE>`, `<H1>`...`<H6>`, `<P>`
- ☐ Tags for comments

What HTML Is...and What It Isn't

There's just one more thing to note before you dive into actually writing Web pages: you should know what HTML is, what it can do, and most specifically what it can't do.

HTML stands for HyperText Markup Language. HTML is based on SGML (the Standard Generalized Markup Language), a much bigger document-processing system. SGML is used to describe the general structure of various kinds of documents. It is not a page description language like PostScript, nor is it a language that can be easily generated from your favorite page layout program. The primary focus of SGML, and therefore HTML, is the content of the document, not its appearance. This section explains a little bit more about that.

HTML Describes the Structure of a Document

HTML, by virtue of its SGML heritage, is a language for describing *structured documents*. The theory behind this is that most documents have common elements—for example, titles, paragraphs, or lists—and if you define a set of elements that a document has before you start writing, you can label those parts of the document with the appropriate names. (See Figure 3.1.)

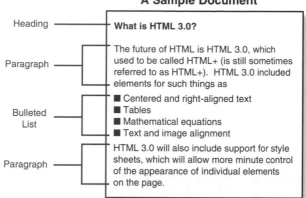

A Sample Document

Heading ——— **What is HTML 3.0?**

Paragraph ——— The future of HTML is HTML 3.0, which
used to be called HTML+ (is still sometimes
referred to as HTML+). HTML 3.0 included
elements for such things as

Bulleted
List
■ Centered and right-aligned text
■ Tables
■ Mathematical equations
■ Text and image alignment

Paragraph ——— HTML 3.0 will also include support for style
sheets, which will allow more minute control
of the appearance of individual elements
on the page.

Figure 3.1. *Document elements.*

If you've worked with word processing programs that use style sheets (such as Microsoft Word) or paragraph catalogs (such as FrameMaker), then you've done something similar; each section of text conforms to one of a set of styles that are defined before you start working.

The elements of a Web document are labeled through the use of HTML tags. It is the tags that describe the document; anything that it not a tag is part of the document itself.

HTML Does Not Describe Page Layout

What style sheets and templates in word processors provide that HTML doesn't is the appearance of each part of the document on the page or screen. For example, styles in Microsoft Word not only have a name ("heading1," for example, for a heading), they also describe the font, the size, and the indentation, among other things, of that heading.

With a few exceptions, HTML does not describe the appearance or layout of a document. HTML does very little to allow you to specify the exact placement or appearance of any element on the page. The designers of HTML did this on purpose. Why? Because you don't know the capabilities of the platform where the document is going to be viewed, the size of the screen, the fonts that are installed, or if there are any fonts at all. By separating the structure of a document and its appearance, a program that reads and understands HTML can make formatting decisions based on the capabilities of the individual platform.

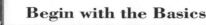

Web browsers, in addition to providing the networking functions to retrieve documents over the Net, are also HTML formatters. When you load an HTML document into a browser such as Mosaic or Lynx, that browser reads, or *parses*, the HTML information and formats the text and images on the screen. If you use different browsers, you may notice that the same document may appear differently in each browser—the headings may be centered in one, or in a larger font.

This does put a wrinkle in how you write and design your Web documents, however, and it may often frustrate you. The number one prevailing rule of designing documents for the Web, as I mention throughout this book, is this:

DO   **DON'T**

DON'T design your documents based on what they look like in one browser. Focus instead on providing clear, well-structured content that is easy to read and understand.

HTML Is Limited

So now you know that HTML isn't WYSIWYG, and that everything you're used to in creating documents for paper isn't going to work when you write pages for the Web. There's more bad news.

With the current state of HTML, the choices you have for the elements in your document (the tags) are also very limited. There are very few kinds of elements you have to choose from: headings, paragraphs, and a few lists are essentially it. You can include images, but what you can do with them is limited. You can't indent text, align text (left, center, justified), use multiple fonts, and you don't have tabs.

You also cannot make up your own elements (tags); if you could, how would browsers know how to interpret them?

Working with HTML is, in many ways, like working with a very stupid word processor, but with the added annoyance that you can't change to a better one. As long as you want to use HTML, you are stuck with its limitations.

HTML's Advantages (Yes, There Are Some)

Working in a text-only markup language, with little control over the appearance of the text and a limited set of tags to choose from, may seem frustratingly archaic in this age of fully WYSIWYG desktop publishing. But for the kind of environment that the Web provides, HTML does have significant advantages over other forms of document publishing that would include more features and allow you more control. For example:

☐ Each HTML document is small, so it can be transferred over the Net and displayed as fast as possible. You don't have to include font or formatting information that would slow down the time it would take to load and display the document.

☐ HTML documents are cross-platform compatible and device-independent, which is a fancy way of saying that they can be read on any platform as long as you have a browser that can read and understand HTML. As I mentioned earlier, you don't have to worry about font formats (or font names or whether a font is installed), or display resolutions, or screen size, or graphics formats, or a host of other issues that make creating documents that work across systems a close to impossible task. Because HTML allows the browser to make those formatting decisions, the language itself is highly portable to just about anywhere.

Also, although HTML is a markup language, it is an especially small and simple-to-learn markup language. There are very few tags to memorize, and there are simple editors that can even insert HTML tags for you. Other markup or page layout languages (such as the PostScript page description language, or troff on the UNIX system) are much larger. Because of their size and complexity, they require a lot of initial learning before you can write simple documents. With HTML you can get started right away.

Will It Get Better?

Yes, it will. But it may take some time.

Currently, most browsers support what is called HTML 2.0—the second major revision of the HTML standard. HTML 2.0 contains most of the page structure—headings, paragraphs, lists, images, and forms.

The future of HTML is HTML 3.0, which used to be called HTML+ (and is still referred to as HTML+). HTML 3.0 includes elements for such things as

☐ Centered and right-aligned text
☐ Tables

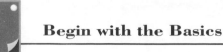

- [ ] Mathematical equations
- [ ] Text and image alignment

HTML 3.0 will also include support for style sheets, which will allow more minute control of the appearance of individual elements including fonts and font sizes, color, indents, automatic numbering, and many other features. Style sheets will be separate from the HTML language itself, allowing the language to remain small and for different style sheets to be matched up to the same text.

HTML 3.0 is still very much open for discussion, although some browsers (notably Netscape and Mosaic) have already begun to implement the more settled parts, such as tables. But HTML 3.0 is still evolving, and it will most likely be some time before available browsers can take advantage of all of its features. You'll learn about HTML 3.0 in Chapter 16.

A Note on the Netscape Extensions

In addition to the existing HTML 2.0 standard and the forthcoming HTML 3.0, there are also the Netscape extensions. The Netscape extensions are a set of tags that were introduced by Netscape with the first release of its browser. The Netscape extensions are tags to allow Web authors to get around some of HTML's current limitations, including centered text, aligning text next to images, and varying font sizes.

The problem with the Netscape extensions is that they are not part of the HTML standard as defined by the Web community at large—they were unilaterally added to the browser without discussion. Although Netscape has been lobbying to get its tags added to HTML 3.0, few browsers other than Netscape support the Netscape extensions. This makes pages that include those extensions strange-looking or even unreadable in other browsers.

You'll learn more about the Netscape extensions tomorrow, but now let's get started exploring the basics of HTML as most browsers understand it.

What HTML Files Look Like

Documents written in HTML are in plain text (ASCII) and contain two things:

- [ ] The text of the document itself
- [ ] HTML *tags* that indicate document elements, structure, formatting, and hypertext links to other documents or to included media.

Most HTML tags look something like this:

```
<TheTagName> affected text </TheTagName>
```

The tag name itself (here, `TheTagName`) is enclosed in brackets (<>).

HTML tags generally have a beginning and an ending tag, surrounding the text that they affect. The beginning tag "turns on" a feature (such as headings, bold, and so on), and the ending tag turns it off. Closing tags have the tag name preceded by a slash (/).

Not all HTML tags have a beginning and an end. Some tags are only one-sided, and still other tags are "containers" that hold extra information and text inside the brackets. You'll learn about these tags as the book progresses.

All HTML tags are case-insensitive; that is, you can specify them in upper- or lowercase, or in any mixture. So, `<HTML>` is the same as `<html>` is the same as `<HtMl>`. I like to put my tags in all caps (`<HTML>`) so I can pick them out from the text better. That's how I show them in the examples in this book.

Exercise 3.1. Take a look at HTML sources.

Before you actually start writing your own HTML documents, it helps to get a feel for what an HTML document looks like. Luckily, there's plenty of unformatted source material out there for you to look at—every document that comes over the wire to your browser is in HTML format. (You usually only see the formatted version after the browser gets done with it.)

Most Web browsers have a way of letting you see the unformatted HTML source of a Web page. You may have a menu item or a button for View Source or View HTML. In Lynx, the \ (backslash) command toggles between source view and formatted view.

Some browsers do not have the capability to directly view the source of a Web document, but do allow you to save the current page as a file to your local disk. Under a dialog box for saving the file, there may be a menu of formats; for example, Text, PostScript, or HTML. You can save the current page as HTML and then open that file in a text editor or word processor to see the HTML source.

Try going to a typical home page, then viewing the source for that page. For example, Figure 3.2 shows what the normal NCSA Mosaic home page (URL `http://www.ncsa.uiuc.edu/SDG/Software/Mosaic/NCSAMosaicHome.html`) looks like.

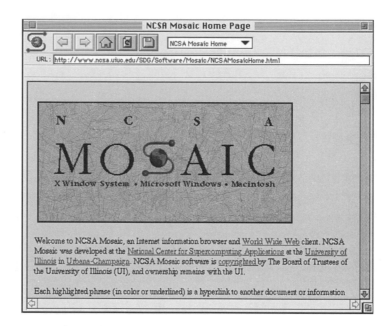

Figure 3.2. *Mosaic home page.*

The HTML source of that page should look something like Figure 3.3.

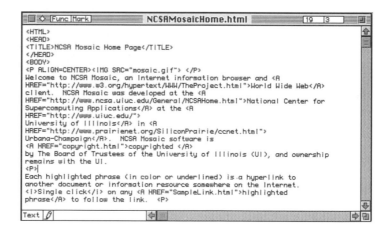

Figure 3.3. *Some HTML source.*

Try viewing the source of your own favorite Web pages. You should start seeing some similarities in the way pages are organized, and get a feel for the kinds of tags that HTML uses. You can learn a lot about HTML by comparing the text on the screen with the source for that text.

Exercise 3.2. Creating an HTML document.

You've seen what HTML looks like—now it's your turn. Let's start with a really simple example so you can get a basic feel for HTML.

To get started writing HTML, you're not going to need a Web server, a Web provider, or even a connection to the Web itself. All you really need is something to edit your HTML files, and at least one browser to view them. You can create, link, and test whole suites of Web pages without even touching a network. In fact, that's what we're going to do for the majority of this book—we'll talk about publishing everything on the Web so other people can see it later.

First, you'll need a text editor. A text editor is a program that saves files in ASCII format. That is, as just plain text, with no font formatting or special characters. On UNIX, vi, emacs, or pico are all text editors. On Windows, the built-in Notepad or DOS edit are good basic text editors, or a shareware editor such as WED or WinEdit will work as well. On the Macintosh, you can use the built-in SimpleText, or a more powerful text editor such as BBedit or Alpha (both of which are shareware).

If all you have is a word processor such as Microsoft Word, don't panic. Usually when you use the Save or Save As command there will be a menu of formats you can use to save the file. One of those should be "Text Only" or "Text Only with Line Breaks." Both of these options will save your file as plain ASCII, just as if you were using a text editor. For HTML files, you'll want to use the Text Only with Line Breaks option if you have it.

What about the plethora of editors that claim to help you write HTML easier? Most of them are actually simple text editors with some buttons that stick the tags in for you. If you've got one of those, go ahead and use it (I'll talk a little more about HTML editors after you try your first example).

Open up that text editor, and type the following code. You don't have to understand what any of this means at this point. You'll learn about it later in this chapter. This is just a simple example to get you started:

```
<HTML><HEAD>
<TITLE>My Sample HTML Document</TITLE></HEAD>
<BODY>
<H1>This is an HTML Document</H1>
</BODY></HTML>
```

After you create your HTML file, save it to disk—and remember to save it as a text-only file if you're using a word processor. When you pick a name for the file, there are two rules to follow:

☐ The file name should have an extension of .html (.htm on DOS systems), for example, myfile.html or text.html. Most Web software will require your files to have this extension, so get into the habit of using it now.

☐ Use small, simple names. Avoid using spaces or special characters (bullets, accented characters and so on) in the filename, and be aware that upper- and lowercase are considered different in most Web software.

Now, start up your Web browser. You don't have to be connected to the network since you're not going to be opening documents at any other site. Your browser or network connection software may complain about the lack of a network connection, but usually it will eventually give up and let you use it anyway.

> **Tip:** If you're using a Web browser from Windows, using that browser without a network is unfortunately more complicated than on other systems. Most Windows browsers are unable to run without a network, preventing you from looking at your local files without running up online charges. If your browser has this problem, there are several things you can try. Depending on your network software, you may be able to start your network package (Trumpet or Chameleon), but not actually dial the network. This often is sufficient for many browsers. If this doesn't work, you'll have to replace the file winsock.dll in your windows directory with what's called a "null sock"—a special file that makes your system think it's on a network when it's not.
>
> Rename the null sock file to winsock.dll and copy it to your Windows directory (Be sure and put your original winsock.dll in a safe place first! You'll need to put everything back the way it was to get back onto the Web). With the null sock installed, you should then be able to use your Windows browser without a network.
>
> If all this is too complex, you may be forced to connect to a network to test your Web files in Windows.

Once your browser is running, look for a menu item or button labeled Open Local, Open File, or sometimes just Open. It's a menu item that will let you browse your local disk. (In Lynx simply use the command `lynx myfile.html` from a command line.) The Open Local command (or its equivalent) tells the browser to read an HTML file from your disk, parse it, and display it, just as if it were a page already on the Web. Using your browser and the Open Local command, you can write and test your HTML files on your computer in the privacy of your own home.

Try opening up the little file you just created in your browser. You should see something like the picture shown in Figure 3.4.

If you don't see something like what's in the picture (for example, if parts are missing, or if everything looks like a heading), go back into your text editor and compare your file to the example. Make sure all your tags have closing tags, and that all your < characters are matched by > characters. You don't have to quit your browser to do this; just fix the file and save it again under the same name.

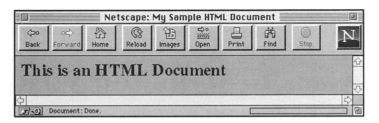

Figure 3.4. *The sample HTML file.*

3

Then go back to your browser. There should be a command called "Reload." (In Lynx, it's Control+R.) The browser will read the new version of your file, and voilà, you can edit and preview and edit and preview until you get it right.

A Note About Formatting

When an HTML document is parsed by a browser, any formatting you may have done by hand—that is, any extra spaces, tabs, returns, and so on—are all ignored. The only thing that formats an HTML document is an HTML tag. If you spend hours carefully editing a plain text file to have nicely formatted paragraphs and columns of numbers, but do not include any tags, when you read the document into an HTML browser, all the text will flow all into one paragraph. All your work will have been in vain.

Note: There's one exception to this rule: a tag called <PRE>. You'll learn about this tag tomorrow in Chapter 5, "Still More HTML."

The advantage of having all white space (spaces, tabs, returns) ignored is that you can put your tags wherever you want. The following examples all produce the same output. (Try it!)

```
<H1>If music be the food of love, play on.</H1>

<H1>
If music be the food of love, play on.
</H1>

<H1>
If music be the food of love, play on. </H1>

<H1> If music be the food of love,
play on. </H1>
```

Programs to Help You Write HTML

You may be thinking that all this tag stuff is a real pain, especially if you didn't get that small example right the first time. (Don't fret about it; I didn't get that example right the first time, and I created it.) You have to remember all the tags. And you have to type them in right and close each one. What a hassle.

There are programs that can help you write HTML. These programs tend to fall into two categories: editors in which you write HTML directly, and converters, which convert the output of some other word processing program into HTML.

Editors

Many freeware and shareware programs are available for editing HTML files. Most of these programs are essentially text editors with extra menu items or buttons that insert the appropriate HTML tags into your text. HTML-based text editors are particularly nice for two reasons: You don't have to remember all the tags, and you don't have to take the time to type them all.

I discuss some of the available HTML-based editors in Chapter 6, "HTML Assistants: Editors and Converters." For now, if you have an HTML editor, feel free to use it for the examples in this book. If all you have is a text editor, no problem; it just means you'll have to do a little more typing.

What about WYSIWYG editors? The problem is that there's really no such thing as WYSIWYG when you're dealing with HTML, since WYG can vary wildly based on the browser used to read your document. So you could spend hours in a so-called WYSIWYG HTML editor (say, one that makes your documents look just like Mosaic or Netscape), only to discover that when the HTML output of that editor is read on some other browser, it looks truly awful. So although there are semi-WYSIWYG editors for HTML, keep in mind HTML's design and limitations when you use them.

Converters

In addition to the HTML editors, there are also converters, which take files from many popular word-processing programs and convert them to HTML. This is the closest HTML gets to being WYSIWYG. With a simple set of templates, you can write your documents entirely in your favorite program. Then, convert the result. You'll almost never have to deal with all this non-WYSIWYG text-only tag nonsense.

In many cases, converters can be extremely useful, particularly for putting existing documents on the Web as fast as possible. However, converters are in no way an ideal environment for HTML development. Most converter programs are fairly limited, not necessarily by their own features, but mostly by the limitations in HTML itself. No amount of fancy converting is going to make HTML do things that it can't yet do. If a particular capability doesn't exist in HTML, there's nothing the converter can do to solve that (and it may end up doing strange things to your HTML files, causing you more work than if you just did all the formatting yourself).

The other problem with converters is that, even though you can do most of your writing and development in a converter with a simple set of formats and low expectations, you will usually have to go "under the hood" and edit the HTML text yourself. Most converters do not convert images, or automate links to documents out on the Web.

In other words, even if you've already decided that you want to do the bulk of your Web work using a converter, you'll still need to know HTML. So press onward; there's not that much to learn.

Structuring Your HTML

HTML defines three tags that are used to describe the document's overall structure and provide some simple "header" information. These three tags identify your document to browsers or HTML tools. They also provide simple information about the document (such as its title or who wrote it) before loading the entire thing. The document structure tags don't affect what the document looks like when it's displayed; they're only there to help tools that interpret or filter HTML files.

According to the strict HTML definition, these tags are optional. If your document does not contain them, browsers will be able to read it anyway. However, it is possible that these document structure tags might become required elements in the future. It's also possible that tools may come along that need them. If you get into the habit of including the document structure tags now, you won't have to worry about updating all your files later.

<HTML>

The first document structure tag in every HTML document is the <HTML> tag. It indicates that the content of this file is in the HTML language.

All the text and HTML commands in your HTML document should go within the beginning and ending HTML tags, like this:

```
<HTML>
...your document...
</HTML>
<HEAD>
```

The <HEAD> tag specifies that the lines within the beginning and ending points of the tag are the prologue to the rest of the file. There are generally only a few tags that go into the <HEAD> portion of the document (most notably, the document title, described below). You should never put any of the text of your document into the header.

Here's a typical example of how you would properly use the <HEAD> tag (you'll learn about </TITLE> later):

```
<HTML>
<HEAD>
<TITLE>This is the Title.</TITLE>
</HEAD>
....
</HTML>
<BODY>
```

The remainder of your HTML document, including all the text and other content (links, pictures, and so on) is enclosed within a <BODY> tag. In combination with the <HTML> and <HEAD> tags, this looks like:

```
<HTML>
<HEAD>
<TITLE>This is the Title. It will be explained later on</TITLE>
</HEAD>
<BODY>
....
</BODY>
</HTML>
```

The Title

Each HTML document needs a title to indicate what the document describes. The title is used by your browser's bookmarks or hotlist program, and also by other programs that catalogue Web pages. To give a document a title, use the <TITLE> tag. <TITLE> tags always go inside the document header (the <HEAD> tags), and describe the contents of the page, like this:

```
<HTML>
<HEAD>
<TITLE>The Lion, The Witch, and the Wardrobe</TITLE>
</HEAD>
<BODY>
....
</BODY>
</HTML>
```

You can only have one title in the document, and that title can only contain plain text; that is, there shouldn't be any other tags inside the title.

When you pick a title, try to pick one that is both short and descriptive of the content on the page. Additionally, your title should also be relevant out of context. If someone browsing on the Web followed a random link and ended up on this page, or if they found your title in a friend's browser history list, would they have any idea what this page is about? You may not intend the page to be used independently of the documents you specifically linked to it, but because anyone can link to any page at any time, be prepared for that consequence and pick a helpful title.

Additionally, because many browsers put the title in the title bar of the window, you may have a limited number of words available. (Although the text within the <TITLE> tag can be of any length, it may be cut off by the browser when it's displayed.) Here are some other examples of good titles:

```
<TITLE>Poisonous Plants of North America</TITLE>
<TITLE>Image Editing: A Tutorial</TITLE>
<TITLE>Upcoming Cemetery Tours, Summer 1995</TITLE>
<TITLE>Installing The Software: Opening the CD Case</TITLE>
<TITLE>Laura Lemay's Awesome Home Page</TITLE>
```

And some not-so-good titles:

```
<TITLE>Part Two</TITLE>
<TITLE>An Example</TITLE>
<TITLE>Nigel Franklin Hobbes</TITLE>
<TITLE>Minutes of the Second Meeting of the Fourth Conference of the
Committee for the Preservation of English Roses, Day Four, After Lunch</TITLE>
```

The following examples show how titles look in both Netscape (Figure 3.5) and Lynx (Figure 3.6).

3

59

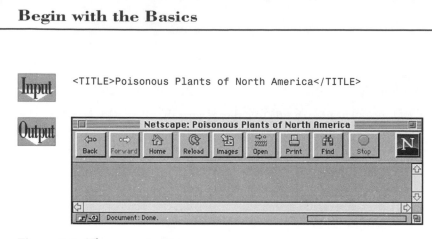

Input

```
<TITLE>Poisonous Plants of North America</TITLE>
```

Output

Figure 3.5. *The output in Netscape.*

```
Poisonous Plants of North America
```

Figure 3.6. *The output in Lynx.*

Headings

Headings are used to divide sections of text, just like this book is divided. ("Headings," above, is a heading.) HTML defines six levels of headings. Heading tags look like this:

```
<H1>Installing Your Safetee Lock</H1>
```

The numbers indicate heading levels (H1 through H6). The headings, when they're displayed, are not numbered. They are displayed either in bigger or bolder text, or are centered or underlined, or are capitalized—something that makes them stand out from regular text.

Think of the headings as items in an outline. If the text you're writing has a structure, use the headings to indicate that structure, as shown in the next code lines. (Note that I've indented the headings in this example to show the hierarchy better. They don't have to be indented in your document, and, in fact, the indenting will be ignored by the browser.)

```
<H1>Engine Tune-Up</H1>
    <H2>Change The Oil</H2>
    <H2>Adjust the Valves</H2>
    <H2>Change the Spark Plugs</H2>
        <H3>Remove the Old Plugs</H3>
```

```
          <H3>Prepare the New Plugs</H3>
               <H4>Remove the Guards</H4>
               <H4>Check the Gap</H4>
               <H4>Apply Anti-Seize Lubricant</H4>
               <H4>Install the Plugs</H4>
     <H2>Adjust the Timing</H2>
```

Note that (unlike titles), headings can be any length, including lines and lines of text (although because headings are emphasized, having lines and lines of emphasized text may be tiring for your reader).

It's a common practice to use a first-level heading at the top of your document to either duplicate the title (which is usually displayed elsewhere), or to provide a shorter or less contextual form of the title. For example, if you had a page that showed several examples of folding bedsheets, part of a long document on how to fold bedsheets, the title might look something like this:

```
<TITLE>How to Fold Sheets: Some Examples</TITLE>
```

The top-most heading, however, might just say:

```
<H1>Examples</H1>
```

Don't use headings to display text in boldface type, or to make certain parts of your document stand out more. Although it may look cool on your browser, you don't know what it'll look like when other people use their browsers to read your document. Other browsers may number headings, or format them in a manner that you don't expect. Also, tools to create searchable indexes of Web pages may extract your headings to indicate the important parts of a document. By using headings for something other than an actual heading, you may be foiling those search programs and creating strange results.

The following examples show headings and how they appear in Netscape (Figure 3.7) and Lynx (Figure 3.8):

```
     <H1>Engine Tune-Up</H1>
          <H2>Change The Oil</H2>
          <H2>Change the Spark Plugs</H2>
               <H3>Prepare the New Plugs</H3>
                    <H4>Remove the Guards</H4>
                    <H4>Check the Gap</H4>
```

3 Begin with the Basics

Figure 3.7. *The output in Netscape.*

Figure 3.8. *The output in Lynx.*

Paragraphs

Now that you have a document title and several headings, let's add some ordinary paragraphs to the document.

Unfortunately, paragraphs in HTML are slippery things. Between the three versions of HTML, the definition of a paragraph has changed. The only thing the three versions agree on is that you indicate a plain text paragraph using the <P> tag.

62

The first version of HTML specified the `<P>` tag as a one-sided tag. There was no corresponding `</P>`, and the `<P>` tag was used to indicate the *end* of a paragraph (a paragraph break), not the beginning. So paragraphs in the first version of HTML looked like this:

```
The blue sweater was reluctant to be worn, and wrestled with her as she at-
tempted to put it on. The collar was too small, and would not fit over her head,
and the arm holes moved seemingly randomly away from her searching hands.<P>
Exasperated, she took off the sweater and flung it on the floor. Then she
vindictively stomped on it in revenge for its recalcitrant behavior.<P>
```

Most browsers that were created early on in the history of the Web—and many browsers—still assume that paragraphs will be formatted this way. When they come across a `<P>` tag, they start a new line and add some extra vertical space between the line they just ended and the one that they just began, as shown in Figure 3.9.

Space between paragraphs

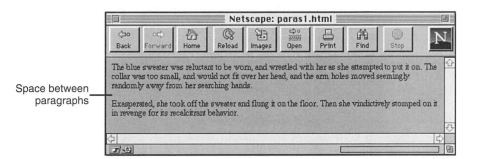

Figure 3.9. *How paragraphs are formatted.*

In the HTML 2.0 and the proposed HTML 3.0 specifications, the paragraph tag has been revised. In these versions of HTML, the paragraph tags are two-sided (`<P>`...`</P>`), but `<P>` indicates the *beginning* of the paragraph. Also, the closing tag (`</P>`) is optional. So the sweater story would look like this in the newer versions of HTML:

```
<P>The blue sweater was reluctant to be worn, and wrestled with her as she
attempted to put it on. The collar was too small, and would not fit over her
head, and the arm holes moved seemingly randomly away from her searching hands.
</P><P>Exasperated, she took off the sweater and flung it on the floor. Then she
vindictively stomped on it in revenge for its recalcitrant behavior.</P>
```

It's a good idea to get into the habit of using `<P>` at the start of a paragraph, as this will become important in HTML 3.0 where you can define the alignment and other features of each paragraph. Older browsers will accept this form of paragraphs just fine.

However, note that because many browsers still expect <P> to indicate the end of a paragraph, if you use it at the beginning you may end up with extra space in between the first paragraph and the element before it, as shown in Figure 3.10.

Note extra space —

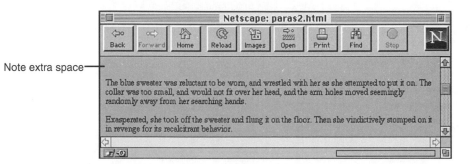

Figure 3.10. *Extra space before paragraphs.*

If this bothers you overly much, you can do one of the following:

☐ Go back to the old style of defining paragraphs.

☐ Use <P> as a paragraph separator, rather than indicating the beginning or ending of a paragraph.

☐ Leave off the first <P> in each set of paragraphs.

Some people like to use <P> tags to spread out the text on the page. Once again, the cardinal reminder: Design for content, not for appearance. Someone with a text-based browser is not going to care much about the extra space you so carefully put in, and some browsers may even collapse multiple <P> tags into one, erasing all your careful formatting.

The following example shows a sample paragraph and how it appears in Netscape (Figure 3.11) and Lynx (Figure 3.12).

```
<P>The sweater lay quietly on the floor, seething from its ill treat-
ment. It wasn't its fault that it didn't fit right. It hadn't wanted to
be purchased by this ill-mannered woman.</P>
```

Output

```
Netscape: paras3.html
```
Back Forward Home Reload Images Open Print Find Stop

The sweater lay quietly on the floor, seething from its ill treatment. It wasn't its fault that it didn't fit right. It hadn't wanted to be purchased by this ill-mannered woman.

Figure 3.11. *The output in Netscape.*

```
The sweater lay quietly on the floor, seething from its ill treatment.
It wasn't its fault that it didn't fit right. It hadn't wanted to be
purchased by this ill-mannered woman.
```

Figure 3.12. *The output in Lynx.*

Comments

You can put comments into HTML documents to describe the document itself or to provide some kind of indication of the status of the document; some source code control programs can put document status into comments, for example. Text in comments is ignored when the HTML file is parsed; comments don't ever show up on screen—that's why they're comments. Comments look like this:

```
<!-- This is a comment -->
```

Each line should be individually commented, and it's usually a good idea not to include other HTML tags within comments. (Although this practice isn't strictly illegal, many browsers may get confused when they encounter HTML tags within comments and display them anyway.)

Here are some examples:

```
<!-- Rewrite this section with less humor -->
<!-- Neil helped with this section -->
<!-- Go Tigers! -->
```

Exercise 3.3. Creating a real HTML document.

At this point, you should know enough to get started creating simple HTML documents. You understand what HTML is, you've been introduced to a handful of tags, and you've even tried browsing an HTML file. You haven't done any links yet, but you'll get to that soon enough, in the next chapter.

This exercise shows you how to create an HTML file that uses the tags you've learned about in this chapter. It will give you a feel for what the tags look like when they're displayed on-screen and for the sorts of typical mistakes you're going to make. (Everyone makes them, and that's why it's often useful to use an HTML editor that does the typing for you. The editor doesn't forget the closing tags, or leave off the slash, or misspell the tag itself.)

So, create a simple example in that text editor of yours. It doesn't have to say much of anything; in fact, all it needs to include are the structure tags, a title, a couple of headings, and a paragraph or two, Here's an example:

```
<HTML>
<HEAD>
<TITLE>Company Profile, Camembert Incorporated</TITLE>
</HEAD>
<BODY>
<H1>Camembert Incorporated</H1>
"Many's the long night I dreamed of cheese -- toasted, mostly." -- Robert Louis
Stevenson
<H2>What We Do</H2>
We make cheese. Lots of cheese; more than eight tons of cheese a year. Your
Brie, your Gouda, your Havarti, we make it all.
<H2>Why We Do It</H2>
<P>We are paid an awful lot of money by people who like cheese. So we make
more.</P>
</BODY>
</HTML>
```

Save your example to an HTML file, open it in your browser, and see how it came out.

If you have access to another browser on your platform, or on another platform, I highly recommend opening the same HTML file there so you can see the differences in appearance between browsers. Sometimes the differences can surprise you; lines that looked fine in one browser will look strange in another browser.

For example, the cheese factory example looks like Figure 3.13 in Netscape (the Macintosh version) and like Figure 3.14 in Lynx.

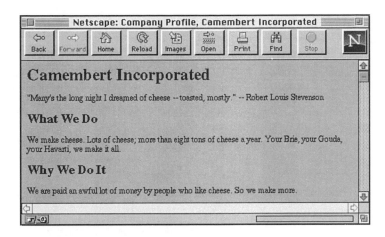

Figure 3.13. *The cheese factory in Netscape.*

```
                              Company Profile, Camembert Incorporated
                         CAMEMBERT INCORPORATED

     "Many's the long night I dreamed of cheese -- toasted, mostly." --
     Robert Louis Stevenson

What We Do

     We make cheese. Lots of cheese; more than eight tons of cheese a year.
     Your Brie, your Gouda, your Havarti, we make it all.

Why We Do It



     We are paid an awful lot of money by people who like cheese. So we
     make more.
```

Figure 3.14. *The cheese factory in Lynx.*

See what I mean?

Summary

HTML, a text-only markup language used to describe hypertext documents on the World Wide Web, describes the structure of a document, not its appearance.

In this chapter, you've learned what HTML is and how to write and preview simple HTML files. You've also learned about the HTML tags shown in Table 3.1.

Table 3.1. HTML tags from Chapter 3.

Tag	Use
`<HTML> ... </HTML>`	The entire HTML document
`<HEAD> ... </HEAD>`	The head, or prologue, of the HTML document
`<BODY> ... </BODY>`	All the other content in the HTML document
`<TITLE> ... </TITLE>`	The title of the document
`<H1> ... </H1>`	First-level heading
`<H2> ... </H2>`	Second-level heading
`<H3> ... </H3>`	Third-level heading
`<H4> ... </H4>`	Fourth-level heading
`<H5> ... </H5>`	Fifth-level heading
`<H6> ... </H6>`	Sixth-level heading
`<P> ... </P>`	Paragraph
`<!-- ... -->`	Comment

Q&A

Q Why was HTML chosen as the language for the Web when it's so limited?

A At the time, the goal was simply to put hypertext information up on the Net so that it could be easily downloaded and formatted on-the-fly in a simple, device-independent way. Given those goals, HTML was an ideal language: simple, small, fast to download, and easy to parse. Since then, new features like images and forms and other media have been added. The limitations of HTML didn't become readily apparent until these new browsers and capabilities came along, and more and more people wanted to publish other kinds of information (most particularly, very visual information). And it happened so fast!

HTML 3.0 should solve many of these limitations. But there's a long way to go yet before HTML allows full control over formatting and layout, simply because of the speed with which it needs to be downloaded over the Net and formatted. If each Web page you viewed took half an hour to load, would you want to read it?

Q **Can I do *any* formatting of text in HTML?**

A You can do some formatting to strings of characters; for example, making a word or two bold. And the Netscape extensions allow you to change the font size and color of the text in your Web page (for readers using Netscape). You'll learn about these features tomorrow, in Chapters 5 and 6.

Q **I've noticed in most Web pages that the document structure tags (`<HTML>`, `<HEAD>`, `<BODY>`) aren't often used. Do I really need to include them if pages work just fine without them?**

A You don't need to, no. Most browsers will handle plain HTML without the document structure tags. But including the tags will allow your documents to be read by more general SGML tools, and to take advantage of features of future browsers. And, it's the "correct" thing to do if you want your documents to conform to true HTML format.

Q **I've seen comments in some HTML files that look like this:**

```
<!-- this is a comment>
```

Is that legal?

A That's the old form of comments that was used in very early forms of HTML. Although many browsers may still accept it, you should use the new form (and comment each line individually) in your documents.

4

Putting the Hyper in Hypertext: All About Links and URLs

After finishing the last chapter, you have two documents that have some headings and text in them. This is all well and good, but rather boring. The real fun starts when you learn how to do hypertext links and link up all your documents to the Web. This chapter starts you going on creating links. Specifically, you'll learn

☐ All about the HTML link tag (<A>) and its various parts

☐ How to link to other documents on your local disk using relative and absolute path names

☐ How to link to other documents on the Web using URLs

Creating Links

To create a link in HTML, you need two things:

☐ The name of the file (or the URL of the file) you want to link to

☐ The text that will serve as the "hot spot"—that is, the text that will be highlighted in the browser, which your readers can then select to follow the link

Only the second element is actually visible in your document. When your reader selects the text that points to a link, the browser uses the first element to "jump" to the appropriate document. That is, the browser uses the first element to retrieve the linked document from the disk or from over the Net, to parse the HTML that document contains (if necessary), and to display it.

The Link Tag <*A*>

To create a link in an HTML document, you use the HTML link tag <A>...</A>. The <A> tag is often called an anchor tag, as it can also be used to create anchors for links. (You'll learn more about creating anchors later on in this chapter.) The most common use of the link tag, however, is to create links to other documents.

Unlike the simple tags you learned about in the last chapter, the <A> tag has some extra features: the opening tag, <A>, includes both the name of the tag ("A") and extra information

about the link itself. The extra features are called *attributes* of the tag. So instead of the opening tag just having a name inside brackets, it looks something like this:

```
<A NAME="Up" HREF="../menu.html" TITLE="Ostrich Care">
```

The extra attributes (in this example, NAME, HREF, and TITLE) describe the link itself. Many of the attributes are only useful for special HTML tools and browsers that can do fancy things with the links. The attribute you'll probably use the most often is the HREF attribute, short for "Hypertext REFerence." The HREF attribute is used to specify the name or URL of the file where this link points.

Like most HTML tags, the link tag also has a closing tag, </A>. All of the text between the opening and closing tags will become the actual link on the screen and be highlighted or underlined or blue or red when the Web page is displayed. That's the text you or your reader will click on (or select, in browsers that don't use mice) to jump to the document specified by the HREF attribute.

Figure 4.1 shows the parts of a typical link using the <A> tag, including the HREF, the text of the link, and the closing tag:

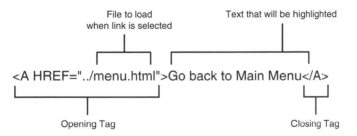

Figure 4.1. *An HTML link using the* <A> *tag.*

The following two examples show a simple link and what it looks like in Netscape (Figure 4.2) and Lynx (Figure 4.3).

Input
```
Go back to <A HREF="../menu.html">Main Menu</A>
```

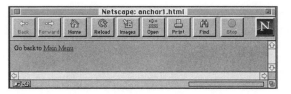

Figure 4.2. *The output in Netscape.*

Figure 4.3. *The output in Lynx.*

Exercise 4.1: Link two documents.

Let's try a really simple example, with two HTML documents on your local disk. You'll need your text editor and a Web browser for this, but since both the documents you'll be fooling with are on your local disk, you won't need to be connected to the network. (Be patient; you'll get to do network stuff in the next section of this chapter.)

First, create two HTML documents, and save them in separate files. Here's the code for the two HTML files I created for this section, which I called `menu.html` and `feeding.html`. It really doesn't matter what your two documents look like or what they're called, but make sure you put in your own file names if you're following along with this example.

Don't want to type in these examples? They're contained on this book's Web site at `http://www.lne.com/Web/Examples/`.

The first file is called `menu.html` file, and it looks like this:

```
<HTML>
<HEAD>
<TITLE>How To Care For Your Ostrich</TITLE>
</HEAD><BODY>
<H1>Caring for Your New Ostrich</H1>
<P>Your new ostrich is a delicate and sensitive creature. This document
describes how to care for your ostrich so that he can be a happy and
healthy ostrich and give you hours of fun and friendship.</P>
<P>Feeding Your Ostrich</P>
<P>Grooming Your Ostrich</P>
<P>Cleaning Up After Your Ostrich</P>
<P>Taunting Your Ostrich</P>
</BODY>
</HTML>
```

The list of menu items ("Feeding Your Ostrich," "Grooming Your Ostrich," and so on) will be links to other documents. For now, just type them as regular text; you'll turn them into links later.

The second file, `feeding.html`, looks like this:

```
<HTML>
<HEAD>
<TITLE>How To Care For Your Ostrich: Feeding Your Ostrich</TITLE>
</HEAD><BODY>
<H1>Feeding Your Ostrich</H1>
<P>This section describes what, how often, and how to feed your ostrich
</P>
<H2>What to Feed Your Ostrich</H2>
Ostriches benefit best from a balanced diet such as that provided by United
Bird Food's Ostrich Kibble 102. We recommend feeding your ostrich a cup of
kibbles once a day, with ample water.
<H2>How to Feed Your Ostrich</H2>
<P>To feed your ostrich, leave the ostrich kibbles in a container by the
edge of the ostrich's pen.</P>
<P>NOTE: Ostriches do not like being watched while eating, and may attack
you if you stand too close. We recommend leaving your ostrich to eat in peace.
</P>
<P>Go back to Main Menu</P>
</BODY>
</HTML>
```

Make sure both your files are in the same directory or folder, and if you haven't called them menu.html and feeding.html, make sure that you take note of the names because you'll need them later.

First, create a link from the menu file to the feeding file. Edit the menu.html file, and put the cursor at the line that says `<P>Feeding Your Ostrich</P>`.

Link tags do not define the format of the text itself, so leave in the paragraph tags and just add the link inside the paragraph. First, put in the link tags themselves (the `<A>` and `</A>` tags) around the text that you want to use as the link:

```
<P><A>Feeding Your Ostrich</A></P>
```

Now add the name of the file you want to link to as the HREF part of the opening link tag. Enclose the name of the file in quotes, with an equals sign between HREF and the name. Note that upper and lower case are distinct, so make sure you type the file name exactly as it appears on the disk. Here I've used feeding.html; if you used different files, use a different file name.

```
<P><A HREF="feeding.html">Feeding Your Ostrich</A></P>
```

4

Note: When you include tags inside other tags, make sure that the closing tag closes the tag that you most recently opened. That is, do this:

`<P> <A> ... </A> </P>`

Instead of this:

`<P> <A> ... </P> </A>`

Some browsers may become confused if you overlap tags in this way, so it's best to always make sure that you close the most recently opened tag first.

Now, start up your browser, select Open Local (or its equivalent), and open the `menu.html` file. The paragraph that you used as your link should now show up as a link that is in a different color, underlined, or otherwise highlighted. Figure 4.4 shows how it looked when I opened it in the Macintosh version of Netscape:

And now, when you click on the link, your browser should load in and display the `feeding.html` document, as shown in Figure 4.5.

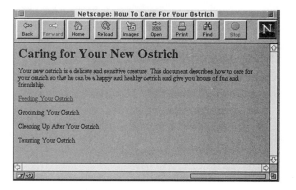

Figure 4.4. *The* `menu.html` *file with link.*

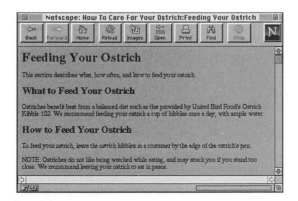

Figure 4.5. *The* `feeding.html` *document.*

If your browser can't find the file when you choose the link, make sure that the name of the file in the HREF part of the link tag is the same as the name of the file on the disk and that both of the files are in the same directory. Remember to close your link, using the `</A>` tag, at the end of the text that serves as the link. Also, make sure that you have quotes at the end of the file name (sometimes its easy to forget). All of these things can confuse the browser and make it not find the file or display the link properly.

Now, let's create a link from the feeding document back to the menu. There is a paragraph at the end of the `feeding.html` document intended for just this purpose:

```
<P>Go back to Main Menu</P>
```

Add the link tag with the appropriate HREF to that line, like this, where `menu.html` is the original menu file:

```
<P><A HREF="menu.html">Go back to Main Menu</A></P>
```

Now when you reload the "feeding" file, the link will be active, and you can jump between the menu and the feeding file by selecting those links.

Linking Local Documents Using Relative and Absolute Path Names

The example in the previous section shows how to link together documents that are contained in the same folder on your local disk (called, appropriately, *local* documents). This section continues that thread, linking documents that are still on the local disk, but may be contained in different directories on that disk.

Putting the Hyper in Hypertext: All About Links and URLs

When you specify the path name of a linked file within quotes, as you did earlier, the browser looks for it in the same directory as the current file. This is so, even if that browser is looking at that file over the Net from some faraway place. This is the simplest form of a relative path name.

Relative path names can also include directories, or they can point to the path you would take to navigate to that file if you started at the current directory or folder. A path name might include directions, for example, to go up two directory levels, and then go down two other directories to get to the file.

To specify relative path names in links, use UNIX-style path names, regardless of the system you actually have. This means that directory or folder names are separated by forward slashes (/), and you use two dots to refer to the directory above the current one ("..").

Table 4.1 shows some examples of relative path names and what they mean.

Table 4.1. Relative path names.

Path name	Means
HREF="file.html"	file.html is located in the current directory.
HREF="files/file.html"	file.html is located in the directory (or folder) called files (and the files directory is located in the current directory).
HREF="files/morefiles/file.html"	file.html is located in the morefiles directory, which is located in the files directory, which is located in the current directory.
HREF="../file.html"	file.html is located in the directory (or folder) one level up from the current directory.
HREF="../../files/file.html"	file.html is located two directory levels up, in the directory files.

If you're linking files on a personal computer (Mac or PC) and you want to link to a file on a different disk, use the name or letter of the disk as just another directory name in the relative path.

On the Macintosh, the name of the disk is used just as it appears on the disk itself. Assume you have a disk called Hard Disk 2, and your HTML files are contained in a folder called HTML Files. If you wanted to link to a file called jane.html in a folder called Public on a shared disk called Jane's Mac, you could use the following relative path name:

```
HREF="../../Jane's Mac/Public/jane.html"
```

On DOS systems, the disks are referred to by letter, just as you would expect them to be, but instead of being c:, d:, and so on, substitute a vertical bar (¦) for the colon (the colon has a special meaning in link path names), and don't forget to use forward slashes like on UNIX. So, if the current file is located in C:\FILES\HTML\, and you want to link to D:\FILES.NEW\HTML\MORE\INDEX.HTM, the relative path name to that file would be:

```
HREF="../../d¦/files.new/html/more/index.htm"
```

Absolute Path Names

You can also specify the link to another document on your local system using an absolute path name. Relative path names, as described above, point to the document you want to link by describing its relation to the current document. Absolute path names, on the other hand, point to the document by starting at the top level of your directory hierarchy and working downward through all the intervening directories to reach the file.

Absolute path names always begin with a slash, which is the way they are differentiated from relative path names. Following the slash are all directories in the path from the top level to the file you are linking.

> **Note:** "Top" has different meanings depending on how you're publishing your HTML files. If you're just linking to files on your local disk, the "top" is the top of your file system (/ on UNIX, or the disk name on a Mac or PC). When you're publishing files using a Web server, the "top" may or may not be the top of your file system (and generally isn't). You'll learn more about absolute path names and Web servers on Day Seven, "Putting it All Online."

Table 4.2 shows some examples of absolute path names and what they mean.

Table 4.2. Absolute path names.

Path name	Means
HREF="/u1/lemay/file.html"	file.html is located in the directory /u1/lemay.
HREF="/d¦/files/html/file.htm"	file.htm is located on the D: disk in the directories files/html (DOS systems).
HREF="/Hard Disk 1/HTML Files/file.html"	file.html is located on the disk Hard Disk 1, in the folder HTML Files (typically a Macintosh).

Should You Use Relative or Absolute Path Names?

To link your own documents, 99 percent of the time you should use relative path names instead of the absolute path names. Using absolute path names may seem easier for complicated links between lots of documents, but absolute path names are not portable. If you specify your links as absolute path names and you move your files elsewhere on the disk, or rename a directory or a disk listed in that absolute path, then all your links will break and you'll have to laboriously edit all your HTML files and fix them all. Using absolute path names also makes it very difficult to move your files to a Web server when you decide to actually make them available on the Web—and that's what you're reading this book for, isn't it?

Specifying relative path names allows you to move your documents around on your own system and to move them to other systems with little to no file modifications to fix the links. It's much easier to maintain HTML documents with relative path names, so the extra work of setting them initially is often well worth the effort.

Links to Other Documents on the Web

So now you have a whole set of documents, all linked to each other. In some places in your documents, however, you would like to refer to a page somewhere else on the Net; for example, to the Palo Alto Zoo home page for more information on the socialization of ostriches. You can also use the link tag to link those other documents on the Net, which I'll call *remote* documents.

The HTML code you use to link documents on the Web looks exactly the same as the code you used for links between local documents. You still use the <A> tag with an HREF attribute, and include some text to serve as the link on your Web page. But instead of a file name or a path in the HREF, use the URL of that document on the Web, as Figure 4.6 shows.

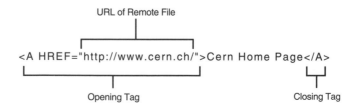

Figure 4.6. *Link to remote files.*

Exercise 4.2: Linking your ostrich pages to the Web.

Let's go back to those two documents you linked together earlier in this chapter, the ones about ostriches. The menu.html file contained several links to other local documents that described how to take care of your ostrich.

Now let's say you want to add a link to the bottom of the menu file to point to the ostrich archives at the Palo Alto Zoo (the world's leading authority on the care of ostriches), whose URL is http://www.zoo.palo-alto.ca.us/ostriches/home.html.

> **Note:** I'm making most of this up. Although the city of Palo Alto, California, has a Web page (URL http://www.city.palo-alto.ca.us/home.html), Palo Alto doesn't have a zoo with ostriches (they do have a petting zoo, however). For the purposes of this example, just pretend that there's a Web page for the Palo Alto Zoo.

First, add the appropriate text for the link to your menu page:

```
<P>The Palo Alto Zoo has more information on ostriches</P>
```

What if you don't know the URL of the home page for the Palo Alto Zoo (or the document you want to link to), but you do know how to get to it by following several links on several different people's home pages? Not a problem. Use your browser to find the home page for the document you want to link to. (Figure 4.7 shows what the home page for the Palo Alto Zoo might look like, if it existed.)

> **Note:** If you set up your system (for the last chapter) so that it would not connect to the network, you might want to put it back now to follow along with this example.

Most browsers display the URL of the file they're currently looking at in a box somewhere near the top of the page. This makes it particularly easy for you to link to other documents; all you have to do is go there with your browser, copy the URL from the window, and paste it into the HTML page you're working on. No typing!

Figure 4.7. *The Palo Alto Zoo home page.*

Once you have the URL of the zoo (the URL for that page is in the box in the top corner, and you can usually copy from that box), you can construct a link tag in your menu file and paste the appropriate URL into the link:

```
<P>The <A HREF="http://www.zoo.palo-alto.ca.us/ostriches/home.html">Palo Alto
Zoo</A>
has more information on ostriches</P>
```

Of course, if you already know the URL of the page you want to link to, you can just type it into the HREF part of the link. Keep in mind, however, that if you make a mistake your browser won't be able to find the file on the other end. Most URLs are a little too complex for normal humans to be able to remember them; I prefer to copy and paste whenever I can to cut down on the chances of typing them wrong.

Figure 4.8 shows how the menu.html file, with the new link in it, looks when it is displayed by Netscape.

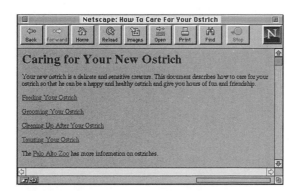

Figure 4.8. *The Palo Alto Zoo link.*

Linking to Specific Places Within Documents

You already have learned how to link from one page to another, where the page you were linking to was either a local page or one elsewhere on the Web. But what if, instead of linking to that second document, you wanted to link to a specific place within that document; for example, to the fourth major section down?

You can do this in HTML by creating an *anchor* within the second document, and then creating a link in the first document that points to both the second document *and* that anchor. Then, when you follow the link with your browser, the browser will open the second document and scroll down to the location of the anchor (Figure 4.9 shows an example).

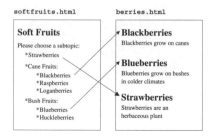

Figure 4.9. *Links and anchors.*

Creating Links and Anchors

You create an anchor in nearly the same way that you create a link, using the <A> tag. If you had wondered why the link tag uses an <A> name instead of an <L> name, now you know: A actually stands for Anchor.

When you specified links using <A>, there were two parts of the link: the HREF attribute in the opening <A> tag, and the text between the opening and closing tags that served as a hot spot for the link.

Anchors are created in much the same way, but instead of using the HREF attribute in the <A> tag, you use the NAME attribute. The NAME attribute takes a keyword (or words) that will be used to reference the anchor.

Anchors also require some amount of text between the opening and closing <A> tags. This text will be used by the browser when a link that is attached to this anchor is selected. The browser scrolls the document to the text within the anchor so that it is at the top of the screen and then highlights it.

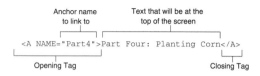

Figure 4.10. *The* <A> *tag and anchors.*

Unlike links, anchors do not show up in the final document. Anchors are invisible until you follow a link that points to them.

To reference an anchor in a link, you use the same form of link that you would when linking the document as a whole, with the file name or URL of the document in the HREF attribute.

After the name of the document, however, you include a hash sign (#) and the name of the anchor exactly as it appears in the NAME attribute of that anchor, like this:

```
<A HREF="../mybigdoc.html#Part4">Go to Part 4</A>
```

This link tells the browser to load the document mybigdoc.html, located one directory level up from the current document, and then to scroll down to the anchor name Part4: the selected text will appear at the top of the screen.

▼ Exercise 4.3. Link sections between two documents.

Let's do an example with two documents. These two documents are part of an online reference to classical music, where each Web page contains all the references for a particular letter of the alphabet (A.html, B.html, and so on). The reference could have been organized such that each section was its own document. Organizing it that way, however, would have involved an awful lot of documents to manage, as well as an awful lot of documents the reader would have to load if they were exploring the reference. It's more efficient in this case to bunch the related sections together under lettered groupings. (Chapter 11, "Writing and Designing Web Pages: Do's and Don'ts," goes into more detail about the trade-offs between short and long documents.)

The first document we'll look at is the one for "M," the first section of which looks like this in HTML (Figure 4.11 shows how it looks when it's displayed):

```
<HTML>
<HEAD>
<TITLE>Classical Music: M</TITLE>
</HEAD>
<BODY>
<H1>M</H1>
<H2>Madrigals</H2>
<ul>
<LI>William Byrd, <EM>This Sweet and Merry Month of May</EM>
<LI>William Byrd, <EM>Though Amaryllis Dance</EM>
<LI>Orlando Gibbons, <EM>The Silver Swan</EM>
<LI>Roland de Lassus, <EM>Mon Coeur se Recommande &agrave; vous</EM>
<LI>Claudio Monteverdi, <EM>Lamento d'Arianna</EM>
<LI>Thomas Morley, <EM>My Bonny Lass She Smileth</EM>
<LI>Thomas Weelkes, <EM>Thule, the Period of Cosmography</EM>
<LI>John Wilbye, <EM>Sweet Honey-Sucking Bees</EM>
</UL>
<P>Secular vocal music in four, five and six parts, usually a capella.
15th-16th centuries.</P>
<P><EM>See Also</EM>
Byrd, Gibbons, Lassus, Monteverdi, Morley, Weelkes, Wilbye</P>
</BODY>
</HTML>
```

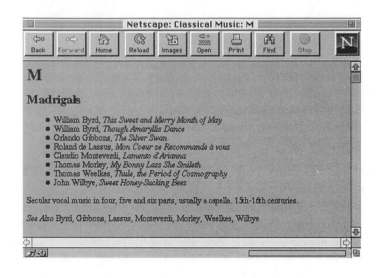

Figure 4.11. *Part M of the Online Music Reference.*

In that last line (the See Also), it would be useful to link those composer names to their respective sections elsewhere in the reference. If you used the procedure you learned previously in this chapter, you'd create a link here around the word Byrd to the document B.html. When your reader selected the link, the browser would drop him or her at the top of the Bs. That hapless reader would then have to scroll down through all the composers that start with B (and there are lots of them: Bach, Beethoven, Brahms, Bruckner) to get to Byrd; a lot of work for a system that claims to link information so you can find what you want quickly and easily.

What you want is to be able to link the word Byrd in M.html directly to the section for Byrd in B.html. Here's the relevant part of B.html you want to link (I've deleted all the Bs before Byrd to make this file shorter for this example. Pretend they're still there.)

```
<HTML>
<HEAD>
<TITLE>Classical Music: B</TITLE>
</HEAD>
<BODY>
<H1>B</H1>
<!-- I've deleted all the Bs before Byrd to make things shorter -->
<H2>Byrd, William, 1543-1623</H2>
<ul>
<LI>Madrigals
<ul>
<LI><EM>This Sweet and Merry Month of May</EM>
<LI><EM>Though Amaryllis Dance</EM>
<LI><EM>Lullabye, My Sweet Little Baby</EM>
</UL>
```

```
<LI>Masses
<ul>
<LI><EM>Mass for Five Voices</EM>
<LI><EM>Mass for Four Voices</EM>
<LI><EM>Mass for Three Voices</EM>
</UL>
<LI>Motets
<ul>
<LI><EM>Ave verum corpus a 4</EM>
</UL>
</UL>
<P><EM>See Also</EM>
Madrigals, Masses, Motets</P>
</BODY>
</HTML>
```

What you'll need to do here is to create an anchor at the section heading for Byrd. You can then link that anchor later on.

As I described in the last section, you need two things for each anchor: an anchor name and the text that will be highlighted when this document is loaded at the tail end of a link. The latter is easy; the section heading itself makes excellent highlighted text.

For the anchor name, you can choose any name you want, but each anchor in the document must be unique. (If you had two or more anchors with the name "fred" in the same document, how would the browser know which one to choose when a link to that anchor is selected?) A good unique anchor name for this example would be simply "Byrd."

With the two parts decided on, you can create the anchor itself in your HTML file. Add the <A> tag to the William Byrd section heading, but be careful here. If this was normal text within a paragraph, you'd just surround the whole line with <A>. But when you're adding an anchor to a big section of text that is also contained within an element—like a heading, paragraph, address, quote, or so on—always put the anchor *inside* the element. In other words, do this:

```
<H2><A NAME="Byrd">Byrd, William, 1543-1623</A></H2>
```

But not this:

```
<A NAME="Byrd"><H2>Byrd, William, 1543-1623</H2></A>
```

The second example could confuse your browser. Is it an anchor, formatted just like the text before it, with mysteriously placed heading tags, or is it a heading that also happens to be an anchor? If you use the right code in your HTML file, with the anchor inside the heading, you solve the confusion.

It's easy to forget about this, especially if you're like me and you create text first and then add links and anchors. It makes sense to just surround everything with an <A> tag. Think of it this way: If you were linking just one word, and not to the entire element, you'd put the <A> tag inside the <H2>. Working with the whole line of text isn't any different. Keep that rule in mind and you'll get less confused.

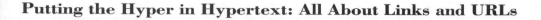

Note: If you're still confused, Appendix B has a summary of all the HTML tags and rules for which tags can and cannot go inside each one.

So you've added your anchor to the heading, and its name is "Byrd." Now go back to your M.html file, to the line with See Also.

```
<P><EM>See Also</EM>
Byrd, Gibbons, Lassus, Monteverdi, Morley, Weelkes, Wilbye</P>
```

You're going to create your link here around the word Byrd, just as you would for any other link. But what's the URL? As you learned in the previous section, path names to anchors look like this:

```
document#anchor_name
```

So if you were creating a link to the to the document itself, the HREF would be this:

```
<A HREF="B.html">
```

Then add the anchor name to link that section, so that it looks like this:

```
<A HREF="B.html#Byrd">
```

Note the capital B in Byrd. Anchor names and links are case sensitive; if you put #byrd in your HREF the link might not work properly in some browsers. Make sure that the anchor name you used in the NAME attribute and the anchor name in the link after the # are exactly the same.

Tip: A common mistake is to put a hash sign in both the anchor name and in the link to that anchor. The hash sign is only used to separate the document and the anchor in the link; anchor names should never have hash signs in them.

So, with the new link to the new section, the See Also line looks like this:

```
<P><EM>See Also</EM>
<A HREF="B.html#Byrd">Byrd</A>,
Gibbons, Lassus, Monteverdi, Morley, Weelkes, Wilbye</P>
```

And, of course, you could go ahead and add anchors and links to the other parts of the reference for the remaining composers.

With all your links and anchors in place, test everything. Figure 4.12 shows the Madrigals section with the link to Byrd ready to be selected.

Figure 4.13 shows what pops up when you select the Byrd link.

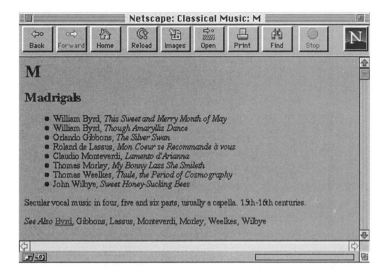

Figure 4.12. *The Madrigals section with link.*

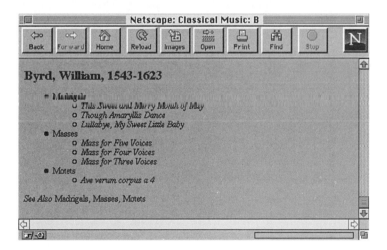

Figure 4.13. *The Byrd section.*

Linking to Anchors in the Same Document

What if you only have one document, and you want to link to sections within that document? You can use anchors for this, too. All you need to do is set up your anchors at each section, the way you usually would. Then, when you link those anchors, leave off the name of the document itself, but include the hash sign and the name of the anchor. So, if you were linking to an anchor name called Section5 in the same document as the link, the link would look like this:

```
Go to <A HREF=#Section5>The Fifth Section</A>
```

When you leave off the document name, the browser assumes you are linking with the current document and will scroll to the appropriate section.

Anatomy of a URL

So far in this book you've encountered URLs twice—in Chapter 1, as part of the introduction to the Web; and in this chapter, when you created links to remote documents. And if you've ever done much exploring on the Web, you've encountered URLs as a matter of course. You couldn't start exploring without a URL.

As I mentioned in Chapter 1, URLs are Uniform Resource Locators. URLs are effectively street addresses for bits of information on the Internet. Most of the time, you can avoid trying to figure out your own URLs by simply navigating to the bit of information you want with your browser, and then copying and pasting the long string of gobbledygook into your link. But it's often useful to understand what a URL is all about, and why it has to be so long and complex. Also, when you put your own information up on the Web, it'll be useful to know something about URLs so that you can tell people where your Web page is.

In this section, you'll learn what the parts of a URL are, how you can use them to get to information on the Web, and the kinds of URLs you can use (HTTP, FTP, mailto, and so on).

Parts of URLs

Most URLs contain (roughly) three parts: the protocol, the host name, and the directory or filename. (See Figure 4.14.)

Figure 4.14. *URL parts.*

The *protocol* is the way in which the document is accessed; that is, the type of protocol or program your browser will use to get to the file. If the browser is using HTTP to get to the file,

the protocol part is http. If the browser uses FTP, it's ftp. If you're using Gopher, it's gopher, and so on. The protocol matches to an information service that must be installed on the system for it to work. You can't use an FTP URL on a machine that does not have an FTP server installed, for example.

The *host name* is the system on the Internet where the information is stored, such as www.netcom.com, ftp.apple.com, or aol.com. You can have the same host name but have different URLs with different protocols, like this:

```
http://mysystem.com
ftp://mysystem.com
gopher://mysystem.com
```

Same machine, three different information servers, and the browser will use different methods of connecting to that same machine. As long as all three servers are installed on that system and available, there's not a problem.

The host-name part of the URL may include a port number. The port number tells your browser to open a connection of the appropriate protocol on a specific network port other than the default port. The only time you'll need a port number in a URL is if the server handling the information has been explicitly installed on that port. (This is covered in Day Seven, "Putting It All Online.")

If a port number is necessary, it goes after the host name but before the directory, like this:

```
http://my-public-access-unix.com:1550/pub/file
```

Finally, the *directory* is the location of the file or other form of information on the host. The directory may be an actual directory and filename, or it may be another indicator that the protocol uses to refer to the location of that information. (For example, Gopher directories are not explicit directories.)

Special Characters in URLs

A "special character" in a URL is anything that is not an upper- or lowercase letter, a number (0–9), or the following symbols: dollar sign ($), dash (-), underscore (_), period (.), or plus sign (+). Any other characters may need to be specified using special URL escape codes to keep them from being interpreted as parts of the URL itself.

URL escape codes are indicated by a percent sign (%) and a two-character hex symbol from the ISO-Latin-1 character set (a superset of standard ASCII). For example %20 is a space, %3f is a question mark, and %2f is a slash.

Say you had a directory named All My Files, probably on a Macintosh, since there are spaces in the filename. Your first pass at a URL with that name in it might look like this:

```
http://myhost.com/harddrive/All My Files/www/file.html
```

4

If you put this URL in quotes in a link tag, it might work (but only if you put it in quotes). But because the spaces are considered special characters to the URL, some browsers may have problems with them and not recognize the path name correctly. For full compatibility with all browsers, use %20:

```
http://myhost.com/harddrive/All%20My%20Files/www/file.html
```

Kinds of URLs

There are many kinds of URLs defined by the Uniform Resource Locator specification. (See Appendix A , "Sources for Further Information," for a pointer to the most recent version.) This section describes some of the more popular URLs and some things to look out for when using them.

HTTP

HTTP URLs are the most popular form of URL on the World Wide Web. HTTP stands for HyperText Transfer Protocol and is the protocol that World Wide Web servers use to send HTML documents over the Net.

HTTP URLs follow the basic URL form:

```
http://www.foo.com/home/foo/
```

If the URL ends in a slash, the last part of the URL is considered to be a directory name. The file that you get using a URL of this type is the "default" file for that directory as defined by the HTTP server, usually a file called index.html. (If the Web page you are designing is the top-level file for all the files in a directory, it's a good idea to call it index.html.)

You can also specify the filename directly in the URL. In this case, the file at the end of the URL is the one that is loaded.

```
http://www.foo.com/home/foo/index.html
http://www.foo.com/home/foo/homepage.html
```

Avoid using HTTP URLs like this, where foo is a directory:

```
http://www.foo.com/home/foo
```

Note that foo is a directory, but there is no slash at the end of the URL. Although most Web servers are smart enough to figure out that foo is a directory and not a file, some may have difficulties resolving this URL. Always make sure you are indicating either a file or a directory explicitly, and that if you are indicating a directory, that a default file is available.

Anonymous FTP

FTP URLs are used to point to files located on FTP servers—and usually anonymous FTP servers; that is, those which you can log into using anonymous as the login ID and your e-mail address as the password. FTP URLs also follow the "standard" URL form.

```
ftp://ftp.foo.com/home/foo
ftp://ftp.foo.com/home/foo/homepage.html
```

Because you can retrieve either a file or a directory list with FTP, the restrictions on whether you need a trailing slash at the end of the URL are not the same. The first URL above retrieves a listing of the foo directory. The second URL retrieves and parses the file homepage.html in the foo directory.

Note that although your browser uses FTP to fetch the file, you can get an HTML file from that server just as if it were an HTTP server. Web browsers don't care *how* they get a hypertext file. As long as they can recognize it as HTML, either by the extension or by the <HTML> tag, depending on the browser, they will parse and display it as an HTML file. If they don't recognize it as an HTML file, it's not a big deal; the browser can either display it if it knows what kind of file it is, or just save it to disk.

> **Note:** Navigating FTP servers using a Web browser can often be much slower than navigating them using FTP itself, as the browser does not hold the connection open. Instead, it opens the connection, finds the file or directory listing, displays it, and then closes down the FTP connection. If you select a link to open a file or another directory in that listing, the browser will construct a new FTP URL from the items you selected, re-open the FTP connection using the new URL, get the next directory or file, and close it again. For this reason, FTP URLs are best when you know exactly which file you want to retrieve, rather than for browsing an archive.

Non-Anonymous FTP

All of the FTP URLs in the previous section were used for anonymous FTP servers. You can also specify an FTP URL for named accounts on an FTP server, like this:

```
ftp://username:password@ftp.foo.com/home/foo/homepage.html
```

In this form of the URL, the username part is your login ID on the server, and password is that account's password. Note that no attempt is made to hide that password in the URL. Be very careful that no one is watching you when you are using URLs of this form—and don't put them into a link that someone else can find!

File

File URLs are intended to reference files contained on the local disk. In other words, they refer to files that are on the same system as the browser. For local files, file URLs take one of these two forms:

```
file:///dir1/dir2/file
file://localhost/dir1/dir2/file
```

Depending on your browser, one or the other will usually work.

File URLs are very similar to FTP URLs, and in fact, if the host part of a file URL is not empty or localhost, your browser uses FTP to find the referenced file anyway. Both of the following URLs result in the same file being loaded in the same way:

```
file://somesystem.com/pub/dir/foo/file.html
ftp://somesystem.com/pub/dir/foo/file.html
```

Probably the best use of file URLs is in startup pages for your browser (which are also called "home pages"). In this instance, since you will always be referring to a local file, a file URL makes sense.

The problem with file URLs is that they reference local files, where local means on the same system as the browser that is pointing to the file—*not* the same system that the document was retrieved from! If you use file URLs as links in your document, and then someone from elsewhere on the Net encounters your document and tries to follow those links, their browser will attempt to find the file on *their* local disk (and generally fail). Also, because file URLs use the absolute path name to the file, if you use file URLs in your document, you will not be able to move that document elsewhere on the system or to any other system.

If your intention is to refer to files that are on the same file system or directory as the current document, use relative path names instead of file URLs. With relative path names for local files and other URLs for remote files, there's no reason why you should need to use a file URL at all.

Mailto

The mailto URL is used to send electronic mail. If the browser supports mailto URLs, when a link that contains one is selected, the browser will prompt you for a subject and the body of the mail message, and send that message to the appropriate address when you're done.

Many browsers do not support mailto and produce an error if a link with a mailto URL is selected.

The mailto URL is different from the standard URL form. It looks like this:

```
mailto:internet_email_address
```

For example:

```
mailto:lemay@netcom.com
```

> **Note:** If the e-mail address includes a percent sign (%), you'll have to use the escape character %25 instead.

Gopher

Gopher URLs use the standard URL file format up to and including the host name. After that, they use special Gopher protocols to encode the path to the particular file. The directory in Gopher does not indicate a directory path name as HTTP and FTP URLs do and is too complex for this chapter. See the URL specification if you're really interested.

Most of the time you'll probably be using a Gopher URL just to point to a Gopher server, which is easy. A URL of this sort looks like this:

```
gopher://gopher.myhost.com/
```

If you really want to point directly to a specific file on a Gopher server, probably the best way to get the appropriate URL is not to try to build it yourself. Instead, navigate to the appropriate file or collection using your browser and then copy and paste the appropriate URL into your HTML document.

Usenet

Usenet news URLs have one of two forms:

```
news:name_of_newsgroup
news:message-id
```

The first form is used to read an entire newsgroup, such as comp.infosystems.www.providers or alt.gothic. If your browser supports Usenet news URLs (either directly or through a newsreader), it will provide you with a list of articles in that newsgroup.

The second form enables you to retrieve a specific news article. Each news article has a unique ID, called a message ID, which usually looks something like this:

```
<lemayCt76Jq.CwG@netcom.com>
```

To use a message ID in a URL, remove the angle brackets and include the news: part:

```
news:lemayCt76Jq.CwG@netcom.com
```

Note that news articles do not exist forever—they "expire" and are deleted— so a message ID that was valid at one point may become invalid a short time later. If you want a permanent link to a news article, it is best to just copy the article to your Web presentation and link it as you would any other file.

Both forms of URL assume that you are reading news from an NNTP server. Both can only be used if you have defined an NNTP server somewhere in an environment variable or preferences file for your browser. Because of this, news URLs are most useful simply for reading specific news articles locally, and not necessarily for using in links in documents.

> **Note:** News URLs, like mailto URLs, may not be supported by all browsers.

Summary

In this chapter, you learned all about links. They are the things that turn the Web from a collection of unrelated pages into an enormous interrelated information system (there are those big words again). You also learned how to use anchors to link specific sections in documents and learned more about URLs and how to use them.

To create links, you use the `<A>...</A>` tag, called the link or link tag, which has three parts:

1. The tag itself, `<A>...</A>`
2. The HREF attribute, which specifies the path name of the file to load (for local documents), or the URL of the file to load (for remote documents)
3. The text in between the opening and closing tags, which is the text that will be highlighted (and able to be selected using a browser) to activate the link

When linking documents that are all stored on the local disk, you can specify their path names as relative or absolute paths. For local links, relative path names are preferred because they let you move those local documents more easily to another directory or to another system. If you use absolute path names, your links will break if you change anything in that hard-coded path.

To link to a document on the Web (a remote document), the value of the HREF attribute is the URL of that document. You can easily copy the URL of the document you want to link. Just go to that document using your favorite Web browser and then copy and paste the URL from your browser into the appropriate place in your link tag.

Linking explicitly between documents is fine if each document cnotains only one discrete piece of information. But if you have several bits of information in each document, linking

between documents isn't specific enough. You need a method for linking to smaller bits of information within documents. That's where anchors come in.

To create anchors to parts of a document you want to link to, use the <A>...</A> tag as you would with a link, but instead of the HREF attribute, you use the NAME attribute to name the anchor. You can then link directly to it using a hash sign (#) and the anchor name.

URLs (Uniform Resource Locators) are used to point to documents, files, and other information on the Internet. Depending on the type of information, URLs can contain several parts, but most contain a protocol type and location or address. URLs can be used to point to many kinds of information, but are most commonly used to point to Web documents (http), FTP directories or files (ftp), information on Gopher servers (gopher), electronic mail addresses (mailto), or Usenet news (news).

Q&A

Q I put a URL into a link, and it shows up as highlighted in my browser, but when I click on it, the browser says "unable to access document." If it can't find the document, why did it highlight the text?

A The browser highlights text within a link tag whether or not the link is valid. In fact, you can even be off the network, load in a local document full of links, and have them all highlighted, even though there's no way to get to them. The only way a you can tell if a link is valid to select it and try to view the document.

As to why the browser couldn't find the document you linked to—make sure you're connected to the network and that you entered the URL into the link correctly. Try opening that URL directly in your browser and see if that works. If directly opening the link doesn't work either, there might be several reasons why. Two common ones are

☐ The server is overloaded or is not on the Net.

Machines go down, as do network connections. If a particular URL doesn't work for you, perhaps there's something wrong with the machine or the network. Or maybe it's a popular site, and too many people are trying to access it at once. Try again later, or during non-peak hours for that server. If you know the people who run the server, you can try sending them electronic mail or calling them.

☐ The URL itself is bad.

Sometimes URLs become invalid. Since a URL is a form of absolute path name, if the file to which it refers moves around, or if a machine or directory name gets changed, the URL won't be any good any more. Try contacting the person or site you got the URL from in the first place. See if they have a more recent link.

Q **Can I put any URL in a link?**

A You bet. If you can get to a URL using your browser, you can put that URL in a link. Note, however, that some browsers support URLs that others don't. For example, Lynx is really good with mailto URLs (URLs that allow you to send electronic mail to a person's e-mail address). When you select a mailto URL in Lynx, it prompts you for a subject and the body of the message. When you're done, it sends the mail.

Other browsers, on the other hand, may not handle mailto URLs, and insist that a link containing the mailto URL is invalid. The URL itself may be fine, but the browser can't handle it.

Q **Can I use images as links?**

A Yup. You'll learn how to do this in Chapter 9, "Using Images."

Q **You've only described two attributes of the <A> tag: HREF and NAME. Aren't there others?**

A Yes; the <A> tag has several attributes including REL, REV, URN, METHODS, and TITLE. However, most of those attributes can only be used by tools that automatically generate links between documents, or by browsers that can manage links better than most of those now available. Because 99 percent of you reading this book won't care about (or ever use) those links or browsers, I'm sticking to HREF and NAME and ignoring the other attributes.

If you're really interested, I've summarized the other attributes in Appendix B, and there are pointers to the various HTML specifications in Appendix A, as well.

Q **My links are not pointing to my anchors; when I follow a link, some other random bit of text is selected. What's going on here?**

A Are you specifying the anchor name in the link after the hash sign exactly the same way that it appears in the anchor itself, with all the upper- and lowercase letters and spaces and other characters the same? Anchors are case-sensitive, so if your browser cannot find an anchor name with an exact match, it may try to select something else in the document that is closer. This is dependent on browser behavior, of course, but if your links and anchors aren't working, it's usually because your anchor names and your anchors do not match. Also, remember that anchor names don't contain hash signs—only the links to them do.

Q **It sounds like file URLs aren't overly useful. Is there any reason you'd want to use them?**

A I can think of two. The first one is if you have many users on a single system (for example, on a UNIX system) and you want to give those local users (but nobody else) access to files on that system. By using file URLs you can point to files on the local system, and anyone on that system can get to them. Readers from outside the system won't have direct access to the disk and wont be able to get to those files.

A second good reason for using file URLs is that you actually want to point to a local disk. For example, you could create a CD full of information in HTML form, and then create a link from a page on the Web to a file on the CD using a file URL. In this case, since your presentation depends on a disk your readers must have, using a file URL makes sense.

Q Is there any way to indicate a subject in a mailto URL?

A Not at the moment. According to the current mailto URL definition, the only thing you can put in a mailto URL is the address to mail to. If you really need a subject or something in the body of the message, consider using a form instead (you'll learn more about forms on Day Eight).

DAY

3

DAY

5

THREE

Still More HTML

Now that you know the basics of laying out HTML pages and linking them together, you are ready to learn more about what HTML can do. This chapter explains most of the remaining tags in the HTML language as of version 2.0, including tags to

- ☐ Create numbered lists, unnumbered lists, and other forms of lists
- ☐ Format the appearance of individual characters (bold, italic, typewriter)
- ☐ Include special characters
- ☐ Create preformatted text (text with spaces and tabs retained)
- ☐ Create other miscellaneous elements including line breaks, rule lines, addresses, and quotations

In addition, at the end of this chapter, you'll create a complete Web page that uses many of the tags presented in this chapter as well as the information from the previous four chapters.

This chapter covers a lot of tags, and it's all going to be a bit overwhelming. But don't worry about remembering everything now; just get a grasp of what sorts of formatting you can do in HTML and then you can look up the specific tags later.

> **Note:** This chapter focuses on the standard HTML 2.0 as it is currently defined and supported by most browsers. I talk in the next chapter about the new HTML 3.0 standard. In addition, Netscape and Microsoft have defined several additions to the tags you'll read about here, for example, attributes to the rule line tag that allow you to modify its length and width. I'll discuss these separately in Chapter 7, "New Features in HTML and the Netscape 2.0 and Internet Explorer 2.0 Extensions."

Lists, Lists, and More Lists

In addition to headings and paragraphs, probably the most common HTML element you'll be using is the list. After this section, you'll not only know how to create a list in HTML, but how to create five different kinds of lists—a list for every occasion!

HTML defines five kinds of lists:

- ☐ Numbered, or ordered lists, typically labeled with numbers
- ☐ Bulleted, or unordered lists, typically labeled with bullets or some other symbol
- ☐ Glossary lists, in which each item in the list has a term and a definition for that term, arranged so that the term is somehow highlighted or drawn out from the text

- Menu lists, for lists of short paragraphs (typically one line)
- Directory lists, for lists of short items that can be arranged vertically or horizontally

> **Note:** The menu and directory lists are defined as official HTML 2.0 tags, but are not commonly used on the Web at large. In fact, many browsers may format both as unordered (bulleted) lists.

List Tags

All the list tags have common elements:

- The entire list is surrounded by the appropriate opening and closing tag for the kind of list (for example, `<UL>` and `</UL>`, or `<MENU>` and `</MENU>`).
- Each list item within the list has its own tag: `<DT>` and `<DD>` for the glossary lists and `<LI>` for all the other lists.

Although the tags and the list items can appear in any arrangement in your HTML code, I prefer to arrange list code so that the list tags are on their own lines, and each new item also starts on a new line. This makes it easy to pick out the whole list as well as the individual elements. In other words, I find an arrangement like this:

```
<P>Dante's Divine Comedy consists of three books:</P>
<UL>
<LI>The Inferno
<LI>The Purgatorio
<LI>The Paradiso
</UL>
```

easier to read than an arrangement like this:

```
<P>Dante's Divine Comedy consists of three books:</P>
<UL><LI>The Inferno<LI>The Purgatorio<LI>The Paradiso
</UL>
```

even though both result in the same output in the browser.

Numbered Lists

Numbered lists are surrounded by the `<OL>`...`</OL>` tags (OL stands for Ordered List), and each item within the list begins with the `<LI>` (List Item) tag.

The `<LI>` tag is one-sided; you do not have to specify the closing tag. The existence of the next `<LI>` (or the closing `</OL>` tag) indicates the end of that item in the list.

When the browser interprets an ordered list, it numbers (and often indents) each of the elements sequentially. You do not have to do the numbering yourself, and if you add or delete items, the browser will renumber them the next time the document is loaded.

```
<P>Laura's Awesome Nachos</P>
<OL>
<LI>Warm up Refried beans with chili powder and cumin.
<LI>Glop refried beans on tortilla chips.
<LI>Grate equal parts Jack and Cheddar cheese, spread on chips.
<LI>Chop one small onion finely, spread on chips.
<LI>Heat under broiler 2 minutes.
<LI>Add guacamole, sour cream, fresh chopped tomatoes, and cilantro.
<LI>Drizzle with hot green salsa.
<LI>Broil another 1 minute.
<LI>Nosh.
</OL>
```

Use numbered lists only when you want to indicate that the elements are ordered; that is, that they must appear or occur in that specific order. Ordered lists are good for steps to follow or instructions to the reader. If you just want to indicate that something has some number of elements that can appear in any order, use an unordered list instead.

The following input and output examples show a simple ordered list and how it appears in Netscape (Figure 5.1) and Lynx (Figure 5.2).

```
<P>To summon the demon, use the following steps:</P>
<OL>
<LI>Draw the pentagram
<LI>Sacrifice the goat
<LI>Chant the incantation
</OL>
```

Figure 5.1. *The output in Netscape.*

Figure 5.2. *The output in Lynx.*

Unordered Lists

Unordered lists are lists in which the elements can appear in any order. Unordered lists look just like ordered lists in HTML, except that the list is indicated using <UL>...</UL> tags instead of <OL>. The elements of the list are separated by <LI>, just as with ordered lists. For example:

```
<P>Lists in HTML</P>
<UL>
<LI>Ordered Lists
<LI>Unordered Lists
<LI>Menus
<LI>Directories
<LI>Glossary Lists
</UL>
```

Browsers usually format unordered lists by inserting bullets or some other symbolic marker; Lynx inserts an asterisk (*).

The following input and output example shows an unordered list and how it appears in Netscape (Figure 5.3) and Lynx (Figure 5.4).

Input

```
<P>The three Erinyes, or Furies, were:</P>
<UL>
<LI>Tisiphone
<LI>Megaera
<LI>Alecto
</UL>
```

Output

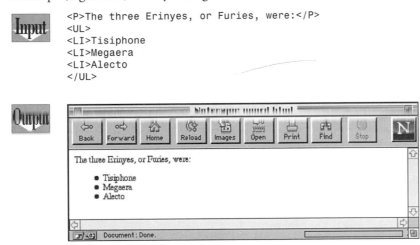

Figure 5.3. *The output in Netscape.*

```
The three Erinyes, or Furies, were:
   * Tisiphone
   * Megaera
   * Alecto
```

Figure 5.4. *The output in Lynx.*

Menu and Directory Lists

Menus are lists of items or short paragraphs with no bullets or numbers or other label-like things. They are similar to simple lists of paragraphs, except that some browsers may indent them or format them in some way differently from normal paragraphs. Menu lists are surrounded by <MENU> and </MENU> tags, and each list item is indicated using <LI>.

Directory lists are for items that are even shorter than menu lists, and are intended to be formatted by browsers horizontally in columns—like doing a directory listing on a UNIX system. As with menu lists, directory lists are surrounded by <DIR> and </DIR>, with <LI> for the individual list items.

> **Note:** Menu and directory lists are not commonly used in Web pages, and in HTML 3.0, they no longer exist (there are other available tags that produce the same effect). Considering that most browsers seem to format menus and directories in similar ways to the glossary lists (or as unordered lists), and not in the way they are described in the specification, it is probably best to stick with the other three forms of lists.

The following input and output example shows a menu and a directory list, and how they appear in Netscape (Figure 5.5) and Lynx (Figure 5.6).

```
<MENU>
<LI>Canto 1: The Dark Wood of Error
<LI>Canto 2: The Descent
<LI>Canto 3: The Vestibule
<LI>Canto 4: Circle One: Limbo
<LI>Canto 5: Circle Two: The Carnal
</MENU>

<DIR>
<LI>files/
<LI>applications/
<LI>mail/
<LI>stuff/
<LI>phone_numbers
</DIR>
```

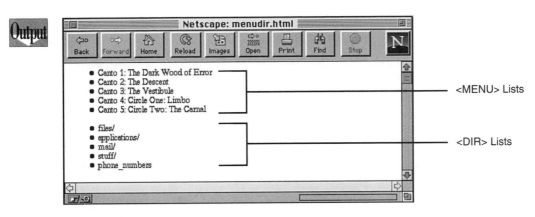

Figure 5.5. *The output in Netscape.*

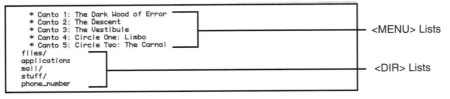

Figure 5.6. *The output in Lynx.*

Glossary Lists

Glossary lists, sometimes called definition lists, are slightly different from other lists. Each list item in a glossary list has two parts:

☐ A term

☐ That term's definition

Each part of the glossary list has its own tag: <DT> for the term, and <DD> for its definition. <DT> and <DD> are both one-sided tags, and they usually occur in pairs, although most browsers can handle single terms or definitions. The entire glossary list is indicated by the tags <DL>...</DL>:

```
<DL>
<DT>Basil<DD>Annual. Can grow four feet high; the scent of its tiny white
flowers is heavenly
<DT>Oregano<DD>Perennial. Sends out underground runners and is difficult
to get rid of once established.
<DT>Coriander<DD>Annual. Also called cilantro, coriander likes cooler
weather of spring and fall.
</DL>
```

Glossary lists are usually formatted with the terms and definitions on separate lines, and the left margins of the definitions are indented.

Glossary lists don't have to be used for terms and definitions, of course. They can be used anywhere the same sort of list is needed. Here's an example:

```
<DL>
<DT>Macbeth<DD>I'll go no more. I am afraid to think of what I have done; look
on't agin I dare not.
<DT>Lady Macbeth<DD>Infirm of purpose! Give me the daggers. The sleeping and the
dead are as but
pictures. 'Tis the eye of childhood that fears a painted devil. If he do bleed,
I'll gild the faces
of the grooms withal, for it must seem their guilt. (Exit. Knocking within)
<DT>Macbeth<DD>Whence is that knocking? How is't with me when every noise apalls
me? What hands are
here? Ha! They pluck out mine eyes! Will all Neptune's ocean wash this blood
clean from my hand?
No. This my hand will rather the multitudinous seas incarnadine, making the
green one red.
(Enter lady Macbeth)
<DT>Lady Macbeth<DD>My hands are of your color, but I shame to wear a heart so
white.
</DL>
```

HTML also defines a "compact" form of glossary list in which less space is used for the list, perhaps by placing the terms and definitions on the same line and highlighting the term, or by lessening the amount of indent used by the definitions.

 Note: Most browsers seem to ignore the COMPACT attribute and format compact glossary lists in the same way that normal glossary lists are formatted.

To use the compact form of the glossary list, use the COMPACT attribute inside the opening <DL> tag, like this:

```
<DL COMPACT>
<DT>Capellini<DD>Round and very thin (1-2mm)
<DT>Vermicelli<DD>Round and thin (2-3mm)
<DT>Spaghetti<DD>Round and thin, but thicker than vermicelli (3-4mm)
<DT>Linguine<DD>Flat, (5-6mm)
<DT>Fettucini<DD>flat, (8-10mm)
</DL>
```

This input and output example shows how a glossary list is formatted in Netscape (Figure 5.7) and Lynx (Figure 5.8):

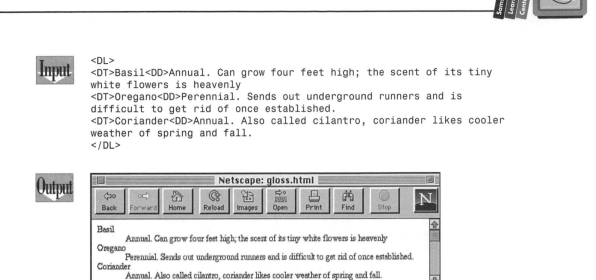

```
<DL>
<DT>Basil<DD>Annual. Can grow four feet high; the scent of its tiny
white flowers is heavenly
<DT>Oregano<DD>Perennial. Sends out underground runners and is
difficult to get rid of once established.
<DT>Coriander<DD>Annual. Also called cilantro, coriander likes cooler
weather of spring and fall.
</DL>
```

Figure 5.7. *The output in Netscape.*

```
Basil   Annual. Can grow four feet high; the scent of its tiny white
        flowers is heavenly

Oregano
        Perennial. Sends out underground runners and is difficult to
        get rid of once established.

Coriander
        Annual. Also called cilantro, coriander likes cooler weather of
        spring and fall.
```

Figure 5.8 *The output in Lynx*

Nesting Lists

What happens if you put a list inside another list? This is fine as far as HTML is concerned; just put the entire list structure inside another list as one of its elements. The nested list just becomes another element of the first list, and it is indented from the rest of the list. Lists like this work especially well for menu-like entities in which you want to show hierarchy (for example, in tables-of-contents), or as outlines.

Indenting nested lists in HTML code itself helps show their relationship to the final layout:

```
<OL>
<UL>
<LI>WWW
<LI>Organization
```

```
<LI>Beginning HTML
     <UL>
     <LI>What HTML is
     <LI>How to Write HTML
     <LI>Doc structure
     <LI>Headings
     <LI>Paragraphs
     <LI>Comments
     </UL>
<LI>Links
<LI>More HTML
</OL>
```

Many browsers format nested ordered and nested unordered lists differently from their enclosing lists; for example, they might use a symbol other than a bullet for a nested list, or number the inner list with letters (a, b, c) instead of numbers. Don't assume that this will be the case, however, and refer back to "section 8, subsection b" in your text, as you cannot determine what the exact formatting will be in the final output.

Here's an input and output example of a nested list and how it appears in Netscape (Figure 5.9) and Lynx (Figure 5.10):

Input
```
<H1>Peppers</H1>
<UL>
<LI>Bell
<LI>Chile
     <UL>
     <LI>Serrano
     <LI>Jalapeno
     <LI>Habanero
     <LI>Anaheim
     </UL>
<LI>Schezuan
<LI>Cayenne
</UL>
```

Output

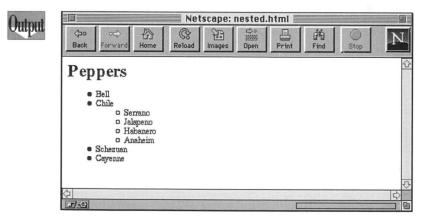

Figure 5.9. *The output in Netscape.*

```
                              PEPPERS
        * Bell
        * Chile
                + Serrano
                + Jalapeno
                + Habanero
                + Anaheim
        * Schezuan
        * Cayenne
```

Figure 5.10. *The output in Lynx.*

Exercise 5.1. Creating a link menu.

Now that you've learned how to do lists, in this chapter and links in the last chapter, you can create what is called a link menu. Link menus are links on your Web page that are arranged in list form or in some other short, easy-to-read and easy-to-understand format. Link menus are terrific for pages that are organized in a hierarchy, for tables of contents, or for navigation among several documents. Web pages that consist of nothing but links often organize those links in menu form.

The idea of a link menu is that you use short, descriptive terms as the links, with either no text following the link or with further description following the link itself. Link menus look best in a bulleted or unordered list format, but you can also use glossary lists or just plain paragraphs.

Link menus let your reader scan the list of links quickly and easily, something that may be difficult to do if you bury your links in body text.

In this exercise, you'll create a Web page for a set of restaurant reviews. This page will serve as the index to the reviews, so the link menu you'll create is essentially a menu of restaurant names.

Start with a simple page framework: a first-level head and some basic explanatory text:

```
<HTML>
<HEAD>
<TITLE>Laura's Restaurant Guide</TITLE>
</HEAD><BODY>
<H1>Laura's Restaurant Reviews</H1>
<P>I spend a lot of time in restaurants in the area, having lunches or dinners
with friends or meeting with potential clients. I've written up several reviews
of many of the restaurants I frequent (and a few I'd rather not go back to).
Here are reviews for the following restaurants:</P>
</BODY></HTML>
```

Now add the list that will become the links, without the link tags themselves. It's always easier to start with link text and then attach actual links afterwards. For this list, we'll use a <UL> tag to create a bulleted list of individual restaurants. You could use a <MENU> tag here just as easily,

5

but the <OL> tag wouldn't be appropriate, because the numbers would imply that you were ranking the restaurants in some way. Here's the HTML list of restaurants; Figure 5.11 shows the page in Netscape as it currently looks with the introduction and the list.

```
<UL>
<LI>Szechuan Supreme
<LI>Mel's Pizza
<LI>Tomi
<LI>The Summit Inn
<LI>Cafe Milieu
</UL>
```

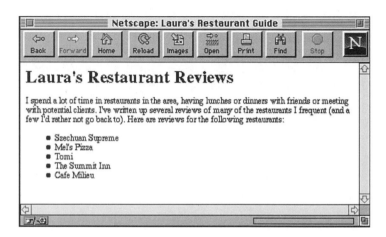

Figure 5.11. *A list of restaurants.*

Now, modify each of the list items so that they include link tags. You'll need to keep the <LI> tag in there, since that indicates where the list items begin. Just add the <A> tags around the text itself. Here we'll link to filenames on the local disk in the same directory as this file, with each individual file containing the review for the particular restaurant:

```
<UL>
<LI><A HREF="schezuan.html">Szechuan Supreme</A>
<LI><A HREF="mels.html">Mel's Pizza</A>
<LI><A HREF="tomi.html">Tomi</A>
<LI><A HREF="summitinn.html">The Summit Inn</A>
<LI><A HREF="millieu.html">Cafe Milieu</A>
</UL>
```

The menu of restaurants looks fine, although it is a little sparse. Your reader doesn't know what kinds of food each restaurant serves (although some of the restaurant names indicate the kind of food they serve), or if the review is good or bad. An improvement would be to add some short explanatory text after the links to provide a hint of what is on the other side of the link itself:

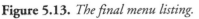

```
<UL>
<LI><A HREF="schezuan.html">Szechuan Supreme</A>. Chinese food. Prices are
excellent, but service is slow
<LI><A HREF="mels.html">Mel's Pizza</A>. Thin-crust New York style pizza.
Awesome, but loud.
<LI><A HREF="tomi.html">Tomi</A>. Sushi. So-so selection, friendly chefs.
<LI><A HREF="summitinn.html">The Summit Inn</A>. California food. Creative
chefs, but you pay extra for originality and appearance.
<LI><A HREF="millieu.html">Cafe Milieu</A>. Lots of atmosphere, sullen
postmodern waitrons, but an excellent double espresso none the less.
</UL>
```

Figure 5.12. *The final link menu.*

The revised list then looks like Figure 5.13.

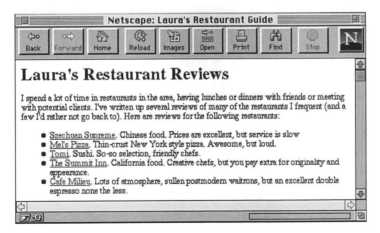

Figure 5.13. *The final menu listing.*

115

Character Styles

When you use an HTML tag for paragraphs, headings, and lists, those tags affect the text as a whole, changing the font, changing the spacing above and below the line, or adding characters (in the case of bulleted lists). *Character styles* are tags that affect words or characters within other HTML entities and change the appearance of that text so that it is somehow different from the surrounding text—making it boldface or underline, for instance.

To change the appearance of a set of characters within text, you can use one of two kinds of tags: *logical* style tags, which indicate the way the text is used (emphasis, citation, definition), and *physical* style tags, which indicate exactly the way the text is to be formatted (boldface, underline).

Logical Styles

Logical style tags indicate how the given highlighted text is to be used, not how it is to be displayed. This is similar to the common element tags for paragraphs or headings. They don't indicate how the text is to be formatted, just how it is to be used in a document. Logical style tags indicate text that is a definition, or code, or emphasized from the text around it.

It is up to the browser to determine the actual way text within these tags is presented, be it in boldface, italic, or any other change in appearance. You cannot guarantee that text highlighted using these tags will always be in boldface, or always be italic (and, therefore, you should not depend on it, either).

Each character style tag has both opening and closing sides, and affects the text within those two tags. There are eight logical style tags currently in use:

☐ `<EM>`: indicates that the characters are to be emphasized in some way; that is, they are formatted differently from the rest of the text. In graphical browsers, `<EM>` is typically italic. For example:

```
<P>We'd all get along much better if you'd stop being so
<EM>silly.</EM></P>
```

☐ `<STRONG>`: the characters are to be more strongly emphasized than with `<EM>`. `<STRONG>` text is highlighted differently from `<EM>` text, for example, in boldface. For example:

```
<P>You <STRONG>must </STRONG> open the can before drinking</P>
```

- [ ] `<CODE>`: a code sample (a fixed-width font such as Courier in graphical displays):

  `<P><CODE>#include "trans.h"</CODE></P>`

- [ ] `<SAMP>`: example text, similar to `<CODE>`:

  `<P>The URL for that page is <SAMP>http://www.cern.ch/</SAMP></P>`

- [ ] `<KBD>`: text intended to be typed by a user:

  `<P>Type the following command: <KBD>find . -name "prune" -print</KBD></P>`

- [ ] `<VAR>`: the name of a variable, or some entity to be replaced with an actual value. Often displayed as italic or underline, for example:

  `<P><CODE>chown </CODE><VAR>your_name the_file</VAR></P>`

- [ ] `<DFN>`: a definition. `<DFN>` is used to highlight a word that will be defined or has just been defined:

  `<P>Styles that are named after how they are actually used are called <DFN>logical character styles</DFN></P>`

- [ ] `<CITE>`: a short quote or citation:

  `<P>Eggplant has been known to cause nausea in many unsuspecting people<CITE> (Lemay, 1994)</CITE></P>`

Note: Of the above tags, all except `<DFN>` are part of the official HTML 2.0 specification. `<DFN>` is commonly supported by most browsers, however, so I've included it here.

Got all those memorized now? Good! There will be a pop quiz at the end of the chapter. Figures 5.14 and 5.15 illustrate how all eight tags are displayed in Netscape and Lynx.

Input

```
<P>We'd all get along much better if you'd stop being so <EM>silly.</
EM>
<P>You <STRONG>must</STRONG> open the can before drinking</P>
<P><CODE>#include "trans.h"</CODE></P>
<P>Type the following command: <KBD>find . -name "prune" -print</KBD></
P>
<P><CODE>chown </CODE><VAR>your_name the_file</VAR></P>
<P>The URL for that page is <SAMP>http://www.cern.ch/</SAMP></P>
<P>Styles that are named on how they are used are called <DFN>character
styles</DFN></P>
<P>Eggplant has been known to cause extreme nausea in many unsuspecting
people<CITE> (Lemay, 1994)</CITE></P>
```

5

Output

```
┌─────────────────────────────────────────────────────────────┐
│ ▣ ▣         Netscape: logicals.html                      ▣ │
├─────────────────────────────────────────────────────────────┤
│  ⇦o    o⇨     ⌂      ⊛      📷      ⇨o      🖨      🔍     ◯  │
│ Back  Forward Home  Reload  Images  Open   Print   Find  Stop │
├─────────────────────────────────────────────────────────────┤
│                                                               │
│ We'd all get along much better if you'd stop being so silly.  │
│                                                               │
│ You must open the can before drinking.                        │
│                                                               │
│ #include "trans.h"                                            │
│                                                               │
│ Type the following command: find . -name "prune" -print       │
│                                                               │
│ chown your_name the_file                                      │
│                                                               │
│ The URL for that page is http://www.cern.ch/                 │
│                                                               │
│ Styles that are named on how they are used are called character styles │
│                                                               │
│ Eggplant has been known to cause extreme nausea in many unsuspecting people (Lemay, 1994) │
│                                                               │
└─────────────────────────────────────────────────────────────┘
```

Figure 5.14. *The output in Netscape.*

```
┌─────────────────────────────────────────────────────────────┐
│ We'd all get along much better if you'd stop being so silly.  │
│                                                               │
│ You must open the can before drinking.                        │
│                                                               │
│ #include "trans.h"                                            │
│                                                               │
│ Type the following command: find . -name "prune" -print       │
│                                                               │
│ chown your_name the_file                                      │
│                                                               │
│ The URL for that page is http://www.cern.ch/                 │
│                                                               │
│ Styles that are named on how they are used are called character styles │
│                                                               │
│ Eggplant has been known to cause extreme nausea in many unsuspecting │
│ people (Lemay, 1994)                                          │
└─────────────────────────────────────────────────────────────┘
```

Figure 5.15. *The output in Lynx.*

Physical Styles

In addition to the tags for style in the previous section, there is also a set of tags that change the actual presentation style of the text—to make it bold, italic, or monospaced.

Like the character style tags, each formatting tag has a beginning and ending tag. There are three physical style tags:

- ☐ <B> for boldface
- ☐ <I> for italic
- ☐ <TT> for monospaced typewriter font

In addition, the <U> tag, for underlining, is implemented in some browsers, but not others. It is not part of the official HTML 2.0 specification.

If you choose to use the physical style tags, be forewarned that if a browser cannot handle one of the physical styles, it may substitute another style for the one you're using.

You can nest character tags—for example, use both bold and italic for a set of characters—like this:

```
<B><I>Text that is both bold and italic</I></B>
```

However, the result on the screen, like all HTML tags, is browser-dependent. You will not necessarily end up with text that is both bold and italic. You may end up with one or the other.

This input and output example shows the physical style tags and how they appear in Netscape and Lynx.

```
<P>In Dante's <I>Inferno</I>, malaboge was the eighth circle of hell,
and held the malicious and fraudulent</P>
<P>All entries must be received by <B>September 26, 1994</B>.</P>
<P>Type <TT>lpr -Pbirch myfile.txt</TT> to print that file.</P>
```

Figure 5.16. *The output in Netscape.*

In Dante's *Inferno*, malaboge was the eighth circle of hell, and held the malicious and fraudulent.

All entries must be received by **September 26, 1994**.

Type lpr -Pbirch myfile.txt to print that file.

```
In Dante's Inferno, malaboge was the eighth circle of hell, and held
the malicious and fraudulent.

All entries must be received by September 26, 1994.

Type lpr -Pbirch myfile.txt to print that file.
```

Figure 5.17. *The output in Lynx.*

Preformatted Text

Most of the time, text in an HTML file is formatted based on the HTML tags used to mark up that text. As I mentioned in Chapter 3, "Begin with the Basics," any extra white space (spaces, tabs, returns) that you put in your text are stripped out by the browser.

The one exception to this rule is the preformatted text tag <PRE>. Any white space that you put into text surrounded by the <PRE> and </PRE> tags is retained in the final output. With the <PRE> and </PRE> tags, you can format the text the way you want it to look, and it will be presented that way.

The one catch is that preformatted text is also rendered (in graphical displays, at least), in a monospaced font such as Courier. Preformatted text is excellent for things like code examples, where you want to indent and format lines appropriately. Because it also enables you to align text by padding it with spaces, you can also use the <PRE> tag for tables. However, the fact that those tables are presented in a monospaced font may make them less than ideal (real tables are part of HTML 3.0 and are currently supported by Netscape and Mosaic—you'll learn about them in the next chapter). Here's an example of a table created with <PRE>. (Figure 5.18 shows how it looks in Netscape.)

```
<PRE>
            Diameter    Distance    Time to     Time to
            (miles)     from Sun    Orbit       Rotate
                        (millions
                        of miles)
- - - - - - - - - - - - - - - - - - - - - - - - - - - - - - - - - - -
Mercury     3100           36       88 days     59 days
Venus       7700           67       225 days    244 days
Earth       7920           93       365 days    24 hrs
Mars        4200          141       687 days    24 hrs 24 mins
Jupiter     88640         483       11.9 years  9 hrs 50 mins
Saturn      74500         886       29.5 years  10 hrs 39 mins
Uranus      32000        1782       84 years    23 hrs
Neptune     31000        2793       165 days    15 hrs 48 mins
Pluto       1500         3670       248 years   6 days 7 hrs
</PRE>
```

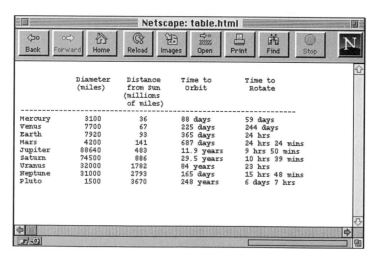

Figure 5.18. *A table created using <pre>, shown in Netscape.*

When creating text for the <PRE> tag, you can use link tags and character styles, but not element tags such as headings or paragraphs. Break your lines using a return, and try to keep your lines at 60 characters or less. Some browsers may have limited horizontal space in which to display text, and since browsers cannot reformat preformatted text to fit that space, you should make sure you stay within the boundaries.

Be careful with tabs in preformatted text. The actual number of characters for each tab stop varies from browser to browser. One browser may have tabs stops at every fourth character, while another may have them at every eighth character. If your preformatted text relies on tabs at a certain number of spaces, consider using spaces instead of tabs.

The <PRE> tag is also excellent for converting files that were originally in some sort of text-only form, such as mail messages or Usenet news postings, to HTML quickly and easily. Just surround the entire content of the article within <PRE> tags, and you have instant HTML, for example:

```
<PRE>
To: lemay@netcom.com
From: jokes@lorelei.com
Subject: Tales of the Move From Hell, pt. 1
Date: Fri, 26 Aug 1994 14:13:38 +0800

I spent the day on the phone today with the entire household
services division of northern california, turning off services,
turning on services, transferring services and other such fun
things you have to do when you move.

It used to be you just called these people and got put on hold for
and interminable amount of time, maybe with some nice music, and
then you got a customer representative who was surly and hard of
hearing, but with some work you could actually get your phone
turned off.
</PRE>
```

The following HTML input and output example shows a simple ASCII art cow and how it appears in Netscape (Figure 5.19) and Lynx (Figure 5.20):

```
<PRE>
       (   )
Moo  (oo)
       \/------\
        ||      | \
        ||--W|| |   *
        ||      ||
        ||      ||
</PRE>
```

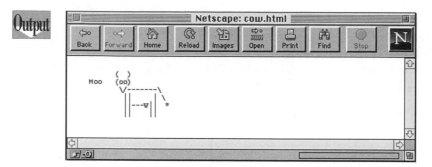

Figure 5.19. *The output in Netscape.*

Figure 5.20. *The output in Lynx.*

Horizontal Rules

The <HR> tag, which has no closing tag and no text associated with it, creates a horizontal line on the page. Rule lines are excellent for visually separating sections of the Web page; just before headings, for example, or to separate body text from a list of items. Figure 5.21 illustrates a rule line.

If one is good, more must be better, right? Not really. Be selective when you use rule lines; more than one together, or separating too many things on the page, makes a page look busy and distracts readers from the rest of its content—like the page in Figure 5.22.

> **Note:** If you've used Netscape, you've probably seen rule lines of varying widths and lengths. This is a Netscape-only extension to HTML—you'll learn about these in Chapter 7; "New Features in HTML and the Netscape 2.0 and Internet Explorer 2.0 Extensions."

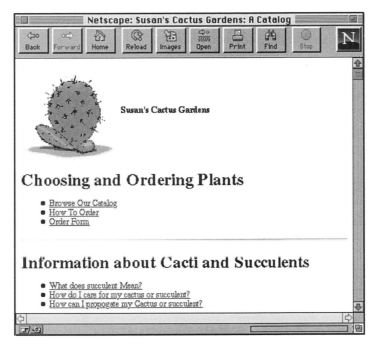

Figure 5.21. *Just enough rules.*

Figure 5.22. *Too many rules.*

This input and output example shows a rule line and a list and how they appear in Netscape (Figure 5.23) and Lynx (Figure 5.24).

```
<HR>
<H2>To Do on Friday</H2>
<UL>
<LI>Do laundry
<LI>Send Fedex with pictures
<LI>Have lunch with Mollie
<LI>Read Email
<LI>Set up Ethernet
</UL>
<HR>
```

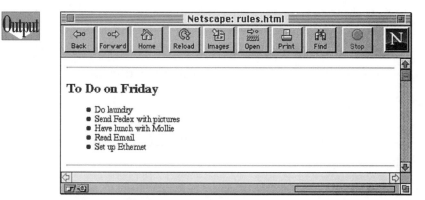

Figure 5.23. *The output in Netscape.*

```
To Do on Friday

      * Do laundry
      * Send Fedex with pictures
      * Have lunch with Mollie
      * Read Email
      * Set up Ethernet
```

Figure 5.24. *The output in Lynx.*

Line Break

The <BR> tag breaks a line of text at the point where it appears. When a Web browser encounters a <BR> tag, it restarts the text after the tag at the left margin (whatever the current left margin happens to be for the current element). You can use <BR> within other elements such as paragraphs or list items;
 will not add extra space above or below the new line

or change the font or style of the current entity. All it does is restart the text at the next line. This example shows a simple paragraph where each line ends with a <BR>. Figures 5.25 and 5.26 show how it appears in Netscape and Lynx.

```
<P>Tomorrow, and tomorrow, and tomorrow<BR>
Creeps in this petty pace from day to day<BR>
To the last syllable of recorded time;<BR>
And all our yesterdays have lighted fools<BR>
The way to dusty death. Out, out, brief candle!<BR>
Life's but a walking shadow, a poor player,<BR>
That struts and frets his hour upon the stage<BR>
And then is heard no more. It is a tale <BR>
Told by an idiot, full of sound and fury, <BR>
Signifying nothing.</P>
```

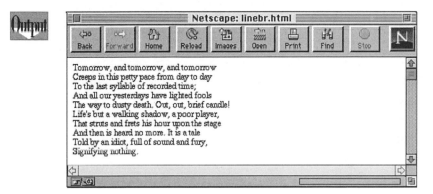

Figure 5.25. *The output in Netscape.*

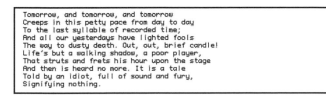

Figure 5.26. *The output in Lynx.*

Addresses

The address tag <ADDRESS> is used for signature-like entities on Web pages. Address tags usually go at the bottom of each Web page and are used to indicate who wrote the Web page, who to contact for more information, the date, any copyright notices or other warning, and anything else that seems appropriate. Addresses are often preceded with a rule line (<HR>), and the <BR> tag can be used to separate the lines, for example:

```
<HR>
<ADDRESS>
Laura Lemay lemay@netcom.com <BR>
A service of Laura Lemay, Incorporated <BR>
last revised September 30 1994 <BR>
Copyright Laura Lemay 1994 all rights reserved <BR>
Void where prohibited. Keep hands and feet inside the vehicle at all times.
</ADDRESS>
```

Without an address or some other method of "signing" your Web pages, it becomes close to impossible to find out who wrote it, or who to contact for more information. Signing each of your Web pages using the <ADDRESS> tag is an excellent way to make sure that if people want to get in touch with you, they can.

This simple input and output example shows an address in Netscape (Figure 5.27) and Lynx (Figure 5.28).

```
<HR>
<ADDRESS>
lemay@netcom.com Laura Lemay
</ADDRESS>
```

Output

```
┌─────────────────────────────────────────────────┐
│ ▨  Netscape: address.html                    ▨   │
│ ⇦o  o⇨  🏠  Ⓒ  📄  ⇨o  🖨  🔍  ○  N             │
│ Back Forward Home Reload Images Open Print Find Stop │
│─────────────────────────────────────────────────│
│                                                  │
│ lemay@netcom.com Laura Lemay                     │
│                                                  │
│ ◁ ◁Ō Document: Done.                             │
└─────────────────────────────────────────────────┘
```

Figure 5.27. *The output in Netscape.*

```
lemay@netcom.com Laura Lemay
```

Figure 5.28. *The output in Lynx.*

Quotations

The `<BLOCKQUOTE>` tag is used to create a quotation. (unlike the `<CITE>` tag, which highlights small quotes, `<BLOCKQUOTE>` is used for longer quotations that should not be nested inside other paragraphs.) Quotations are generally set off from regular text by indentation or some other method. For example, the Macbeth dialogue I used in the example for line breaks would have worked better as a `BLOCKQUOTE` than as a simple paragraph. Here's another example:

```
<BLOCKQUOTE>
"During the whole of a dull, dark, and soundless day in the autumn
of the year, when the clouds hung oppressively low in the heavens,
I had been passing alone, on horseback, through a singularly dreary
trace of country, and at length found myself, as the shades of evening
grew on, within view of the melancholy House of Usher."--Edgar Allen Poe
</BLOCKQUOTE>
```

As in paragraphs, you can separate lines in a `<BLOCKQUOTE>` using the line-break tag `<BR>`. This input and output example shows a sample of this, and how it appears in Netscape (Figure 5.29).

```
<BLOCKQUOTE>
        Guns aren't lawful, <BR>
        nooses give.<BR>
        gas smells awful.<BR>
        You might as well live.<BR>
        --Dorothy Parker
        </BLOCKQUOTE>
```

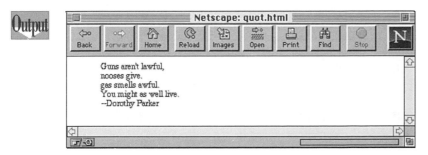

Figure 5.29. *The output in Netscape.*

Special Characters

As you learned earlier in the week, HTML files are ASCII text and should contain no formatting or fancy characters. In fact, the only characters you should be putting in your HTML files are characters that are actually printed on your keyboard. If you have to hold down any key other than Shift, or type an arcane series of keys to produce a single character, you can't use that character in your HTML file. That includes characters you may use every day, such as em dashes and curly quotes (and, if your word processor is set up to do automatic curly quotes, you should turn them off when you write your HTML files).

But wait a minute, I can hear you say. If I can type a character, like a bullet or an accented "a" on my keyboard using a special key sequence, include it in an HTML file, and my browser can display it just fine when I look at that file, what's the problem?

The problem is that the internal encoding your computer does to produce that character (which allows it to show up properly in your HTML file and in your browser's display) most likely will not translate to other computers. Someone else on the Net reading your HTML file with that funny character in it may very well end up with some other character, or garbage. Or, depending on how your page gets shipped over the Net, the character may be lost before it ever gets to the computer where the file is being viewed.

> **Note:** In technical jargon, this means that the characters in HTML files must be from the standard (7-bit) ASCII character set, and cannot include any characters from "extended" (8-bit) ASCII, as every platform has a different definition of the characters that are included in the upper ASCII range. HTML browsers interpret codes from upper ASCII as characters in the ISO-Latin-1 (ISO-8859-1) character set, a superset of ASCII.

So what can you do? HTML provides a reasonable solution. It defines a special set of codes, called character entities, which you can include in your HTML files to represent the characters you want to use. When interpreted by a browser, these character entities are displayed as the appropriate special characters for the given platform and font.

Character Entities for Special Characters

Character entities take one of two forms: named entities and numbered entities.

Named entities begin with an ampersand (&) and end with a semicolon (;). In between is the name of the character (or, more likely, a shorthand version of that name like agrave for an a with a grave accent or reg for a registered trademark sign). The names, unlike other HTML tags, are case sensitive, so you should make sure to type them exactly. Named entities look something like this:

```
&quot;
&laquo;
&copy;
```

The numbered entities also begin with an ampersand and end with a semicolon, but instead of a name, they have a hash sign and a number. The numbers correspond to character positions in the ISO-Latin-1 (ISO 8859-1) character set. Every character that you can type or use a named entity for also has a numbered entity. Numbered entities look like this:

```
&#130;
&#245;
```

You use either numbers or named entities in your HTML file by including them in the same place that the character they represent would go. So, to have the word "resumé" in your HTML file, you would use either:

```
resum&eacute;
```

or

```
resum&#233;
```

I've included a table in Appendix B that lists the named entities currently supported by HTML Levels 1 and 2. See that table for specific characters.

> **Note:** HTML's use of the ISO-Latin-1 character set allows it to display most accented characters on most platforms, but it has its limitations. For example, common characters such as bullets, em dashes, and curly quotes are simply not available in the ISO-Latin-1 character set. This means you cannot use these characters at all in your HTML files. Also, many ISO-Latin-1 characters may be entirely unavailable in some browsers depending on whether or not those characters exist on that platform and in the current font. Future versions of HTML will allow multiple character sets (including the Unicode character set, which includes most of the known characters and symbols in the world).

5

Character Entities for Reserved Characters

For the most part, character entities exist so that you can include special characters that are not part of the standard ASCII character set. There are several exceptions, however, for the few characters that have special meaning in HTML itself. You must also use entities for these characters.

For example, say you wanted to include a line of code in an HTML file that looked something like this:

```
<P><CODE>if x < 0 do print i</CODE></P>
```

Doesn't look unusual, does it? Unfortunately, HTML cannot display this line as written. Why? The problem is with the < (less than) character. To an HTML browser, the less than character means "this is the start of a tag." Because in this context the less than character is not actually the start of a tag, the browser will get confused. You'll have the same problem with the greater than character (>) because it means the end of a tag in HTML, and with the ampersand (&), meaning the beginning of a character escape. Written correctly for HTML, that line of code would look like this:

```
<P><CODE>if x &lt; 0 do print i</CODE></P>
```

HTML provides named escape codes for each of these characters, and one for the double-quote, as well, as shown in Table 5.1.

Table 5.1. Escape codes for characters used by tags.

Entity	Result
<	<
>	>
&	&
"	"

The double-quote escape is the mysterious one. Technically, to produce correct HTML files, if you want to include a double-quote in text, you should be using the escape sequence and not typing the quote character. However, I have not noticed any browsers having problems displaying the double-quote character when it is typed literally in an HTML file, nor have I seen many HTML files that use it. For the most part, you are probably safe using plain old " in your HTML files rather than the escape code.

Exercise 5.2. Create a real HTML page.

Here's your chance to apply what you've learned and create a real Web page. No more disjointed or overly silly examples. The Web page you'll create in this section is a real one, suitable for use in the real world (or the real world of the Web, at least).

Your task for this example: to design and create a home page for a bookstore called The Bookworm, which specializes in old and rare books.

Plan the Page

In Chapter 2, "Get Organized," I mentioned that planning your Web page before writing it usually makes things easier to build and to maintain. So first, consider the content you want to include on this page. Here are some ideas for topics for this page:

- ☐ The address and phone number of the bookstore
- ☐ A short description of the bookstore and why it is unique
- ☐ Recent titles and authors
- ☐ Upcoming events

Now, come up with some ideas for the content you're going to link from this page. Each title in a list of recently acquired books seems like a logical candidate. You can also create links to more information about the book, its author and publisher, its pricing, maybe even its availability.

The Upcoming Events section might suggest a potential series of links, depending on how much you want to say about each event. If you only have a sentence or two about each one, describing them on this page might make more sense than linking them to another page. Why make your reader wait for each new page to load for just a couple of lines of text?

Other interesting links may arise in the text itself, but for now, the basic link plan will be enough to start with.

5

5   Still More HTML

Begin With a Framework

First, create the framework that all HTML files must include: the document structuring commands, a title, and an initial heading. Note that the title is descriptive but short; you can save the longer title for the <H1> element in the body of the text.

```
<HTML>
<HEAD>
<TITLE>The Bookworm Bookshop</TITLE>
</HEAD>
<BODY>
<H1>The Bookworm: A Better Book Store</H1>
</BODY></HTML>
```

Add Content

Now begin adding the content. Since this is a literary endeavor, a nice quote about old books to start the page would be a nice touch. Because it's a quote, you can use the <BLOCKQUOTE> tag to make it stand out as such. Also, the name of the poem is a citation, so use <CITE> there, too.

```
<BLOCKQUOTE>
"Old books are best--how tale and rhyme<BR>
Float with us down the stream of time!"<BR>
- Clarence Urmy, <CITE>Old Songs are Best</CITE>
</BLOCKQUOTE>
```

The address of the bookstore is a simple paragraph, with the lines separated by line breaks.

```
<P>The Bookworm Bookshop<BR>
1345 Applewood Dr<BR>
Springfield, CA 94325<BR>
 (415) 555-0034
</P>
```

After the address comes the description of the bookstore. I've arranged the description to include a list of features, to make the features stand out from the text better:

```
<P>Since 1933, The Bookworm Bookshop has offered rare and hard-to-find titles for the
discerning reader. Unlike the bigger bookstore chains, the Bookworm offers:
<UL>
<LI>Friendly, knowledgeable, and courteous help
<LI>Free coffee and juice for our customers
<LI>A well-lit reading room so you can "try before you buy"
<LI>Four friendly cats: Esmerelda, Catherine, Dulcinea and Beatrice
</UL>
```

Add one more note about the hours the store is open, and emphasize the actual numbers:

```
<P>Our hours are <STRONG>10am to 9pm</STRONG> weekdays,
<STRONG>noon to 7</STRONG> on weekends.</P>
```

Add More Content

After the description come the other major topics of this home page: the recent titles and upcoming events sections. Since these are topic headings, we'll label them with second-level head tags:

```
<H2>Recent Titles (as of 9/25/94)</H2>
<H2>Upcoming Events</H2>
```

The Recent Titles section itself is a classic link menu, as I described earlier on in this section. Here we'll put the list of titles in an unordered list, with the titles themselves as citations (the `<CITE>` tag).

```
<H2>Recent Titles (as of 9/25/94)</H2>
<UL>
<LI>Sandra Bellweather, <CITE>Belladonna</CITE>
<LI>Jonathan Tin, <CITE>20-Minute Meals for One</CITE>
<LI>Maxwell Burgess, <CITE>Legion of Thunder</CITE>
<LI>Alison Caine, <CITE>Banquo's Ghost</CITE>
</UL>
```

Now, add the anchor tags to create the links. How far should the link extend? Should it include the whole line (author and title), or just the title of the book? This is a matter of preference, but I like to link only as much as necessary to make sure the link stands out from the text. I prefer this approach to overwhelming the text. Here, I've linked only the titles of the books.

```
<UL>
<LI>Sandra Bellweather, <A HREF="belladonna.html">
<CITE>Belladonna</CITE></A>
<LI>Johnathan Tin, <A HREF="20minmeals.html">
<CITE>20-Minute Meals for One</CITE></A>
<LI>Maxwell Burgess, <A HREF="legion.html">
<CITE>Legion of Thunder</CITE></A>
<LI>Alison Caine, <A HREF="banquo.html">
<CITE>Banquo's Ghost</CITE></A>
</UL>
```

Note that I've put the `<CITE>` tag inside the link tag `<A>`. I could have just as easily put it outside the anchor tag; character style tags can go just about anywhere. But as I mentioned once before, be careful not to overlap tags. Your browser may not be able to understand what is going on. In other words, don't do this:

```
<A HREF="banquo.html"><CITE>Banquo's Ghost</A></CITE>
```

Next, let's move on to the Upcoming Events section. In the planning section we weren't sure if this would be another link menu, or if the content would work better solely on this page.

Again, this is a matter of preference. Here, because the amount of extra information is minimal, it doesn't make much sense to create links for just a couple of sentences. So for this section we'll create a menu list (using the MENU tag), which results in short paragraphs (bulleted in some browsers). I've boldfaced a few phrases near the beginning of each paragraph. Those phrases emphasize a summary of the event itself so that each paragraph can be scanned quickly and ignored if the reader isn't interested.

```
<H1>Upcoming Events</H1>
<MENU>
<LI><B>The Wednesday Evening Book Review</B> meets, appropriately, on Wednesday
evenings at
PM for coffee and a round-table discussion. Call the Bookworm for information on
joining
the group and this week's reading assignment.
<LI><B>The Children's Hour</B> happens every Saturday at 1pm and includes
reading,
games, and other activities. Cookies and milk are served.
<LI><B>Carole Fenney</B> will be at the Bookworm on Friday, September 16, to
read
from her book of poems <CITE>Spiders in the Web.</CITE>
<LI><B>The Bookworm will be closed</B> October 1 to remove a family
of bats that has nested in the tower. We like the company, but not
the mess they leave behind!
</MENU>
```

Review What You've Got

Here's the HTML code for the page, so far:

```
<HTML>
<HEAD>
<TITLE>The Bookworm Bookshop</TITLE>
</HEAD>
<BODY>
<H1>The Bookworm: A Better Book Store</H1>
<BLOCKQUOTE>
"Old books are best--how tale and rhyme<BR>
Float with us down the stream of time!"<BR>
- Clarence Urmy, <CITE>Old Songs are Best</CITE>
</BLOCKQUOTE>
<P>The Bookworm Bookshop<BR>
1345 Applewood Dr<BR>
Springfield, CA 94325<BR>
 (415) 555-0034
</P>
<P>Since 1933, The Bookworm Bookshop has offered rare and hard-to-find titles
for the discerning reader. Unlike the bigger bookstore chains,the Bookworm
offers:
<UL>
```

```
<LI>Friendly, knowledgeable, and courteous help
<LI>Free coffee and juice for our customers
<LI>A well-lit reading room so you can "try before you buy"
<LI>Four friendly cats: Esmerelda, Catherine, Dulcinea and Beatrice
</UL>
<P>Our hours are <STRONG>10am to 9pm</STRONG> weekdays,
<STRONG>noon to 7</STRONG> on weekends.</P>
<H2>Recent Titles (as of 9/25/94)</H2>
<UL>
<LI>Sandra Bellweather, <A HREF="belladonna.html">
<CITE>Belladonna</CITE></A>
<LI>Johnathan Tin, <A HREF="20minmeals.html">
<CITE>20-Minute Meals for One</CITE></A>
<LI>Maxwell Burgess, <A HREF="legion.html">
<CITE>Legion of Thunder</CITE></A>
<LI>Alison Caine, <A HREF="banquo.html">
<CITE>Banquo's Ghost</CITE></A>
</UL>
<H2>Upcoming Events</H2>
<MENU>
<LI><B>The Wednesday Evening Book Review</B> meets, appropriately, on
Wednesday evenings at PM for coffee and a round-table discussion. Call
the Bookworm for information on joining the group and this week's
reading assignment.
<LI><B>The Children's Hour</B> happens every Saturday at 1pm and includes
reading, games, and other activities. Cookies and milk are served.
<LI><B>Carole Fenney</B> will be at the Bookworm on Friday, September 16,
to read from her book of poems <CITE>Spiders in the Web.</CITE>
<LI><B>The Bookworm will be closed</B> October 1 to remove a family
of bats that has nested in the tower. We like the company, but not
the mess they leave behind!
</MENU>
</BODY></HTML>
```

So, now we have some headings, some text, some topics, and some links. This is the basis for an excellent Web page. At this point, with most of the content in, consider what else you might want to create links for, or what other features you might want to add to this page.

For example, in the introductory section, a note was made of the four cats owned by the bookstore. Although you didn't plan for it in the original organization, you could easily create Web pages describing each cat (and showing pictures), and then link them back to this page, one link (and one page) per cat.

Is describing the cats important? As the designer of the page, that's up to you to decide. You could link all kinds of things from this page if you had interesting reasons to link them (and something to link *to*). Link the bookstore's address to the local chamber of commerce. Link the quote to an online encyclopedia of quotes. Link the note about free coffee to the Coffee Home Page.

5

I'll talk more about good things to link (and how not to get carried away when you link) on Day Five, when you learn about Do's and Don'ts for good Web pages. My reason for bringing this point up here is that once you have some content in place in your Web pages, opportunities for extending the pages and linking to other places may arise, opportunities you didn't think of when you created your original plan. So, when you're just about finished with a page, it's often a good idea to stop and review what you have, both in the plan and in your Web page.

For the purposes of this example, we'll stop here and stick with the links we've got. We're close enough to being done that I don't want to make this chapter longer than it already is!

Sign the Page

You're finished; sign what you have so your readers know who did the work. Here, I've separated the signature from the text with a rule line. I've also included the most recent revision date, my name as the "Web Master" (cute Web jargon meaning the person in charge of a Web site), and a basic copyright (with a copyright symbol indicated by the numeric escape ©):

```
<HR>
<ADDRESS>
Last Updated: 9/25/94<BR>
WebMaster: Laura Lemay lemay@bookworm.com<BR>
&#169; copyright 1994 the Bookworm<BR>
</ADDRESS>
```

And that's it! Save the file as ASCII and open up your browser.

Test the Result

Now that all the code is in place, you can preview the results in a browser. Figure 5.30 shows how it looks in Netscape. Actually, this is how it looks after you fix the spelling errors and forgotten closing tags and other strange bugs that always seem to creep into an HTML file the first time you create it. This always seems to happen no matter how good you get at it. If you use an HTML editor or some other help tool it will be easier, but there always seems to be mistakes. That's what previewing is for, so you can catch those problems before you actually make the document available to other people.

Looks good so far, but in the browsers I used to tested it, the description of the store and the Recent Titles sections tend to run together; there isn't enough distinction between them. (See Figure 5.31.)

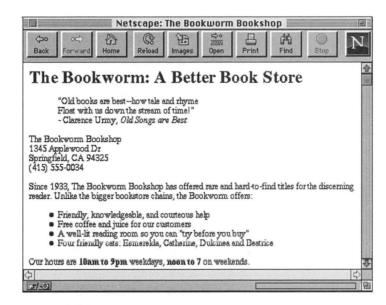

Figure 5.30. *The Bookworm home page, almost done.*

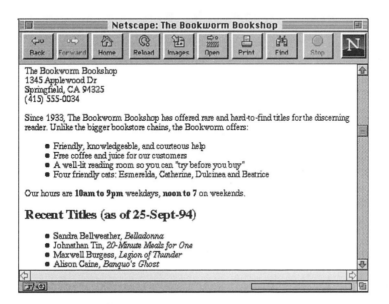

Figure 5.31. *A problem section.*

You have two choices for making them more distinct:

☐ Add rule lines (<HR>) in between sections.

☐ Change the <H2> tags to <H1> for more emphasis of the individual sections.

With design issues like this, it often comes down to a matter of preference and what looks the best in as many browsers as you can get your hands on. Either choice is equally correct, as both are visually interesting, and you haven't had to do strange things in HTML in order to get it to do what you want.

I settled on a single rule line between the description and the Recent Titles section. Figure 5.32 shows how it came out.

```
Netscape: The Bookworm Bookshop
Back  Forward  Home  Reload  Images  Open  Print  Find  Stop   N

1345 Applewood Dr
Springfield, CA 94325
(415) 555-0034

Since 1933, The Bookworm Bookshop has offered rare and hard-to-find titles for the discerning
reader. Unlike the bigger bookstore chains, the Bookworm offers:

  • Friendly, knowledgeable, and courteous help
  • Free coffee and juice for our customers
  • A well-lit reading room so you can "try before you buy"
  • Four friendly cats: Esmerelda, Catherine, Dulcinea and Beatrice

Our hours are 10am to 9pm weekdays, noon to 7 on weekends.

Recent Titles (as of 25-Sept-94)

  • Sandra Bellweather, Belladonna
  • Johnathan Tin, 20-Minute Meals for One
  • Maxwell Burgess, Legion of Thunder
  • Alison Caine, Banquo's Ghost
```

Figure 5.32. *The final Bookworm home page.*

Summary

Tags, tags, and more tags! In this chapter, you've learned about most of the remaining tags in the HTML language for presenting text, and put together a real-life HTML home page. You could stop now and create quite presentable Web pages. But there's more cool stuff to come, so don't put the book down yet.

Table 5.2 presents a quick summary of all the tags you've learned about in this chapter.

Table 5.2. HTML Tags from Chapter 5.

Tag	Use
`<OL>...</OL>`	An ordered (numbered) list. Items in the list each begin with `<LI>`.
`<UL>...</UL>`	An unordered (bulleted or otherwise marked) list. Items in the list each begin with `<LI>`.
`<MENU>...</MENU>`	A menu list (a list of short items or paragraphs).
`<DIR>...</DIR>`	A list of especially short (1–2 word) items. Directory lists are not often used in most HTML files.
`<LI>`	Individual list items in ordered, unordered, menu, or directory lists.
`<DL>...</DL>`	A glossary or definition list. Items in the list consist of pairs of elements: a term and its definition.
`<DT>`	The term part of an item in a glossary list.
`<DD>`	The definition part of an item in a glossary list.
`<EM>...</EM>`	Emphasized text.
`<STRONG>...</STRONG>`	Strongly emphasized text.
`<CODE>...</CODE>`	A code sample.
`<KBD>...</KBD>`	Text to be typed in by the user.
`<VAR>...</VAR>`	A variable name.
`<SAMP>...</SAMP>`	Sample text.
`<DFN>...</DFN>`	A definition, or a term about to be defined.
`<CITE>...</CITE>`	A citation.
`<B>...</B>`	Bold text.
`<I>...</I>`	Italic text.
`<TT>...</TT>`	Text in typewriter font (a monospaced font such as Courier).
`<HR>`	A horizontal rule line at the given position in the text.
` `	A line break; start the next character on the next line (but do not create a new paragraph or list item).
`<BLOCKQUOTE>`	A quotation longer than a few words.
`<ADDRESS>`	A "signature" for each Web page; typically occurs near the bottom of each document and contains contact or copyright information.

5

Q&A

Q **If there are line breaks in HTML, can I also do page breaks?**

A There is no page break tag in HTML. Consider what the term "page" means in a Web document. If each document on the Web is a single "page," then the only way to produce a page break is to split your HTML document into separate files and link them.

Even within a single document, browsers have no concept of a page; each HTML document simply scrolls by continuously. If you consider a single screen a page, you still cannot have what results in a page break in HTML. This is because the screen size in each browser is different, and is based on not only the browser itself but the size of the monitor on which it runs, the number of lines defined, the font being currently used and other factors that you cannot control from HTML.

When designing your Web pages, don't get too hung up on the concept of a "page" the way it exists in paper documents. Remember, HTML's strength is its flexibility for multiple kinds of systems and formats. Think instead in terms of creating small chunks of information and how they link together to form a complete presentation.

Q **My glossaries came out formatted really strangely! The terms are indented farther in than the definitions!**

A Did you mix up the <DD> and <DT> tags? The <DT> tag is always used first (the definition term), and then the DD follows (the definition). I mix these up all the time. There are too many D tags in glossary lists.

Q **I've seen HTML files that use <LI> outside of a list structure, alone on the page, like this:**

```
<LI>And then the duck said, "put it on my bill"
```

A Most browsers will at least accept this tag outside a list tag, and will format it either as a simple paragraph or as a non-indented bulleted item. However, according to the true HTML definition, using an <LI> outside a list tag is illegal, so "good" HTML pages shouldn't do this. And since we are all striving to write good HTML (right?), you shouldn't do this either. Always put your list items inside lists where they belong.

Q **What about that pop quiz you threatened?**

A OK, smarty. Without looking at Table 5.2, list all eight logical style tags and what they're used for. Explain why you should use the logical tags instead of the physical tags. Then create an HTML page that uses each one in a sentence, and test it in several browsers to get a feel for how it looks in each.

6

DAY

THREE

HTML Assistants: Editors and Converters

HTML Assistants: Editors and Converters

After all the information presented in the last chapter, you're probably wondering what other terrors I have left to describe in this chapter. Fear not; I'm not going to describe any more HTML tags. In this chapter you'll just learn about tools that are designed to make writing HTML documents easier.

Writing HTML documents by hand in a text editor is probably the most cumbersome way to write HTML. You have to type all the tags, remember what the tags are called, remember to close your two-sided tags, remember to include closing quotes on attributes, and a host of other details. Not to mention knowing something about what tags can go where. With all that to keep in mind as you produce an HTML page, it sometimes becomes difficult to remember what you're actually writing.

On the other hand, if you go looking for a full-featured HTML editor that lets you quickly see the results of your work, insert links, anchors, and inline graphics quickly and easily, build a form using element widgets you can drag from a toolbox, or manage multiple sets of documents and the structure amongst them, you'll be looking for a very long time.

Which is not to say that tools for writing HTML files don't exist; on the contrary, there are lots of them, and there are even more converters and filters available that allow you to work in a program you know well and then output HTML. But none of these tools really creates a good HTML environment. A truly excellent HTML environment has yet to be produced. I recommend trying several editors and converters to see what works for you. You may end up finding an editor that makes writing HTML documents fast and easy…or you might find that none of them work as well as a dumb text editor and a list of tags.

In this chapter, I'll describe some of the more common tools that claim to make writing HTML easier. They fall into several categories:

- ☐ Tag editors—text editors that help you create HTML files by inserting tags or managing links
- ☐ Near-WYSIWYG editors
- ☐ Converters—programs that let you convert files created by popular word processing programs or other formats to HTML
- ☐ The advantages and disadvantages of using a converter versus working directly in HTML

This chapter is by no means a complete catalog of the available editors and converters for HTML, only a sample of some of the more popular tools. Also, this is a rapidly growing field, and by the time you read this, it is likely that there will be newer, better, and more powerful tools for HTML development. For this reason, Appendix A, "Sources for Further Information," provides some pointers to lists of editors and filters. These lists are being constantly updated and are the best source for finding tools that may not be described in this chapter.

Tag Editors

A *tag editor* is a term I use to describe a simple stand-alone text editor or an extension to another editor. Tag editors help you write HTML documents by inserting the tags for you. They make no claim to being WYSIWYG—all they do is save you some typing. Tag editors generally provide shortcuts to creating HTML files. Instead of trying to remember whether selections in forms are specified by the <SELECT> tag or the <SELECTION> tag, or having to type both the opening and closing parts of a long tag by hand, tag editors usually provide windows or buttons with meaningful names that insert the tag into the text for you at the appropriate spot. You're still working with text, and you're still working directly in HTML, but tag editors take away a lot of the drudgery involved in creating HTML documents.

Most tag editors work best if you already have a document prepared in regular text with none of the tags. Using tag editors as you type a document is slightly more difficult; it's best to type the text and then apply the style after you're done.

For Microsoft Windows

If you use Windows to develop HTML files, you have no shortage of tag editors. There are seemingly hundreds of them. Here are four of the most popular: HTML Assistant, HotDog, HTML Easy!, and WebEdit.

HTML Assistant

HTML Assistant is one of the older but still most popular tag editors for Windows. HTML Assistant allows you to insert tags by clicking buttons in a toolbar and to preview your work with your favorite browser. The interface is simple and intuitive, with all the important tags available on a toolbar. With a basic understanding of HTML, you can get started right away with HTML Assistant.

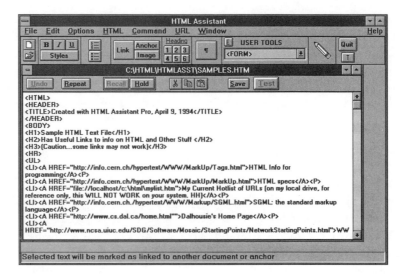

Figure 6.1. *HTML Assistant.*

One of its best features is the capability to collect URLs from hotlists or bookmark files generated by Mosaic and Cello and to enable you to create links to those URLs. With this feature, you may never have to type a URL into your HTML documents.

HTML Assistant comes in several incarnations: a freeware version with enough features for most HTML files, and a commercial Pro version that includes more features (HTML tags, filtering, searching, and so on). The free version of HTML Assistant supports HTML 2.0, including forms, with the Pro version supporting more of the recent tags. You can also add new tags through a User Tools menu.

The FAQ (Frequently Asked Questions) for HTML Assistant is at `ftp://ftp.cs.dal.ca/htmlasst/htmlafaq.html`. (You can get to the actual program from that URL as well.)

HotDog

HotDog, from Sausage Software, is a full-featured HTML tag editor with support for just about every HTML feature, either existing or proposed, including HTML 2.0, tables, forms, all of the Netscape extensions.

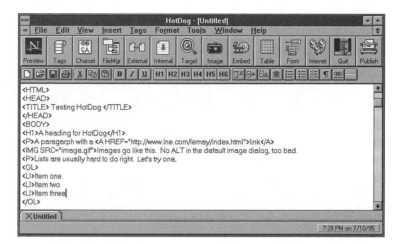

Figure 6.2. *HotDog.*

Using HotDog is reasonably intuitive, allowing you to insert tags through the use of a toolbar or through menu items. One very nice feature is that when you start a new document, all the HTML structuring tags are inserted for you: <HTML>, <HEAD>, and <BODY>. Since I include these tags in all my HTML files, having them included saves some time over inserting them by hand. HotDog's linking feature is also quite nice, allowing you to build a URL from parts and showing you the result as you build it.

HotDog's biggest drawback is the fact that it tries to support everything. If you're actually working with HTML 3.0 you may need all these tags, but if you just want to create something simple, all the extra tags and features can be overwhelming. (I was confused, and I've worked with HTML 3.0!) And given that most browsers don't even support most of HTML 3.0 right now and that the standard is changing, including support for all of HTML 3.0 is a bit premature. It complicates the use of an otherwise terrific editor.

You can get more information about the shareware HotDog and its forthcoming commercial equivalent from Sausage Software's Web site at http://www.sausage.com/

HTML Easy!

HTML Easy!, although not as striking to look at as HotDog, lives up to its name in that it is far easier to use. It supports HTML 2.0 and the Netscape extensions, including forms and tables.

![HTML Easy! Pro screenshot]

```
<HEAD>
<TITLE>HTML Easy! Testing Page</TITLE>
</HEAD>
<BODY>
<H1>This is a heading for Html Easy</H1>
Paragraph, anyone?<P>
<UL>
<LI>Ahh, lists are done nicely.  Item <A HREF="http://www.lne.com/">one </A>(with link)
<LI>Item two
</UL>
This is an image: <IMG SRC="image.gif" ALT="ALT"></IMG> (what's that closing tag doing there?)
</BODY>
<FORM ACTION="/cgi-bin/post-query" METHOD=GET>
<SELECT NAME="sdfsdfsd" >
<OPTION>one
<OPTION>two
</SELECT>
```

Figure 6.3. *HTML Easy!.*

There were some oddities in its use. For example, although it supports the HTML tags for <HEAD> and <BODY>, it does not support the <HTML> tag itself—you have to include it by hand. Also, when it inserts tags for you, it then selects both tags, requiring you to click the mouse in between them so that you can type the content of the tag (other editors will set the insertion point for you after inserting the tags).

You can find out more about HTML Easy! from `http://www.seed.net.tw/~milkylin/`.

WebEdit

Like HotDog, the shareware WebEdit purports to support the full suite of HTML 2.0, 3.0, and Netscape tags. Also like HotDog, this means dozens of tags and options and alternatives to choose from without any distinction of which tags are actually useful for real-life Web presentations and needlessly complicating the use of the editor for creating simple pages.

WebEdit's interface for inserting elements—where you choose an element and then select features of that element—is quite elegant and easy to use—if you have a reason to use all the features of that element. For most common uses, however, all the extra features get in the way.

Find out more about WebEdit from `http://wwwnt.thegroup.net/webedit/webedit.htm`.

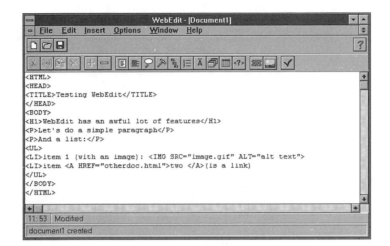

Figure 6.4. *WebEdit.*

For Macintosh

If you're developing HTML files on the Macintosh, HTML.edit provides a hypercard-like environment for inserting HTML tags into text files and managing related documents. If you're used to working on a more fully featured text editor such as Alpha or BBedit, there are also HTML extensions for both these packages.

HTML.edit

HTML.edit is a HyperCard-based HTML tag editor, but it does not require HyperCard to run. It provides menus and buttons for inserting HTML tags into text files, as well as features for automatic indexing (for creating those hyperlinked table-of-contents lists) and automatic conversion of text files to HTML.

Its most interesting feature, however, is its Index page, which enables you to collect a set of related HTML documents, sort of like a project in THINK C or a book file in FrameMaker. Once a file is listed on the Index page, that file appears in a list of files that you can link, so you can create navigation links between related files quickly and easily.

I found the interface to HTML.edit somewhat confusing to figure out, but a quick read through the online help answered most of my questions. HTML.edit supports all of HTML 2.0, including forms as well as tables. It does not support the Netscape extensions.

6

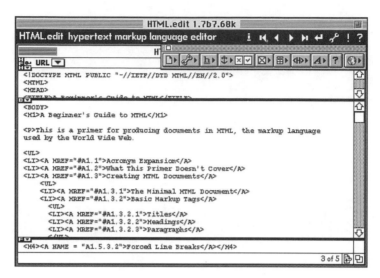

Figure 6.5. *HTML.edit.*

You can get information about HTML.edit from `http://ogopogo.nttc.edu/tools/HTMLedit/HTMLedit.html`.

HTML Extensions for Alpha and BBedit

Alpha and BBedit are two of the more popular shareware text editors available for the Macintosh. Both provide mechanisms to add extensions for working in particular languages and writing text that conforms to a particular style. Extensions exist for both Alpha and BBedit to help with writing HTML tags.

There are significant advantages to using a standard text editor with extensions as opposed to using a dedicated HTML tag editor. For one thing, general text editors tend to provide more features for writing than a simple HTML text editor, including search and replace and spell-checking. Also, if you're used to working in one of these editors, being able to continue to use it for your HTML development means that you don't have to take the time to learn a new program to do your work.

If you use the Alpha editor, versions after 5.92b include the HTML extensions in the main distribution. You can get Alpha and its HTML extensions from `ftp://cs.rice.edu/public/Alpha/`.

There are actually two extension packages for HTML development in BBedit: the first, called HTML Extensions for BBedit, was written by Carles Bellver. You can get information about this package from `http://www.uji.es/bbedit-html-extensions.html`.

The second package, HTML BBedit Tools, was based on Carles Bellver's extensions, and includes some additional features. You can get more information about it at http://www.york.ac.uk/~ld11/BBEditTools.html.

For UNIX

tkHTML is a nice graphical HTML tag editor for the X11 Window System that uses the tcl language and the tk toolkit. It lets you insert tags into text files, convert existing text easily to HTML, and automatically preview your HTML files using a WWW browser called WWwish. You can get more information about tkHTML from http://alfred1.u.washington.edu:8080/~roland/tkHTML/tkHTML.html, or download the source directly from ftp://ftp.u.washington.edu:/public/roland/tkHTML.

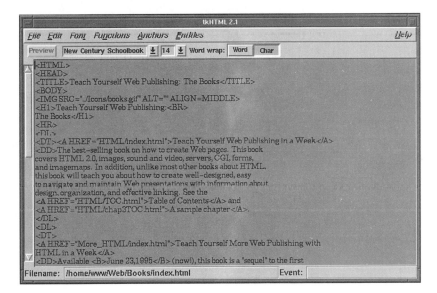

Figure 6.6. *tkHTML.*

If you prefer to work in Emacs, the popular text editor-slash-kitchen sink, you have three HTML-mode packages to choose from:

☐ html-mode, the original, available at ftp://ftp.ncsa.uiuc.edu/Web/elisp/html-mode.el.

☐ html-helper-mode, an enhanced version of the above. You can get information about it at http://www.santafe.edu/~nelson/tools/.

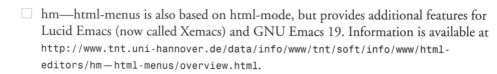

☐ hm—html-menus is also based on html-mode, but provides additional features for Lucid Emacs (now called Xemacs) and GNU Emacs 19. Information is available at `http://www.tnt.uni-hannover.de/data/info/www/tnt/soft/info/www/html-editors/hm—html-menus/overview.html`.

If you use Emacs extensively, you might also want to look at William Perry's Emacs w3-mode, which turns Emacs into a fully-featured Web browser with support for most advanced features of HTML. It includes support for quite a bit of HTML 3.0, many of the Netscape extensions, and just about anything else you can imagine. Get more information about w3-mode from `http://www.cs.indiana.edu/elisp/w3/docs.html`.

WYSIWYG Editors

The concept of a true WYSIWYG editor for HTML files is a bit of a fallacy, since (as I've harped on throughout this book) each browser formats HTML documents in different ways, and most allow the reader to configure their browser to use their favorite fonts. The closest an editor could come to WYSIWYG would be if it allowed you to select the browser that would be viewing your document—and you could look at your document under Lynx, then under Mosaic for X, and then under Cello.

Because HTML's design relies on the fact that is not truly WYSIWYG, be suspicious of any editor that claims to be fully WYSIWYG or that claims you need absolutely no knowledge of HTML to use it. Many of these editors generate very poor HTML code and may betray a lack of understanding of HTML by their authors.

There are some editors that purport to be near-WYSIWYG; that is, they provide some WYSIWYG capabilities while still reminding you of the existence of the HTML underneath. This section describes a few.

For Microsoft Windows

For near-WYSIWYG HTML editing under Windows, you have essentially two choices: any of a number of template packages for Microsoft Word 2.0 or 6.0, and SoftQuad HoTMetaL.

Template Packages for MS Word

If you like Microsoft Word Version 2.0 or Version 6.0, several template packages exist, assigning styles as you would in any Word document and selecting HTML features (such as links and inline images) from a toolbar. All also let you export your files to HTML format. Note, however, that if you make changes to the HTML document you've exported, you cannot import it back into Word.

There are three well-known template packages:

- [ ] CU_HTML (from Chinese University of Hong Kong, hence the CU). Information is available at `http://www.cuhk.hk/csc/cu_html/cu_html.htm`.

- [ ] GT_HTML (from Georgia Tech Research Institute). See the information at `http://www.gatech.edu/word_html/release.htm`.

- [ ] ANT_HTML (by Jill Smith; according to an information file that comes with the package, "the acronym is a secret"). You can retrieve the entire package from `ftp://ftp.einet.net/einet/pc/ANT_HTML.ZIP`.

Microsoft Internet Assistant

Microsoft is in the HTML editor market with a tool called Internet Assistant. Internet Assistant is a plug-in for Word for Windows 6.0 which allows you to create your HTML files in Word and then save them as HTML. If you stick to the style sheet included with Internet Assistant, and understand HTML's limitations, this can make creating HTML documents almost easy.

Internet Assistant also doubles as a Web browser, allowing you to visit sites on the Web from within Word. The browser support is quite slow in comparison to dedicated browsers such as Netscape or Mosaic, however.

You can get Internet Assistant from Microsoft's Web site (information is at `http://www.microsoft.com/MSOffice/Word/ia/default.htm`), or by calling their support lines.

WordPerfect Internet Publisher

Similar to Microsoft's Word plug-in is WordPerfect's Internet Publisher for WordPerfect for Windows 6.1. Internet Publisher includes a template for editing files for the Web, and a converter program that allows you to add links and convert the document to HTML.

You can get more information about WordPerfect Internet Publisher from the WordPerfect (Novell) Web site at `http://wp.novell.com/elecpub/intpub.htm`. You can also download it from that page by calling the WordPerfect support lines.

SoftQuad HoTMetaL

SoftQuad HoTMetaL is an excellent stand-alone editor that allows very near-WYSIWYG capabilities without trying to hide the fact that you're still working in HTML. You still work with tags in HoTMetaL, and you can only insert tags where they are legal. (You can't, for example, put regular paragraphs into a `<HEAD>` section.) This is a good thing; it means that if you use HoTMetaL, you cannot write an HTML document that does not conform to correct HTML style. HoTMetaL supports all of HTML 2.0 as well as the Netscape extensions and HTML 3.0.

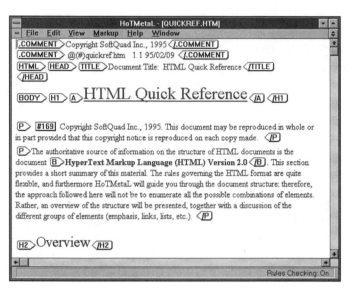

Figure 6.7. *HoTMetaL.*

HoTMetaL comes in several different configurations: a free version, a PRO version that offers more features, and a forthcoming 2.0 PRO version with still more advanced features and an improved interface. Information about HoTMetaL and SoftQuad's other SGML-based tools is available at `http://www.sq.com/`.

For Macintosh

Several near-WYSIWYG HTML editors exist for the Macintosh. Only two, however, stand out as being easy to use and having enough features to make them worthwhile for day-to-day use: HTML Editor and HTML Web Weaver.

The commercial version of SoftQuad's HoTMetaL is also available for the Macintosh, although the free tryout version had not been released as I was writing this book. Given HoTMetaL's respect in the Windows and UNIX worlds, I recommend trying it out when the free version becomes available.

HTML Editor

HTML Editor is a wonderful application that lets you insert tags into your file and see the result in a WYSIWYG fashion—at the same time. The tags are shown in a lighter color than the surrounding text, and the text looks like it would look in Mosaic, although you can change the appearance of any style and apply it across the document. There are options to hide the

tags in your document to get the full effect, and you can also preview the document using your favorite browser.

Figure 6.8. *HTML Editor.*

HTML Editor's current version is 1.0. It supports only the basic HTML 2.0 tags, not including forms. It does not include any of the Netscape extensions or HTML 3.0 tags. It has a feature for including custom tags, however, so you can customize the application to include these new tags.

The documentation for HTML Editor is available at `http://dragon.acadiau.ca/~giles/HTML_Editor/Documentation.html`. You can get the actual package from `ftp://cs.dal.ca/giles/HTML_Editor_1.0.sit.hqx`.

HTML Web Weaver

HTML Web Weaver (formerly called HTML Super Text) is like HTML Editor in that it shows the text of a document in a semi-WYSIWYG form, with the tags in a smaller font and a different color. HTML Web Weaver's interface is quite elegant, making it easy to create lists and links. However, because it splits the URL over several different text fields, creating a link the first time can be confusing.

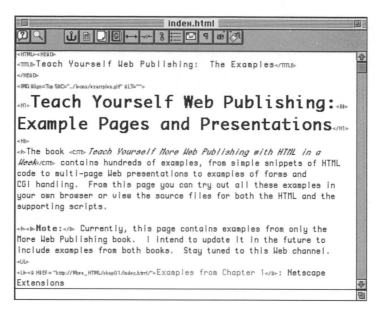

Figure 6.9. *HTML Web Weaver.*

One very odd part of HTML Web Weaver is that it doubles as a regular editor. You can create documents and apply different fonts, sizes, and styles to the text, and never end up with HTML as the final result. This can be very confusing to a beginner who might assume that all they have do is Save As and end up with HTML. The only way to create an HTML document in HTML Web Weaver is to make use of the HTML tags.

HTML Web Weaver supports HTML 2.0, minus forms, and includes the Netscape extensions. You can also create custom tags.

You can get more information about HTML Web Weaver and the latest version from `http://137.143.111.3/web.weaver/about.html`

For UNIX

Two WYSIWYG tools are available for UNIX systems running X: SoftQuad HoTMetaL and tkWWW.

SoftQuad HoTMetaL

SoftQuad's HoTMetaL HTML editor, described in the section on Windows editors, is also available for many UNIX workstations running X11 (Motif). See `http://www.sq.com/` for more information.

tkWWW

tkWWW is a World Wide Web browser and editor that runs using the tcl language and tk toolkit under X. Because it is both an editor and browser, it can rightfully claim WYSIWYG-ness if you use tkWWW as your only browser. In tkWWW, you choose items and styles from menus, and correct HTML is produced when you save the document. This is nice if you can't stand looking at HTML tags—using tkWWW, you never have to see one.

tkWWW requires tcl and tk. An overview of its features is available at `http://uu-gna.mit.edu:8001/tk-www/help/overview.html`. You can retrieve the package itself from `ftp://ftp.aud.alcatel.com:/tcl/extensions`.

Converters

What if you'd prefer not to work in HTML at all—you have your own tool or language that you're familiar with, and you'd prefer to work in that? Many programs exist that will convert different formats into HTML. This section describes many of those converters.

If you use a commercial word processor, and you don't see a converter listed here or among the lists of converters in Appendix A, try calling the vendor of that word processor. Conversion to HTML has been a hot topic for most word processing and desktop publishing companies, and that company may have a converter available.

For Windows

Converters for Windows are available for two of the most popular word processing systems: Microsoft Word and WordPerfect.

Microsoft Word

The CU_HTML, ANT_HTML, and GT_HTML packages, as well as Microsoft's Internet Assistant can be used to convert Word documents to HTML. See the section about these packages earlier in this chapter for information.

Microsoft Word can also export files in RTF (Rich Text Format), which can then be converted to HTML using the RTFTOHTM filter for Windows. You can get more information about this filter from `http://info.cern.ch/hypertext/WWW/Tools/RTFTOHTM.html`.

WordPerfect

In addition to the Internet Publisher program I mentioned previously in this chapter, other converters exist. WPTOHTML is a set of WordPerfect macros that converts

HTML Assistants: Editors and Converters

WordPerfect 5.1 and 6.0 for DOS files to HTML. WordPerfect can also export RTF files, enabling you to use the RTF converter mentioned in the previous section on Microsoft Word.

The WPTOHTML macros are described at `gopher://black.ox.ac.uk/h0/ousu_dir/.html-stuff/wptohtml.html`.

For Macintosh

Converters for Macintosh files lag behind other platforms, but good ones do exist, including rtftohtml, an excellent RTF to HTML converter. Since many popular word processing and desktop publishing programs can export RTF (including Microsoft Word, PageMaker, QuarkXPress, and FrameMaker), this may be the only converter you need. You can get information about RTFTOHTML at `ftp://ftp.cray.com/src/WWWstuff/RTF/rtftohtml_overview.html`.

If you use ClarisWorks, definitely check out `http://ai.eecs.umich.edu/highc/software/translator/XTND_HTML_Translator.html`, which contains information about a Claris XTND translator for HTML files.

If you use QuarkXPress, you can either use the RTF converter mentioned above, or export your Quark files to tagged text and then use the converter mentioned in the section on Quark under UNIX converters.

For UNIX

UNIX, of course, has all the good converters. Many of these are written in the Perl language, which means that if you have a port of Perl for your system, these converters may work there as well.

Here's a quick rundown of the more popular converters.

Plain Text

If you have files in plain text format that you want to convert to HTML quickly and easily, there are two simple filters that will do it for you, both called txt2html. See either `http://www.seas.upenn.edu/~mengwong/txt2html.html` or `http://www.cs.wustl.edu/~seth/txt2html/` for more information.

RTF (Rich Text Format)

Although RTF is a more popular format for desktop word processors, the filter mentioned under Macintosh converters also exists for UNIX systems. That URL, once again, is `ftp://ftp.cray.com/src/WWWstuff/RTF/rtftohtml_overview.html`.

LaTeX

For converting LaTeX files to HTML, you can use latex2html. latex2html is quite enthusiastic in its conversion, including converting equations into GIF files for inclusion in the HTML document. You can get latex2html at `http://cbl.leeds.ac.uk/nikos/tex2html/doc/latex2html/latex2html.html`.

FrameMaker

Several filters to convert FrameMaker files exist for UNIX.

☐ Frame2HTML from Norwegian Telecom does an excellent job of converting whole books to HTML, including preserving inter-document hypertext links as HTML tags and also converting internal graphics into GIF files with the GhostScript and PBM filter packages installed. See `http://www.w3.org/hypertext/WWW/Tools/fm2html.html` for more information.

☐ WebMaker is a similar package for converting FrameMaker documents to HTML. It is available in binary form for several popular platforms including SunOS, Solaris, HPUX, and IRIX. You can get more information from `http://www.w3.org/WebMaker/`.

FrameMaker has advertised its support for exporting files to HTML in its newest version (5.0), which is available for many different platforms including Macintosh and Windows. This filter promises to be interesting, and FrameMaker files can contain images, tables, and hypertext links within pages in the file and elsewhere on the Web.

QuarkXPress

QuarkXPress files themselves cannot yet be converted to HTML, but Quark can output tagged text that can then be converted to HTML. More information is contained at `http://the-tech.mit.edu/~jeremy/qt2www.html`.

PostScript

Information about a general-purpose PostScript to HTML converter can be found at `http://stasi.bradley.edu/ftp/pub/ps2html/ps2html-v2.html`. You will need Ghostscript to use this converter.

Working Directly in HTML versus Using a Converter

With all these converters from word processors to HTML, you can often do most of your HTML development in those programs and deal with converting the files to HTML at the last minute. For many projects, this may be the way to go.

Consider the advantages of using a converter:

☐ Authors do not have to keep track of tags. Having to memorize and know the rules of how tags work is a major issue if all one wants to do is write.

☐ Fewer errors end up in HTML documents (misspellings, forgetting to close tags, using overlapping tags). Because the HTML is automatically generated, there's less chance of "operator error" in the final output.

☐ Authors can use a tool they're familiar with. If they know MS Word and live and die by MS Word, they can work in MS Word.

On the other hand, working in a converter is not a panacea. There are pitfalls, which include:

☐ No tools can provide all the features of HTML, particularly with links to external documents. Some handworking of the final HTML files will generally be required after you convert.

☐ The split-source issue. Once you convert your files from their original form to HTML, you have two sources you are going to have to monitor. To make changes after you do the conversion, you will either have to change the original and regenerate the HTML (wiping out any hand-massaging you did to those files), or you'll have to make sure you make the change to BOTH the original source and the HTML documents. For large projects, splitting the source at any time except the very last minute can create enormous headaches for everyone involved.

Working directly in HTML, for all its hideous text-only markup what-you-see-is-nothing-like-what-you-get glory, does have advantages, including:

☐ All your work is done in one file; no extra step to generate the final version is needed.

☐ HTML files are text only, making it possible for them to be filtered through programs that can easily do automatic tasks such as generating tables of contents of major headings (and hyperlinking them back to those headings), or testing for the validity of the links in those files. The files can also easily be put under source code control.

☐ You have the full flexibility of the HTML language, including the ability to code new features as they appear, rather than having to wait for the next revision of the converter.

Summary

To wind down, I've simply provided some simple lists of HTML editors and converters to help you in your HTML development. After everything you've learned so far, the prospect of tools to help you must come as a welcome relief. Consider using one or more of the tools mentioned in this chapter; they may be able to help you in producing HTML documents.

6

4

New Features in HTML and the Netscape 2.0 and Internet Explorer 2.0 Extensions

Up to this point in the week I've been talking primarily about HTML 2.0, the current official version of HTML that most browsers on the Web today are expected to understand. If you write your Web pages using the tags you've learned about up to this point, you can be sure that your pages will be readable and correct for the vast majority of your readers.

HTML 2.0, however, is not the only set of HTML tags you have to choose from when designing your Web pages. More recent browsers such as Netscape and recent versions of Mosaic include new HTML tags that are either part of the proposed HTML 3.0 specification or are new inventions. Some of these tags provide additional features, such as real tables. Others provide greater control over the display of existing features—for example, changing the width and length of a rule line. The new features allow you slightly more flexibility in page design than standard HTML allows. The disadvantage, of course, is that they are not supported in as many browsers as standard HTML. By using them you risk creating unreadable, confusing, or ugly pages.

In this chapter you'll learn about the Netscape and Internet Explorer 2.0 extensions—new HTML tags that are available in the Netscape Navigator and Internet Explorer 2.0 browser. In particular, you'll learn about:

- ☐ Centering text
- ☐ Specifying the width, length, and alignment of rule lines
- ☐ Changing the size of the font
- ☐ Specifying different labels for bulleted and numbered lists
- ☐ Creating a background for your pages of either a solid color or a tiled image
- ☐ Changing the color of the text in your page

Note: This chapter won't talk about all of the Netscape extensions. A few of them relate to HTML elements we haven't talked about yet, like images and search prompts. You'll learn about those extensions when we cover those topics.

The Status of HTML 2 and HTML 3

There are two major revisions of HTML on the Web today: HTML 2 and HTML 3.

HTML 2 has become the standard for Web page design, and the vast majority of browsers on the Web today support most (if not all) of the features in HTML 2.

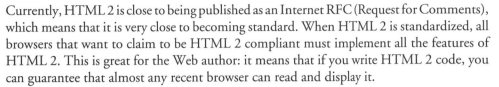
Currently, HTML 2 is close to being published as an Internet RFC (Request for Comments), which means that it is very close to becoming standard. When HTML 2 is standardized, all browsers that want to claim to be HTML 2 compliant must implement all the features of HTML 2. This is great for the Web author: it means that if you write HTML 2 code, you can guarantee that almost any recent browser can read and display it.

The next big step is HTML 3, a major revision that will finally solve many of the limitations of HTML 2 and provide an enormous amount of flexibility for Web authors. HTML 3 used to be called HTML+ and has incorporated most of the proposed features that HTML+ included. HTML 3 includes text alignment (left, right, center, justified), wrapping text alongside images, tables, math, tabs, notes, and a whole host of smaller features that make HTML a lot more pleasant to work with.

The actual structure of HTML 3—that is, what the tags look like and how you use them—is very much in discussion by standards organizations, browser developers, and members of the World Wide Web Consortium. Some parts of HTML 3, such as tables, are settling down, but others are in flux and likely to change as the discussion goes on. You'll learn all about HTML 3 in Chapter 16.

The Great Netscape Controversy

For the most part, the discussions of HTML 2 have been winding down as the standard is solidified, and more attention has been paid to HTML 3 as developers look to the future for more interesting developments. But there was one major wrinkle in the standards discussions: the HTML extensions made by Netscape Communications Corporation as part of the first release of its browser, the Netscape Navigator (usually just called Netscape).

In addition to the browser itself, Netscape Corp. included support for a suite of HTML tags that were not part of the HTML specification—tags that were neither part of HTML 2 nor part of the proposed HTML 3 and only worked if the page was being viewed in Netscape. If you've run into pages with tags such as <FONT> and <CENTER>, you've witnessed the Netscape extensions firsthand.

An enormous flurry of controversy followed the release of the Netscape extensions, with the sides falling into two major camps.

Web developers (both page authors and browser developers) argued that Netscape had set a dangerous precedent by branching off on its own and implementing tags that were not part of the standard. If every browser decided unilaterally to add its own tags, they argued, then the Web would splinter into several browser-specific Webs, making it impossible for authors of Web pages to keep up with the different tags in different browsers and write a page that works in every browser on the market (the way you can write pages now).

On the other side, Netscape and its proponents argued that the standards discussions were moving too slowly and that the features offered by the Netscape extensions were desperately wanted by page authors. They also pointed out that pages written to include the new Netscape tags would not break in other browsers; the new tags and the features they provided would just be ignored. In this way, Netscape's HTML extensions weren't breaking the standard; they were just adding to it and allowing added features to the users of the Netscape browser (Web authors and Web readers).

Both sides have valid points, and fortunately the result of the release of the Netscape extensions has been a positive one. The Netscape extensions still exist, and you can use them in your pages if you choose to do so (more about that later). Due to the controversy, however, Netscape Corp. and other browser developers are making a concerted effort to become members of, and contributors to, the WWW Consortium and to actively participate in the discussions of HTML 3. As a result of the closer cooperation, the HTML 3 standard is moving forward and Netscape and other browser developers can propose new features and incorporate parts of HTML 3 into their browsers much earlier than they could have previously. Tables, part of HTML 3, are a good example of this. Both NCSA (Mosaic) and Netscape Corp. (Netscape) have been involved in the discussions, so now the same tags for tables are supported by the new releases of both browsers. You'll learn about tables in the next chapter.

How Should You Deal with the Changes?

Even with the cooperation between browser developers in providing new features, the simple fact that new HTML tags are appearing faster than ever on the Web means that your job as a Web author has suddenly become much more difficult. Before, all you had to do was deal with HTML 2, and the vast majority of the browsers on the Web would be able to read your pages without a problem. Now, you've got several groups of tags to work with:

- The HTML 2 tags
- The Netscape extensions, which are only supported by Netscape
- Upcoming HTML 3 tags such as tables, which are supported by a few but not all browsers (you'll learn about tables in the next chapter)
- Other proposed HTML 3 tags that will eventually show up in other browsers and might eventually include some of the Netscape tags

If you're finding all of this rather boggling, you're not alone. Authors and developers just like you are all trying to sort out the mess and make decisions based on how they want their pages to look. You'll have to make these decisions as well.

It might be easier for you to look at the choices you have as a sort of continuum between the conservative and the experimental Web author (see Figure 7.1).

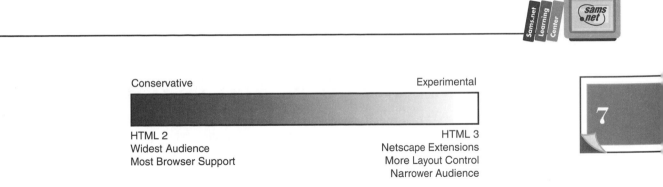

Figure 7.1. *The Web author continuum.*

Note: Don't think of these endpoints as value judgments; conservative isn't worse than experimental, or vice versa. There are advantages at both ends and significant advantages in the middle.

The conservative Web developer wants the widest possible audience for her Web pages. The conservative Web developer sticks to HTML 2 tags as defined by the standard. This is not to say that the conservative Web developer is boring. You can create magnificent Web content with the HTML 2 tags, and that content has the advantage over more experimental content in that it is supported without a hitch by the greatest number of browsers and, therefore, will reach the widest possible audience.

The experimental Web developer, on the other hand, wants the sort of control over layout that Netscape or the HTML 3 tags give her and is willing to shut out a portion of her audience to get it. Her pages are designed for a single browser, tested only in a single browser, and might even have a big announcement on the pages that says "These Pages Must be Read Using Browser X." Much of the time, if you use some other browser to read those pages, the result is confusing if not entirely unreadable.

The best position, in terms of choosing between interesting design and a wide audience, is probably a balance between the two.

With some knowledge beforehand of the effects that the Netscape and HTML 3 tags will have on your pages, both in browsers that support them and those that don't, you can make slight modifications to your design that will enable you to take advantage of both sides. Your pages are still readable and useful in older browsers over a wider range of platforms, but they can also take advantage of the advanced features in the newer browsers. Learning about the effects of the new tags is considerably more work, and the importance of testing your pages is increased, but the result is a page that is closer to the spirit of the Web in the first place: a page that is viewable in any browser, on any platform, at any speed network connection, and so on.

What Are the Netscape Extensions?

With the news and the warnings out of the way, let's get to the new tags. In this chapter, you'll learn about the Netscape extensions to HTML, and in the next chapter you'll learn about tables.

As I noted in the previous section, the Netscape extensions are a set of HTML tags that Netscape implemented in the first release of its browser, the Netscape Navigator. Although these tags have been proposed by Netscape to be part of the HTML 3 standard, only a few have made it in so far. For now, Netscape is the only browser in which the majority of these tags will work.

All the Netscape tags can be used in such a way that the pages you develop are still usable in other browsers. If you design and test your pages carefully, you can create pages so that readers looking at them in a browser other than Netscape might not even be able to tell that you have used the Netscape extensions. Throughout this chapter, I'll give you hints on how to accomplish this.

Centering Text

One of the most obvious extensions Netscape made to HTML was the capability to center text on the page. Netscape actually has two ways of doing this: the <CENTER> tag and the ALIGN=CENTER attribute.

The <CENTER> tag enables you to center whole portions of pages. You put the <CENTER> tag before the text you want centered, and the </CENTER> tag after you're done.

```
<CENTER>
<H1>Northridge Paints, Inc.</H2>
<P>We don't just paint the town red.</P>
</CENTER>
```

Note that <CENTER> is not itself a paragraph type. You still need regular element tags (<P>, <H1>, <UL>, <BLOCKQUOTE>, and so on) inside the opening and closing <CENTER> tags. If you center plain text with no <P> tag, the result ends up on a separate line in Netscape, but might blend into the surrounding text in other browsers, which is not what you expect. For example, note the following bit of code:

```
<P>The result is that 90% of Penguins die from this disease.</P>
<CENTER><B>The Solution</B></CENTER>
<P>The solution, therefore, is to make sure penguins get enough
herring in their diet.</P>
```

Figures 7.2 and 7.3 show the result in both Netscape and in an older version of Mosaic.

To get around this problem, make sure you include a <P>, <H1>, or other text element tag inside your <CENTER> tags. Also, if you're going to center text to make it look like a heading (as this example did), it's a good idea to actually use a heading tag so that other browsers will display it as a heading.

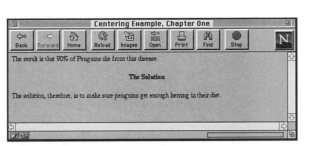

Figure 7.2. *The effect of the* <CENTER> *tag in Netscape.*

Figure 7.3. *The effect of the* <CENTER> *tag in Mosaic.*

To avoid all these problems with the <CENTER> tag, consider using the ALIGN=CENTER attribute to center your text instead. You can use that attribute on most of the standard element tags such as paragraphs, headings, and so on. So instead, the earlier Northridge Paints example might look like this:

```
<H1 ALIGN=CENTER>Northridge Paints, Inc.</H2>
<P ALIGN=CENTER >We don't just paint the town red.</P>
```

ALIGN=CENTER is part of the HTML 3 specification, is already starting to be accepted by more browsers, and might be widely available by the time you read this. <CENTER>, on the other hand, is a Netscape-only extension and might not end up in the official HTML 3 proposal. By using ALIGN=CENTER instead of <CENTER>, your text will still be centered in other browsers that support centering.

So why use <CENTER> at all? It does have the advantage of only needing two tags—one on either side of the bit you want centered—as opposed to having to add ALIGN=CENTER to every single tag in between. Additionally, in Netscape, it centers elements that haven't had ALIGN=CENTER implemented yet, such as images and tables. Who knows? Maybe <CENTER> will end up in the HTML 3 specification. But to be safe and standard, stick with ALIGN=CENTER.

One last thing to note is that if your pages are read in a browser that doesn't support centering at all, your centered text appears as plain left-justified text. If you've used centering to provide some sort of emphasis effect (for example, to give the appearance of a heading), you might actually want to use heading or emphasis tags so that if the text isn't centered, it is still emphasized. In the following input and output examples, you see the effects of using ALIGN=CENTER with two different browsers: in Netscape and in Mosaic.

```
<H1 ALIGN=CENTER>Iphigenia in Tauris</H1>
<P ALIGN=CENTER>A Tragedy by Euripides</P>
<P><B>Cast:</B></P>
<UL>
<LI>Iphigenia
<LI>Pylades
<LI>Orestes
<LI>King Thoas
<LI>Athena
<LI>Temple Maidens, Herdsmen, Soldiers
</UL>
```

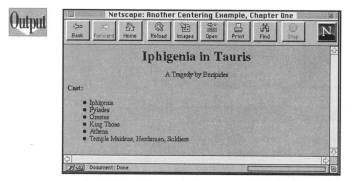

Figure 7.4. *The output in Netscape.*

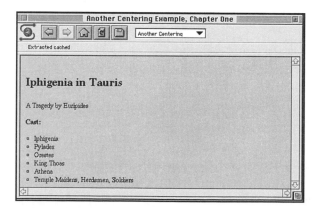

Figure 7.5. *The output in Mosaic.*

Rule Lines

The <HR> tag, as you learned in Chapter 4, creates a rule line on the page. The attributes Netscape has added to the <HR> tag give you greater control over the appearance of that line.

The SIZE attribute indicates the thickness, in pixels, of the rule line. The default is 2, and this is also the smallest thickness that you can make the rule line. Figure 7.6 shows some sample rule line thicknesses.

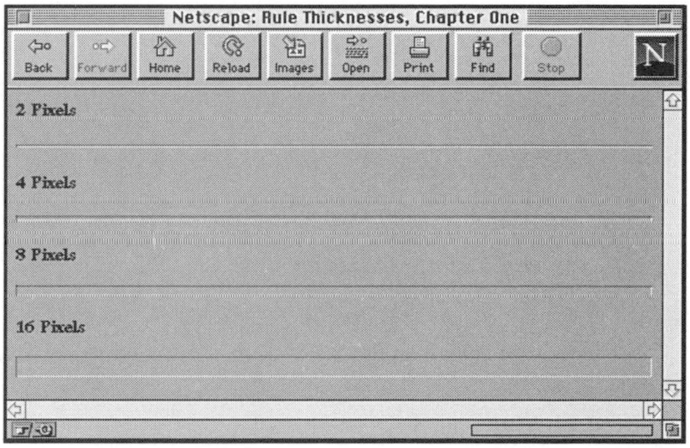

Figure 7.6. *Examples of rule line thicknesses.*

The WIDTH attribute indicates the horizontal width of the rule line. You can specify either the exact width, in pixels, or the value as a percentage of the screen width (for example, 30 percent or 50 percent), which will change if you resize the window. Figure 7.7 shows some sample rule line widths.

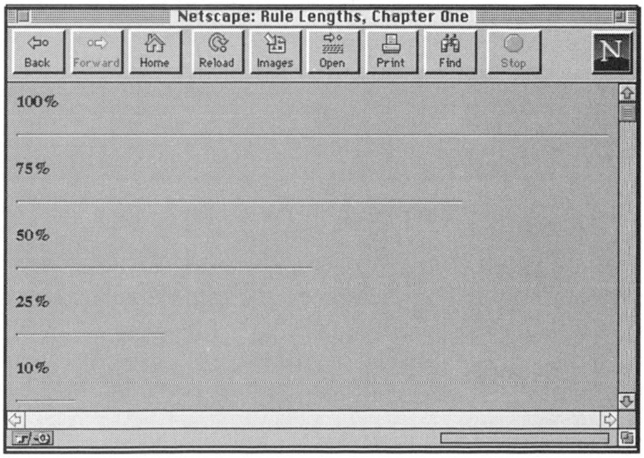

Figure 7.7. *Examples of rule line widths.*

If you specify a WIDTH smaller than the actual width of the screen, you can also specify the alignment of that rule line with the ALIGN attribute, making it flush left (ALIGN=LEFT), flush right (ALIGN=RIGHT), or centered (ALIGN=CENTER). By default, rule lines are centered.

A popular trick that Netscape-centric Web designers are using is to create patterns with several small rule lines, as shown in Figure 7.8.

Figure 7.8. *An example of patterns created with several small rule lines.*

This is one of those instances in which Netscape-specific design looks awful in other browsers. When viewed in browsers without the SIZE attribute, each of the small rule lines now covers the entire width of the screen, as shown in Figure 7.9.

Figure 7.9. *The small rule lines in Mosaic.*

If you must have these rule line patterns, consider using small images instead (which will work in other browsers).

Finally, the NOSHADE attribute causes Netscape to draw the rule line as a plain black line, without the three-dimensional shading, as shown in Figure 7.10.

The following examples show how rule lines with Netscape extensions appear both in Netscape (Figure 7.11) and Mosaic (Figure 7.12).

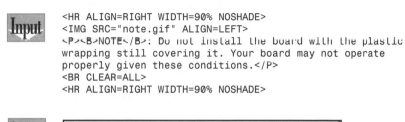

Figure 7.10. *Rule lines without shading.*

Input

```
<HR ALIGN=RIGHT WIDTH=90% NOSHADE>
<IMG SRC="note.gif" ALIGN=LEFT>
<P><B>NOTE</B>: Do not install the board with the plastic
wrapping still covering it. Your board may not operate
properly given these conditions.</P>
<BR CLEAR=ALL>
<HR ALIGN=RIGHT WIDTH=90% NOSHADE>
```

Output

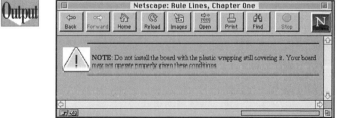

Figure 7.11. *The output in Netscape.*

Figure 7.12. *The output in Mosaic.*

Font Sizes

One of Netscape's more controversial extensions enables you to change the size of the font for a character, word, phrase, or on any range of text. The `<FONT>...</FONT>` tags enclose the text, and the `SIZE` attribute indicates the size to which the font is to be changed. The values of `SIZE` are 1 to 7, with 3 being the default size. Look at the following example:

```
<P>Bored with your plain old font?
<FONT SIZE=5>Change it.</FONT></P>
```

Figure 7.13 shows the typical font sizes for each value of `SIZE`.

Figure 7.13. *Font sizes in Netscape.*

You can also specify the size in the `<FONT>` tag as a relative value using the + or - characters in the value for `SIZE`. Because the default size is 3, you can change relative font sizes from to -3 to +4, like this:

```
<P>Change the <FONT SIZE=+2>Font</FONT> size again.</P>
```

In the preceding example, the word Font (inside the `<FONT>` tags) will be two size levels larger than the default font when you view that example in Netscape.

Relative font sizes are actually based on a value that you can define using the `<BASEFONT>` tag, another Netscape extension. The `<BASEFONT>` tag also has the required attribute `SIZE`. `SIZE` can have a value of 1 to 7. All relative font changes in the document after the `<BASEFONT>` tag will be relative to that value.

Try to avoid using the `<FONT>` tag to simulate the larger-font effect of the HTML content-based tags such as the heading tags (`<H1>`, `<H2>`, and so on), or to emphasize a particular word or phrase. If your documents are viewed in browsers other than Netscape, you'll lose the font sizes, and your text will appear as if it were any other paragraph. If you stick to the content-based tags, however, a heading is a heading, regardless of where you view it. Try to limit your use of the font tag to small amounts of special effects.

These examples show how to use the <FONT> tags that appear in both Netscape (Figure 7.14) and Mosaic (Figure 7.15).

```
<P>Acme Brand Sticky Notes give you <B><FONT SIZE=5>BIG SAVINGS
</FONT></B> over name brand alternatives.</P>
```

Acme Brand Sticky Notes give you **BIG SAVINGS** over name brand alternatives.

Figure 7.14. *The output in Netscape.*

Acme Brand Sticky Notes give you **BIG SAVINGS** over name brand alternatives.

Figure 7.15. *The output in Mosaic.*

Lists

Normally, when you create lists in HTML, the browser determines the size and type of the bullet in an unordered list (the <UL> tag) or the numbering scheme in numbered lists (usually simply 1, 2, and so on for each item in the list). In Netscape, several attributes to the list tags were added to allow greater control over how individual items are labeled.

For unordered lists (the <UL> tag), the TYPE attribute indicates the type of bullet used to mark each item. The possible values are as follows:

- ☐ TYPE=DISC, for a solid bullet (the default)
- ☐ TYPE=CIRCLE, for a hollow bullet
- ☐ TYPE=SQUARE, for a square hollow bullet

For example, the following code shows a list with hollow squares as the labels. Figure 7.16 shows the result.

```
<UL TYPE=SQUARE>
<LI>The Bald Soprano
<LI>The Lesson
<LI>Jack, or the Submission
<LI>The Chairs
</UL>
```

Figure 7.16. *Bullet types in Netscape.*

For ordered lists (the <OL> tag), the TYPE attribute also applies but has a different set of values that indicate the numbering scheme used for the list:

☐ TYPE=1, the default, which labels the list items with numbers (1, 2, 3)

☐ TYPE=A, which orders the list items with capital letters (A, B, C, and so on)

☐ TYPE=a, which orders the list items with lowercase letters (a, b, c, and so on)

☐ TYPE=I, which labels the list items with capital roman numerals (I, II, III, IV, and so on)

☐ TYPE=i, which labels the list items with lowercase roman numerals (i, ii, iii, iv, and so on)

For example, the following code numbers the outer list with roman numerals (I, II, III), and the inner list with Arabic numerals (1, 2, 3). Figure 7.17 shows the result.

```
<OL TYPE=I>
<LI>Income
    <OL TYPE=1>
    <LI>Wages, Salaries and other Earnings
    <LI>Interest and Dividend Income
    <LI>Gains and Losses
    </OL>
<LI>Itemized Deductions
<LI>Figuring your Tax
</OL>
```

In addition, the START attribute indicates the number from which the list is to be started. The start attribute takes a number regardless of the TYPE. So, if you have an OL tag of TYPE=A with a START=3 attribute, the list starts from C and progress through D, E, and so on.

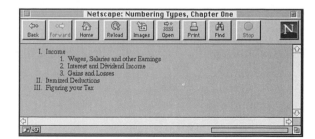

Figure 7.17. *Numbered list types in Netscape.*

Note that because other browsers ignore the START attribute, your lists might be numbered differently in browsers other than Netscape. To prevent such renumbering, either avoid using START altogether, or don't refer to specific list items by number in your text.

Finally, each list item tag (<LI>) also has added attributes to control list labels within a single list. The TYPE attribute can take any of the same values that it had in <UL> and <OL>. If you use numbering types in a <UL> list or bullet types in an <OL>, they will be ignored. Changing the TYPE for a list item affects that list item and all the items following it.

Within ordered lists, the <LI> tag can also have the VALUE attribute, which sets the value of this item to a particular number. This also affects all list items after this one, enabling you to restart the numbering within a list at a particular value.

Both TYPE and VALUE are ignored in other browsers, so relying on the effect they produce (for example, to mark specific items within a list as different from other items in a list) is probably not a good idea, because you will lose that emphasis in browsers other than Netscape.

These examples show how use of the TYPE attribute to the <OL> tag appears in both Netscape (Figure 7.18) and Mosaic (Figure 7.19).

```
<P>Planting Instructions:</P>
    <UL TYPE=SQUARE>
    <LI>Bare root plants should be planted immediately,
    or submerged in water until planting
    <LI>Roses should be submerged in water for 4-6 hours
    <LI>Avoid letting other plants dry out
    </UL>
<LI>Dig appropriate-sized holes in planting location
<LI>Dust with fertilizer
<LI>Plant with crown level with soil surface, firming as the hole is
filled in
<LI>Water well and keep damp for the first week.
</OL>
```

177

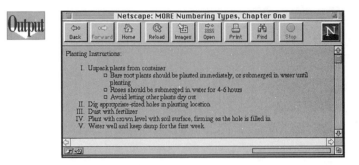

Figure 7.18. *The output in Netscape.*

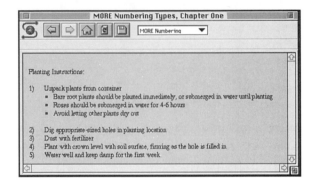

Figure 7.19. *The output in Mosaic.*

Backgrounds (Netscape 1.1 and Up Only)

Up to this point, I've described the Netscape extensions that have been available in Netscape 1.0 and above. In the newest version of Netscape (1.1) you can also, from your HTML files, change the background of the page from the basic gray to any color you want, or use a pattern for the background. Both of these are accomplished using an extension to the <BODY> tag.

The <BODY> tag, in case you've forgotten, is the tag that surrounds all of the content of your HTML file. <HEAD> contains the title, and <BODY> contains almost everything else.

Solid Color Backgrounds

The easiest and fastest way to change the background of the page in Netscape is to decide what color you want it to be and then use the BGCOLOR attribute to the <BODY> tag to change the color.

But before you can add the BGCOLOR attribute to <BODY>, you'll have to find out the RGB (red, green, blue) values for the color you want. You should be able to figure this out from most image-editing programs that allow you to set the colors; the numbers are usually 0 to 255, with 0 0 0 being black and 255 255 255 being white.

The catch in Netscape is that once you have the RGB numbers in ASCII, you have to convert them to hexadecimal. To get the hexadecimal numbers, you can use any scientific calculator that converts between ASCII and hex. Alternatively, you can use rgb.html, a form that will do the conversion for you, which you'll learn how to implement later on in this book. For now, if you're really interested, you can try out the rgb.html form at http://www.lne.com/Web/rgb.html.

When you have the hexadecimal numbers, you can give the BGCOLOR attribute a value. That value has all the two-digit hex numbers in one string beginning with a hash (#), like this: #000000. (That particular number is for a black background, by the way.)

So, the final HTML to produce your colored background looks something like this:

```
<BODY BGCOLOR=#FFFFFF>
<BODY BGCOLOR=#934CE8>
```

> **Note:** If you make your background too dark, you won't be able to read the text on top of it. Fortunately, you can also change the color of the text to compensate for this. You'll learn about text and link colors in the next section.

Tiled-Image Backgrounds

Instead of a solid colored background, you can also specify an image file that will be tiled by Netscape (each image laid side by side and in rows to fill the screen) to produce a graphical background for your pages.

To create an image for the tile, you'll want to make sure that when the image is tiled, that the pattern flows smoothly from one tile to the next. You can usually do some careful editing of the image in your favorite image-editing program to make sure the edges line up. The goal is to have the edges meet cleanly so that there isn't a "seam" between the tiles after you've laid them end to end. (See Figure 7.20 for an example of tiles that don't line up very well.) You can also try commercial clip art packages for patterns that are often designed specifically to be tiled in this fashion. As always with clip art, make sure you have the right to use the image before you put it up on the Web.

7 New Features in HTML and the Extensions

Note: Tiled-image backgrounds considerably slow down the speed with which your pages are displayed, especially on slow connections. Try to keep your background images as small as possible (even files over 5 KB seriously degrade performance), or better yet, use a flat color background instead.

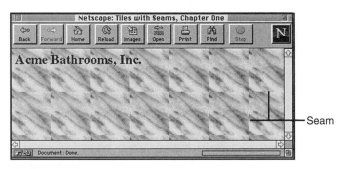

Figure 7.20. *Tiled images with "seams."*

When you have an image that can be cleanly tiled, all you need to create a tiled-image background is the BACKGROUND attribute, part of the <BODY> tag. The value of BACKGROUND is a file name or URL that points to your image file, as in the following example:

```
<BODY BACKGROUND="tiles.gif">
<BODY BACKGROUND="backgrounds/rosemarble.gif">
```

Figure 7.21 shows the result of a simple tiled background.

Figure 7.21. *A tiled background in Netscape.*

Note: You'll learn more about images, including background images, in Chapter 9.

180

Be careful with tiled backgrounds. It is all too easy to create incredibly hideous pages if you get carried away with the tiles. Try to resist the urge to create strange backgrounds or those that distract from the text and the images on top of them. (See Figure 7.22.) Subtle patterns are always better than wild patterns. Remember, your readers are still visiting your pages for the content on them, not to marvel at your ability to create faux marble.

Figure 7.22. *Interfering patterns and text.*

Text and Link Colors (Netscape 1.1 and Up Only)

When you can change the background colors, it makes sense to be able to change the color of the text itself. Netscape 1.1 provides this feature with more additional attributes to the `<BODY>` tag.

To change the text and link colors, you'll need your color values in the same form as the ones for the backgrounds—that is, as hexadecimal numbers preceded by a hash sign. With those numbers scribbled down, you can then add any of the following attributes to the body tag:

☐ `TEXT` controls the color of all the document's body text that isn't a link, including headings, body text, text inside tables, and so on.

☐ `LINK` controls the color of normal, unfollowed links in the document (the ones that are blue by default).

☐ `VLINK` controls the color of links you have visited (the ones that are purple by default).

☐ `ALINK` controls the color of a link that has had the mouse button pressed on it, but not released (an *activated* link). These are red by default.

For example, to create a page with a black background, white text, and bright purple unfollowed links, you might use the following `<BODY>` tag:

```
<BODY BGCOLOR=#000000 TEXT=#FFFFFF LINK=#9805FF>
```

181

This would produce a file that looks something like the one shown in Figure 7.23.

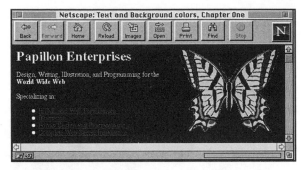

Figure 7.23. *Background and text colors.*

Note: Text colors for body text and links can be changed only once per page. You don't have control over the color of individual elements or words.

Using colors for your backgrounds and fonts can be tempting, but be very careful if you decide to do so. The capability to change the document and font colors and provide fancy backdrops can give you the ability to quickly and easily make your pages entirely unreadable. Here are some hints for avoiding this:

☐ Make sure you have enough contrast between the background and foreground (text) colors. Low contrast can be hard to read. Also, light-colored text on a dark background is harder to read than dark text on a light background.

☐ Avoid changing link colors at all. Because your readers have semantic meanings attached to the default colors (blue means unfollowed, purple means followed), changing the colors can be very confusing.

☐ Sometimes, increasing the font size of all the text in your document using `<BASEFONT>` can make it more readable on a background. Both the background and the bigger text will be missing in other browsers that don't support the Netscape tags.

When in doubt, ask a friend to look at your pages. Because you are familiar with the content and the text, you might not realize how hard your pages are to read. Someone who hasn't read them before won't have your biases and will be able to tell you that your colors are too close or that the pattern is interfering with the text. Of course, you'll have to find a friend who will be honest with you.

The Dreaded *<BLINK>*

You won't find the `<BLINK>` tag listed in Netscape's official documentation of its extensions. The capability to cause text to blink was included in Netscape as a hidden undocumented feature or *Easter egg*. Still, a good percentage of pages on the Web seem to use this feature.

The `<BLINK>`...`</BLINK>` tags cause the text between the opening and closing tags to have a blinking effect. Depending on the version of Netscape you are using, this can mean that the text itself vanishes and comes back at regular intervals or that a large white block appears and disappears behind the text. Blink is usually used to draw attention to a portion of the page.

But, similar to how too much normal emphasis (boldface, link text, and so on) on a page detracts from the content, the `blink` can be far worse. Because it repeats, the blink continues to drag attention to that one spot and, in some cases, can make it nearly impossible to absorb any of the content of the page. The use of `<BLINK>` is greatly discouraged by most Web designers (including myself), because many people find it extremely intrusive and annoying. Blink is the HTML equivalent of fingernails on a blackboard.

If you must use blink, use it very sparingly (no more than a few words on a page). Also, be aware that in some versions of Netscape, blinking can be turned off. If you want to emphasize a word or phrase, you should use a more conventional way of doing so, in addition to (or in place of) blink, because you cannot guarantee that blink will be available even if your reader is using Netscape to view your pages.

Other Extensions

In addition to the extensions I've mentioned so far in this chapter, there are also the following miscellaneous extensions for line and word breaks, search prompts, and character entities.

<NOBR> and *<WBR>*

The `<NOBR>`...`</NOBR>` tags are the opposite of the `<BR>` tag. The text inside the NOBR tags always remains on one line, even if it would have wrapped to two more lines without the NOBR. NOBR is used for words or phrases that must be kept together on one line, but be careful: long unbreakable lines can look really strange on your page, and if they are longer than the page width, they might extend beyond the right edge of the screen.

The `<WBR>` tag (*word break*) indicates an appropriate breaking point within a line (typically one inside a `<NOBR>`...`</NOBR>` sequence). Unlike `<BR>`, which forces a break, `<WBR>` is only used where it is appropriate to do so. If the line will fit on the screen just fine, the `<WBR>` is ignored.

To get around this problem, Netscape added the PROMPT attribute to <ISINDEX>. The value of PROMPT is the string you want to use as the prompt, as in this example:

```
<ISINDEX PROMPT="Enter your Height:">
<ISINDEX PROMPT="Type four numbers, separated by spaces:">
```

Copyright and Registered Trademark Symbols

Netscape introduced two new named-character entities for the copyright (©) and registered (®) symbols: © and ®, respectively. The HTML 2 specification doesn't have named entities for these characters, although you can always use the numeric escapes © and ® in the ISO Latin-1 character encoding for the same result.

Frames (Netscape 2.0 and up)

If you want to include frames in your documents, use the new <FRAMES>, <FRAMESET>, and <NOFRAMES> tags. The <FRAMESET> tag—and matching end tag—acts as the container for the frame document (it has no <BODY> to speak of), and can include <FRAMES>, nested <FRAMESET>, or <NOFRAMES> tags.

<FRAMESET> has two attributes that you'd expect, <ROWS> and <COLS>. Both attributes use comma-separated values to measure in either absolute pixels, percentage (from 1 to 100), or relative scale. Because the people viewing your frame document will, no doubt, have varying sizes of windows, the fixed value of pixels becomes tricky; it's best to balance absolute pixel values with a percentage or relative scale value to make sure you fill the width and height of any viewer's window.

To define a single frame within a <FRAMESET>, use the <FRAMES> tag, with its six attributes. The <SRC> attribute identifies the URL of the document to be displayed in the specific frame.

You can name the frame, optionally, using <NAME>, which makes it easy for the frame to be targeted by links from other frames or documents. You control the margins for your frame with <MARGINWIDTH> and <MARGINHEIGHT>, specifying a value in pixels that allows enough space for the content.

Choosing yes, no, or auto as values, the <SCROLLBAR> attribute indicates whether or not the frame has a scrollbar. The auto value allows the browser to guess whether the particular frame needs a scrollbar.

The <NORESIZE> attribute is a flag that indicates the frame isn't resizable. Because the default is that frames are resizable, any frames adjacent to one with this attribute will be affected by the flag.

Lastly, the <NOFRAMES> tag is for when you want to create frames to be viewed by browsers that would ignore the <FRAMESET> and <FRAMES> tags. A frames-capable browser ignores the data between the start and end <NOFRAMES> tags.

Internet Explorer

Netsape isn't the only company offering new tags and attributes. Content authors can take advantage of Microsoft Internet Explorer 2.0's added HTML tags. For more information about these new features, check out `http://www.microsoft.com/windows/ie/ie20html.htm`.

Here is a brief overview of Internet Explorer's enhancements:

- [ ] <BODY>—You can add BGPROPERTIES=FIXED to the <BODY> tag to get a nonscrolling background.
  ```
  <BODY BACKGROUND="mybackground.gif" BGPROPERTIES=FIXED>
  ```

- [ ] <TABLE>—Internet Explorer 2.0 fully supports tables as specified in the HTML 3.0 draft standard. Using the ALIGN=RIGHT or ALIGN=LEFT attributes, you can set the alignment of your tables. Using the BGCOLOR=#nnnnnn attribute, you can specify a different color for each cell in a table.

- [ ] <IMG>—You can add video clips (.AVI files) to your pages with a string of new attributes to the <IMG> tag, most notably the dynamic source feature, DYNSRC=URL. You can integrate video clips in such a way as to not exclude viewers without video-enabled browsers. If your browser supports inline clips, you see the video; if not, you see a still image.
  ```
  <IMG SRC="earth.gif" DYNSRC="spinearht.avi">
  ```

- [ ] <BGSOUND>—You can now use soundtracks for your web pages. Samples or MIDI formats are accepted.
  ```
  <BGSOUND SRC="whistle.wav">
  ```

- [ ] <MARQUEE>—As you might guess, this new tag offers your pages a scrolling text marquee. Using alignment and behavior attributes, you can plug in the text and make it appear as gracefully on the screen as you desire.
  ```
  <MARQUEE ALIGN=MIDDLE>Buy Low, Sell High!<MARQUEE>
  ```

The supported colors for the BGCOLOR attribute for <MARQUEE> and individual tables cells read like the latest fashion catalog: black, olive, teal, red, blue, maroon, gray, lime, fuchsia, white, green, purple, silver, yellow, aqua, and classic navy.

Internet Explorer 2.0 Tags

<BODY>

You can add `BGPROPERTIES=FIXED` to the `<BODY>` tag to get a nonscrolling background.

`<BODY BACKGROUND="`*mybackground.gif*`" BGPROPERTIES=FIXED>`

<TABLE>

Internet Explorer 2.0 fully supports tables as specified in the HTML 3.0 draft standard. Using the `ALIGN=RIGHT` or `ALIGN=LEFT` attributes, you can set the alignment of your tables. Using the `BGCOLOR=#`*nnnnnn* attribute, you can specify a different color for each cell in a table.

<IMG>

You can add video clips (.AVI files) to your pages with a string of new attributes to the `<IMG>` tag, most notably the dynamic source feature, DYNSRC=*URL*. You can integrate video clips in such a way as to not exclude viewers without video-enabled browsers. If your browser supports inline clips, you see the video; if not, you see a still image.

`<IMG SRC="earth.gif" DYNSRC="spinearht.avi">`

You can use `START=FILEOPEN` or `START=MOUSEOVER` and a variety of `LOOP` commands to guage when and for how long the clip is played.

<BGSOUND>

You can now use soundtracks for your web pages. Samples or MIDI formats are accepted.

`<BGSOUND SRC="whistle.wav">`

You can use `LOOP` features to specify the repetition of the background sound.

<MARQUEE>

As you might guess, this new tag offers your pages a scrolling text marquee. Your text can appear using different attributes, such as `ALIGN=RIGHT` and can have behaviors of `SLIDE`, `SCROLL` (the default), and `ALTERNATE`.`<MARQUEE ALIGN=MIDDLE>Buy Low, Sell High!<MARQUEE>`

Summary

In this chapter, you've read about two major subjects:

☐ You've learned about all the changes that have been happening with HTML and the Web, and how best to handle them in your own documents.

☐ You've become familiar with the Netscape extensions to HTML and learned some ways in which you can use them, so that you can take advantage of the extra features while still retaining compatibility with other browsers.

Table 7.1 contains a quick summary of the tags you've learned about in this chapter.

Table 7.1. The Netscape extensions.

Tag or Entity	Attribute	Use
<CENTER>...</CENTER>		(New tag.) Centers all the text, images, tables, and so on between the two tags.
(many tags)	ALIGN=CENTER	Implemented on many text tags, such as <P>, <H1-6>, and so on. Centers the text within that tag.
<HR>	SIZE	The thickness of the rule, in pixels.
<HR>	WIDTH	The width of the rule, either in exact pixels or as a percentage of page width (for example, 50 percent).
<HR>	ALIGN	The alignment of the rule on the page. Possible values are LEFT, RIGHT, and CENTER.
<HR>	NOSHADE	Display the rule without three-dimensional shading.
<FONT>...</FONT>		(New tag.) Changes the size of the font for the enclosed text.
<FONT>	SIZE	The size of the font to change to, either from 1 to 7 (default is 3) or as a relative number using +N or -N. Relative font sizes are based on the value of <BASEFONT>.
<BASEFONT>	SIZE	(New tag.) The default font size on which relative font changes are based.

continues

187

Table 7.1. continued

Tag or Entity	Attribute	Use
<UL>	TYPE	The type of bullet to label the list items. Possible values are DISC, CIRCLE, and SQUARE.
<OL>	TYPE	The type of number to label the list items. Possible values are A, a, I, i, and 1.
<OL>	START	The number with which to start the list.
<LI>	TYPE	The type of bullet (in <UL> lists), or the type of number (in <OL> lists). TYPE has the same values as its <UL> or <OL> equivalent and affects this item and all those following it.
<LI>	VALUE	(In <OL> lists only.) The number with which to label this item. Affects the numbering of all list items after it.
<BODY>	BGCOLOR	The color of the page's background, in a hexadecimal triplet (#NNNNNN).
<BODY>	BACKGROUND	The name of an image file to use as the background for this page (will be tiled to fit the space).
<BODY>	TEXT	The color of the page's body text, in a hexadecimal triplet (#NNNNNN).
<BODY>	LINK	The color of the page's unfollowed links, in a hexadecimal triplet (#NNNNNN).
<BODY>	VLINK	The color of the page's followed links, in a hexadecimal triplet (#NNNNNN).
<BODY>	ALINK	The color of the page's activated links, in a hexadecimal triplet (#NNNNNN).
<FRAME>	MARGINHEIGHT	The height of the frame, in pixels.
	MARGINWIDTH	The width of the frame, in pixels.
	NAME	Naming the frame enables it for targeting by links in other documents. (Optional)
	NORESIZE	A flag to denote the frame cannot be resized.

Tag or Entity	Attribute	Use
	SCROLLING	Indicates (*yes/no/auto*) whether a frame has scrollbars.
	SRC	The URL of the document displayed in the frame.
<FRAMESET>	COLS	The size of the frame's columns in pixels, percentages, or relative scale.
	ROWS	The size of the frame's rows in pixels, percentages, or relative scale.
<NOFRAMES>		Creates frames that can be viewed by non-frame browsers only.
<BLINK>...</BLINK>		(New tag.) Causes the enclosed text to have a blinking effect.
<NOBR>...</NOBR>		(New tag.) Do not wrap the enclosed text.
<WBR>		(New tag.) Wrap the text at this point only if necessary.
&reg;		Named entity for registered symbol (®).
&copy;		Named entity for copyright symbol (©).

Q&A

Q You've left out a significant Netscape extension: the ability to wrap text next to images.

A I left it out because we haven't discussed images yet. I'll discuss that extension tomorrow when we talk about images.

Q So Netscape supports <CENTER> and ALIGN=CENTER, and you say that more browsers will be accepting the latter. Why don't we have right-aligned text, too?

A Odd, isn't it? The proposal for HTML 3 states that the ALIGN attribute can have values of LEFT (the default), CENTER, RIGHT, and JUSTIFIED. Several browsers support the full alignment suite. (I know of two: Arena, which supports all of HTML 3, and emacs-w3.) But, for the most part, browser authors simply haven't gotten around to implementing right-alignment yet. I expect that the full suite of alignments is close to the top of the stack for future developments, however.

Q I've seen statistics on the Web that say between 60 percent and 90 percent of people on the Web are using Netscape. Why should I continue designing my pages for other browsers and testing my pages in other browsers when most of the world is using Netscape anyhow?

A You can design explicitly to Netscape if you want to; your pages are your pages, and the decision is yours. But, given how easy it is to make small modifications that allow your pages to be viewed and read in other browsers without losing much of the design, why lock out 10 to 40 percent of your audience for the sake of a few tags? Remember, with the Web the size that it is, 10 percent could very well be half a million people or more. The readership of the Web is increasing every day.

Q Why is the `<FONT>` tag controversial?

A It's controversial because you can specify information about the actual presentation of your page in the HTML code. Panic! Horror! Death of the Web!

I'll explain a little bit more about this controversy on Day 14 when I talk about HTML 3. The gist of it, however, is that HTML is defined by a language called SGML, which specifies that documents should be marked up based on their content, not how they are going to appear on the page. Think in terms of the tags that you're used to—headings, quotations, character emphasis. Those tags don't say anything about how the page should be displayed. All they do is specify the elements of that page. This allows the various browser developers to decide how to actually display each element, based on the capabilities of the system they are working on.

According to the SGML purists, all of HTML should be that way. In fact, tags such as `<B>` and `<I>` (part of the HTML 2 standard) are already really bad because these tags say too much about presentation. When confronted with a tag such as `<FONT>`, which says nothing about why the font should be changed, the purists go into a tizzy. And they do have a point: How is one supposed to display the `<FONT>` tag on a text-based browser? Does increasing or decreasing the font size imply that one bit of text is more or less important than the surrounding text? How can you know what the author intended?

The counterargument is that presentation hints such as `<FONT>` are just that—hints. If a browser isn't capable of changing the font, it can just ignore the tags. Of course, this theory relies on you, the Web author, not using presentation-based tags to imply meaning. If you want to emphasize some text, use a tag intended for emphasis (and also change the font size if you want to). That way, the meaning comes across in all browsers but also looks cool in those browsers that can change the font.

Q **"Blink is the HTML equivalent of fingernails on a blackboard"? Isn't that a little harsh?**

A I couldn't resist. :)

Many people absolutely detest blink and will tell you so at a moment's notice, with a passion usually reserved for politics and religion. There are people who might ignore your pages simply because you use blink. Why alienate your audience and distract from your content for the sake of a cheesy effect?

8

Tables

DAY

FOUR

In this chapter, you'll learn about tables, a new HTML 3 feature and the most interesting thing to hit the Web since forms. In particular, you'll learn about the following:

- ☐ The state of tables on the Web today
- ☐ How to use (or not use) tables in your Web documents
- ☐ Creating captions, rows, and heading and data cells
- ☐ Modifying cell alignment
- ☐ Creating cells that span multiple rows or columns

Who Supports Tables?

Tables are the first part of HTML 3 to hit the Web. At the time you are reading this, tables are very new and are unsupported by most browsers. Fortunately, the two most popular browsers on the Web do support them:

- ☐ NCSA Mosaic, as of the 2.5 beta release for X and the 2.0 beta release for Mac and Windows and onward
- ☐ Netscape Navigator 1.1, as of 1.1b1 and onward

Check the documentation of your favorite browser to see whether it does tables, or try one of the examples in this chapter.

Tables Are Still Changing

The very definition of what a table looks like in HTML is still under discussion by the committee working on the HTML specification and is subject to change. NCSA and Netscape Corporation have implemented tables as they were defined at the time, but that definition might have changed by the time you read this, and might change even after that.

If you decide to use tables as I've described them here, or so that they work in your version of Netscape or Mosaic, be prepared to tweak your tables to get them to work if the definition changes.

Should I Use Tables in My Web Pages?

Tables are great for summarizing large amounts of information in a way that can be quickly and easily scanned. In terms of information design, tables are right up there with link menus

(as described earlier in this book) for structuring data so that your reader can get in and out of your pages. When tables become more standardized and more widely used, you should make use of tables wherever they seem appropriate.

Right now, however, support for tables is limited to readers who are using Netscape and Mosaic. If you use tables in your pages, those tables will not work in other browsers. You won't lose all the data in the table, but you will lose the formatting, which can make your data just as unreadable as if it hadn't been included at all. For example, Figure 8.1 shows a table that looks pretty nice in Netscape.

8

Figure 8.1. *A table in Netscape 1.1.*

Figure 8.2 shows the same table as viewed by an earlier version of Netscape that didn't support tables.

Figure 8.2. *The same table in Netscape 1.0.*

Pretty gross, huh? It's also really confusing for your readers if they're not using a browser that supports tables and you haven't warned them about it.

Admittedly, Netscape and Mosaic make up the vast majority of browsers on the Web today, so this might not be an issue for you. But, if you prefer your documents to be viewable on any browser and any platform, you might want to consider the alternatives to tables.

Alternatives to Tables

What if you want to use tables in your pages, but you're wary of the fact that they're still too new? There are several alternatives you can use.

Use a List

If the information you want to put in a table is small enough, try organizing it into a list or multiple lists instead of a table. You might have to reorganize your information, and it won't look as structured as it did in table form, but lists are part of HTML 2 and are supported by every browser out there.

For example, Figure 8.3 shows a simple table.

Figure 8.3. *A simple table.*

Figure 8.4 shows the same table reformatted as a set of lists.

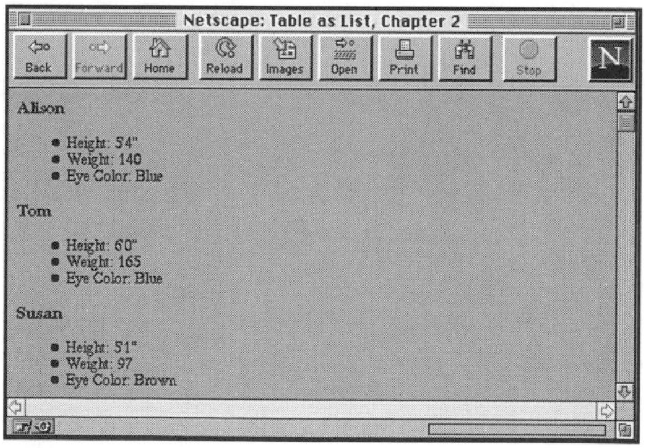

Figure 8.4. *The same table as a definition list.*

Use an Image

Instead of using HTML tables, why not draw your table as an image, and then put that image on your page (see Figure 8.5)? If the table is small enough and you only use black and white, this can be an excellent workaround to the lack of tables. And, with an image, you can also use preformatted text inside the ALT tag to mock the effect of the table in browsers that can't view images.

Figure 8.5. *The same table as an image.*

Use Preformatted Text

If you must have the table format but you don't want to use the table tags, you can use preformatted text (the <PRE> tag) to line up your information in table-like columns. However, keep in mind that preformatted text is usually displayed in a monospaced font such as Courier, so the appearance of the table will not be as nice as it was in table form. Figure 8.6 shows that simple table again as preformatted text.

Figure 8.6. *The same table as preformatted text.*

197

Link the Table Externally

Finally, instead of putting the table directly on your page, consider putting the table on a separate page by itself and create a link to it on the original page with a suitable description.

```
<P><A HREF="conversion.html">A Table</A> of conversions between English
and Metric distances. Your browser must support tables to be able to view
this.</P>
```

Creating Basic Tables

If you've made it this far, you've read (I hope) all my warnings about the fact that tables are new and changing and they'll make your documents unreadable in other browsers. If you've come this far, I assume you still want to go ahead with it. Therefore, in this section, you'll learn how to create a basic table with headings, data, and a caption.

But first, one more warning (the last one, really): Creating tables by hand in HTML is no fun. The code for tables was designed to be easy to generate by programs, not to be written by hand, and as such it's rather confusing. You'll do a lot of experimenting, testing, and going back and forth between your browser and your code to get a table to work out right. Unfortunately, until tools show up that can automatically convert tables from, say, a word processor or a spreadsheet, you'll have to go through this process to use tables in your pages.

Table Parts

Before we get into the actual HTML code to create a table, let me define some terms so we both know what we're talking about:

- ☐ The *caption* indicates what the table is about: for example, "Voting Statistics, 1950–1994," or "Toy Distribution Per Room at 1564 Elm St." Captions are optional.

- ☐ The *table headings* label the rows or columns, or both. Table headings are usually in a larger or emphasized font that is different from the rest of the table.

- ☐ Table *data* is the values in the table itself. The combination of the table headings and table data make up the sum of the table.

- ☐ Table *cells* are the individual squares in the table. A cell can contain normal table data or a table heading.

Figure 8.7 shows a typical table and its parts.

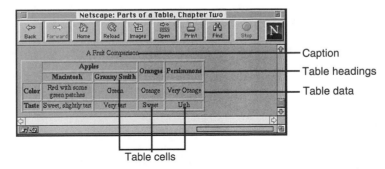

Figure 8.7. *The parts of a table.*

The *<TABLE>* Tag

To create a table in HTML, you use the <TABLE>...</TABLE> tags, which contain the code for a caption and then the contents of the table itself.

```
<TABLE>
...table contents...
</TABLE>
```

Although the HTML 3 specification defines several attributes for the TABLE tag, the only one in common use is the BORDER attribute. BORDER causes the table to be drawn with a border around it, which can be a special, fancy border in a graphical browser or just a series of dashes and pipes (¦) in a text-based browser (when tables are added to a text-based browser).

Borderless tables are useful when you want to use the table structure for layout purposes, but you don't necessarily want the outline of an actual table on the page. For example, if you put form elements in table cells, you could have far greater control over form layout than you normally would, but having the table borders between the elements of your form would distract from the form itself.

Rows and Cells

Inside the <TABLE>...</TABLE> tags, you define the actual contents of the table. Tables are specified in HTML row by row, and each row definition contains definitions for each of the cells in that row. So, to define a table, you start by defining a top row and each cell in turn, and then you define a second row and its cells, and so on. The columns are automatically calculated based on how many cells there are in each row.

Each table row is indicated by the <TR> tag and ends with the appropriate closing </TR>. Within a table row, you use the <TH> and <TD> tags to indicate individual cells. You can have as many rows as you want to and as many cells in each row as you need for your columns, but you should make sure each row has the same number of cells so that the columns line up.

Here's a simple example: a table with only one row, four cells, and one heading on the left side.

```
<TABLE>
<TR>
    <TH>Heading</TH>
    <TD>Data</TD>
    <TD>Data</TD>
    <TD>Data</TD>
</TR>
</TABLE>
```

The <TH> tag indicates a cell that is also a table heading, and the <TD> tag is a regular cell within the table (TD stands for Table Data). Headings are generally displayed in a different way than table cells, such as in a boldface font. Both <TH> and <TD> must be closed with their respective closing tags </TH> and </TD>.

If it's a heading along the top edge of the table, the <TH> tags for that heading go inside the first row. The HTML for a table with a row of headings along the top and one row of data looks like this:

```
<P>A Table with Headings Across the Top</P>
<TABLE BORDER>
<TR>
    <TH>Drive Plate</TH>
    <TH>Front Cover</TH>
</TR>
<TR>
    <TD>39-49</TD>
    <TD>19-23</TD>
</TR>
</TABLE>
```

If the headings are along the left edge of the table, put each <TH> in the first cell in each row, like this:

```
<P>A Table with Headings Along the Side</P>
<TABLE BORDER>
<TR>
    <TH>Drive Plate</TH>
    <TD>39-49</TD>
</TR>
<TR>
    <TH>Front Cover</TH>
    <TD>19-23</TD>
</TR>
</TABLE>
```

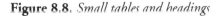

Figure 8.8 shows the results of both these tables.

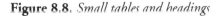

Figure 8.8. *Small tables and headings*

Both table headings and data can contain any text or HTML code or both, including links, lists, forms, and other tables.

The following input and output example shows a simple table. Figure 8.9 shows its result in Netscape.

```
<HTML>
<HEAD>
<TITLE>Empty</TITLE>
</HEAD>
<BODY>
<TABLE BORDER>
<CAPTION>Soup of the Day</CAPTION>
<TR>
    <TH>Monday</TH>
    <TH>Tuesday</TH>
    <TH>Wednesday</TH>
    <TH>Thursday</TH>
    <TH>Friday</TH>
</TR>
<TR>
    <TD>Split Pea</TD>
    <TD>New England<BR>Clam Chowder</TD>
    <TD>Minestrone</TD>
    <TD>Cream of<BR>Broccoli</TD>
    <TD>Chowder</TD>
</TR>
</TABLE>
</BODY>
</HTML>
```

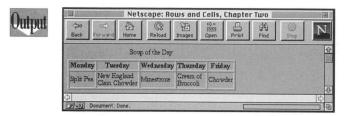

Figure 8.9. *Rows and cells.*

Empty Cells

What if you want a cell with nothing in it? That's easy. Just define a cell with a `<TH>` or `<TD>` tag with nothing inside it.

```
<TR>
    <TD></TD>
    <TD>10</TD>
    <TD>20</TD>
</TR>
```

Sometimes, an empty cell of this sort is displayed as if the cell doesn't exist (as shown in Figure 8.10).

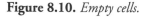

An empty cell—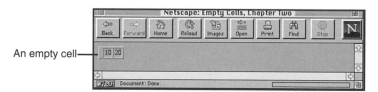

Figure 8.10. *Empty cells.*

If you want to force a truly empty cell, you can add a line break in that cell by itself with no other text (see Figure 8.11).

```
<TR>
    <TD><BR></TD>
    <TD>10</TD>
    <TD>20</TD>
</TR>
```

The empty cell, really empty—

Figure 8.11. *Really empty cells.*

The following input and output example creates a pattern of empty cells. (See Figure 8.12.)

Input

```
<HTML>
<HEAD>
<TITLE>Empty</TITLE>
</HEAD>
<BODY>
<TABLE BORDER>
<TR>
    <TH></TH><TH><BR></TH><TH></TH><TH></TH>
    <TH><BR></TH><TH></TH><TH><BR></TH><TH></TH>
    <TH></TH><TH><BR></TH><TH></TH><TH></TH>
    <TH><BR></TH><TH></TH><TH><BR></TH><TH></TH>
</TR>
<TR>
    <TH></TH><TH><BR></TH><TH></TH><TH></TH>
    <TH><BR></TH><TH></TH><TH><BR></TH><TH></TH>
    <TH></TH><TH><BR></TH><TH></TH><TH></TH>
    <TH><BR></TH><TH></TH><TH><BR></TH><TH></TH>
</TR>
</TABLE>
</BODY>
</HTML>
```

Output

```
Netscape: A Pattern of Empty Cells, Chapter Two
Back  Forward  Home  Reload  Images  Open  Print  Find  Stop   N
```

Figure 8.12. *A pattern of empty cells.*

Captions

Table captions tell your reader what the table is for. Although you could just use a regular paragraph or a heading as a label for your table, there is a <CAPTION> tag for just this purpose. Because the <CAPTION> tag labels captions as captions, tools to process HTML files could extract them into a separate file, or automatically number them, or treat them in special ways simply because they are captions.

But what if you don't want a caption? You don't have to include one. Captions are optional. If you just want a table and don't care about a label, leave the caption off.

The <CAPTION> tag goes inside the <TABLE> tag just before the table rows, and it contains the title of the table. It closes with the </CAPTION> tag.

```
<TABLE>
<CAPTION>Decapitated Tulips in Virginia, 1960-1980</CAPTION>
<TR>
```

The optional ALIGN attribute to the caption determines whether the caption is placed at the top of the table or at the bottom. By default, the caption is placed at the top of the table (ALIGN=TOP). You can use the ALIGN=BOTTOM attribute to the caption if you want to put the caption at the bottom of the table, like this:

```
<TABLE>
<CAPTION ALIGN=BOTTOM>Torque Limits for Various Fruits</CAPTION>
```

In general, unless you have a very short table, you should put your caption at the top so that your readers will see it first and know what they are about to read, instead of seeing it after they're already done reading the table (at which point they've usually figured out what it's about anyway).

Exercise 8.1. Create a simple table.

So now that you know the basics of how to create a table, let's try a simple example. For this example, we'll create a table that indicates the colors you get when you mix the three primary colors together.

Figure 8.13 shows the table we're going to re-create in this example.

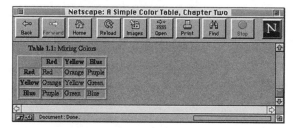

Figure 8.13. *The simple color table.*

Here's a quick hint for laying out tables: because HTML defines tables on a row-by-row basis, it can sometimes be difficult to keep track of the columns, particularly with very complex tables. Before you start actually writing HTML code, it's useful to make a sketch of your table so you know what the heads are and the values of each cell. You might find it is easiest to use a word processor with a table editor (such as Microsoft Word) or a spreadsheet to lay out your tables. Then when you have the layout and the cell values, you can write the HTML code for that table. Of course, eventually there will be filters so that you can simply save the file and automatically get HTML code out of the other end, but for now this is a good way of keeping track of everything.

Let's start with a simple HTML framework for the page that contains a table. Like all HTML files, you can create this file in any text editor.

```
<HTML><HEAD>
<TITLE>Colors</TITLE>
</HEAD>
<BODY>
<TABLE BORDER>
...
</TABLE>
</BODY></HTML>
```

Note that the <TABLE> tag has the BORDER attribute. This draws the highlighted borders around the table.

Now start adding table rows. The first row is the three headings along the top of the table. The table row is indicated by </TR>, and each cell by a <TH> tag:

```
<TR>
    <TH>Red</TH>
    <TH>Yellow</TH>
    <TH>Blue</TH>
</TR>
```

> **Note:** You can format the HTML code any way you want to; like all HTML, the browser ignores most extra spaces and returns. I like to format it like this, with the contents of the individual rows indented and the cell tags on separate lines, so I can pick out the rows and columns more easily.

Now add the second row. The first cell in the second row is the Red heading on the left side of the table, so it will be the first cell in this row, followed by the cells for the table data:

```
<TR>
    <TH>Red</TH>
    <TD>Red</TD>
    <TD>Orange</TD>
    <TD>Purple</TD>
</TR>
```

Continue by adding the remaining two rows in the table, with the Yellow and Blue headings. Here's what you have so far for the entire table:

```
<TABLE BORDER>
<CAPTION><B>Table 1.1:</B> Mixing Colors</CAPTION>
<TR>
    <TH>Red</TH>
    <TH>Yellow</TH>
    <TH>Blue</TH>
</TR>
<TR>
    <TH>Red</TH>
    <TD>Red</TD>
```

```
    <TD>Orange</TD>
    <TD>Purple</TD>
</TR>
<TR>
    <TH>Yellow</TH>
    <TD>Orange</TD>
    <TD>Yellow</TD>
    <TD>Green</TD>
</TR>
<TR>
    <TH>Blue</TH>
    <TD>Purple</TD>
    <TD>Green</TD>
    <TD>Blue</TD>
</TR>
</TABLE>
```

Finally, let's add a simple caption. The `<CAPTION>` tag goes just after the `<TABLE>` tag and just before the first `<TR>` tag:

```
<TABLE BORDER>
<CAPTION><B>Table 1.1:</B> Mixing Colors</CAPTION>
<TR>
```

Now, with a first draft of the code in place, test the HTML file in your favorite browser that supports tables. Figure 8.14 shows how it looks in Netscape.

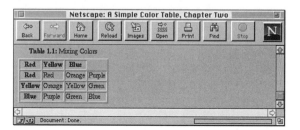

Figure 8.14. *The color table.*

Oops! What happened with that top row? The headings are all messed up. The answer, of course, is that you need an empty cell at the beginning of that first row to space the headings out over the proper columns. HTML isn't smart enough to match it all up for you (this is exactly the sort of error you're going to find the first time you test your tables).

Let's add an empty table heading cell to that first row:

```
<TR>
    <TH></TH>
    <TH>Red</TH>
    <TH>Yellow</TH>
    <TH>Blue</TH>
</TR>
```

> **Note:** I used `<TH>` here, but it could just as easily be `<TD>`. Because there's nothing in the cell, its formatting doesn't matter.

If you try it again, you should get the right result with all the headings over the right columns.

How Tables Are Displayed

Both Netscape and Mosaic currently put the table on a line by itself, with no text to either side of the table and the table flush with the left margin. The Netscape table documentation notes that, in Netscape at least, this will change and you'll eventually have much more control over the placement of a table, as well as have the ability to wrap text around the table. Currently, you can center the table in Netscape with the `<CENTER>` tag, but neither Netscape nor Mosaic implements the various table alignment features defined in the HTML 3 specification.

When a browser parses the HTML code for a table, the cell widths and lengths are automatically calculated based on the width and length of the data within the cells and the current width of the page. Although HTML 3 defines a method for specifying exact column and table widths (using the `COLSPEC` and `WIDTH` attributes to the `<TABLE>` tag), Mosaic has not yet implemented it, and Netscape implements only the `WIDTH` attribute but uses it differently from the HTML 3 definition. (You'll learn about the `WIDTH` attribute, as Netscape defines it, later in this chapter.)

You can slightly modify the way a table is laid out with line breaks (`<BR>` tags) inside your cells, by using the `NOWRAP` attribute or both `<BR>` and `NOWRAP` together.

Line breaks are particularly useful if you have a table in which most of the cells are small and only one or two cells have longer data. As long as the screen width can handle it, the browser generally just creates really long rows, which looks rather funny in some tables (see Figure 8.15).

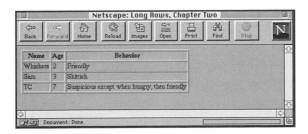

Figure 8.15. *A table with one long row.*

By putting in line breaks, you can wrap that row in a shorter column so that it looks more like the table shown in Figure 8.16.

Figure 8.16. *The long row fixed with <BR>.*

On the other hand, you might have a table in which a cell is being wrapped for which you want all the data on one line. (This can be particularly important for things such as form elements within table cells where you want the label and the input field to stay together.) In this instance, you can add the NOWRAP attribute to the <TH> or <TD> tags and the browser keeps all the data in that cell on the one line. Note that you can always add <BR> tags by hand to that same cell and get line breaks exactly where you want them.

Be careful when you hard-code table cells with line breaks and NOWRAP attributes. Remember, your table might be viewed in many different screen widths. Try resizing the window in which your table is being viewed and see whether your table can still hold up under different widths with all your careful formatting in place. For the most part, you should try to let the browser itself format your table and to make minor adjustments only when necessary.

Cell Alignment

When you have your rows and cells in place, you can align the data within each cell for the best effect based on what your table contains. HTML tables give you several options for aligning the data within your cells both horizontally and vertically. Figure 8.17 shows a table (a real HTML one!) of the various alignment options.

Horizontal alignment (the ALIGN attribute) defines whether the data within a cell is aligned with the left cell margin (LEFT), the right cell margin (RIGHT), or centered within the two (CENTER).

Vertical alignment (the VALIGN attribute) defines the vertical alignment of the data within the cell, meaning whether the data is flush with the top of the cell (TOP), flush with the bottom of the cell (BOTTOM), or vertically centered within the cell (MIDDLE). Netscape also implements VALIGN=BASELINE, which is similar to VALIGN=TOP, except that it aligns the baseline of the first line of text in each cell (depending on the contents of the cell, this might or might not produce a different result than ALIGN=TOP).

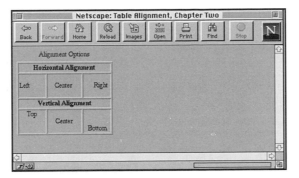

Figure 8.17. *Cell alignment.*

By default, heading cells are centered both horizontally and vertically, and data cells are centered vertically but aligned flush left.

You can override the defaults for an entire row by adding the ALIGN or VALIGN attributes to the <TR> tag, as in this example:

```
<TR ALIGN=CENTER VALIGN=TOP>
```

You can override the row alignment for individual cells by adding ALIGN to the <TD> or <TH> tags:

```
<TR ALIGN=CENTER VALIGN=TOP>
    <TD>14</TD>
    <TD>16</TD>
    <TD ALIGN=LEFT>No Data</TD>
    <TD>15</TD>
</TR>
```

The following input and output example shows the various cell alignments and how they look in Netscape (Figure 8.18).

```
<HTML>
<HEAD>
<TITLE>Cell Alignments</TITLE>
</HEAD>
<BODY>
<TABLE BORDER>
<TR>
    <TH></TH>
    <TH>Left</TH>
    <TH>Centered</TH>
    <TH>Right</TH>
</TR>
<TR>
    <TH>Top</TH>
    <TD ALIGN=LEFT VALIGN=TOP><IMG SRC="button.gif"></TD>
    <TD ALIGN=CENTER VALIGN=TOP><IMG SRC="button.gif"></TD>
```

209

```
        <TD ALIGN=RIGHT VALIGN=TOP><IMG SRC="button.gif"></TD>
    </TR>
    <TR>
        <TH>Centered</TH>
        <TD ALIGN=LEFT VALIGN=MIDDLE><IMG SRC="button.gif"></TD>
        <TD ALIGN=CENTER VALIGN=MIDDLE><IMG SRC="button.gif"></TD>
        <TD ALIGN=RIGHT VALIGN=MIDDLE><IMG SRC="button.gif"></TD>
    </TR>
    <TR>
        <TH>Bottom</TH>
        <TD ALIGN=LEFT VALIGN=BOTTOM><IMG SRC="button.gif"></TD>
        <TD ALIGN=CENTER VALIGN=BOTTOM><IMG SRC="button.gif"></TD>
        <TD ALIGN=RIGHT VALIGN=BOTTOM><IMG SRC="button.gif"></TD>
    </TR>
    </TABLE>
    </BODY>
    </HTML>
```

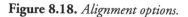

Figure 8.18. *Alignment options.*

▼ Exercise 8.2. A vegetable planting guide.

Tables are great when you have a lot of information—particularly technical or numeric information—that you want to present in a way that enables your readers to find what they need quickly and easily. Perhaps they're only interested in one bit of that information or a range of it. Presented in a paragraph or in a list, it might be more difficult for your readers to glean what they need.

For example, say you want to summarize information about planting vegetables, which includes the time in the year each vegetable should be planted, how long it takes before you can harvest that vegetable, whether you can transplant an already growing plant, and some common varieties that are known to grow especially well. You can present this information as a list, one paragraph per vegetable; but, because the data falls into neat categories, the data will look better and be more accessible as a table. Figure 8.19 shows the vegetable-planting chart, the table you'll be building in this exercise. Like the last example, it's a rather simple table, but it does use links, images, and lists inside the table cells. In addition, it takes advantage of some of the alignment options that I described in the previous section. In this example, we'll start with a basic HTML framework, lay out the rows and the cells, and then adjust and fine-tune the alignment of the data within those cells. You'll find, as you work with more tables, that this plan is the easiest way to develop a table. If you worry about the alignment at the same time that you're constructing the table, it's easy to get confused.

210

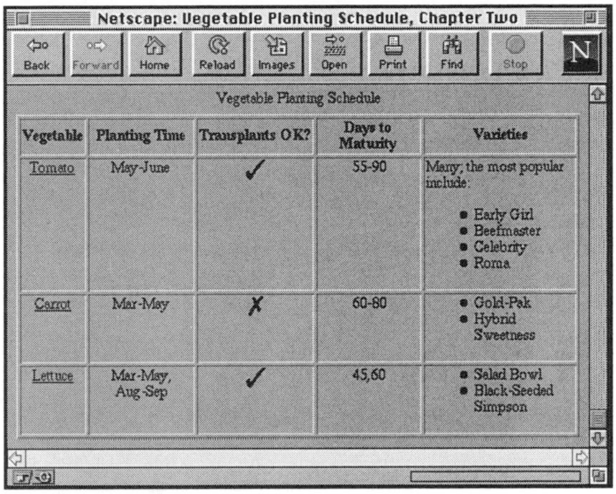

Figure 8.19. *The vegetable planting schedule.*

Here's the basic framework for the table, including the caption:

```
<HTML>
<HEAD>
<TITLE>Vegetable Planting Schedule</TITLE>
</HEAD>
<BODY>
<TABLE BORDER>
<CAPTION>Vegetable Planting Schedule</CAPTION>

</TABLE>
</BODY>
</HTML>
```

The first row is the heading for the table, which is easy enough. It's a row with five heading cells:

```
<TR>
    <TH>Vegetable</TH>
    <TH>Planting Time</TH>
    <TH>Transplants OK?</TH>
    <TH>Days to Maturity</TH>
    <TH>Varieties</TH>
</TR>
```

The remaining rows are for the data for the table. Note that within a table cell (a `<TH>` or `<TD>` tag), you can put any HTML markup, including links, images, forms, or other tables. In this example, we've used links for each vegetable name (pointing to further information), a checkmark or X image for whether you can plant transplants of that vegetable, and an unordered list for the varieties. Here's the code so far for three rows of the table:

```
<TABLE BORDER>
<CAPTION>Vegetable Planting Schedule</CAPTION>
```

```
<TR>
    <TD ><A HREF="tomato.html">Tomato</A></TD>
    <TD>May-June</TD>
    <TD><IMG SRC="check.gif"></TD>
    <TD>55-90</TD>
    <TD>Many; the most popular include:
        <UL>
        <LI>Early Girl
        <LI>Beefmaster
        <LI>Celebrity
        <LI>Roma
        </UL>
    </TD>
</TR>
<TR>
    <TD><A HREF="tomato.html">Carrot</A></TD>
    <TD>Mar-May</TD>
    <TD><IMG SRC="ex.gif"></TD>
    <TD>60-80</TD>
    <TD><UL>
        <LI>Gold-Pak
        <LI>Hybrid Sweetness
        </UL>
    </TD>
</TR>
<TR>
    <TD><A HREF="tomato.html">Lettuce</A></TD>
    <TD>Mar-May, Aug-Sep</TD>
    <TD><IMG SRC="check.gif"></TD>
    <TD>45,60</TD>
    <TD><UL>
        <LI>Salad Bowl
        <LI>Black-Seeded Simpson
        </UL>
    </TD>
</TR>
</TABLE>
```

One exception to the rule that whitespace in your original HTML code doesn't matter in the final output exists in tables in Netscape. For images in cells, say you've formatted your code with the <IMG> tag on a separate line, like this:

```
<TD>
    <IMG SRC="check.gif">
</TD>
```

With this code, the return between the <TD> and the <IMG> tag is significant; your image will not be properly placed within the cell (this particularly shows up in centered cells). To correct the problem, just put the <TD> and the <IMG> on the same line:

```
<TD><IMG SRC="check.gif"></TD>
```

Figure 8.20 shows what the table looks like so far.

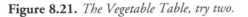

Figure 8.20. *The Vegetable Table, try one.*

So far, so good, but the columns would look better centered. We can do this globally for each row by adding the ALIGN=CENTER attribute to each <TR> tag. (Note that you only need to do it for the data rows; the headings are already centered.)

```
<TR ALIGN=CENTER>
    <TD ><A HREF="tomato.html">Tomato</A></TD>
    <TD>May-June</TD>
    ....
```

Figure 8.21 shows the new table with the contents of the cells now centered:

Figure 8.21. *The Vegetable Table, try two.*

213

Now the table looks much better, except for the bullets in the varieties column. They got centered, too, so now they're all out of whack. But that doesn't matter; we can fix that by adding the ALIGN=LEFT attribute to the <TD> tag for that cell in every row (see Figure 8.22).

```
<TD ALIGN=LEFT>Many; the most popular include:
    <UL>
    <LI>Early Girl
    ...
```

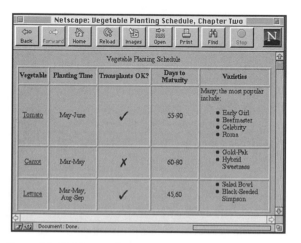

Figure 8.22. *The Vegetable Table, try three.*

> **Note:** You could have just kept the default alignment for each row and then added an ALIGN=CENTER attribute to every cell that needed to be centered. But that would have been a lot more work. It's usually easier to change the default row alignment to the alignment of the majority of the cells and then change the cell alignment for the individual cells that are left.

We're getting close, but let's try one more thing. Right now, all the cells are vertically centered. Let's add a VALIGN=TOP to each data row (next to the ALIGN=CENTER) so that they'll hug the top of the cells.

```
<TR ALIGN=CENTER VALIGN=TOP>
    <TD ><A HREF="tomato.html">Tomato</A></TD>
    <TD>May-June</TD>
```

You're done! Here's the final HTML text for the example:

```
<HTML>
<HEAD>
<TITLE>Vegetable Planting Schedule</TITLE>
</HEAD>
<BODY>
<TABLE BORDER>
<CAPTION>Vegetable Planting Schedule</CAPTION>
<TR ALIGN=CENTER>
    <TH>Vegetable</TH>
    <TH>Planting Time</TH>
    <TH>Transplants OK?</TH>
    <TH>Days to Maturity</TH>
    <TH>Varieties</TH>
</TR>
<TR ALIGN=CENTER VALIGN=TOP>
    <TD ><A HREF="tomato.html">Tomato</A></TD>
    <TD>May-June</TD>
    <TD><IMG SRC="check.gif"></TD>
    <TD>55-90</TD>
    <TD ALIGN=LEFT>Many; the most popular include.<UL>
        <LI>Early Girl
        <LI>Beefmaster
        <LI>Celebrity
        <LI>Roma
        </UL>
    </TD>
</TR>
<TR ALIGN=CENTER VALIGN=TOP>
    <TD><A HREF="carrot.html">Carrot</A></TD>
    <TD>Mar-May</TD>
    <TD><IMG SRC="ex.gif"></TD>
    <TD>60-80</TD>
    <TD ALIGN=LEFT><UL>
        <LI>Gold-Pak
        <LI>Hybrid Sweetness
        </UL>
    </TD>
</TR>
<TR ALIGN=CENTER VALIGN=TOP>
    <TD><A HREF="carrot.html">Lettuce</A></TD>
    <TD>Mar-May, Aug-Sep</TD>
    <TD><IMG SRC="check.gif"></TD>
    <TD>45,60</TD>
    <TD ALIGN=LEFT><UL>
        <LI>Salad Bowl
        <LI>Black-Seeded Simpson
        </UL>
    </TD>
</TR>
</TABLE>
</BODY>
</HTML>
```

Cells That Span Multiple Rows or Columns

The tables we've created up to this point all had one value per cell or had the occasional empty cell. You can also create cells that span multiple rows or columns within the table. Those *spanned* cells can then hold headings that have subheadings in the next row or column, or can create other special effects within the table layout. Figure 8.23 shows a table with spanned columns and rows.

This cell spans two rows and two columns.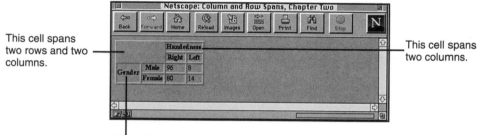

This cell spans two columns.

This cell spans two rows.

Figure 8.23. *Tables with spans.*

To create a cell that spans multiple rows or columns, you add the ROWSPAN or COLSPAN attribute to the <TH> or <TD> tags, along with the number of rows or columns you want the cell to span. The data within that cell then fills the entire width or length of the combined cells, as in the following example:

```
<TR>
    <TH COLSPAN=2>Gender
</TR>
<TR>
    <TH>Male</TH>
    <TH>Female</TH>
</TR>
<TR>
    <TD>15</TD>
    <TD>23</TD>
</TR>
```

Figure 8.24 shows how this table might appear when displayed.

Note that if a cell spans multiple rows, you don't have to redefine that cell as empty in the next row or rows. Just ignore it and move to the next cell in the row; the span will fill in the spot for you.

Cells always span downward and to the right. So to create a cell that spans several columns, you add the COLSPAN attribute to the leftmost cell in the span, and for cells that span rows, you add ROWSPAN to the topmost cell.

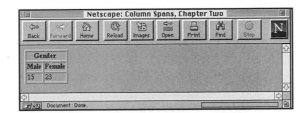

Figure 8.24. *Column spans.*

The following input and output example shows a cell that spans multiple rows (the cell with the word "Piston" in it). Figure 8.25 shows the result in Netscape.

```
<HTML>
<HEAD>
<TITLE>Ring Clearance</TITLE>
</HEAD>
<BODY>
<TABLE BORDER>
<TR>
    <TH COLSPAN=2></TH>
    <TH>Ring<BR>Clearance</TH>
</TR>
<TR ALIGN=CENTER>
    <TH ROWSPAN=2>Piston</TH>
    <TH>Upper</TH>
    <TD>3mm</TD>
</TR>
<TR ALIGN=CENTER>
    <TH>Lower</TH>
    <TD>3.2mm</TD>
</TR>
</TABLE>
</BODY>
</HTML>
```

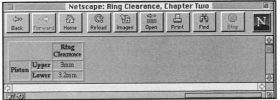

Figure 8.25. *Cells that span multiple rows and columns.*

Exercise 8.3. A table of service specifications.

Had enough of tables yet? Let's do one more example that takes advantage of everything you've learned here: tables with headings and normal cells, alignments, and column and row spans. This is a very complex table, so we'll go step by step, row by row to build it.

Figure 8.26 shows the table, which indicates service and adjustment specifications from the service manual for a car.

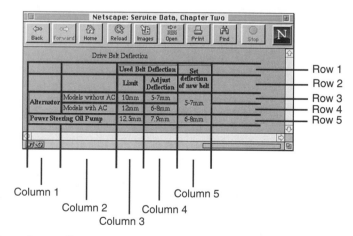

Figure 8.26. *The really complex service specification table.*

There are actually five rows and columns in this table. Do you see them? Some of them span columns and rows. Figure 8.27 shows the same table with a grid drawn over it so you can see where the rows and columns are.

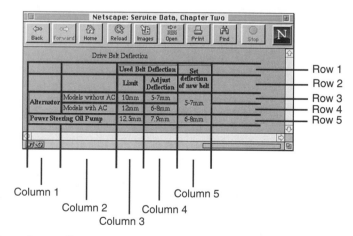

Figure 8.27. *Five columns, five rows.*

With tables such as this one that use many spans, it's helpful to draw this sort of grid to figure out where the spans are and in which row they belong. Remember, spans start at the topmost row and the leftmost column.

Ready? Start with the framework, just as you have for the other tables in this chapter:

```
<HTML>
<HEAD>
<TITLE>Service Data</TITLE>
</HEAD>
<BODY>
<TABLE BORDER>
<CAPTION>Drive Belt Deflection</CAPTION>

</TABLE>
</BODY>
</HTML>
```

Now create the first row. With the grid on your picture, you can see that the first cell is empty and spans two rows and two columns (see Figure 8.28). Therefore, the HTML for that cell would be as follows:

```
<TR>
<TH ROWSPAN=2 COLSPAN=2></TH>
```

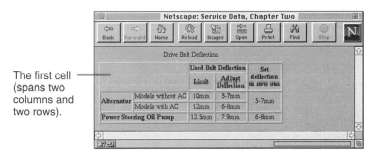

The first cell (spans two columns and two rows).

Figure 8.28. *The first cell.*

The second cell in the row is the Used Belt Deflection header, which spans two columns (for the two cells beneath it). So the code for that cell is

```
<TH COLSPAN=2>Used Belt Deflection</TH>
```

Now that you have two cells that span two columns each, there's only the one left in this row. But this one, like the first one, spans the row beneath it:

```
<TH ROWSPAN=2>Set deflection of new belt</TH>
</TR>
```

Now go on to the second row. This isn't the one that starts with the Alternator heading. Remember that the first cell in the previous row has a ROWSPAN and a COLSPAN of two, meaning that it bleeds down to this row and takes up two cells. You don't need to redefine it for this row; you just move on to the next cell in the grid. The first cell in this row is the Limit header, and the second cell is the Adjust Deflection cell.

```
<TR>
    <TH>Limit</TH>
    <TH>Adjust Deflection</TH>
</TR>
```

What about the last cell? Just like the first cell, the cell in the row above this one had a ROWSPAN of two, which takes up the space in this row. So the only values you need for this row are the ones you already defined.

Are you with me so far? Now is a great time to try this out in your browser to make sure that everything is lining up. It will look kind of funny because we haven't really put anything on the left side of the table yet, but it's worth a try. Figure 8.29 shows what we've got so far.

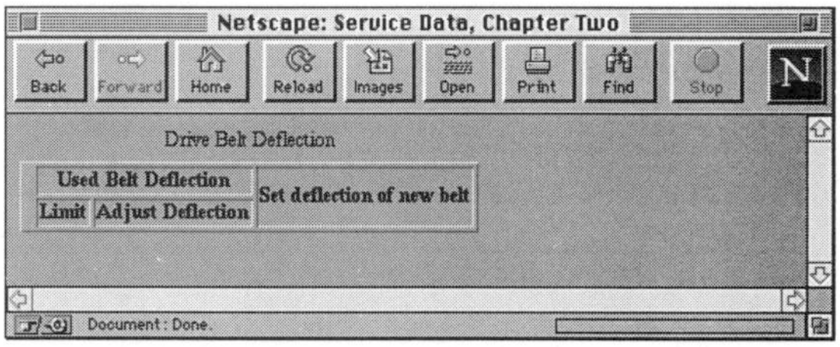

Figure 8.29. *The table so far.*

Next row! Check your grid if you need to. Here, the first cell is the heading for Alternator, and it spans this row and the one below it. Are you getting the hang of this yet?

```
<TH ROWSPAN=2>Alternator</TD>
```

The next three are pretty easy because they don't span anything. Here are their definitions:

```
<TD>Models without AC</TD>
<TD>10mm</TD>
<TD>5-7mm</TD>
```

The last cell is just like the first one:

```
<TD ROWSPAN=2>5-7mm</TD>
```

We're up to row number four. In this one, because of the ROWSPANs from the previous row, there are only three cells to define: the cell for Models with AC and the two cells for the numbers.

```
<TD>Models with AC</TD>
<TD>12mm</TD>
<TD>6-8mm</TD>
```

> **Note:** In this table, I've made the Alternator cell a header and the AC cells plain data. This is mostly an aesthetic decision on my part; I could just as easily have made all three headings.

Now for the final row—this one should be easy. The first cell (Power Steering Oil Pump) spans two columns (the one with Alternator in it, and the With/Without AC column). The remaining three are just one cell each.

```
<TH COLSPAN=2>Power Steering Oil Pump</TD>
<TD>12.5mm</TD>
<TD>7.9mm</TD>
<TD>6-8mm</TD>
```

That's it. You're done laying out the rows and columns. That was the hard part; the rest is just fine-tuning. Let's try looking at it again to make sure there are no strange errors (see Figure 8.30).

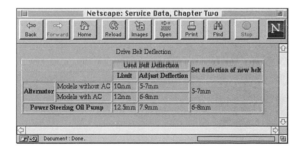

Figure 8.30. *The table: the next step.*

Now that you have all the rows and cells laid out, adjust the alignments within the cells. The numbers, at least, should be centered. Because they make up the majority of the table, let's make centered the default alignment for each row:

```
<TR ALIGN=CENTER>
```

But the labels along the left side of the table look funny if they're centered, so align them left:

```
<TH ROWSPAN=2 ALIGN=LEFT>Alternator</TD>
```

Finally, the last bit of fine-tuning I've done is to put some line breaks in the longer headings so that the columns are a little narrower. Because the text in the headings is pretty short to start with, I don't have to worry too much about the table looking funny if it gets too narrow. Here are the lines I modified:

```
<TH ROWSPAN=2>Set<BR>deflection<BR>of new belt</TH>
<TH>Adjust<BR>Deflection</TH>
```

Voilà—the final table, with everything properly laid out and aligned!

> **Note:** If you got lost at any time, the best thing you can do is pull out your handy text editor and try it yourself, following along tag by tag. After you've done it a couple of times, it becomes easier.

Here's the full text for the table example:

```
<HTML>
<HEAD>
<TITLE>Service Data</TITLE>
</HEAD>
<BODY>
<TABLE BORDER>
<CAPTION>Drive Belt Deflection</CAPTION>
<TR>
    <TH ROWSPAN=2 COLSPAN=2></TH>
    <TH COLSPAN=2>Used Belt Deflection</TH>
    <TH ROWSPAN=2>Set<BR>deflection<BR>of new belt</TH>
</TR>
<TR>
    <TH>Limit</TH>
    <TH>Adjust<BR>Deflection</TH>
</TR>
<TR ALIGN=CENTER>
    <TH ROWSPAN=2 ALIGN=LEFT>Alternator</TD>
    <TD ALIGN=LEFT>Models without AC</TD>
    <TD>10mm</TD>
    <TD>5-7mm</TD>
    <TD ROWSPAN=2>5-7mm</TD>
</TR>
<TR ALIGN=CENTER>
    <TD ALIGN=LEFT>Models with AC</TD>
    <TD>12mm</TD>
    <TD>6-8mm</TD>
</TR>
<TR ALIGN=CENTER>
    <TH COLSPAN=2 ALIGN=LEFT>Power Steering Oil Pump</TD>
    <TD>12.5mm</TD>
    <TD>7.9mm</TD>
    <TD>6-8mm</TD>
</TR>
</TABLE>
</BODY>
</HTML>
```

The Netscape Extensions to Tables

In addition to the Netscape extensions you learned about in the previous chapter, Netscape has also made several extensions to the HTML 3 definition of tables. These tags and attributes will only work in Netscape's version of tables and might not be incorporated into the standard, so all the usual warnings go double for these tags.

Table Widths

The HTML 3 proposal defines a WIDTH attribute to the <TABLE> tag, which enables you to specify the exact width of the table when it is displayed. Width is measured in the current units that are specified by the UNITS attribute.

Netscape implements the WIDTH attribute but does so in a slightly different way. WIDTH can have a value that is either the exact width of the table (in pixels) or a percentage (such as 50 percent or 75 percent) of the current screen width, which can therefore change if the window is resized. If WIDTH is specified, the width of the columns within the table can be compressed or expanded to fit the required width. For example, Figure 8.31 shows a table that would have been quite narrow if it had been left alone. But this table has stretched to fit a 100 percent screen width using the WIDTH attribute, which causes Netscape to spread out all the columns to fit the screen.

Note: Trying to make the table too narrow for the data it contains might be impossible, in which case Netscape tries to get as close as it can to your desired width.

Name	Height	Weight	Eye Color
Alison	5'4"	140	Blue
Tom	6'0"	165	Blue
Susan	5'1"	97	Brown

Figure 8.31. *Table widths in Netscape.*

Column Widths

The WIDTH attribute can also be used on individual cells (<TH> or <TD>) to specify the width of individual columns. As with table width, the WIDTH tag in calls can be an exact pixel width or a percentage (which is taken as a percentage of the full table width).

Column widths are useful when you want to have multiple columns of exactly the same width, regardless of their contents (for example, for some forms of page layout). Figure 8.32 shows that same table from the previous example that spans the width of the screen, although this time the first column is 10 percent of the table width and the remaining three columns are 30 percent. Netscape adjusts the column widths to fit both the width of the screen and the given percentages.

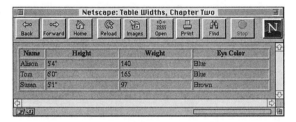

Figure 8.32. *Column widths.*

Border Widths

Netscape has slightly modified the BORDER attribute to the <TABLE> tag. BORDER, as you know from the last chapter, is used to draw a border around the table. In Netscape, if BORDER has a numeric value, the border around the outside of the table is drawn with that pixel width. The default is BORDER=1; BORDER=0 suppresses the border (just as if you had omitted the BORDER attribute altogether).

Note: The border value applies only to the shaded border along the outside edge of the table, not to the borders around the cells. See the next section for that value.

Figure 8.33 shows an example of a table with a border of 10 pixels.

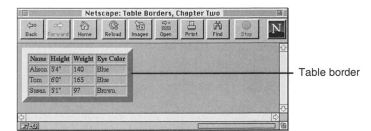

Figure 8.33. *Table border widths.*

8

Cell Spacing

Cell spacing is similar to cell padding except that it affects the amount of space between cells—that is, the width of the shaded lines that separate the cells. The CELLSPACING attribute in the <TABLE> tag affects the spacing for the table. Cell spacing is 2 by default.

Cell spacing also includes the outline around the table, which is just inside the table's border (as set by the BORDER attribute). Experiment with it and you can see the difference. For example, Figure 8.34 shows an example of a table with cell spacing of 8 and a border of 4.

Figure 8.34. *Cell spacing (and borders).*

Cell Padding

Cell padding is the amount of space between the edges of the cells and the cell's contents. By default, Netscape draws its tables with a cell padding of 1 pixel. You can add more space by adding the CELLPADDING attribute to the <TABLE> tag, with a value in pixels for the amount of cell padding you want. Figure 8.35 shows an example of a table with cell padding of 10 pixels.

The CELLPADDING attribute with a value of 0 causes the edges of the cells to touch the edges of the cell's contents (which doesn't look very good).

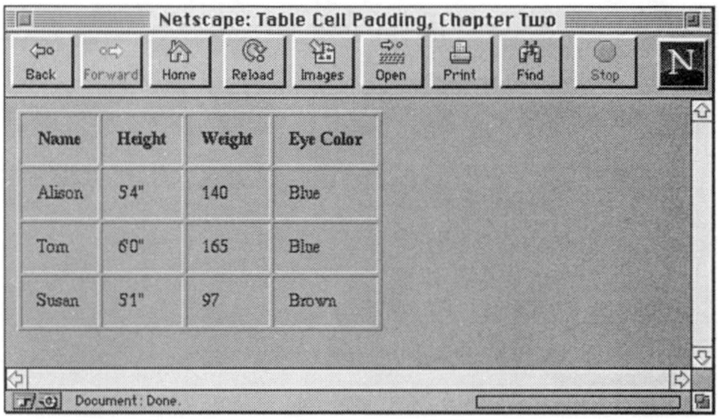

Figure 8.35. *Cell padding.*

Summary

In this chapter, you've learned all about the Next Big Thing in HTML: tables, as currently supported by Netscape and Mosaic. Tables enable you to arrange your information in rows and columns so that your readers can scan the table quickly and get to the information they need.

While working with tables in this chapter, you've learned about headings and data, captions, defining rows and cells, aligning information within cells, and creating cells that span multiple rows or columns. With these features you can create tables for most purposes.

As you're constructing tables, it's helpful to keep the following steps in mind:

☐ Sketch your table and where the rows and columns fall. Mark which cells span multiple rows and columns.

☐ Start with a basic framework and lay out the rows, headings, and data row by row and cell by cell in HTML. Include row and column spans as necessary. Test frequently in a browser to make sure it's all working correctly.

☐ Modify the alignment in the rows to reflect the alignment of the majority of the cells.

☐ Modify the alignment for individual cells.

☐ Adjust line breaks, if necessary.

☐ Test your table in multiple browsers (at the moment, at least NCSA Mosaic and Netscape). Different browsers can have different ideas of how to lay out your table or be more accepting of errors in your HTML code.

Table 8.1 presents a quick summary of the HTML table-creating tags that you've learned about in this chapter.

Table 8.1. The table tags.

Tag	Use
`<TABLE>...</TABLE>`	Indicates a table.
`BORDER`	An attribute of the `<TABLE>` tag, indicating whether the table will be drawn with a border. The default is no border. In Netscape, if `BORDER` has a value, that value is the width of the shaded border around the table.
`CELLSPACING`	(Netscape only.) Defines the amount of space between the cells in the table.
`CELLPADDING`	(Netscape only.) Defines the amount of space between the edges of the cell and its contents.
`<CAPTION>...</CAPTION>`	Creates an optional caption for the table.
`<TR>...</TR>`	Defines a table row, which can contain heading and data cells.
`<TH>...<TH>`	Defines a table cell containing a heading. Heading cells are usually indicated by boldface and centered both horizontally and vertically within the cell.
`<TD>...<TD>`	Defines a table cell containing data. Table cells are in a regular font, and are left-justified and vertically centered within the cell.
`ALIGN`	When used with `<CAPTION>`, the possible values are `TOP` and `BOTTOM`. `ALIGN` indicates whether the caption will be placed at the top of the table (the default) or the bottom. When used with `<TR>`, the possible values are `LEFT`, `CENTER`, and `RIGHT`, which indicate the horizontal alignment of the cells within that row (overriding the default alignment of heading and table cells). When used with `<TH>` or `<TD>`, the possible values are also `LEFT`, `CENTER`, and `RIGHT`, which override both the row's alignment and any default cell alignment.

8

continues

227

Table 8.1. continued

Tag	Use
VALIGN	When used with `<TR>`, possible values are TOP, MIDDLE, and BOTTOM. VALIGN indicates the vertical alignment of the cells within that row (overriding the defaults).
	When used with `<TH>` or `<TD>`, the same possible values are used, and VALIGN overrides both the row's vertical alignment and the default cell alignment.
	In Netscape, VALIGN can also have the value BASELINE.
ROWSPAN	Used within a `<TH>` or `<TD>` tag, ROWSPAN indicates the number of cells below this one that this cell will span.
COLSPAN	Used within a `<TH>` or `<TD>` tag, COLSPAN indicates the number of cells to the right of this one that this cell will span.
NOWRAP	Used within a `<TH>` or `<TD>` tag, NOWRAP prevents the browser from wrapping the contents of the cell.
WIDTH	(Netscape only.) When used with `<TABLE>`, indicates the width of the table, in exact pixel values or as a percentage of page width (for example, 50 percent).
	When used with `<TH` or `<TD>`, WIDTH indicates width of the cell, in exact pixel values or as a percentage of table width (for example, 50 percent).

Q&A

Q   **Tables are a real hassle to lay out, especially when you get into row and column spans. That last example was awful.**

A   You're right. Tables are a tremendous pain to lay out by hand like this. However, if you're writing filters and tools to generate HTML code, having the table defined like this makes more sense because you can programmatically just write out each row in turn. Sooner or later, we'll all be working in HTML filters anyhow (let's hope), so you won't have to do this by hand for long.

Q   **My tables work fine in Netscape, but they're all garbled in Mosaic. What did I do wrong?**

A   Did you remember to close all your `<TR>`, `<TH>`, and `<TD>` tags? Make sure you've put in the matching `</TR>`, `</TH>`, and `</TD>` tags, respectively.

Why does Netscape work with this and Mosaic doesn't? Netscape is more forgiving of bad HTML code. One could argue that Netscape is doing the right thing by "fixing" poorly written HTML, but that also means that if you're using Netscape to test your HTML, you could be producing files that are entirely scrambled when viewed in other browsers. As I said repeatedly, never rely on only one browser to test your HTML code. If you can test your code against an HTML validator, that's even better because all the validator cares about is the correctness of your code.

Q **Can you nest tables, putting a table inside a single table cell?**

A Sure! As I mentioned in this chapter, you can put any HTML code you want to inside a table cell, and that can include other tables.

DAY

5

9

Using Images

Using Images

Some people would argue that the sole reason the World Wide Web has become so popular is that formatted text and graphics can be viewed together on the page. Text is fine, but there's nothing like a flashy color picture to really draw people's attention to your Web page.

This chapter explains almost everything you need to use images in Web pages:

☐ The kinds of images you can use

☐ How to include images on your Web page, either alone or alongside text

☐ How to use images as clickable links

☐ The Netscape extensions for images

☐ Providing alternatives for browsers that cannot view images

☐ Using images with transparent backgrounds

☐ How (and when) to use images in your Web page

Image Formats

There are two kinds of images that your Web browser can deal with: *inline* images and *external* images.

Inline images are images that appear directly on the Web page and are loaded when you load the page itself—assuming, of course, that you have a graphical browser, and that you have automatic image-loading turned on. To be displayed directly on a Web page, your images should be in GIF format. All graphical Web browsers are expected to be able to display GIF files.

Some newer browsers, notably Netscape, can now display inline images in JPEG format as well as GIF. However, support for inline JPEG files is not widespread, so sticking with GIF is the safest method of making sure your images can be viewed by the widest possible audience.

External images are images that are not directly displayed when you load a page. They are only downloaded at the request of your reader, usually on the other side of a link. Because browsers can be configured to handle different file types, and helper applications can be used to display many different image formats, you have more flexibility in the kind of image formats you can use for external images, for example JPEG, PCX, XBM, or PICT. External images are covered in the next chapter.

So how do you get images, and once you have them, how do you get them into GIF format?

You can get images by drawing them, scanning them, or buying a commercial clip art package. You can also find GIF images on the Net, in the many image archives that are out there. But watch out for these images; many people scan and upload images without being aware of (or ignoring) the fact that those images may be copyrighted and owned by someone else who may not be pleased that you are using their work on the Web.

If you intend to use images on your home pages, your safest bet is to use images you create yourself, or get explicit permission from the owner of the image to use those images online, or take advantage of CD-ROMs that are full of royalty-free clip art and stock photography (as I have in this book).

After you have an image, you'll need to convert it to GIF format to use it on your Web page. Many image editing programs such as Adobe Photoshop, Color It, Paint Shop Pro, or XV will read common input formats and output GIF files; look for an option called CompuServe GIF, or GIF87, or GIF89, or just plain GIF. There are also converter programs available (DeBabelizer on the Mac or the PBM filter package for UNIX) that do nothing except convert images to and from other formats.

Inline Images in HTML: The <IMG> Tag

After you have an image in GIF format, ready to go, you can put it in your Web page. Inline images are specified in HTML using the <IMG> tag. The <IMG> tag, like the <HR> and <BR> tags, has no closing tag. It does, however, have three attributes: SRC, ALT, and ALIGN. You'll learn about ALT and ALIGN later in this chapter; let's start here with SRC.

> **Note:** In the HTML 2.0 specification, IMG only has these three attributes. If you have seen other attributes used for <IMG> on the Web, those attributes are most likely Netscape extensions. I'll discuss the Netscape extensions to images later on in this chapter.

The SRC attribute indicates the filename or URL of the image you want to include, in quotes. The path name to the file uses the same rules as path names in links to other documents. So, for a GIF file named image.gif in the same directory as this file, you can use the following tag:

```
<IMG SRC="image.gif">
```

For an image file one directory up from the current directory, use

```
<IMG SRC="../image.gif">
```

And so on, using the same rules as for document names in the HREF part of the <A> tag.

Note: For your GIF files to be recognized as GIF files by a Web server or browser, make sure you name them with a .gif extension.

Note: If you use the same image several times in the same document, use relative path names over full path names or URLs in the <IMG> tag. Using relative path names for each repeated image allows the browser to only download the image once, and then just redisplay it at each point on the page. If you specify the image using a full path name, the browser may repeatedly download it, slowing down the time it takes for your document to load.

Exercise 9.1. Try it!

Every year for Halloween, you've volunteered as a vampire for a local haunted house. This year, using all the excellent advice I've given you in the last six chapters, you've created a home page to advertise the "Halloween House of Terror," in halloween.html. Here's the HTML code for the top part of the file, and Figure 9.1 shows how it looks so far:

```
<HTML>
<HEAD>
<TITLE>Welcome to the Halloween House of Terror</TITLE>
<BODY>
<H1>Welcome to the Halloween House of Terror!!</H1>
<HR>
<P>Voted the most frightening haunted house three years in a row, the
<STRONG>Halloween House of Terror</STRONG> provides the ultimate in
Halloween thrills. Over <STRONG>20 rooms of thrills and excitement</STRONG> to
make your blood run cold and your hair stand on end!</P>
<P>The Halloween House of Terror is open from <EM>October 20 to November
1st</EM>, with a gala celebration on Halloween night. Our hours are:</P>
<ul>
<LI>Mon-Fri 5pm-midnight
<LI>Sat & Sun 5pm-3AM
<LI><STRONG>Halloween Night (10/31)</STRONG>: 3pm-???
</UL>
<P>The Halloween House of Terror is located at:<BR>
The Old Waterfall Shopping Center<BR>
1020 Mirabella Ave<BR>
Springfield, CA 94532<BR>
    </P>
    </BODY>
    </HTML>
```

Figure 9.1. *The Halloween House home page.*

So far, so good, although it looks a little plain. Conveniently, you happen to have an image of a spider web kicking around in a clip art library (Figure 9.2) that would look excellent at the top of that Web page.

Figure 9.2. *The spider web image.*

The image is called web.gif, and is in GIF format and in the same directory as the halloween.html page, so it's ready to go into the Web page. To include it, add the following line to the HTML file just before the initial heading:

```
<BODY>
<IMG SRC="web.gif">
<H1>Welcome to the Halloween House of Terror!!</H1>
```

And now, when you reload the halloween.html page, your browser should open and include the spider web image.

If the image doesn't load (if your browser displays a funny-looking icon in its place), first make sure you've specified the name of the file properly in the HTML file. Image filenames are case-sensitive.

If that doesn't work, double-check the image file to make sure that it is indeed a GIF image.

Finally, make sure that you have image loading turned on in your browser. (The option is called Auto Load Images in both Netscape and Mosaic)

Figure 9.3 shows the result with the spider web image included.

Figure 9.3. *The Halloween House home page, with spider.*

If one spider is good, two would be really good, right? Try adding another <IMG> tag next to the first one, and see what happens.

Note how this appears in your particular browser, and if you have multiple browsers available, try testing the file in each one. Different browsers will format adjacent images differently; some will format it as shown in Figure 9.4, whereas others will arrange the images on separate lines.

Figure 9.4. *Multiple images.*

Images and Text

The previous exercise showed how to put an inline image on a page on its own separate line, with text above or below the image. HTML also enables you to put an image next to (or inside) a line of text. (In fact, this is what the phrase "inline image" actually means.)

To include an image inline with a line of text, simply include it in the text, inside the element tags (<H1>, <P>, <ADDRESS>, and so on). Figure 9.5 shows the difference putting the image inline with the text makes. (I've also shortened the title itself.)

```
<H1><IMG SRC="web.gif">The Halloween House of Terror!!</H1>
```

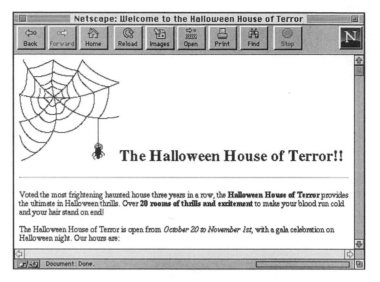

Figure 9.5. *The Halloween House page with image inside the heading.*

The image doesn't have to be large, and it doesn't have to be at the beginning of the text. You can include an image anywhere in a block of text:

```
<BLOCKQUOTE>
Love, from whom the world <IMG SRC="world.gif"> begun,<BR>
Hath the secret of the sun. <IMG SRC="sun.gif"> <BR>
Love can tell, and love alone,
Whence the million stars <IMG SRC="star.gif"> were strewn <BR>
Why each atom <IMG SRC="atom.gif"> knows its own. <BR>
—Robert Bridges
</BLOCKQUOTE>
```

Figure 9.6 shows how this looks.

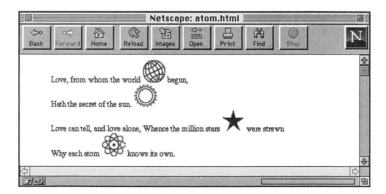

Figure 9.6. *Images can go anywhere in text.*

One very important thing to note about including images inside text: In HTML 2.0, you can only put a single line of text next to the image. All other lines following the image will wrap underneath the image, as shown in Figure 9.7.

Figure 9.7. *Text does not wrap around images.*

What if you want to include multiple lines of text next to an image? You can do this with a Netscape extension, but as I've warned before, it will only work in Netscape and other browsers that support it. I'll discuss the ability to wrap text next to images later on in this chapter in the section on Netscape Extensions.

Text and Image Alignment

The ALIGN attribute of the <IMG> tag allows you to control the alignment of an image with the line of text next to it (and with any other images in that line). There are three possible values in HTML 2.0:

- [ ] ALIGN-TOP, which aligns this image with the topmost part of the line (either the top of the text or the top of the tallest image in the line)
- [ ] ALIGN=MIDDLE, which aligns this image with the middle of the line (usually the baseline of the line of text, not its middle)
- [ ] ALIGN=BOTTOM, which aligns this image with the bottom of the line (either the bottom of the text or the bottom of the largest image in the line)

Figure 9.8 shows how each alignment attribute affects the appearance of the text and the image.

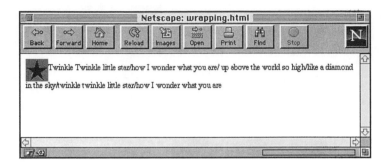

Figure 9.8. *Images and text alignment.*

Images and Links

If you include an `<IMG>` tag inside the opening and closing parts of a link tag (`<A>`), that image serves as a clickable hot spot for the link itself:

```
<A HREF="index.html"><IMG SRC="uparrow.gif"></A>
```

Images that are also hot spots for links appear with a border around them to distinguish them from ordinary non-clickable images, as Figure 9.9 shows.

Figure 9.9. *Images that are also links.*

Note: You can change the width of this border or hide it entirely using a Netscape extension. More about this later on in the chapter.

If you include both an image and text in the anchor, both the image and the text itself become hot spots, pointing to the same document:

```
<A HREF="index.html"><IMG SRC="uparrow.gif">Up to Index</A>
```

▼ Exercise 9.2. Navigation icons.

When you have a set of related Web pages between which the navigation takes place in a consistent way (for example, moving forward, or back, up, home, and so on), it makes sense to provide a menu of navigation options at the top or bottom of each page so that your readers know exactly how to find their way through your documents.

This example shows you how to create a set of icons that are used to navigate through a linear set of documents. You have three icons in GIF format: one for forward, one for back, and a third to enable the reader to jump to a global index of the entire document structure.

First, we'll write the HTML structure to support the icons. Here, the document itself isn't all that important, so I'll just include a shell document. Figure 9.10 shows how the document looks to begin with.

```
<HTML>
<HEAD>
<TITLE>Motorcycle Maintenance: Removing Spark Plugs</TITLE>
<H1>Removing Spark Plugs</H1>
<P>(include some info about spark plugs here)</P>
<HR>
</BODY>
</HTML>
```

Figure 9.10. *The basic document, no icons.*

Now, at the bottom of the document, add your images using IMG tags (Figure 9.11 shows the result):

```
<IMG SRC="arrowright.gif">
<IMG SRC="arrowleft.gif">
<IMG SRC="arrowup.gif">
```

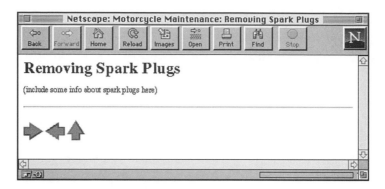

Figure 9.11. *The basic document with icons.*

Now, add the anchors to the images to activate them. Figure 9.12 shows the result.

```
<A HREF="replacing.html"><IMG SRC="arrowright.gif"></A>
<A HREF="ready.html"><IMG SRC="arrowleft.gif"></A>
<A HREF="index.html"><IMG SRC="arrowup.gif""></A>
```

Figure 9.12. *The basic document with iconic links.*

Now when you click on the icons, the browser jumps to the document in the link just as it would have if you had used text links.

Speaking of text, are the icons usable enough as they are? How about adding some text describing exactly what is on the other side of the link? You can add the text inside or outside the anchor, depending on whether you want the text to be a hot spot for the link as well. Here, we'll include it outside the link, so only the icon serves as the hot spot. We'll also align the bottoms of the text and the icons using the ALIGN attribute of the <IMG> tag. Finally, because the extra text causes the icons to move onto two lines, we'll arrange each one on its own line instead. See Figure 9.13 for the final menu.

```
<P>
<A HREF="replacing.html"><IMG SRC="arrowright.gif" ALIGN=BOTTOM></A>
On to "Gapping the New Plugs"<BR>
<A HREF="ready.html"><IMG SRC="arrowleft.gif" ALIGN=BOTTOM></A>
Back to "When You Should Replace your Spark Plugs"<BR>
<A HREF="index.html"><IMG SRC="arrowup.gif" ALIGN=BOTTOM></A>
Up To Index
</P>
```

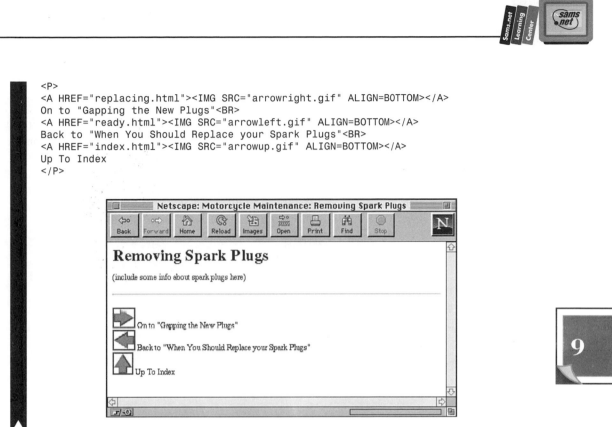

Figure 9.13. *The basic document with iconic links and text.*

Image Interlacing and Transparent Backgrounds

Two nifty features of GIF files are the ability to create transparent backgrounds and the ability to save those images in an interlaced format. This section describes each of these features and how to create GIF files with them.

Note: Only GIF files have these features (and only the special GIF89 format, at that). You can't create transparent or interlaced JPEG images).

Transparency

Transparent images are images that have an invisible background so that the color (or pattern) of the page background shows through, giving the image the appearance of floating on the page. Figure 9.14 illustrates the difference between normal and transparent GIFs.

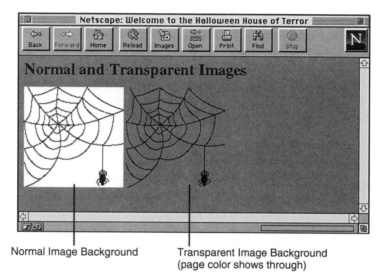

Normal Image Background   Transparent Image Background
(page color shows through)

Figure 9.14. *Normal and transparent backgrounds.*

Transparency is a feature of newer GIF files (called GIF89 format). In order to create a GIF file with a transparent background, you'll need an image tool or program that can create transparent backgrounds. I discuss programs to do this later on in this chapter.

Before you can convert the image, however, you need an image with an appropriate background. The easiest images to convert have transparent backgrounds or are icons or other simple art in which the image and the background are distinct. (See Figure 9.15.) Although you can have photographs with transparent backgrounds, the results might not be as nice if the defining line between the image and the background is not clear.

The goal is to make sure that your background is all one single color. If that background is made up of several colors that are sort of close to each other (as they might be in a photograph), then only one of those colors will be transparent.

You can isolate the background of your image using any image-editing program. Simply edit the pixels around the image so they are all one color. Also, be careful that the color you're using for the background isn't also used extensively in the image itself because the color will become transparent there, too.

Figure 9.15. *Good and bad images for transparent backgrounds.*

> **Note:** Even if you have a GIF image in the proper format with a transparent background, some browsers that do not understand GIF89 format may not be able to display that image or may display it with an opaque background. Transparent GIFs are still a new phenomenon, and full support for them in browsers has not yet become commonplace.

Interlacing

Unlike transparency, *interlacing* a GIF image doesn't change the appearance of the image on the page. Instead, it affects how the image is saved and its appearance while it is being loaded. As the image comes in over the network, it may have the appearance of fading in gradually, or of coming in at a low resolution and then gradually becoming clearer. To create this effect, you have to both save your GIF files in an interlaced format and have a Web browser such as Netscape that can display files as they are being loaded.

Normally, a GIF file is saved in a file one line at a time (the lines are actually called *scan lines*), starting from the top of the image and progressing down to the bottom (see Figure 9.16). If your browser can display GIFs as they are being loaded (as Netscape can), you'll see the top of the image first and then more of the image line by line as it arrives over the wire to your system.

Interlacing saves the GIF image in a different way. Instead of saving each line linearly, an interlaced GIF file is saved in a stepwise fashion, which saves every eighth row starting from the first, followed by every eighth row starting from the fourth, followed by every fourth row starting from the third, and then the remaining rows (see Figure 9.17).

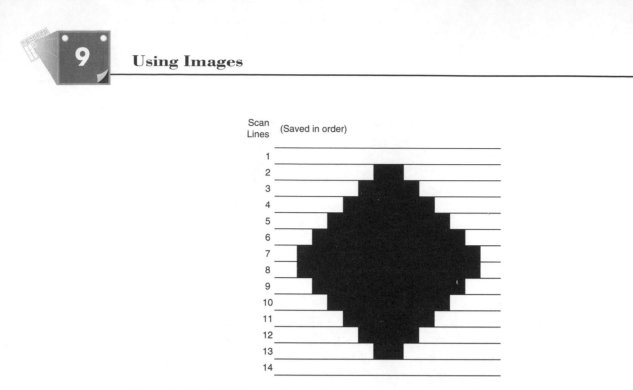

Figure 9.16. *GIF files saved normally.*

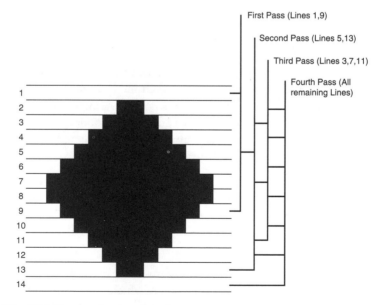

Figure 9.17. *GIF files saved as interlaced.*

When the interlaced GIF file is displayed, the rows are loaded in as they were saved: the first set of lines appears, and then the next set, and so on. Depending on the browser, this can create

a "venetian blind" effect. Or (as in Netscape) the missing lines might be filled in with the information with the initial lines, creating a blurry or blocky effect (as you can see in Figure 9.18), which then becomes clearer as more of the image appears.

Figure 9.18. *Interlaced GIF files being loaded.*

If your browser doesn't support interlaced GIF files, or if it waits until the entire image is loaded before displaying it, you won't get the interlaced effect, but your image will still display just fine. Interlacing doesn't break the GIF for other browsers; it just changes how it's loaded for browsers that can take advantage of it.

Interlacing is great for large images that may take some time to load. With the interlacing effect, your readers can get an idea of what the image looks like before it's finished—which then allows them to stop loading it if they're not interested, or if the image is an image map, to click on the appropriate spot and move on.

On the other hand, interlacing isn't as important for smaller files like icons and small logos. Small images load quickly enough that the interlacing effect is lost.

The next section describes tools for creating transparent and interlaced images.

Tools for Creating Interlaced and Transparent GIF Images

Many image editing programs allow you to save GIF files as interlaced, with transparent backgrounds, or both. If your favorite program doesn't, you might try contacting its author or manufacturer—with transparent and interlaced GIF images becoming more common, a new version of your favorite tool may be out that allows these features.

On Windows, LView Pro is a great shareware image editing program that you can get from one of the SimTel mirrors (I like `http://www.acs.oakland.edu/oak/SimTel/SimTel-win3.html`). LView Pro allows you to create GIF images with both transparency and interlacing (make sure you get the newest version—only versions 1.A and above have these features).

On the Mac, the shareware program Graphic Converter can create both transparent and interlaced GIF images (and it reads Photoshop files, so you don't even have to save as GIF from Photoshop! Now if only Photoshop did interlacing and transparency itself...). You can get Graphic Converter from one of the many Sumex-AIM mirrors (I like `http://hyperarchive.lcs.mit.edu/HyperArchive.html`).

GIF Converter, another shareware program for the Mac, can do minor image editing such as cropping and reducing colors, and can also save GIF files as interlaced. It can't (yet) do transparent backgrounds, but another program called Transparency will do just fine for that. If you use two different programs, always set the interlacing first, then the transparency— otherwise you may end up with small gray ghosts on your transparent background. Check those same Sumex-AIM mirrors for either program.

For UNIX, a program called GIFTool allows you to create both interlaced and transparent images, and it can also batch-convert a whole set of GIF files to interlaced format (great for converting whole directories at once!). You can get information, binaries for several common UNIX platforms, and source for GIF tools from `http://www.homepages.com/tools/`.

The Netscape Extensions to Images

In addition to the Netscape extensions to HTML that you learned about yesterday, there is also a suite of extensions to the `<IMG>` tag that allows you better control over the placement of images on the page. This section describes those extensions, which include:

- [ ] The ability to wrap multiple lines of text next to images
- [ ] Adjusting the space between an image and its surrounding text
- [ ] Adjusting the size of the border, if any, around an image

Wrapping Text Next to Images

One of the more annoying limitations of HTML 2.0 is that you can only put one line of text next to an inline image. This makes long headlines look ugly and restricts the use of images to large blocks on the left margin with a single line of text alongside them.

To get around this limitation, the Netscape extensions include two new values for the ALIGN attribute of the <IMG> tag—LEFT and RIGHT. As you would expect, ALIGN=LEFT aligns an image to the left margin, and ALIGN=RIGHT to the right margin. But they also indicate that any text following those images will be displayed in the space to the right or left of that image, depending on the margin alignment. Figure 9.19 shows an image with some text aligned next to it:

Figure 9.19. *Text and images aligned.*

You can put any HTML text (paragraphs, lists, headings, other images) after an aligned image, and the text will be wrapped into the space between the image and the margin (or, you can also have images on both margins and put the text between them). Netscape will fill in the space with text until the bottom of the image, and then continue filling in the text beneath the image.

What if you want to stop filling in the space and start the next line underneath the image? A normal line break won't do it—it'll just break the line to the current margin alongside the image. A new paragraph will also continue wrapping the text alongside the image. To stop wrapping text next to an image, use a line break with the new attribute CLEAR. With the CLEAR attribute you can break the line so that the next line of text begins after the end of the image (all the way to the margin). See Figure 9.20 for an example. The CLEAR can have one of three values:

- ☐ LEFT: Break to an empty left margin, for left-aligned images
- ☐ RIGHT: Break to an empty right margin, for right-aligned images
- ☐ ALL: break to a line clear to both margins

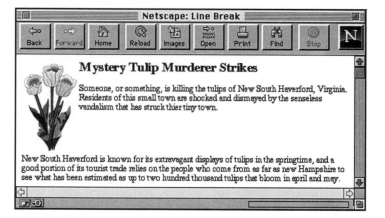

Figure 9.20. *Line break to a clear margin.*

Like all Netscape extensions, the text wrapping features are supported in few other browsers. However, these features have been incorporated into the HTML 3.0 specification, so other browsers are likely to incorporate them in the future. But what about now? What happens if you view pages with text and images aligned in other browsers?

Most of the time, you'll just lose the alignment, but since only the first line of text will appear next to the image, the text may break in odd places. Often, something as simple as putting a <BR> after the image (which does little in Netscape, but pushes all the text after the image

on other browsers) can create an effect that works well both in the browsers that support image and text wrapping and those that don't. Be sure to test your pages in multiple browsers so you know what the effect will be.

For example, the following input and output example shows the HTML code for a page for Papillon Enterprises, who design Web pages. Figure 9.21 shows the result in Netscape, and Figure 9.22 shows the result in MacWeb (which does not have image and text wrapping capabilities).

Input

```
<H1><IMG SRC="butterfly.gif" ALIGN=RIGHT ALIGN=MIDDLE>
Papillon Enterprises</H1>
<P>Design, Writing, Illustration, and Programming for the
<B>World Wide Web</B></P>
<P>Specializing in:</P>
<UL>
<LI>HTML and Web Page Design
<LI>Illustration
<LI>Forms Design and Programming
<LI>Complete Web Server Installation
</UL>
<HR>
```

Output

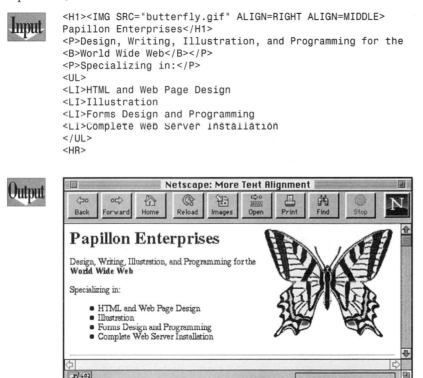

Figure 9.21. *The output in Netscape.*

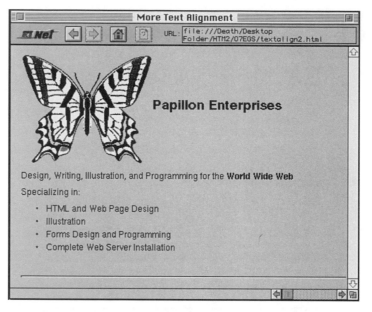

Figure 9.22. *The Output in MacWeb (no image alignment).*

Other Image Alignment Options

In addition to the LEFT and RIGHT alignments, there are also several new Netscape options for aligning images within a line of text and with other images in that line. The new options are listed below, along with comparisons with the original ALIGN options:

☐ ALIGN=TEXTTTOP aligns the top of the image with the top of the tallest text in the line.

☐ ALIGN=TOP aligns the image with the topmost item in the line (which may be another image).

☐ ALIGN=ABSMIDDLE aligns the middle of the image with the middle of the largest item in the line.

☐ ALIGN=MIDDLE aligns the middle image with the middle of the baseline of the text.

☐ ALIGN=BASELINE aligns the bottom of the image with the baseline of the text. ALIGN=BASELINE is the same as ALIGN=BOTTOM, but ALIGN=BASELINE is a more descriptive name.

☐ `ALIGN=ABSBOTTOM` aligns the bottom of the image with the lowest item in the line (which may be below the baseline of the text).

Figure 9.23 shows examples of the new alignment options.

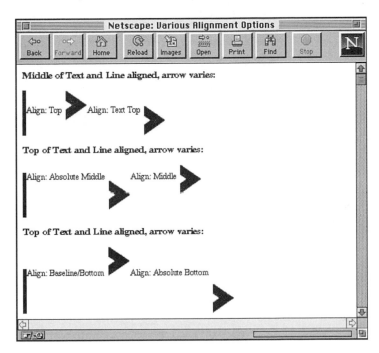

Figure 9.23. *New alignment options.*

Modifying the Space Around Images

With the ability to wrap text around an image, you may also want to adjust the amount of space around that image. The VSPACE and HSPACE attributes allow you to do this. Both take a value in pixels; VSPACE controls the space above and below the image, and HSPACE controls the space to the left and the right.

For example, the following HTML code produces the effect shown in Figure 9.24.

```
<P><IMG SRC="eggplant.gif" VSPACE=30 HSPACE=30 ALIGN=LEFT>
This is an eggplant. We intend to stay a good ways away from it,
because we really don't like eggplant very much.</P>
```

Figure 9.24. *Image spacing.*

Image Dimensions and Scaling

Two attributes of the <IMG> tag, HEIGHT and WIDTH, specify the height and width the of the image, in pixels.

If you use the actual height and width of the image in these values (which you can find out in most image editing programs), you will considerably speed up the time it takes to lay out your Web page in Netscape, particularly if you use lots of images.

Why? Normally when Netscape is parsing the HTML code in your file it has to load and test each image to get its width and height before proceeding, so it can format the text appropriately. If the width and height are already specified in the HTML code itself, Netscape can just make a space for the image of the appropriate size and keep going (see Figure 9.25).

Figure 9.25. *Space for the image.*

If the values for WIDTH and the HEIGHT are different from the actual width and height of the image, Netscape will automatically scale to fit those dimensions. Since smaller images take up less disk space than larger images, and therefore take less time to transfer over the network, this is a sneaky way to get away with large images on your pages—just create a smaller version, and then scale it to the dimensions you want on your Web page. Note, however, that the pixels will also be scaled, so the bigger version may end up looking grainy or blocky. Experiment with different sizes and scaling factors to get the right effect.

Note that both the WIDTH and HEIGHT attributes will be ignored in other browsers. Most of the time this won't have much of an effect on the pages appearance—if you scaled the image in Netscape, it'll just be smaller in another browser. And if you used the actual width and height, there won't be any difference at all.

Image Borders

The BORDER attribute creates a border around an image. Normally, inline images don't have borders unless they are also links. By specifying a value (in pixels) for BORDER, you can draw a border around an inline image or modify the width of the link border. Figure 9.26 shows an example of an image with a border around it.

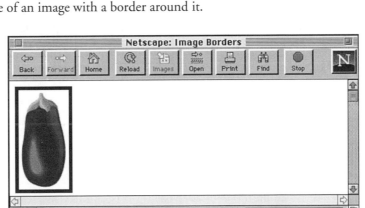

Figure 9.26. *An image border.*

Be very careful when setting BORDER to 0 (zero) on images with links, as this removes the link border entirely. Without the visual indication that the image is also a link it becomes difficult for your reader to know that they *can* click on the image—to them, your linked image looks just like a regular inline image. To get around the problem, you can:

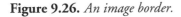

- ☐ Use a small, thin border, for example, BORDER=1.
- ☐ Design your images so that they look like buttons, for example, the images shown in Figure 9.27.

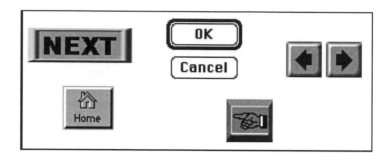

Figure 9.27. *Images that look like buttons.*

LOWSRC

The LOWSRC attribute is the last of the Netscape extensions to the <IMG> tag. The value of LOWSRC is an image file, just like the value of SRC:

```
<IMG SRC="wall.gif" LOWSRC="wallsmall.gif">
```

The difference is that the image specified by LOWSRC is loaded first with all the text, and then after all the layout and LOWSRC images are done loading and displaying, the image specified in SRC is loaded and fades in to replace the LOWSRC image.

Why would you want this? LOWSRC is generally a smaller or lower resolution version of the actual image, one that can load quickly and give the reader an idea of the overall effect of the page. Then, since all the layout is done, they can scroll around and read while the better images are quietly loaded in the background.

Providing Alternatives to Images

Graphics can turn a simple text-only Web page into a glorious visual feast. But what happens if someone is reading your Web page from a text-only browser, or what if he or she has image-loading turned off, so all your careful graphics appear as simple icons? All of a sudden that glorious visual feast isn't looking as nice. And, worse, if you haven't taken these possibilities into consideration while designing your Web page, your work could be unreadable and unusable by that portion of your audience.

There is a simple solution to one of these problems. The ALT attribute of the <IMG> tag, enables you to substitute something meaningful in place of the image on browsers that cannot display that image.

Usually, in a text-only browser such as Lynx, graphics that are specified using the `<IMG>` tag in the original file are "displayed" as the word [IMAGE]. (An example is shown in Figure 9.28.) If the image itself was a link to something else, that link is preserved.

```
                              [IMAGE] Up To Index
```

Figure 9.28. *"Images" in Lynx.*

The `ALT` attribute in the `<IMG>` tag enables you to provide a more meaningful text alternative to the blank [IMAGE] for your readers who are using text-only Web browsers. The `ALT` attribute contains a string with the text you want to substitute for the graphic:

```
<IMG SRC="myimage.gif" ALT="[a picture of a cat]">
```

Note that most browsers will interpret the string you include in the `ALT` attribute as a literal string; that is, if you include any HTML tags in that string they will be printed as typed instead of being parsed and displayed as HTML code. Try to limit the use of `ALT` to a simple string.

For example, in Exercise 9.2, with the arrow icons for navigation, you could provide text alternatives for the icons, or just include an empty string (`""`) to "hide" the image in the text version. Here are two ideas:

1. Use text-only markers (Figure 9.29). Here's the code:

```
<P>
<A HREF="replacing.html"><IMG SRC="arrowright.gif" ALIGN=BOTTOM
ALT="[NEXT]"></A>On to "Gapping the New Plugs"<BR>
<A HREF="ready.html"><IMG SRC="arrowleft.gif" ALIGN=BOTTOM
ALT="[PREVIOUS]"></A> Back to "When You Should Replace your Spark
Plugs"<BR><A HREF="index.html"><IMG SRC="arrowup.gif" ALIGN=BOTTOM
ALT="[UP]"></A>Up To Index</P>
```

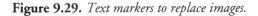
```
     [NEXT] On to "Gapping the New Plugs"
     [PREVIOUS] Back to "When You Should Replace your Spark Plugs"
     [UP] Up To Index
```

Figure 9.29. *Text markers to replace images.*

2. Hide the images altogether and make the text the anchor instead (shown in Figure 9.30). Enter:

```
<P>
<A HREF="replacing.html"><IMG SRC="arrowright.gif" ALIGN=BOTTOM ALT="">On
to "Gapping the New Plugs"<BR></A>
<A HREF="ready.html"><IMG SRC="arrowleft.gif" ALIGN=BOTTOM ALT=""> Back to
"When You Should Replace your Spark Plugs"</A><BR>
<A HREF="index.html"><IMG SRC="arrowup.gif" ALIGN=BOTTOM ALT="">Up To
Index</A>
</P>
```

```
On to "Gapping the New Plugs"
Back to "When You Should Replace your Spark Plugs"
Up To Index
```

Figure 9.30. *Hide the images.*

> **Tip:** A sneaky trick I've seen used for the ALT attribute is to include an ASCII art picture (a picture made up of characters, like the cow in Chapter 5, "Still More HTML") in the ALT tag, which then serves as the "picture" in text-only browsers. To accomplish this trick, you'll need the ASCII art prepared ahead of time. Then, in your HTML code, include the entire <IMG> tag inside <PRE>...</PRE> tags, and the ASCII art inside the ALT attribute, like this:
>
> ```
> <PRE>
> <IMG SRC="cow.gif" ALT="
>         ( )
> Moo    (oo)
>         \/----\
>          ||    | \
>          ||--W||  *
>          ||    ||
>          ||    ||
> ">
> </PRE>
> ```
>
> In this code, the original image (cow.gif) will be replaced by the text version, neatly formatted, in text-only browsers. Note that because the <PRE> tags are outside the <IMG> tag itself (to get around the fact that you can't put HTML code inside the ALT attribute), this trick works best when the image is alone on a line; that is, there is no text on the line before or after it.

Hints for Better Use of Images

The use of images in Web pages is one of the bigger arguments among users and providers of Web pages today. For everyone who wants to design Web pages with more, bigger, and brighter images to take full advantage of the graphical capabilities of the Web, there is someone on a slow network connection who is begging for fewer images so that his or her browser does not take three hours to load a page.

As a designer of Web pages, you should take both of these points of view under consideration. Balance the fun of creating a highly visual, colorful Web page with the need to get your information to everyone you want to get it—and that includes people who may not have access to your images at all.

This section offers some hints and compromises you can make in the design of your Web pages so that you can make everyone happy (or everyone unhappy, depending on how you look at it).

Do You Really Need This Image?

For each image you put inline on your Web page, consider why you are putting it there. What does that image add to the design? Does it provide information that could be presented in the text instead? Is it just there because you like how it looks?

Try not to clutter your Web page with pretty but otherwise unnecessary images. A simple Web page with only a few iconic images is often more effective than a page which opens with an enormous graphic and continues the trend with flashy 3D buttons, drop-shadow bullets, and psychedelic line separators.

Keep Your Images Small

A smaller image takes less time to transfer over the Net; therefore, using smaller images makes your Web page load faster and causes less frustration for people trying to read it over a slow link. What could be easier?

Smaller images can mean smaller in actual physical dimensions on the screen, but you can also create smaller images by reducing the number of colors in the image. Your goal is to reduce the file size of the image so that it transfers faster, but a 4-inch by 4-inch black-and-white image (two colors) may be smaller in file size than a 1/2-inch by 1/2-inch full-color photographic image. With most image-processing programs, you can reduce the number of colors and touch up the result so it looks good even with fewer colors.

A good rule to follow is that you should try to keep your inline images somewhere under 20K. That may seem small, but a single 20K file takes nearly that many seconds to download over a 14.4K bps SLIP connection. Multiply that time by the number of images on your Web page, and it may take a substantial amount of time for that page to load (even if you're using a browser that can load multiple images at once. The pipe is only so wide). Will someone care about what you have in your Web page if they have had to go off and have lunch while it was loading?

> **Note:** The small icons that I used for the arrows in the navigation examples are 300 bytes apiece—less than a third of a single K. The spider web image in the Halloween example is slightly larger than 1K. Small does not mean the image isn't useful.

Provide Alternatives to Images

If you're not using the ALT attribute in your images, you should be. The ALT attribute is extremely useful for making your Web page readable by text-only browsers. But what about people who turn off images in their browser because they have a slow link to the Internet? Most browsers do not use the value of ALT in this case. And sometimes ALT isn't enough; because you can only specify text inside an ALT string, you can't substitute HTML code for the image.

To get around all these problems while still keeping your nifty graphical Web page, consider creating alternative text-only versions of your Web pages and putting links to them on the full-graphics versions of that same Web page, like this:

```
<P>A <A HREF="TextVersion.html">text-only</A> version of this page is
available.</P>
```

The link to the text-only page only takes up one small paragraph on the "real" Web page, but makes the information much more accessible. It's a courtesy that readers with slow connections will thank you for, and it still allows you to load up your "main" Web page with as many graphics as you like for those with fast connections.

Watch Out for Display Assumptions

Many people create problems for their readers by making a couple of careless assumptions about other people's hardware. When developing Web pages, be kind and remember these two guidelines:

☐ Don't assume everyone has screen or browser dimensions the same as yours.

Just because that huge GIF you created is wide enough to fit on your screen in your browser doesn't mean it'll fit someone else's. And coming across an image that is too wide is annoying, as it requires the reader to resize their window all the time or scroll sideways.

To fit in the width of a majority of browsers windows, try to keep the width of your images to less than 450 pixels (most browsers on the Macintosh have a screen width of about 465).

☐ Don't assume everyone has full color displays.

Test your images in resolutions other than full color (you can often do this in your image editing program). Many of your readers may have display systems that have only 16 colors, only have grayscale, or even just black and white. You may be surprised at the results: Colors drop out or dither strangely in grayscale or black and white, and the effect may not be what you had intended.

Make sure your images are visible at all resolutions, or provide alternatives for high- and low-resolution images on the page itself.

Summary

One of the major features that makes the World Wide Web stand out from other forms of Internet information is that documents on the Web can contain full-color graphics. It was arguably the existence of those graphics that allowed the Web to catch on so quickly and to become so popular in so short a time.

To place images on your Web pages, those images must be in GIF or JPEG format (GIF is more widely supported) and small enough that they can be quickly downloaded over a potentially slow link. The HTML tag <IMG> allows you to put an image on the Web page, either inline with text or on a line by itself. The <IMG> tag has three attributes:

- [ ] SRC: the location and filename of the image to include.
- [ ] ALIGN: how to position the image vertically with its surrounding text. ALIGN can have one of three values: TOP, MIDDLE, or BOTTOM.
- [ ] ALT: a text string to substitute for the image in text-only browsers.

You can include images inside a link tag (<A>) and have those images serve as hot spots for the links, same as text.

Netscape has provided a few extensions to the <IMG> tag that allow for greater control over images. Those new attributes include:

- [ ] ALIGN=LEFT and ALIGN=RIGHT: places the image against the appropriate margin, allowing all following text to flow into the space alongside the image.
- [ ] ALIGN=TEXTTOP, ALIGN=ABSMIDDLE, ALIGN=BASELINE, and ALIGN=ABSBOTTOM: allows greater control over the alignment of an inline image and the text surrounding it.
- [ ] VSPACE and HSPACE: defines the amount of space between an image and the text surrounding it.
- [ ] BORDER: defines the width of the border around an image (with or without a link). BORDER=0 hides the border altogether.
- [ ] LOWSRC: defines an alternate, lower-resolution image that is loaded before the image indicated by SRC.

In addition, the Netscape extension to <BR>, CLEAR, allows you to stop wrapping text alongside an image. CLEAR can have three values: LEFT, RIGHT, and ALL.

Q&A

Q How can I create thumbnails of my images?

A You'll have to do that with some kind of image-editing program; the Web won't do it for you. Just open up the image and scale it down to the right size.

Q Can I put HTML tags in the string for the ALT attribute?

A That would be nice, wouldn't it? Unfortunately, you can't. All you can do is put an ordinary string in there. Keep it simple and you should be fine.

Q I've seen some Web pages where you can click on different places in an image and get different link results, like a map of the United States where each state has a different page. How do you do this in HTML?

A That's called an *image map*, and it's an advanced form of Web page development. It involves writing code on the server side to interpret the mouse clicks and send back the right result. I describe image maps in Chapter 15, "Forms and Image Maps."

10

FIVE

Using External Media: Images, Sound, and Video

As the last chapter explains, inline images are images that can be displayed directly on the page along with text. The World Wide Web also supports other media, including images, sound, and video that can be retrieved on demand and loaded in windows separate from the browser window itself. These forms of media on the Web are called external media because they are stored externally from your Web files themselves.

In this chapter, you learn about

- ☐ What "external media" means
- ☐ How different browsers handle different forms of external media
- ☐ Specifying external media in your HTML file
- ☐ Using sound
- ☐ Using video

What's External Media?

In its most general form, external media are any files that are not directly viewable by a Web browser on a Web page. External files can include just about any kind of file you can create: non-inline GIF files, MPEG video, PostScript files, zipped applications, just about anything. You can create a link in an HTML file to an external media file in exactly the same way that you link to another document: using the <A> tag.

When a server sends a browser a file, it also includes information about what kind of file it is, using a special message sent along with the file. If the browser cannot display that kind of file, it matches the file type to an additional list of "helper" applications (sometimes called "viewers") for that platform. If the file type can be recognized and a helper application is listed, the browser starts the helper application and feeds it the file. The helper application in turn displays or runs or plays the external media file that the browser could not read. If the browser can't figure out what kind of file the server is trying to send, it just saves the file to disk (some browsers may ask first).

Browsers also can execute helper applications for files that it loads from the local disk, except it uses the extension of the file (.gif, .jpeg, and so on) to find out the type of the file, and to execute the appropriate helper application. This is why the HTML and GIF files that you've been working with locally must have extensions of .html and .gif, respectively, so that the browser can figure out what they are.

This system works especially well as it keeps the browser small (no need to include viewers or players for every strange media type out there), and it's also configurable for new file types and new and better helper applications as they are written. Each browser has a list that maps file extensions to file types, and another list that maps file types to applications. You should

be able to configure your browser to use the helper applications you want to use, as well as be able to add new file extensions to the list of file types.

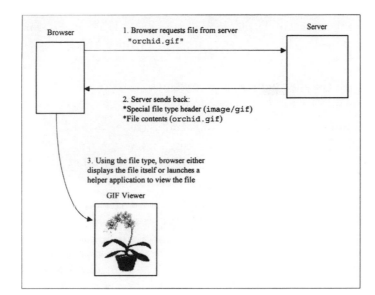

Figure 10.1. *Browsers and other files.*

Note: The list of file types that browsers use in their helper application lists are drawn from a standard called MIME, which was originally intended for encoding media in electronic mail messages. You won't need to know this now, but it may be important once you start dealing with servers in Day Seven.

Specifying External Media in HTML

To specify an external media file in HTML, you link to it just as you would any other document, by using the <A> tag and the HREF attribute. The path to the external file is a path name or URL just as you would use if the file were another HTML document:

```
<A HREF="some_external_file">A media file.</A>
```

If you're going to make use of links to external media files, it is helpful if you include in the body of the link (or somewhere nearby) some information about the format of the media, such as what kind of file format it is and its file size.

Knowing the format of the file ahead of time is useful since it lets your readers know if they can read it or not. They're not going to want to retrieve a file if they can't do anything with it once it's been downloaded.

Telling them how big the file is allows your readers to decide before selecting the link whether they have the time (or the inclination) to sit and wait for the download to take place.

A few words as part of the link satisfies both these suggestions:

```
<A HREF="bigsnail.jpeg">A 59K JPEG Image of a snail</A>
<A HREF="tacoma.mov">The Fall of the Tacoma Narrows Bridge </A>
 (a200K QuickTime File)
```

Using External Images

If you're using images inline on your Web page, the one format that all graphical browsers can read is GIF. Linking to external images, however, gives you slightly more flexibility in the image formats you can use.

Some popular image formats for external media include the following:

☐ **GIF**

Even though GIF files can be read inline, it often makes sense, particularly in the case of larger files, to link to external GIF files.

☐ **JPEG**

Although many browsers are supporting inline JPEG images, many more do not. So it makes sense to use JPEG as an external image. The combination of inline GIFs and external JPEGs is particularly useful.

☐ **XBM**

XBM files are X Window System Bitmaps.

☐ **PICT**

PICT files are a common graphics format for the Macintosh.

Image processing programs such as Adobe Photoshop, Paint Shop Pro for Windows, xv for X, the pbm conversion programs for UNIX, and deBabelizer for Macintosh and Windows should be able to convert between many of these formats.

Once you have a converted file, you must name it with the appropriate extension so your browser can recognize it. Extensions for graphics files are shown in Table 10.1.

Table 10.1. Image formats and extensions.

Format	Extension
GIF	.gif
JPEG	.jpg, .jpeg
XBM	.xbm
PICT	.PICT

Exercise 10.1 uses external image files.

Exercise 10.1: Linking to external GIF and JPEG files.

A common practice in Web pages is to provide a very small GIF image (a "thumbnail") inline on the page itself. You then link that image to its larger counterpart. This has two major advantages over including the entire image inline:

☐ It keeps the size of the Web page small, so that page can be downloaded quickly.

☐ It gives your reader a "taste" of the image before downloading the entire thing.

In this simple example, you'll set up a link between a small image and an external, larger version of that same image. The large image is a photograph of some penguins in GIF format, called `penguinsbig.gif` (shown in Figure 10.2).

First, create a thumbnail version of the penguins photograph in your favorite image editor. The thumbnail can be a scaled version of the original file, a clip of that file (say, one penguin out of the group), or anything else you want to indicate the larger image.

Here, I've created a picture of one penguin in the group to serve as the inline image. (I've called it `penguinslittle.gif`.) Unlike the large version of the file, which is 100K, the small picture is only 3K. Using the `<IMG>` tag, I'll put that image directly on a nearly content-free Web page:

```
<HTML>
<HEAD>
<TITLE>Penguins</TITLE>
</HEAD></BODY>
<H1>Penguins</H1>
<IMG SRC="penguinslittle.gif">
</BODY></HTML>
```

10

Figure 10.2. *Penguins.*

Now, using a link tag, you can link the small icon to the bigger picture by enclosing the `<IMG>` tag inside an `<A>` tag:

```
<A HREF="penguinsbig.gif"><IMG SRC="penguinslittle.gif"></A>
```

The final result of the page is shown in Figure 10.3. Now, if you click on the small penguin image, the big image will be downloaded and viewed by the helper application defined for GIF files for that browser.

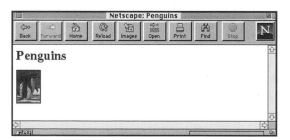

Figure 10.3. *The Penguins home page with link.*

An alternative to linking the small image directly to the large image is to provide the external image in several different formats, and provide descriptive links for each one (as in the hint

in the previous section). In this part of the example, I'll link to a JPEG version of that same penguins file.

To create the JPEG version of the penguin photograph, you need to use your image editor or converter again to convert the original photograph. Here, I've called it penguinsbig.jpg.

To provide both GIF and JPEG forms of the penguin photo, we'll convert the link on the image into a simple link menu to the GIF and JPEG files, providing some information about file size:

Input

```
<IMG SRC="penguinslittle.gif">
<UL>
<LI>Penguins (<A HREF="penguinsbig.gif">100K GIF file</A>)
<LI>Penguins (<A HREF="penguinsbig.jpg">25K JPEG file</A>)
</UL>
```

Output

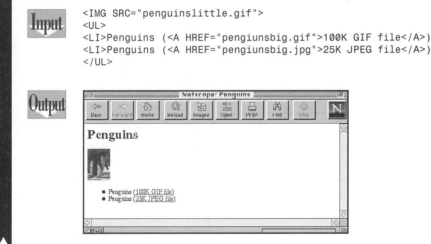

Figure 10.4. *The Penguins link menu.*

Using Sound

Including sound files on your Web page can provide optional annotations to existing text, welcome messages from you or someone important in your organization, or extra information that words and pictures cannot convey. If you're musically inclined, you can provide sound clips of your work on the Web or create archives of clips from your favorite bands—be sure to get their permission first!

To include a link to an external sound on your Web page, you must have that sound sample in the right format, just as you would for an image. Currently, the only fully cross-platform sound file format for the Web is Sun Microsystems's AU format. AU allows several different kinds of sound sample encoding, but the most popular one is 8-bit μ-law. For this reason, AU files are often called simply μ-law files. AU files are of only barely acceptable quality, as the 8-bit sampling causes them to sound a bit like they are being transmitted over a telephone.

271

You can use other better quality sound formats for specific platforms. The most popular are AIFF for the Macintosh and WAV for Windows. In addition, a recent addition to the already mind-boggling array of sound formats is MPEG audio. MPEG is generally better known as a video standard, but the audio portion of the standard allows for very high-quality sound, and players exist for many platforms. Note, however, that if you use one of these formats (or any other unusual formats), those sounds will probably not be playable cross-platform; therefore, you should be sure to indicate the format of the sound file in the link that points to it.

So how does one get or create a sound file, and once you have it, how do you use it? Read on.

Getting Sound Files

Where can you get sound files? From a variety of sources:

- ☐ Many systems allow you to record and digitize sounds or voice using a microphone that came with your system or with inexpensive add-on equipment.

- ☐ Some platforms with CD-ROM drives may allow you to record digital sounds directly off a standard audio CD; you'll need a CD-ROM drive that supports this, of course. Keep in mind if you go this route that most published audio material is copyrighted, and its owners may not appreciate your making their songs or sounds available for free on the Internet.

- ☐ Many Internet archives have collections of small, digitized samples in the appropriate format for the platform they emphasize (for example, SND format files for Macintosh archives, WAV format for Windows, AU for Sun's UNIX, and so on).

Note: Keep in mind that, like images, sounds you find on the Net may be owned by someone who won't like your using them. Use caution when using "found" sounds.

- ☐ Commercial "clip sound" products are available, again, in appropriate formats for your platform. These sounds have the advantage of usually being public domain or royalty-free, meaning that you can use them anywhere without needing to get permission or pay a fee.

Converting Sound Files

Once you have a sound file, it may not be in the right format—that is, the format you want it to be in. The programs introduced in this section can read and convert many popular sound formats.

For UNIX and PC-compatible systems, a program called SOX by Lance Norskog can convert between many sound formats (AU, WAV, AIFF, Macintosh SND) and perform some rudimentary processing including filtering, changing the sample rate, and reversing the sample.

On DOS, WAVany by Bill Neisius converts most common sound formats (including AU and Macintosh SND) to WAV format.

Waveform Hold and Modify (WHAM), for Windows, is an excellent sound player, editor, and converter that also works really well as a helper application for your browser.

For the Macintosh, the freeware SoundApp by Norman Franke reads and plays most sound formats, and converts to WAV, Macintosh SND, AIFF, and NeXT sound formats (but mysteriously, not Sun AU). The freeware program Ulaw will convert Macintosh sounds (SND) to AU format.

FTP sources for each of these programs are listed in Appendix A, "Sources for Further Information."

Including Sound Files on Web Pages

10

In order for a browser to recognize your sound file, it must have the appropriate extension for its file type. Common formats and their extensions are listed in Table 10.2.

Table 10.2. Sound formats and extensions.

Format	Extension
AU/µ-law	.au
AIFF/AIFC	.aiff, .aif
WAV	.wav
MPEG Audio	.mp2

After you have a file in the right format and with the right extension, you can link to it from your Web page like any other external file:

```
Laurence Olivier's "To Be or Not To Be" soliloquy from the film of the play
Hamlet (<A HREF="olivier_hamlet.au">AIFF format, 357K)</A>
```

Two further hints for using sound files in your Web page:

☐ *Always* tell your readers that your link is to a sound file, and also be sure to note that sound files format. This is especially important if you use a format other than AU; otherwise, your readers will have to download it to find out if they can handle it or not.

☐ Sound files tend to be quite large, so consider creating sound files of lesser quality for people on slower connections. In particular, mono sound files generally are smaller than stereo, and 8-bit files are smaller than 16-bit.

☐ If you use multiple sound files on your Web page, consider providing an explanatory note at the top of the page, and then using a small inline GIF icon (such as the one shown in Figure 10.5) as the link to the sound file itself. (Include the size of the file in the link, as well.) Using a sound file icon provides an elegant way to show that a sound lurks on the other side of the link without needing to explain it in text all the time.

Figure 10.5. *A sound file icon.*

Using Video

"Video" refers to any digitally encoded motion picture, which can include both animation as well as "real" video files.

For video files that can be read across platforms, the current standard on the Web is MPEG, but Apple's QuickTime format has been gaining ground as players become more available for platforms other than the Macintosh. QuickTime also has the advantage of being able to include an audio track with the video; although MPEG video files can have audio tracks, few existing players can play it.

Getting and Converting Video Files

Just as with images and sound, you can get video clips by making them yourself, downloading them from the Net, or purchasing royalty-free clips that you can read on your platform. The best and easiest way to get video is to find it. Once again, the best place to get short video clips is through the use of royalty-free video libraries on CD-ROM or through sources over the Internet.

To convert video files between formats on the Macintosh, use the freeware program Sparkle. Sparkle can read and play both MPEG and QuickTime files, and convert between them. In addition, the program AVI->Quick can convert AVI (Video for Windows) files to QuickTime format.

On DOS/Windows systems, a commercial program called XingCD enables you to convert AVI files to MPEG. AVI to QuickTime converters are also available; one is a program called SmartCap from Intel, which can convert between AVI and QuickTime files that use the Indeo compression method. To use AVI files, you'll need the Video for Windows package, available from Microsoft. To use QuickTime movies, you'll need the QuickTime for Windows package, available from Apple. You'll need both to convert from one format to the other.

FTP locations and other information for these programs are in Appendix A.

Including Video Files on Web Pages

Once you have a video file, you must do two things:

- ☐ Name the file appropriately. MPEG files should have an extension of .mpg or .mpeg; QuickTime movies have a .mov extension.
- ☐ Link to the file using the <A> tag just as you did with external images and sounds.

In addition, if you want a QuickTime movie to be read on a platform other than the Macintosh, you will need to "flatten" that movie. On the Macintosh, files contain resource and data forks for different bits of the file. Flattening a QuickTime file involves moving all the data in the QuickTime file into the data fork so other platforms can read it.

A small freeware program called FastPlayer will flatten QuickTime movies on the Mac; on Windows, try a program called Qflat. FTP locations are in Appendix A.

As with all external media files, you should be sure to tell your readers the type and size of file they are linking to; this is especially important for video files, since the sizes are often frighteningly large. As I noted with sound files, linking to an icon on the Web page itself is often a nice design touch. (See Figure 10.6.)

Figure 10.6. *A video file icon.*

Exercise 10.2: Creating a media archive.

One of the uses of Web pages I have only vaguely mentioned up to this point is that of creating a media archive. A media archive is a Web page that serves no purpose other than to provide quick access to image or other media files for viewing and downloading.

Previously on the Net, media was stored in FTP or Gopher archives. The text-only nature of these sorts of archives makes it difficult for people to find what they're looking for in images, sounds, or video. The filename is often the only description they have of the content of the file. Even reasonably descriptive file names, such as `red-bird-in-green-tree.gif` or `verdi-aria.aiff`, aren't all that useful when you're talking about images or sounds. It's only through actually downloading the file itself that people can really decide whether or not they want it.

Through the use of inline images, icons, and splitting up sound and video files into small clips and larger files, you can create a media archive on the Web that is far more usable than any of the text-only archives.

> **Note:** Keep in mind that this sort of archive, in its heavy use of inline graphics and large media files, is optimally useful in graphical browsers attached to fast networks. However, the Web does provide advantages in this respect even for text-only browsers, simply because there is more room available. Rather than having only the filename to describe the file, you can use as many words as you need. For example:
>
> A `<A HREF="organgefish.jpeg">34K JPEG file</A>` of an orange fish with a bright yellow eye, swimming in front of some very pink coral.

In this exercise, you'll create a simple example of a media archive with several GIF images, AU sounds, and MPEG video.

First, start with the framework for the archive, which includes some introductory text, some inline images explaining the kind of files, and headings for each file type:

```
<HTML>
<HEAD>
<TITLE>Laura's Way Cool Image Archive</TITLE>
<H1>Laura's Way Cool Image Archive</H1>
<P>Select an image to download the appropriate file.</P>
<P><IMG SRC="penguinslittle.gif">Picture icons indicate GIF images</P>
<P><IMG SRC="earicon.gif">This icon indicates an AU Sound file</P>
<P><IMG SRC="film.gif">This icon indicates an MPEG Video File</P>
<HR>
<H2>Images</H2>
<H2>Sound Files</H2>
<H2>Video Files</H2>
```

Figure 10.7 shows how it looks so far.

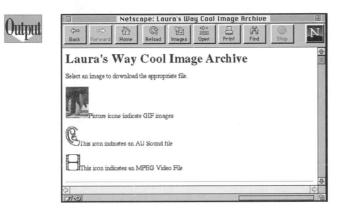

Figure 10.7. *The framework for the media archive.*

For the archive, we have four large GIF images:

- ☐ A drawing of a pink orchid
- ☐ A photograph full of jelly beans
- ☐ The cougar from the Palo Alto Zoo home page
- ☐ A biohazard symbol

Using your favorite image editor, you can create thumbnails of each of these pictures to serve as the inline icons, and insert <IMG> links in the appropriate spots in your archive file:

10

```
<H2>Images</H2>
<IMG SRC="orchidsmall.gif" ALT="a drawing of a pink orchid">
<IMG SRC="jellybeansmall.gif" ALT="a photograph of some jellybeans">
<IMG SRC="cougarsmall.gif" ALT="a photograph of a cougar">
<IMG SRC="biohazardsmall.gif" ALT="a biohazard symbol">
```

Note that I included values for the ALT attribute to the <IMG> tag, which will be substituted for the images in browsers that cannot view those images. Even though you may not intend for your Web page to be seen by nongraphical browsers, it's polite to at least offer a clue to people who stumble onto it. This way, everyone can access the media files you are offering on this page.

Now, link the thumbnails of the files to the actual images:

```
<A HREF="orchid.gif"><IMG SRC="orchidsmall.gif" ALT="a drawing of a pink orchid"></A>
<A HREF="jellybean.gif"><IMG SRC="jellybeansmall.gif" ALT="a photograph of some jellybeans"></A>
<A HREF="cougar.gif"><IMG SRC="cougarsmall.gif" ALT="a photograph of a cougar"> </A>
<A HREF="biohazard.gif"><IMG SRC="biohazardsmall.gif" ALT="a biohazard symbol"> </A>
```

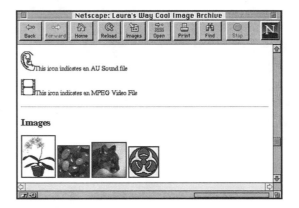

Figure 10.8. *Image links to larger images.*

If I leave the archive like this, it looks nice, but I'm breaking one of my own rules: I haven't noted how large the files themselves are. Here, you have several choices for formatting. You could just put the size of the file inline with the image and let the images wrap on the page however they want, as illustrated in Figure 10.9, as follows:

```
<H2>Images</H2>
<A HREF="orchid.gif"><IMG SRC="orchidsmall.gif" ALT="a drawing of a pink orchid"></A>(67K)
<A HREF="jellybean.gif"><IMG SRC="jellybeansmall.gif" ALT="a photograph of some jellybeans"></A>(39K)
<A HREF="cougar.gif"><IMG SRC="cougarsmall.gif" ALT="a photograph of a cougar"></A>(122K)
<A HREF="biohazard.gif"><IMG SRC="biohazardsmall.gif" ALT="a biohazard symbol"></A>(35K)
```

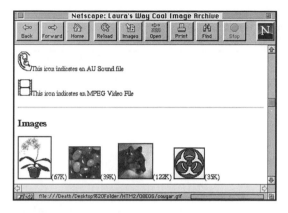

Figure 10.9. *Images with text.*

Or you could put in line breaks after each image to make sure they line up along the left edge of the page. I prefer the first method, as it allows a more compact layout of images.

Now, moving on to the sound and video files. You have three sound files and two videos. Because these files can't be reduced to a simple thumbnail image, we'll describe them in the text in the archive (including the huge sizes of the files):

```
<H2>Sound and Video Files</H2>
<P>A five-part a capella renaissance madrigal called "Flora Gave me Fairest Flowers"
(650K)</P>
<P>Some lovely wind-chime sounds (79K) </P>
<P>Chicken noises (112K)</P>
<P>The famous Tacoma Narrows bridge accident (where the bridge twisted and fell down in
the wind)(13Meg)</P>
<P>A three-dimensional computer animation of a flying airplane over a landscape
(2.3Meg)</P>
```

Now, add the icon images to each of the descriptions—the ear icon to the sounds and the filmstrip icon to the videos. Here we'll also include a value for the ALT attribute to the <IMG> tag, this time providing a simple description that will serve as placeholder for the link itself in text-only browsers.

And finally, just as you did in the image part of the example, link the icons to the external files. Here is the HTML code for the final list:

```
<H2>Sound and Video Files</H2>
<P><A HREF="flora.au"><IMG SRC="earicon.gif" ALT="[madrigal sound]"> A five-part a capella
renaissance madrigal called "Flora Gave me Fairest Flowers" (650K)</A></P>
<P><A HREF="windchime.au"><IMG SRC="earicon.gif" ALT="[windchime sound]"> Some lovely
wind-chime sounds (79K)</A></P>
<P><A HREF="bawkbawk.au"><IMG SRC="earicon.gif" ALT="[chicken sound]"> Chicken noises
(112K)</A></P>
<P><A HREF="tacoma.mpeg"><IMG SRC="film.gif" ALT="[tacoma video]"> The famous Tacoma
Narrows bridge accident (where the bridge twisted and fell down in the wind) (13Meg)</A></
P>
```

```
<P><A HREF="airplane.mpeg"><IMG SRC="film.gif" ALT="[3D airplane]">A three-dimensional
computer animation of a flying airplane over a landscape (2.3Meg) </A></P>
```

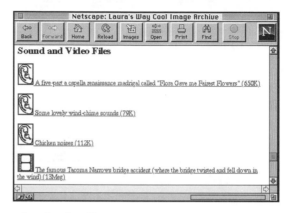

Figure 10.10. *Sound and video files.*

Et voilà, your media archive. It's simple with the combination of inline and external images. And, with the use of the ALT attribute, you can even use it reasonably well in text-only browsers. Figure 10.11 shows how it came out!

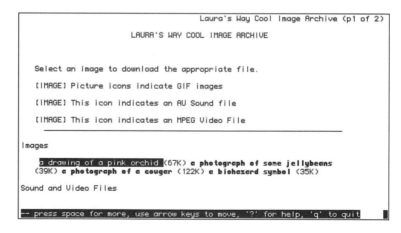

Figure 10.11. *The media archive in Lynx.*

Summary

External media files are files that cannot be read directly by your Web browser. Instead, if you link to an external file, your browser starts up a "helper" application to view or play those files.

Non-inline images, sound, and video are the most popular external media files used on Web pages. In this chapter, you've learned about the popular formats for each of these kinds of media and how to obtain samples of them, as well as other information regarding converting between formats and naming the files appropriately so that they can be recognized by Web browsers.

Q&A

Q My browser has a helper application for JPEG images listed in my helper applications list. But when I downloaded a JPEG file, it complained that it couldn't read the document. How can I fix this?

A Just because an application is listed in the helper application list (or initialization file) doesn't mean that you have that application available on your system. Browsers are generally shipped with a default listing of helper applications that are most commonly used for the common external file formats available on the Web. You have to locate and install each of those helper applications before your browser can use them. The fact that an application is listed isn't enough.

Q If JPEG files are so much smaller than GIF files, with some slight image degradation that is forgivable, why do browsers use only GIF files for inline images?

A At the time that image support was put into Mosaic (the first browser to use inline images), GIF was a much more popular format than JPEG, there were many more viewers across platforms for GIF than JPEG, and the size issue was not as important. Now that JPEG has caught on more, some browsers (such as Netscape) are beginning to accept inline JPEG images in addition to GIFs.

Q I've been using AU files for my sound samples, but there's an awful hiss during the quiet parts. What can I do?

A Some sound editing programs can help remove some of the hiss in AU files, but because of the nature of AU encoding, you'll usually have some amount of noise. If sound quality is that important to you, consider using AIFF or, if you have the converters, MPEG audio.

Q Why don't my MPEG files have sound?

A Maybe they do! The MPEG standard allows for both video and audio tracks, but few players can handle the audio track at this time. You have two choices, if you must have sound for your MPEG movies: wait for better players (or bribe a programmer to write one), or convert your movies to QuickTime and show your readers how to install and use QuickTime players.

DAY
6

DAY

SIX

11

Writing and Designing Web Pages: Do's and Don'ts

You won't learn about any tags in this chapter, or how to convert files from one strange file format to another. You're done with the HTML part of Web page design; next come the intangibles, the things that separate your documents from those of someone who just knows the tags and can fling text and graphics around and call it a presentation.

Armed with the information from the last five days, you could put this book down now and go off and merrily create Web pages to your heart's content. However, armed with both that information and what you'll learn today, you can create *better* Web pages. Do you need any more incentive to continue reading?

This chapter includes hints for creating well-written and well-designed Web pages, and highlights do's and don'ts concerning

- ☐ How to write your Web documents so that they can be easily scanned and read
- ☐ Issues concerning design and layout of your Web pages
- ☐ When and why you should create links
- ☐ Other miscellaneous tidbits and hints

Writing for Online

Writing on the Web is no different from writing in the real world. Even though the writing you do on the Web is not sealed in hardcopy, it is still "published," and still a reflection of you and your work. In fact, because it is online, and therefore more transient to your reader, you'll have to follow the rules of good writing that much more closely because your readers will be less forgiving.

Because of the vast quantities of information available on the Web, your readers are not going to have much patience if your Web page is full of spelling errors or poorly organized. They are much more likely to give up after the first couple of sentences and move on to someone else's page. After all, there are several million pages out there. There isn't time to waste on bad pages.

This doesn't mean that you have to go out and become a professional writer to create a good Web page. But here are a few hints for making your Web page easier to read and understand.

Write Clearly and Be Brief

Unless you are writing the Great American Web Novel, your readers are not going to visit your page to linger lovingly over your words. One of the best ways you can make the writing in your Web documents effective is to write as clearly and concisely as you possibly can, present your points, and then stop. Obscuring what you want to say with extra words just makes it more difficult to figure out your point.

If you don't have a copy of Strunk and White's *The Elements of Style*, put this book down right now and go buy it and read it. And then re-read it, memorize it, inhale it, sleep with it under your pillow, show it to all your friends, quote it at parties, make it your life. There is no better guide to the art of good, clear writing than that book.

Organize Your Documents for Quick Scanning

Even if you write the clearest, briefest, most scintillating prose ever seen on the Web, chances are good your readers will not start at the top of your Web page and carefully read every word down to the bottom.

Scanning, in this context, is the first quick look your readers give to each page to get the general gist of the content. Depending on what your users want out of your documents, they may scan the parts that jump out at them (headings, links, other emphasized words), perhaps read a few contextual paragraphs, and then move on. By writing and organizing your documents for easy "scannability," you can help your readers get the information they need as fast as possible.

To improve the scannability of your Web documents:

- ☐ Use headings to summarize topics. Note how this book has headings and subheadings. You can flip through quickly and find the portions that interest you. The same thing applies to Web pages.

- ☐ Use lists. Lists are wonderful for summarizing related items. Every time you find yourself saying something like, "each widget has four elements," or "use the following steps to do this," the content after that phrase should be an ordered or unordered list.

- ☐ Don't forget link menus. As a form of list, link menus have all the advantages of lists for scannability and double as excellent navigation tools.

- ☐ Don't bury important information in text. If you have a point to make, make it close to the top of the page or at the beginning of a paragraph. Long paragraphs are harder to read and make it more difficult to glean information. The further into the paragraph you put your point, the less likely anybody will read it.

Figure 11.1 shows the sort of writing technique that you should avoid.

Because all the information on this page is in paragraph form, your readers have to read all three paragraphs in order to find out what they want and where they want to go next.

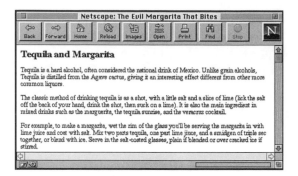

Figure 11.1. *A Web page that is difficult to scan.*

How would you improve this example? Try rewriting this section so that the main points can be better picked out from the text. Consider that:

☐ There are actually two discrete topics in those three paragraphs.

☐ The four ingredients of the drink would make an excellent list.

Figure 11.2 shows what an improvement might look like.

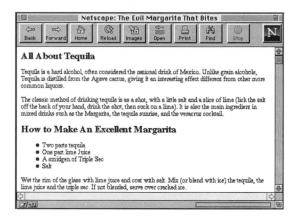

Figure 11.2. *An improvement to the difficult Web page.*

Make Each Page Stand on Its Own

Keep in mind as you write that your reader could jump into any of your Web pages from anywhere. For example, you may structure a page so section four distinctly follows section three and has no other links to it. Then, someone you don't even know might create a link to the page starting section four. From then on, a reader could very well find himself or herself on section four without even being aware that section three exists.

Be careful to write each page so that it stands on its own. These guidelines will help:

☐ Use descriptive titles, as I mention in Chapter 3, "Begin with the Basics." The title should provide not only the direct subject of this page, but its relationship to the rest of the pages in the presentation of which it is a part.

☐ If a document depends on the one before it, provide a navigational link back to the document before it (and preferably also one up to the top level).

☐ Avoid initial sentences like: "You can get around these problems by..." "After you're done with that, do..." and "The advantages to this method are...." The information referred to by "these," "that," and "this" are off on some other page. If those sentences are the first thing your reader sees, he or she is going to be confused.

Be Careful with Emphasis

Use emphasis sparingly in your text. Paragraphs with a whole lot of **boldface** and *italic* or words in ALL CAPS are hard to read, both if you use any of them several times in a paragraph and if you emphasize long strings of text. The best emphasis is used only with small words (such as, **and**, *this*, or, BUT).

Link text is also a form of emphasis. Use single words or short phrases as link text. Do not use entire passages or paragraphs as links.

Figure 11.3 illustrates a particularly bad example of too much emphasis obscuring the rest of the text.

Figure 11.3. *Too much emphasis.*

By removing some of the boldface and using less text for your links, you can considerably reduce the amount of distraction in the paragraph. (See Figure 11.4.)

Figure 11.4. *Less emphasis.*

Don't Use Browser-Specific Terminology

Avoid references in your text to specific features of specific browsers. For example, don't use wording like:

☐ *Click Here.* What if your reader is using a browser without a mouse? A more generic phrase is "select this link." (Of course, you should avoid the "here" syndrome in the first place, which neatly gets around this problem as well.)

☐ *To save this document, pull down the File menu and select Save.* Each browser has a different set of menus and different ways of accomplishing the same action. If at all possible, do not refer to specifics of browser operation in your Web pages.

☐ *Use the Back button to return to the previous page.* As in the previous note, each browser has a different set of buttons and different methods for going "back." If you want your readers to have the ability to go back to a previous page, or to any specific page, link them.

Spell Check and Proofread Your Documents

Spell checking and proofreading may seem like obvious suggestions, but given the number of documents I have seen on the Web that have obviously not had either, it bears mentioning.

Designing a set of Web pages and making them available on the Web is like publishing a book, producing a magazine, or releasing a product. It is, of course, considerably easier to publish Web pages than books, magazines, or other products, but just because it is easy does not mean it can be sloppy.

Thousands of people may be reading and exploring the content you provide. Spelling errors and bad grammar reflect badly on your work, on you, and on the content you are describing. Poor writing may be irritating enough that your reader won't bother to delve any deeper than your home page, even if the subject you're writing about is fascinating.

Proofread and spell check each of your Web documents. If possible, have someone else read them—other people can often pick up errors that you, the writer, can't see. Even a simple edit can greatly improve many documents and make them easier to read and navigate.

Design and Page Layout

Design? What design? I've been noting throughout this book that the Web is not a good place to experiment wildly with visual design, and that you shouldn't take design into consideration when you write your Web pages. Have I changed my mind?

No, not really. Although the design capabilities of HTML and the Web are quite limited, there's still a lot you can work with, and still quite a few opportunities for people without a sense of design to create something that looks simply awful.

Probably the best rule to follow at all times as far as laying out each Web page is this: Keep the design as simple as possible. Reduce the number of elements (images, headings, rule lines), and make sure that the eye is drawn to the most important parts of the page first.

Keep that cardinal rule in mind as you read the next sections, which offer some other suggestions for basic design and layout of Web pages.

Don't Overuse Images

Be careful about including lots of images on your Web page. Besides the fact that each image slows down the time it takes to load the document, including too many images on the same page can make your document look busy and cluttered and distract from the point you are trying to get across. (See Figure 11.5.)

Figure 11.5. *Too many images.*

Remember the hints I gave you in Chapter 9, "Using Images." Consider why you need to use each image before you put it on the page. If it doesn't directly contribute to the content, consider leaving it off.

Use Alternatives to Images

And of course, as soon as I mention images, I have to also mention that not all browsers can view those images. To make your documents accessible to the widest possible audience, you're going to have to take the text-only browsers into account when you design your Web pages. Two possible solutions that can help:

☐ Use the ALT attribute of the <IMG> tag to automatically substitute appropriate text strings for the graphics in text-only browsers. Use either a descriptive label to substitute for the default [image] that appears in the place of each inline image, or use an empty string (" ") to ignore the image altogether.

☐ If providing a single-source page for both graphical and text-only browsers becomes too much work and the result is not turning out to be acceptable, consider creating separate pages for each one: a page designed for the full-color full-graphical browsers, and a page designed for the text-only browsers. Then provide the option of choosing one or the other from your home page.

Be Careful with Backgrounds and Link Colors

Using the Netscape extensions, you can use background colors and patterns and change the color of the text on your pages. Using this feature can be very tempting, but be very careful if you decide to do so. The ability to change the document and font colors and to provide fancy backdrops can give you the ability to quickly and easily make your pages entirely unreadable. Here are some hints for avoiding this:

☐ Make sure you have enough contrast between the background and foreground (text) colors. Low contrast can be hard to read. Also, light-colored text on a dark background is harder to read than dark text on a light background.

☐ Avoid changing link colors at all. Because your readers have semantic meanings attached to the default colors (blue means unfollowed, purple or red means followed), changing the colors can be very confusing.

☐ Sometimes increasing the font size of all the text in your document using <BASEFONT> can make it more readable on a background. Both the background and the bigger text will be missing in other browsers that don't support the Netscape tags.

☐ If you're using background patterns, make sure the pattern does not interfere with the text. Some patterns may look interesting on their own, but can make it difficult to read the text you put on top of them.

When in doubt, try asking a friend to look at your pages. Because you are familiar with the content and the text, you may not realize how hard your pages are to read. Someone who hasn't read them before will not have your biases and will be able to tell you that your colors are too close or that the pattern is interfering with the text. Of course, you'll have to find a friend who will be honest with you.

Use Headings as Headings

Headings are often rendered in graphical browsers in a larger or bolder font. Because of this, it's often tempting to use a heading tag to provide some sort of warning, note, or emphasis in regular text, as shown in Figure 11.6.

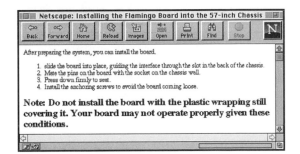

Figure 11.6. *The wrong way to use headings.*

Headings work best when they're used as headings, because they stand out from the text and signal the start of a new topic. If you really want to emphasize a particular section of text, consider using rule lines and a small icon, instead. Figure 11.7 shows an example of the same text in Figure 11.6 with a different kind of visual emphasis.

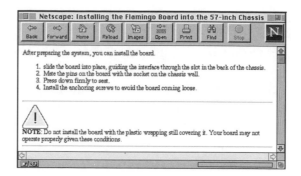

Figure 11.7. *An alternative to the wrong way to use headings.*

Group Related Information Visually

Grouping related information within a page is a task for both writing and design. By grouping related information under headings, as I suggested in the writing hints section, you improve the scannability of that information. Visually separating each section from the others helps to make each section distinct and emphasizes the relatedness of the information.

If a Web page contains several sections of information, find a way to visually separate those sections; for example, with a heading or with a rule line <HR>. (See Figure 11.8.)

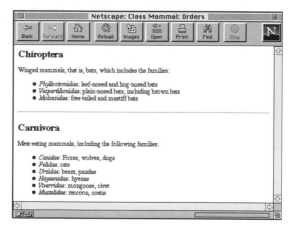

Figure 11.8. *Separate sections visually.*

Use a Consistent Layout

When you're reading a book or a magazine, each page, each section, usually has the same layout. The page numbers are where you expect them, and the first word on each page starts in the same place.

The same sort of consistent layout works equally well in Web pages. A single "look and feel" for each page in your Web presentation is comforting to your readers. After two or three pages, they will know what the elements of each page are and where to find them. With a consistent design, your readers can find the information they need and navigate through your pages without having to stop at every page and try to find where things are.

Consistent layout can include:

☐ Consistent page elements. If you use second-level headings (<H2>) on one page to indicate major topics, then use second-level headings for major topics on all your pages. If you have a heading and a rule line at the top of your page, then use that same layout on all your pages.

☐ Consistent forms of navigation. Put your navigation menus in the same place on every page (usually the top or the bottom of the page), and use the same number of them. If you're going to use navigation icons, make sure you use the same icons in the same order for every page.

Using Links

Without links, Web pages would be really dull, and finding anything interesting on the Web would be close to impossible. The quality of your links, in many ways, can be as important as the writing and design of your actual pages. Here's some friendly advice on creating and using links.

Use Link Menus with Descriptive Text

As I've noted in this chapter and frequently in this book, link menus are a great way of organizing your content and the links on a page. By organizing your links into lists or other menu-like structures, your reader can scan their options for the page quickly and easily.

However, just organizing your links into menus often isn't enough. Make sure when you arrange your links into menus that you aren't too short in your descriptions. It's tempting to use menus of filenames or other marginally descriptive links in menus, like the menu shown in Figure 11.9.

Figure 11.9. *A poor link menu.*

Well, that is a menu of links, and the links are descriptive of the actual document they point to, but they don't really describe the *content* of that document. How do readers know what's on the other side of that link, and how can they make a decision about whether they're interested in it or not from the limited information you've given them? Of these three links, only the last (`pesto.recipe`) gives you a hint about what you will see when you jump to that file.

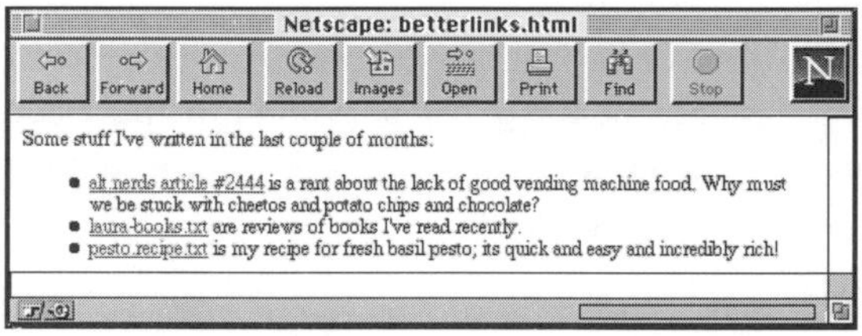

Figure 11.10. *A better link menu.*

A better plan is either to provide some extra text describing the content of the file (Figure 11.10), or to avoid the filenames altogether (who cares?). Just describe the contents of the files in the menu, with the appropriate text highlighted. (See Figure 11.11.)

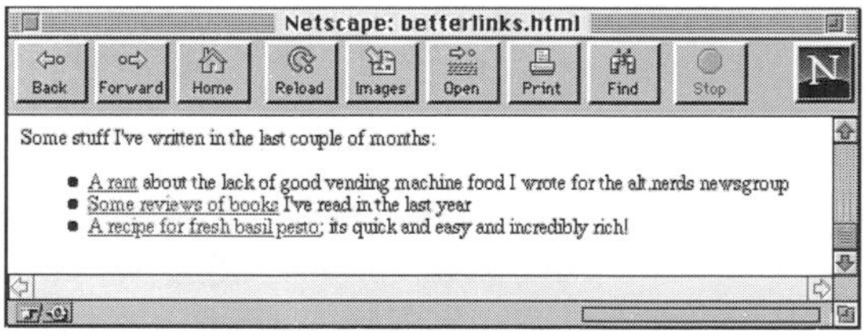

Figure 11.11. *Another better link menu.*

Either one of these forms is better than the first; both give your reader more of a clue of what's on the other side of the link.

Using Links in Text

Instead of putting links on their own lines in menu form, you can also put links directly into paragraphs on the page—to show a footnote-like tangent, for example, or to describe an actual cross-reference to some other document. ("For more information on fainting goats, see The Fainting Goat Primer.") Also, some link menus work better with some extra text, in which some of the words are highlighted as a link. Figure 11.12 shows an example of links in body text. This page is from the documentation for setting up the CERN version of a Web server at `http://www.w3.org/hypertext/WWW/Daemon/User/Guide.html`.

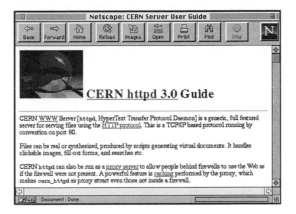

Figure 11.12. *Links in text.*

The best way to provide links in text is to first write the text without the links. Then, highlight the appropriate words that point to the linked document. Make sure that you don't interrupt the flow of the document when you include a link. The idea of links in text is that the text should stand on its own. That way, the links provide additional or tangential information that your readers can choose to ignore or follow based on their own whims.

Here's another example of using links in text (shown in Figure 11.13), but one in which the text itself isn't overly relevant—it's just there to support the links. If you're using text just to describe links, consider using a link menu instead of a paragraph. It'll be easier for your readers to find the information they want. Instead of having to read the entire paragraph, they can skim for the links that interest them.

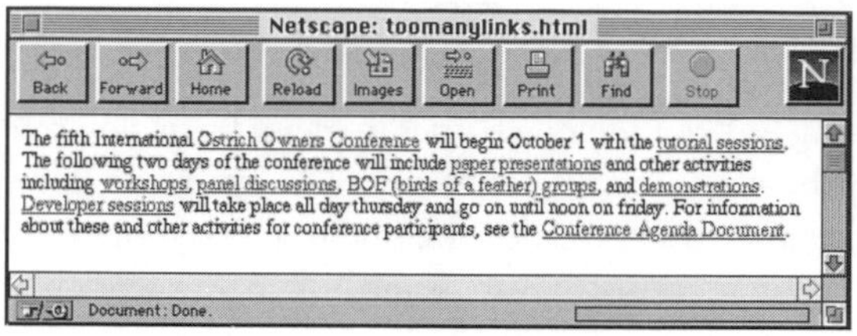

Figure 11.13. *Links in text that don't work well.*

Probably the easiest way to figure out if you're doing links within text properly is to print out the formatted Web page from your browser. In hardcopy, without hypertext, would the paragraph still make sense? If the page reads funny on paper, it'll read funny online as well. Some simple rephrasing of sentences can often help enormously in making the text on your pages more readable and more usable both online and when printed.

Avoid "Here" Syndrome

A common mistake that many Web authors make in creating links in body text is the "here" syndrome. Here syndrome is the tendency to create links with a single highlighted word (here), and to describe the link somewhere else in the text. Here are a couple of examples:

> Information about ostrich socialization is contained **here**.

> Select **this link** for a tutorial on the internal combustion engine.

Because links are highlighted on the Web page, those links visually "pop out" more than the surrounding text (or "draw the eye" in graphic design lingo). Your reader will see the link first, before reading the text. Try it. Here's a picture of a particularly heinous example of here syndrome, in Figure 11.14. Close your eyes, and then open them quickly, pick a "here" at random, and see how long it takes you to find out what the "here" is for.

Figure 11.14. *Here syndrome.*

Now try the same thing with a well-organized link menu of the same information, shown in Figure 11.15.

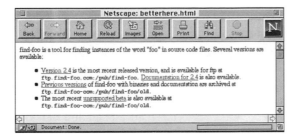

Figure 11.15. *The same page, reorganized.*

Since "here" says nothing about what the link is there for, your poor reader has to search the text before and after the link itself to find out just what is supposed to be "Here." In paragraphs that have lots of "here" or other nondescriptive links, it becomes difficult to match up the links with what they are supposed to link to, forcing your reader to work harder to figure things out.

So instead of a link like this:

> Information about ostrich socialization is contained **here**.

A much better choice of wording would be something like this:

> The Palo Alto Zoo has lots of **information about ostrich socialization**.

or just

> The Palo Alto Zoo has lots of information about **ostrich socialization.**

To Link or Not to Link

Just as with graphics, every time you create a link, consider why you are linking two documents or sections. Is the link useful? Will it give your readers more information or take them closer to their goal? Is the link relevant in some way to the current content?

Each link should serve a purpose. Link for relevant reasons. Just because you mention the word "coffee" deep in a page about some other topic, you don't have to link that word to the coffee home page. It may seem cute, but if a link has no relevance to the current content, it just confuses your reader.

This section describes some of the categories of links that are useful in Web documents. If your links do not fall into one of these categories, consider why you are including them in your document.

> **Note:** Thanks to Nathan Torkington for his "Taxonomy of Tags," published on the www-talk mailing list, which inspired this section.

Explicit navigation links are links that indicate the specific paths one can take through your Web documents: forward, back, up, home. These links are often indicated by navigation icons (Figure 11.16).

Implicit navigation links (Figure 11.17) are different from explicit navigation links in that the link text implies, but does not directly indicate, navigation between documents. Link menus are the best example of this; it is apparent from the highlighting of the link text that you will get more information on this topic by selecting the link, but the text itself does not necessarily say that. Note that the major difference between explicit and implicit navigation links is this: if you print a page containing both, you should no longer be able to pick out the implicit links.

Implicit navigation links can also include table-of-contents-like structures or other overviews made up entirely of links.

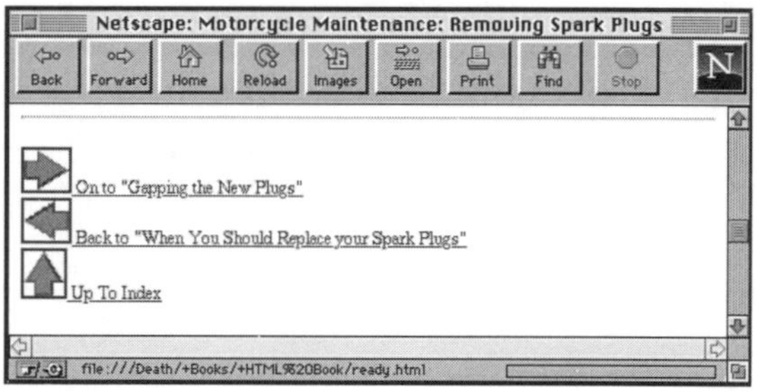

Figure 11.16. *Explicit navigation links.*

Figure 11.17. *Implicit navigation links.*

Word or *concept definitions* make excellent links, particularly if you are creating large networks of documents that include glossaries. By linking the first instance of a word to its definition, you can explain the meaning of that word to readers who don't know what it means while not distracting those who do (Figure 11.18).

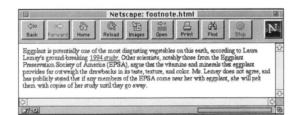

Figure 11.18. *Definition links.*

Finally, links to *tangents* and *related information* are valuable when the text content would distract from the main purpose of the document. Think of tangent links as footnotes or end notes in printed text. They can refer to citations to other works, or to additional information that is interesting but not necessarily directly relevant to the point you're trying to make.

Figure 11.19. *Footnote links.*

Be careful that you don't get carried away with definitions and tangent links. Link to only the *first* instance of a definition or tangent, and resist the urge to link every time you possibly can—for example, linking every instance of the letters "WWW" on your page to the WWW project home page in Switzerland. If you are linking twice or more to the same location on one page, consider removing most of the extra links. Your readers can make the effort to select one of the other links if they are interested in the information.

11

Other Good Habits and Hints

In this section, I've gathered several other miscellaneous hints and advice about good habits to get into when working with groups of Web pages. These include notes on how big to make each document in your presentation and how to sign your documents.

Link Back to Home

Consider including a link back to the top level or home page on every page of your presentation. Providing this link allows readers a quick escape from the depths of your content. Using a home link is much easier than trying to navigate backwards through a hierarchy, or trying to use the "back" facility of a browser.

Don't Split Topics Across Pages

Each Web document works best if it covers a single topic in its entirety. Don't split topics across pages; even if you link between them, the transition can be confusing. It will be even more confusing if someone jumps in on the second or third page and wonders what is going on.

If you think that one topic is becoming too large for a single document, consider reorganizing the content so that you can break that topic up into subtopics. This works especially well in hierarchical organizations. It allows you to determine exactly to what level of detail each "level" of the hierarchy should go, and exactly how big and complete each page should be.

Don't Create Too Many or Too Few Documents

There are no rules for how many pages you must have in your Web presentation, nor for how large each page should be. You can have one page or several thousand, depending on the amount of content you have and how you have organized it.

With this in mind, you may decide to go to one extreme or to another, each of which has advantages and disadvantages. For example, say you put all your content in one big document, and create links to sections within that document (as illustrated in Figure 11.20).

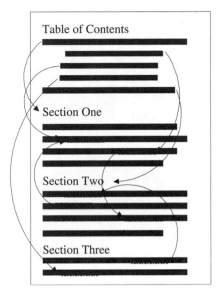

Figure 11.20. *One big document.*

Advantages:

- ☐ One file is easier to maintain, and links within that file won't ever break if you move things around or rename files.
- ☐ Mirrors real-world document structure. If you are distributing documents both in hard copy and online, having a single document for both makes producing both easier.

Disadvantages:

- ☐ A large file takes a very long time to download, particularly over slow network connections and especially if the document includes lots of graphics.
- ☐ Readers must scroll a lot to find what they want. Accessing particular bits of information can become tedious. Navigating at points other than at the top or bottom becomes close to impossible.
- ☐ The structure is overly rigid. A single document is inherently linear. Although you can skip around within sections in the document, the structure still mirrors that of the printed page and doesn't take advantage of the flexibility of smaller documents linked in a non-linear fashion.

11

Or, on the other extreme, you could create a whole bunch of little documents with links between them (illustrated in Figure 11.21).

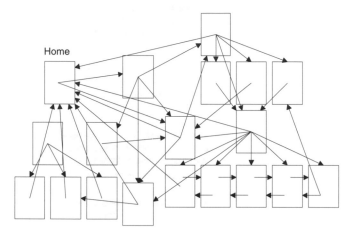

Figure 11.21. *Lots of little documents.*

Advantages:

- ☐ Smaller documents load very quickly.
- ☐ You can often fit the entire page on one screen, so the information in that document can be scanned very easily.

Disadvantages:

- ☐ Maintaining all those links will be a nightmare. Just adding some sort of navigational structure to that many documents may create thousands of links.
- ☐ If you have too many jumps between documents, the jumps may seem jarring. Continuity is difficult when your reader spends more time jumping than actually reading.

So what is the solution? Often the content you're describing will determine the size and number of documents you need, especially if you follow the one-topic-per-page suggestion. Testing your Web pages on a variety of platforms and network speeds (as I discuss tomorrow) will let you know if a single document is too large. If you spend a lot of time scrolling around in it or if it takes more time to load than you expected, it may be too large.

Sign Your Documents

Each document should contain some sort of information at the bottom of the page that acts as the "signature." I mention this briefly in Chapter 5, "Still More HTML," as part of the description of the <ADDRESS> tag; that particular tag was intended for just this purpose.

Here is a list of some useful information to consider putting in the ADDRESS tag on each page:

☐ Contact information for the person who created this Web page or the person responsible for it, colloquially known as the "web master." This should include at least his or her name and preferably an e-mail address.

☐ The status of the document. Is it complete? Is it a work-in-progress? Is it intentionally left blank?

☐ When this document was last revised. This is particularly important for documents that change a lot. Include a date on each document so that people know how old it is.

☐ Copyright or trademark information, if it applies.

☐ The URL of this document. Including a printed URL of a document that is found at that same URL may seem a bit like overkill, but what happens if someone prints out the page and loses any other reference to it in the stack of documents on their desk? Where did it come from? (I've done this many times and often wished for a URL to be typed on the document itself.)

Figure 11.22 shows a nice example of an address block.

Figure 11.22. *An example address.*

A nice touch to include on your Web page is to link a mailto URL to the text containing the e-mail address of the web master, like this:

```
<ADDRESS>
Laura Lemay <A HREF="mailto:lemay@netcom.com">lemay@netcom.com</A>
</ADDRESS>
```

This enables the readers of the document who have browsers that support the mailto URL to simply select the link and send mail to the relevant person responsible for the page without having to retype the address into their mail programs.

Note: This will only work in browsers that support mailto URLs. But even in browsers that don't accept it, the link text will appear as usual, so there's no harm in including the link regardless.

Finally, if you don't want to clutter each page with a lot of personal contact or boilerplate copyright information, a simple solution is to create a separate page for the extra information, and then link the signature to that page, like this:

```
<ADDRESS>
<A HREF="copyright.html">Copyright</A> and
<A HREF="webmaster.html">contact</A> information is available.
</ADDRESS>
```

Provide Non-Hypertext Versions of HyperText Documents

Even though the Web provides a way to create documents in new and exciting ways, some readers still like to read many things offline, on the bus, or at the breakfast table. These kinds of readers have real problems with hypertext documents, because once you start using hypertext to organize a document it becomes difficult to be able to tell your browser to "print the whole thing"—the browser only knows the boundaries of individual pages.

If you are using the Web to publish anything that might be readable and usable outside the Web, consider also creating a single text or PostScript version. You can then make that available as an external document for downloading. That enables your readers both to browse the document online and, if they want to, also to print it out for reading offline. You can even link the location of the hard-copy document to the start of the hypertext version, like this:

```
A <A HREF="ftp://myhome.com/pub/mydir/myfile.ps">PostScript version</A> of
this document is available via ftp at myhome.com in the directory /pub/mydir/
myfile.ps.
```

And, of course, a handy cross-reference for the hardcopy version would be to provide the URL for the hypertext version:

```
<US>"This document is also available on hypertext form on the World Wide Web at
the URL: http://myhome.com/pub/mydir/myfile.index.html."
```

Summary

The main do's and don'ts for Web page design from this chapter are as follows:

- ☐ DO write your documents clearly and concisely.
- ☐ DO organize the text of your document so that your readers can scan for important information.
- ☐ DON'T write Web pages that are dependent on pages before or after them in the structure. DO write context-independent pages.
- ☐ DON'T overuse emphasis (boldface, italic, all caps, link text). DO use emphasis sparingly and only when absolutely necessary.
- ☐ DON'T use terminology specific to any one browser (click here, use the back button, and so on).
- ☐ DO spell check and proofread your documents.
- ☐ DO keep your layout simple.
- ☐ DON'T clutter the page with lots of pretty but unnecessary images.
- ☐ DO provide alternatives to images for text-only browsers.
- ☐ DO be careful with Netscape's backgrounds and colored text so that you do not make your pages flashy but unreadable.
- ☐ DON'T use heading tags to provide emphasis.
- ☐ DO group related information both semantically (through the organization of the content) and visually (through the use of headings or by separating sections with rule lines).
- ☐ DO use a consistent layout across all your pages.
- ☐ DO use link menus to organize your links for quick scanning, and DO use descriptive links.
- ☐ DON'T use the "here" syndrome with your links.
- ☐ DO have good reasons for using links. DON'T link to irrelevant material.
- ☐ DON'T link repeatedly to the same site on the same page.
- ☐ DO always provide a link back to your home page.
- ☐ DO match topics with pages.
- ☐ DON'T split individual topics across pages.
- ☐ DO provide a signature block or link to contact information at the bottom of each page.
- ☐ DO provide single-document, non-hypertext versions of linear documents.

11

Q&A

Q   **I'm converting existing documents into Web pages. These documents are very text-heavy and are intended to be read from start to finish instead of being quickly scanned. I can't restructure or redesign the content to better follow the guidelines you've suggested in this chapter—that's not my job. What can I do?**

A   Some content is going to be like this, particularly when you're converting a document written for paper to online. Ideally, you would be able to rewrite and restructure for online presentation, but realistically you often won't be able to do anything with the content other than throw it online.

All is not lost, however. You can still improve the overall presentation of these documents by providing reasonable indexes to the content (summaries, tables of contents pages, subject indexes, and so on), and by including standard navigation links back out of the text-heavy pages. In other words, you can create an easily navigable framework around the documents themselves, which can go a long way towards improving content that is otherwise difficult to read online.

Q   **I have a standard signature block that contains my name and e-mail address, revision information for the document, and a couple lines of copyright information that my company's lawyers insisted on. It's a little imposing, particularly on small pages, where the signature is bigger than the page itself!**

A   If your company's lawyers agree, consider putting all your contact and copyright information on a separate page, and then linking it on every page instead of duplicating it every time. This way your pages won't be overwhelmed by the legal stuff, and if the signature changes, you won't have to change it on every single page.

12

Producing HTML Documents for Business and Fun: Some Examples

In this chapter, we'll walk through some simple examples of pages and presentations that you might find out on the Web. (Actually, you *won't* find these particular pages out on the Web; I developed these examples specifically for this chapter.) Each of these Web presentations is either typical of the kind of information being provided on the Web today, or shows some unique method for solving problems you might run into while developing your own presentations. In particular, you'll explore the following Web presentations:

- ☐ A company profile for the Foozle Sweater Company
- ☐ An encyclopedia of motorcycles, with images, sounds, and other media clips
- ☐ The catalog for a small nursery, in which you can both browse and order cacti and succulents
- ☐ A Web-based book about making bread

In each example, I note some of the more interesting features of the page as well as some of the issues that you might want to consider as you develop your own pages and presentations.

The code for these examples is available on this book's Web site at `http://www.lne.com/Web/Examples`.

Example One: A Company Profile

Foozle Industries, Inc., makes a wide variety of sweaters for all occasions. (They were responsible for the demon sweater mentioned in Chapter 3, "Begin with the Basics.") Customers visiting the Foozle Industries Web server would be first presented with the Foozle Industries Home Page (Figure 12.1).

Figure 12.1. *Foozle Industries home page.*

From this simple but nonpretentious home page, the customer has several choices of pages to visit on Foozle's Web site, arranged in a link menu. I won't describe all of them in this section, just a few that provide interesting features.

What's New at Foozle?

The first link to check out from the Foozle home page is the What's New page. The link to this page has been time stamped, noting the last time it changed.

Selecting the What's New link takes you, appropriately, to the What's New page (Figure 12.2).

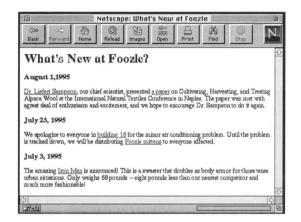

Figure 12.2. *The Foozle What's New page.*

Organized in reverse chronological order (from the most recent event backwards), the What's New page contains information about interesting things going on at Foozle Industries, both inside and outside the company. This page is useful for announcing new products to customers on the Web, or just providing information about the site, the company, or other Foozle information. What's New pages, in general, are useful for sites that are visited repeatedly and frequently, as they allow your readers to find the new information on your site quickly and easily without having to search for it.

In this What's New page, the topmost item in the list of new things is a note about a paper presented by the Foozle chief scientist at a conference in Naples. That item has a link attached to it, implying that the paper itself is on the other side of that link, and, sure enough, it is (Figure 12.3).

Figure 12.3. *All about Foozle Alpaca wool.*

Alpaca wool is fascinating, but where do you go from here? The links at the top of the page indicate that the reader has two navigation choices: back up to the Foozle home page, or to an overview of technical papers.

We've visited the home page already, so let's go on to the overview.

Technical Papers

The Technical Papers section of the Foozle Web site (Figure 12.4) provides a list of the papers Foozle has published describing technical issues surrounding the making of sweaters. (Didn't know there were any, did you?)

Each link in the list takes you to the paper it describes. You can't see it in the figure, of course, but the link to the Alpaca wool paper is in a different color, indicating that it has already been visited.

From here, the reader can move down in the hierarchy and read any of the papers, or go back up the hierarchy to the overview page. From the overview page, the reader would then have the choice of exploring the other portions of the Web site: the company overview, the product descriptions, or the listing of open opportunities.

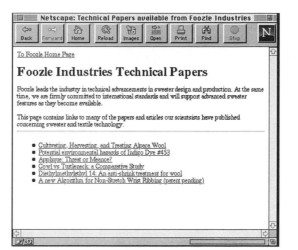

Figure 12.4. *The Technical Papers section.*

Features of this Web Site and Issues for Development

This Web presentation for a simple company profile is quite straightforward in terms of design; the structure is a simple hierarchy, with link menus for navigation to the appropriate pages. Extending it is a simple matter of adding additional "limbs" to the hierarchy by adding new links to the top-level page.

However, note the path we took through the few pages in this Web site. In a classic hierarchy the reader visits each "limb" in turn, exploring downward, and the creeping back up levels to visit new pages. However, remember the link between the What's New page and the paper on Alpaca wool? This link caused the reader to move sideways from one limb (the What's New page) to another (the Technical Papers section).

In this example, of course, given its simplicity, there is little confusion. But given a hierarchy much more complicated than this, with multiple levels and sub-trees, having links that cross hierarchical boundaries and allow the reader to break out of the structure can be confusing. After a few lateral links it is difficult to figure out where you are in the hierarchy. This is a common problem with most hypertext systems, and is often referred to as "getting lost in hyperspace."

12

Few really good solutions exist to the problem of getting lost. I prefer to avoid the problem by trying not to create lateral links across a hierarchy. By sticking with the rigid structure of the hierarchy and providing only navigational links, the reader can usually figure out where they are, and if not, they usually only have two main choices: move back up in the hierarchy to a known point, or drill deeper into the hierarchy for more detailed information.

Example Two: A Multimedia Encyclopedia

The Multimedia Encyclopedia of Motorcycles is a set of Web pages that provides extensive information about motorcycles and their makers. In addition to text information about each motorcycle maker, the multimedia encyclopedia includes photographs, sounds (engine noises!), and video for many of the motorcycles listed.

The index is organized alphabetically, one page per letter (`A.html`, `B.html`, and so on). To help navigate into the body of the encyclopedia, the home page for this presentation is an overview page.

The Overview Page

The overview page is the main entry point into the body of the encyclopedia (Figure 12.5).

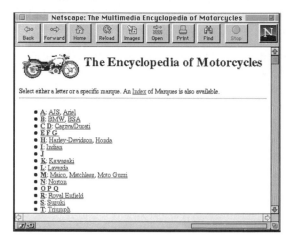

Figure 12.5. *The Motorcycle Encyclopedia overview page.*

This page provides two main ways to get into the encyclopedia: by selecting the first letter of the marque, or by selecting the name of one of the specific marques mentioned in the list itself.

> **Note:** A *marque* is a fancy term used by motorcycle and sports car fanatics to refer to manufacturers of a vehicle.

So, for example, if you wanted to find out information about the Norton motorcycle company, you could select N, for Norton, and then scroll down to the appropriate entry in the N page. But since Norton is one of the major manufacturers listed next to the N link, you could select that link instead, and go straight to the entry for Norton.

The Entry for Norton

Each individual page contains entries for all the marques starting with that letter. If the reader has chosen a specific manufacturer, the link pointed directly to that specific entry (for example, the entry for Norton, shown in Figure 12.6). Each entry contains information about the marque and the various motorcycles they have produced over the years.

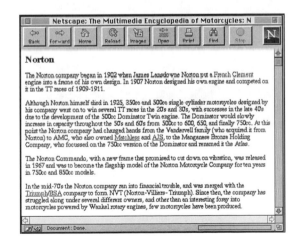

Figure 12.6. *Entry for Norton.*

So where are the pictures? This was supposed to be a multimedia encyclopedia, wasn't it? In addition to the text describing Norton itself, the entry includes a list of external media files: images of various motorcycles, sound clips of what they sound like, and film of famous riders on their Nortons (Figure 12.7).

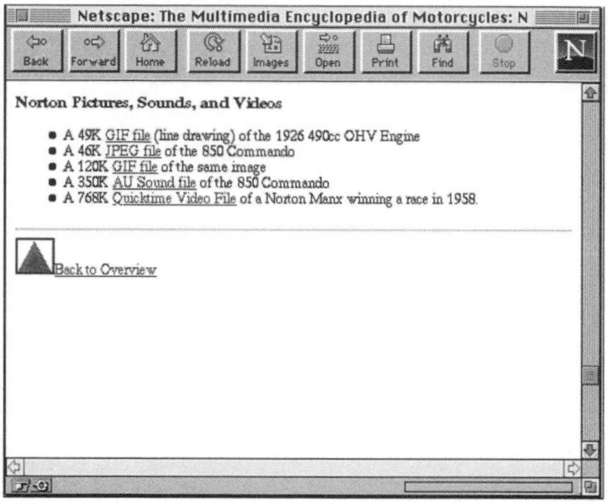

12

Producing HTML Documents for Business and Fun

Netscape: The Multimedia Encyclopedia of Motorcycles: N

Norton Pictures, Sounds, and Videos

- A 49K GIF file (line drawing) of the 1926 490cc OHV Engine
- A 46K JPEG file of the 850 Commando
- A 120K GIF file of the same image
- A 350K AU Sound file of the 850 Commando
- A 768K Quicktime Video File of a Norton Manx winning a race in 1958.

Back to Overview

Figure 12.7. *The list of external media.*

Each media file is described in text, and contains links to those files so you can download them if you want to. For example, selecting the 850 Commando link accesses a JPEG image of the 850 Commando (Figure 12.8).

Figure 12.8. *The Norton 850 Commando.*

Note also that in each point in the text where another manufacturer is mentioned, that manufacturer is linked to its own entry. For example, selecting the word BSA in the last paragraph takes you to the entry for BSA (Figure 12.9).

316

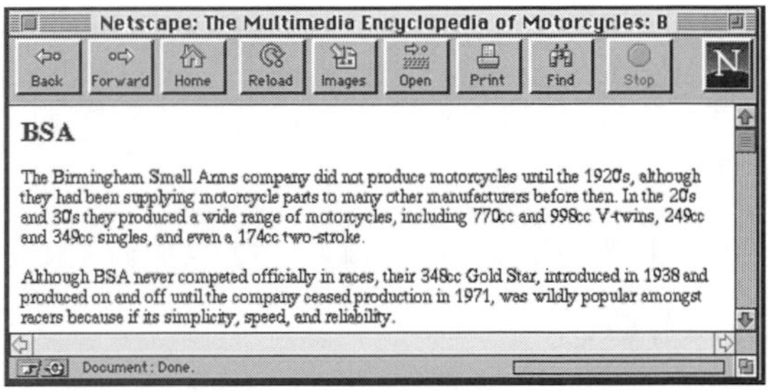

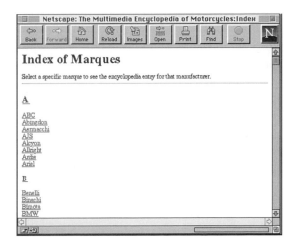

Figure 12.9. *Entry for BSA.*

In this way, the reader can jump from link to link and manufacturer to manufacturer, exploring the information the encyclopedia contains based on what interests them. After they're done exploring, however, getting back to a known point is always important. For just this purpose, each entry in the encyclopedia contains a "Back to Overview" link. The duplication of this link in each entry means that the reader never has to scroll far in order to find the line.

The Index of Marques

Back on the main overview page, there's one more feature I'd like to point out: the overview also contains a link to an Index of Marques, an alphabetical listing of all the manufacturers of motorcycles mentioned in the encyclopedia (Figure 12.10).

Figure 12.10. *The Index of Marques.*

12

Each name in the index is, as you might expect, a link to the entry for that manufacturer in the encyclopedia itself, allowing you yet another way to quickly navigate into the alphabetic listings.

Features of this Web Site and Issues for Development

Probably the best feature of the design of this encyclopedia is the overview page. In many cases, an online encyclopedia of this sort would provide links to each letter in the alphabet, and leave it at that. If you wanted to check out Norton motorcycles, you would select the link for "N" and then scroll down to the entry for Norton. By providing links to some of the more popular motorcycle makers on the overview page itself, the author of this Web page provides a simple quick-reference that shortens the scrolling time and takes its readers directly to where they want to be.

The addition of the Index of Marques is also a nice touch, as it enables readers to jump directly to the entry of a particular manufacturer's name—again, to reduce the amount of scrolling required to find the entry they want. Again, it's the same content in the encyclopedia. The overview page simply provides several different ways to find the information readers might be looking for.

The encyclopedia itself is structured in a loosely based Web pattern, making it possible for readers to jump in just about anywhere and then follow cross-references and graze through the available information, uncovering connections between motorcycles and marques and motorcycle history that might be difficult to uncover in a traditional paper encyclopedia. Also, by providing all the media files external to the pages themselves, the author of this Web presentation not only allows the encyclopedia to be used equally well by graphical and text-only browsers, but also keeps the size of the individual files for each letter small so they can be quickly loaded over the Net.

Finally, note that every listing in each letter has a link back to the overview page. If there were more than a single link, they would clutter the page and look ugly. But because the only explicit navigation choice is back to the overview, including a single link enables readers to quickly and easily get back out of the encyclopedia, rather than having to scroll to the top or the bottom of the document in a more conventional organization.

The biggest issue with developing a Web presentation of this kind is in setup and maintenance. Depending on the amount of material you have to put online, the task of arranging it all (Do you use exactly 26 files, one for each letter of the alphabet? Or more? Or less?) and creating the links for all the cross-references and all the external media can be

daunting indeed. Fortunately, a presentation of this sort does not have to be updated very often, so after the initial work is done, the maintenance is not all that difficult. To add new information, you simply put it in the appropriate spot, create new links to and from the new information, and there you are.

Example Three: A Shopping Catalog

Susan's Cactus Gardens is a commercial nursery specializing in growing and shipping cacti and succulents. They offer over 120 species of cacti and succulents as well as books and other cactus-related items. Figure 12.11 shows the home page for Susan's Cactus Gardens.

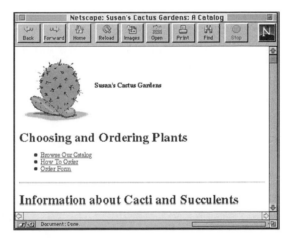

Figure 12.11. *Susan's Cactus Gardens home page.*

From here, customers have several choices: read some background about the nursery itself, get information about specials and new plants, browse the catalog, get information about ordering, and actually order the cacti or succulents they have chosen.

Browsing the Catalog

Selecting the Browse Our Catalog link takes customers to another menu page, where they have several choices for *how* they want to browse the catalog (Figure 12.12).

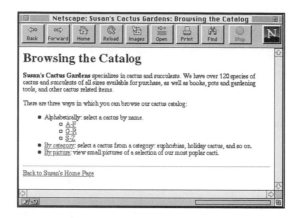

Figure 12.12. *How to browse the catalog.*

By providing several different views of the catalog, the author is serving many different kinds of customers: those who know about cacti and succulents and just want to look up a specific variety, in which case the alphabetic index is most appropriate; those who know they would like, say, an Easter Cactus with pink flowers, but are not sure which particular variety they want (the listing by category); as well as those who don't really know or care about the names but would like something that looks nice (the photo gallery).

The alphabetical links (A–F, G–R, S–Z) take customers to an alphabetical listing of the plants available for purchase. Figure 12.13 shows a sample listing from the alphabetical catalog.

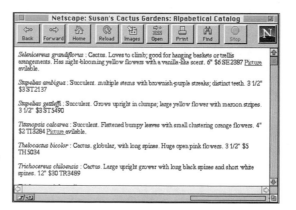

Figure 12.13. *The Cactus Catalog, alphabetical.*

Each item indicates the Latin or scientific name of the cactus; a common name, if any; a simple description; size; order number; and price. If a photograph of this cactus is available in the photo gallery section of the catalog, a link is provided to that photograph, so readers can see what this cactus looks like before they buy it.

The catalog is also cross-referenced by each cactus's common name, if any. The link from the common name takes you back to the primary entry for the cactus. So if you really wanted a plant called Crown of Thorns, selecting that entry would take you to the true entry for that plant, *Euphorbia Milii*.

Each section of the alphabetical catalog also includes navigation buttons for returning back up to the list of catalog views (Browsing the Catalog), or for returning to the home page.

The second view of the catalog (accessible from the Browsing the Catalog page) is the category view. Selecting this link takes the reader to yet another page of menus, listing the available categories (Figure 12.14).

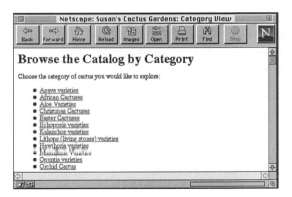

Figure 12.14. *The category view.*

Selecting a particular category—for example, Orchid Cacti—takes customers to a listing of the available plants in that category. Each element in the category listing should look familiar; they're the same elements as in the alphabetical listing, sorted in a different order (Figure 12.15).

From the category index, customers can go back to the list of categories (one step up), or back to the list of catalog views (two steps up). On the Browsing the Catalog page, there's one more catalog view to examine: the photo gallery.

The photo gallery enables customers to browse many of the cacti available at the nursery by looking at pictures of them, rather than having to know their scientific names. This feature is obviously only available to graphical browsers, but provides an excellent way to browse for interesting cacti.

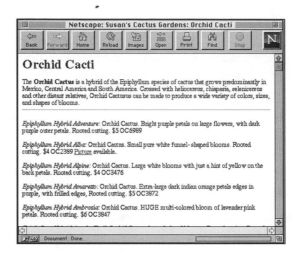

Figure 12.15. *The Cactus Catalog, by category.*

The photo gallery page (shown in Figure 12.16) is organized as a series of icons, with each small picture of the cactus linked to a larger JPEG equivalent. The text description of each picture also takes you back to the appropriate entry in the main catalog.

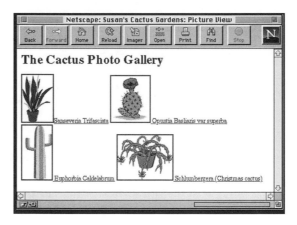

Figure 12.16. *The Cactus Catalog, photo gallery.*

Ordering

After customers have finished browsing the catalog, and they have an idea of the cacti they want to order, they can jump back up to the home page for Susan's Cactus Gardens and find out how to order. (It's the second bullet in the list shown previously in Figure 12.11.)

The page for ordering is just some simple text (Figure 12.17): information about where to call or send checks, tables for shipping costs, notes on when they will ship plants, and so on.

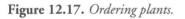

Figure 12.17. *Ordering plants.*

In the section on ordering by mail, there is a link to an order form. The form itself is a PostScript file that customers would download, print out, and then fill out and send to the nursery. (It's an external file, specified in the HREF attribute to a link tag just as you would specify any external media file.)

> **Note:** Why not order online? This page could have easily included an HTML form that allowed readers to order their cactuses online. I didn't include one here because you haven't learned about forms yet; we'll do that later on in the book in Chapter 15, "Forms and Image Maps."

And, lastly, note that the third bullet on the Susan's Cactus Gardens home page is a direct link to the order form file; it's provided here so repeat customers won't have to take the added step of going back to the ordering, shipping, and payment page again.

12

Features of this Web Site and Issues for Development

In any online shopping service, the goals are to allow the reader to browse the items for sale, and then to order those items. Within the browsing goal, there are several subgoals: What if the reader wants a particular item? Can it be found quickly and easily? What if someone just wants to look through the items for sale until he or she finds something interesting?

These two goals for browsing the online inventory may seem conflicting, but in this particular example they've been handled especially well through the use of the multiple views on the content of the catalog. The multiple views do provide a level of indirection (an extra menu between the top-level page and the contents of the catalog itself), but that small step provides a branching in the hierarchy structure that helps each different type of customer accomplish his or her goals.

Probably the hardest part of building and maintaining a set of Web pages of this sort is maintaining the catalog itself, particularly if items need to be added or removed, or if prices change on a frequent basis. If the nursery only had one catalog view (the alphabetical one), this would not be so bad, as you could make changes directly to the catalog files. With additional views and the links between them, however, maintenance of the catalog becomes significantly more difficult.

Ideally, this sort of information could be stored in a database rather than as individual HTML files. Databases are designed to handle information like this, and to be able to generate different views on request. But how do you hook up the database with the Web pages?

The Web has a mechanism for running programs on the server side. This could mean that given enough programming skill (and familiarity with your database) that you could create a program to do database queries from a Web page, and return a neatly formatted list of items. Then, on the Web page, when someone requested the alphabetical listing they would get an automatically generated list that was as up to date as the database was. But to do this you'll need a database that can talk to your Web server, which, depending on the system your Web server runs on, may or may not be technically feasible. And you need the programming skill to make it work.

An alternate solution is to keep the data in the database and then dump it to text and format it in HTML every once in a while. The primary difficulty with that solution, of course, is how much work it would take to do the conversion each time while still preserving the cross-references to the other pages. Could the process be automated, and how much setup and daily maintenance would that involve?

With this kind of application, these are the kind of questions and technical challenges you may have to deal with if you create Web presentations. Sometimes the problem involves more than designing, writing, and formatting information on the screen.

Example Four: An Online Book

In this final example we'll look at an online book called *Bread & Circuses*. This is a book that might very well have been published in hardcopy, and has since been converted to HTML and formatted with few changes—the book-like structure has been retained in HTML, with each chapter a separate page. This is quite common on the Web, not necessarily with books but with other papers, articles, and otherwise linear forms of information. Does it work? Read on.

The home page for *Bread & Circuses* (shown in Figure 12.18) is, appropriately, a table of contents, just as it might be in a real book. Organized as lists within lists, this table of contents is essentially a large link menu with pointers to the various sections in the book.

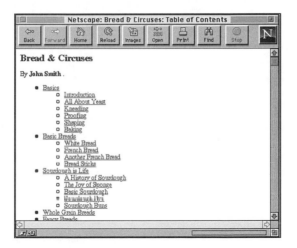

Figure 12.18. *The* Bread & Circuses *table of contents.*

Readers who are interested in all the content the book has to offer could simply select the first link (Basics) and read all the way through from start to finish. Or, they could choose a topic and jump directly to that section in the book

Proofing

Choosing the link for Proofing takes the reader to the file for Chapter One and then scrolls down to the appropriate section in that file (shown in Figure 12.19).

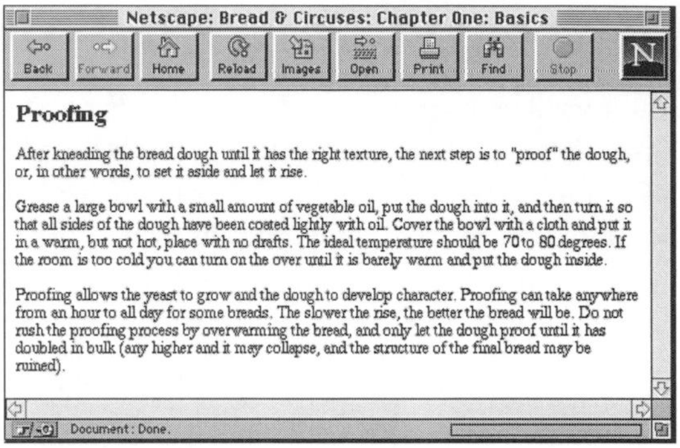

Figure 12.19. *The section on proofing.*

Here, the reader can read all about proofing. At the end of the section is the next section, "Kneading and Proofing Again." And following it is the remainder of the chapter. Finally, at the end of the chapter, there are navigation links back to the table of contents, or on to the next chapter (Figure 12.20).

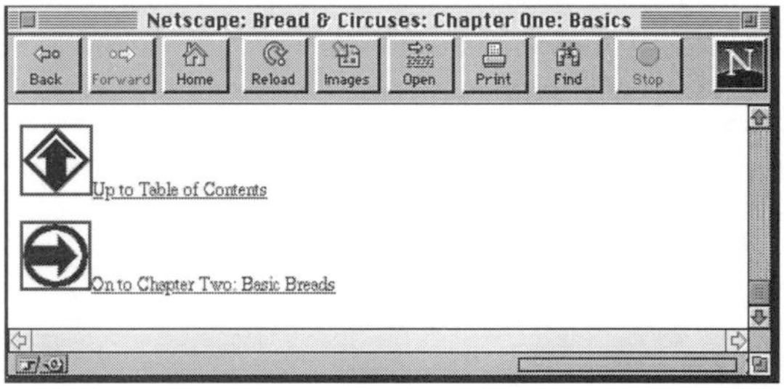

Figure 12.20. *Navigation links.*

The two navigation links allow you to progress linearly through the book by selecting the next chapter link, or to go back to the table of contents and choose another section or chapter to read. Note in this example the placement of the navigation links only at the end of each chapter file. The table of contents makes it easy to jump into the middle of the chapter, but to jump back out again you have to scroll all the way to the bottom (or go back using your browser).

The Index

On the table of contents page, at the bottom of the list, there's a link to an index (the same place it would be in a hardcopy book — at the end). The index is similar to the table of contents in that it provides an overview of the content and links into specific places within the book itself. Like a paper index, the online version contains an alphabetical list of major topics and words, each one linked to the spot in the text where it is mentioned (Figure 12.21).

Figure 12.21. *The index.*

Yeast is mentioned multiple times in the book. Because online books do not (usually) have page numbers, linking index entries to multiple locations becomes more of a chore, as you'll have to construct your index so that each entry includes some kind of location reference.

So is this index useful? Like the table of contents, it does help readers jump to a specific place within the content. But also like the table of contents, it's harder for readers to get back out again once they're in the book—even more so for the index, since the author does not provide a navigation link at the end of the chapter directly back to the index. This makes the index useful only in limited circumstances.

Features of this Web Site and Issues for Development

The biggest problem with putting books or other linear material online is that the material is often more difficult to navigate online than it was on paper. Online, readers can't flip through the pages as quickly and easily as they can on paper, or be able to use hints such as page numbers and chapter headings—both ways in which hardcopy books make finding where you are easy. For this reason, when you convert information intended for hardcopy to HTML it is crucial to include overview pages, such as the table of contents in this example, to enable readers to jump in and out of the content and to find what they want.

More importantly, however, you have to provide methods of jumping back out again. In this example, the table of contents made it possible to jump into the middle of the content, but jumping back out again was less easy because there were few navigation links except at the end of the chapter. And jumping back to the index involved two links: back to the table of contents and then on to the index. In hardcopy, this isn't an issue. Online, it becomes one.

This example provided both a table of contents and an index. Multiple views on the same contents is usually a good thing, as I pointed out in the previous two examples, as it lets your readers choose which way they want to find what they are looking for. Watch out for views that are intended for hardcopy, however, as they might not apply overly well. For example, a typical index, with a word or citations and a list of page numbers, doesn't work overly well in a Web presentation, as you don't have page numbers. Consider some other method of linking to information in your document.

When converting a linear document to the Web, there may also be the temptation to add extra non-navigational links as well, for example, to refer to footnotes or citations or just related material. However, keep in mind with linear structures as with hierarchies that the structure can often keep your reader from getting lost or confused in your material. Links to other sections in the book can be confusing and muddle the structure you've tried to hard to preserve by converting the document to HTML.

Limited forms of non-navigational links can work well, however—for example, an explicit reference to another section of the book in the text such as, "For more information about yeast, see 'yeast' in Chapter One." In this case, it is clear where the link is leading, and the reader understands where they are and where they are going so they can reorient their position in the presentation.

Summary

I've only presented a couple ideas for using and structuring Web pages here; the variations on these themes are unlimited for the Web pages you will design.

Probably the best way to find examples of the sort of Web pages you might want to design and how to organize them is to go out on the Web and browse what's out there. While you're browsing, in addition to examining the layout and design of individual pages and the content they describe, keep an eye out for the structures people have used to organize their pages, and try to guess why they might have chosen that organization. ("They didn't think about it" is a common reason for many poorly organized Web pages, unfortunately.) Critique other people's Web pages with an eye for their structure and design: Is it easy to navigate them? Did you get lost? Can you easily get back to a known page from any other location in their presentation? If you had a goal in mind for this presentation, did you achieve that goal, and if not, how would you have reorganized it?

Learning from other people's mistakes and seeing how other people have solved difficult problems can help you make your own Web pages better.

Q&A

Q **These Web presentations are really cool. What are their URLs?**

A As I noted at the beginning of this chapter, the Web presentations I've described here are mockups of potential Web presentations that *could* exist (and the mockups are on my Web site at `http://www.lne.com/Web/Examples`). Although many of the designs and organizations that I have created here were inspired by existing Web pages, these pages do not actually exist on the Web.

Q **Three out of the four examples here used some sort of hierarchical organization. Are hierarchies that common and do I have to use them? Can't I do something different?**

A Hierarchies are extremely common on the Web, but that doesn't mean that they're bad. Hierarchies are an excellent way of organizing your content, especially when the information you're presenting lends itself to a hierarchical organization.

You can certainly do something different to organize your presentation. But the simplicity of hierarchies allows them to be easily structured, easily navigated, and easily maintained. Why make more trouble for yourself and for your reader by trying to force a complicated structure on otherwise simple information?

12

DAY

7

13

Web Servers

This is the day of reckoning. You've put together a Web presentation with a well-organized structure, included meaningful images (and specified values for the ALT attributes), written your text with wit and care, used only relative links, and tested it extensively on your own system.

Now, on Day Seven, it's finally time to publish it, to put it all online so that other people on the Web can see it and link their pages to yours. In this chapter, you learn nearly everything you need to get started publishing the work you've done:

☐ Where you can find a Web server on which to put your presentation

☐ How to install your Web presentation

☐ How to find out your URL

☐ How to test your Web pages

☐ Some hints for administering your own server

☐ Methods for advertising your presentation

What Does a Web Server Do?

The Web server is a program that sits on a machine on the Net, waiting for a Web browser to connect to it and make a request. Once a request comes over the wire, the server locates and sends the file back to the browser. It's as easy as that.

Web servers and Web browsers communicate using the HyperText Transfer Protocol (HTTP), a special "language" created specifically for transferring hypertext documents over the Web. Because of this, Web servers are often called HTTPD servers.

> **Note:** The "D" stands for "daemon." A daemon is a UNIX term for a program that sits in the background and waits for requests. When it receives a request, it wakes up, processes that request, and then goes back to sleep. You don't have to be on UNIX for a program to act like a daemon, so Web servers on any platform are still called HTTPDs. Most of the time I call them Web servers.

When a server sends a file to a browser, the server also sends information about what kind of file it is sending (for example, a GIF file or a QuickTime movie. The browser uses that information to figure out if it can display the file itself, or if it needs to start up a helper application. You can also extend the behavior of your server to include files that may not be part of the default set.

Finally, Web servers can also be set up to run scripts and programs based on information that your readers provide from their browsers. For example, you could set up a Web page that asks your reader for a search string. When the browser sends back the string (as entered by the reader, using the browser), the server passes that string to a program on the server side which does the search and passes the result to the server, which in turn hands it back to the browser.

These special programs are called CGI scripts, gateway programs, or gateway scripts, and are the basis for creating interactive forms and clickable image maps (images that contain several "hot spots" and do different operations based on the location within the image that has been selected). You'll learn about these scripts in the next chapter, and about forms and image maps tomorrow. For now, let's focus on getting your pages out onto the Web.

Finding a Server to Use

Before you can put your Web presentation on the Web, you'll need to find a Web server that you can use. Depending on how you get your access to the Internet, this may be really easy or not quite so easy.

Using a Web Server Provided by Your School or Work

If you get your Internet connection through school or work, that organization will most likely allow you to publish Web pages on their Web server. Given that these organizations usually have a fast connection to the Internet, and people to administer the site for you, this is an ideal situation if you have it.

If you're in this situation, you'll have to ask your system administrator, computer consultant, or network provider if they have a Web server available, and, if so, where to put your pages so they can be viewed by the Web at large.

Using a Commercial Internet or Web Service

If you pay for your access to the Internet through an Internet service provider or a commercial online service, you may also be able to publish your Web pages using that service, although it may cost you extra to do so, and there may be restrictions on the kind of pages you can publish or whether you can run CGI scripts or not. Ask your provider's help line or online groups or conferences related to Internet services to see how they have set up Web publishing.

Several organizations have popped up in the last year that provide nothing but space on their server so you can publish your Web pages. These services will usually provide you with some method for transferring your files to their site, and they provide the disk space and the network connection. Generally you are charged a flat monthly rate, with some additional cost if you use a large amount of disk space. Some services even allow gateway scripts for forms and image maps and will provide consulting to help you set them up, and a few will even set up their server with your own vanity host name so that it looks as if you've got your own server running on the Web. These features can make commercial Web sites an especially attractive option. Appendix A, "Sources for Further Information," includes pointers to lists of these sites.

Using Anonymous FTP or Gopher

If your service provider doesn't provide a Web server, but does allow you to make files available using FTP or Gopher, you can serve HTML files to the Web using those services instead. You'll have a different URL, and you won't have all the features of a real Web site (forms, scripts, image maps), but if it's all you've got, it'll work just fine. And often it may be a cheaper option than a dedicated Web server.

Setting Up Your Own Server

For the ultimate in Web publishing, running your own Web site is the way to go. If you run your own site, you can not only publish as much as you want to and include any kind of content you want to, but you can also use forms, CGI scripts, image maps, and many other special options that most other Web servers won't let you do.

There is, of course, a drawback. There are several, in fact. To set up your own server, you'll not only need access to a system to run it on, but more importantly, you'll need a fast full-time connection to the Internet. A part-time 14.4 SLIP connection may be fine for browsing other people's Web pages, but if you are publishing information yourself, you'll want your server available all the time, and you'll want the fastest connection you can possibly afford. Although you can serve pages at 14.4KB, your server will be painfully slow to the vast majority of sites trying to access your information. 28.8 is the bare minimum, and a dedicated line such as a 56KB or ISDN line is preferable. But, of course, those lines are considerably more expensive than the little dialup SLIP or PPP connection you get through your normal Internet provider, and can run into hundreds of dollars a month.

In addition, you'll need the technical background to be able to administer the server. For Macintosh and PC systems this may not be that great of a problem, but for UNIX systems you'll need to know something about UNIX and network administration as well as how to set up and administer the server itself and keep it running all the time.

Between the system you'll need to serve documents, the fees for the Internet connection, the amount of knowledge you need, and the time you'll need to spend administering it, setting up your own server may not be a cost-effective method of publishing Web documents, to say the least, particularly when Web services can give you most of what you need for a low monthly fee and none of the hassles. But running your own server does provide the most flexibility and power of all these solutions because you can configure everything the way you want it to be and be able to install and use gateway scripts for interactivity and forms.

Installing Server Software

If you do decide to install your own server on your own system, you can choose from several servers for each platform. This section describes the most popular servers and their major features.

FTP and Web sites for all of the servers in this section are described in Appendix A.

Servers for UNIX Systems

The Web began on UNIX systems, and even today new features are usually being introduced on UNIX systems first. UNIX systems often make the best Web servers because of this advantage they have in Web technology—more tools and hints and publicly available software exist for managing Web servers on UNIX than on any other platform.

Many Web servers are publicly available for UNIX, but the two most widely used are CERN's HTTPD and NCSA's HTTPD. Both are freeware and both serve Web files equally well. Both also provide advanced features such as forms and CGI script.

CERN's HTTPD can also be run as a proxy; that is, it can be set up to handle outgoing Web connections from inside an Internet firewall. Some organizations set up their networks so that the majority of the machines are on an internal network, with only one machine actually talking to the Internet at large, to prevent (or minimize) unauthorized access on the internal network. That one machine is called a firewall, and with CERN's HTTPD running on it, it can pass Web information back and forth between the internal network and the Web at large.

CERN servers running as proxies also have a facility for *caching*—storing frequently retrieved documents on the firewall system instead of retrieving them from the Web every time they are requested. This can significantly speed up the time it takes to access a particular document through a firewall.

NCSA's HTTPD, on the other hand, supports server-side include files, which allow documents to include other documents and be customized at the time a reader requests them. NCSA's server is also somewhat better supported, and is more popular on the Web at large, so more tools and hints provide for using it than CERN's server.

At the time that I'm writing this book, the most current versions of the CERN and NCSA Web servers are 3.0 and 1.4, respectively.

> **Note:** To install either CERN's or NCSA's server to run most effectively in its default configuration, you should have root access on the system that you are running on. But you can run a Web server even if you don't have root access by installing it on a port number above 1024. (See the documentation for your server for instructions on doing this.) If you decide to go this route, be sure to check with your system administrator first. Web servers can be a significant draw on system resources, and the providers of your system may not want you running a Web server at all, in which case you'll have to look for an alternate solution to serving your files.

In addition to the popular CERN and NCSA servers, there are also the server products from Netscape. The Netscape servers have many extra administrative features that the freeware HTTPDs do not have, and can handle extremely busy sites better than those servers as well. The catch, of course, is that the Netscape servers are not freeware.

The Netscape Communications Server is free for educational and charitable institutions. Anyone else can test-drive it for 60 days, after which you're expected to pay for it (it costs $1,495). Technical support is extra and costs $495.

The Netscape Commerce Server provides all the features of the Communications server as well as software to provide encrypted connections between the server and browser for secure transactions over the Internet. The Netscape Commerce Server costs $5,000 with support an extra $995.

You can find out more about the Netscape servers at the Netscape home page (`http://www.netscape.com`).

Servers for Microsoft Windows

Although the Web has been slanted towards UNIX for some time now, this is rapidly changing. If you use a PC running Windows, Windows for Workgroups, Windows NT, or Windows 95, that PC can easily run as a Web server.

For Windows and Windows for Workgroups, WinHTTPD is a popular server. Based on NCSA's HTTPD, WinHTTPD has been very popular and has proved to be as robust and fast as UNIX-based servers. It also provides CGI scripting capabilities through a DOS shell or a Visual Basic interface. Its current version is 1.4c. It's free for personal use, but commercial users are expected to register and pay for it (and registration costs a scant $99).

For Windows NT and Windows 95, a commercial 32-bit version of WinHTTPD called WebSite is provided by O'Reilly and Associates. WebSite costs $379.

Netscape's Communications server is also available for Windows NT. See Netscape's home page for details.

Servers for Macintosh

MacHTTP is an HTTP server for the Macintosh that is exceptionally easy to set up and use and provides extensive CGI scripting capabilities through AppleScript. MacHTTP is shareware; you can use it for 30 days, and after that the cost is $65 for educational users and $95 for everyone else.

Organizing and Installing Your HTML Files

Once you have access to a Web server of some sort, you can publish the Web presentation you've labored so hard to create. But before you actually move it into place on your server, it's best to have your files organized and a good idea of what goes where so you don't lose files or so your links don't break.

Probably the best way to organize each of your presentations is to include all the files for that presentation in a single directory. If you have lots of extra files—for your images, for example—you can put those in a subdirectory to that main directory. Your goal is to contain all your files in a single place rather than scattering them around on your disk. Once you have your files contained, you can set all your links in your files to be relative to that directory. If you follow these hints, you stand the best chance of being able to move that directory around to different servers without breaking the links.

Web servers usually have a default HTML file that is loaded when the reader requests a URL that ends with directory instead of a specific file. For most Web servers, this file is usually called index.html (index.htm for DOS). Your home page or top-level index for each presentation should be called by this name so the server knows which page to load as the default page. Using this default filename will also allow the URL to that page to be shorter, since you don't have to include the actual filename. So, for example, your URL might be http://www.myserver.com/www/ rather than http://www.myserver.com/www/index.html.

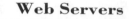

Each file should also have an appropriate extension indicating what kind of file it is so the server can map it to the appropriate file type. When you publish your files, the server uses the file extension to tell the browser what kind of file it's sending (much in the way the browser used the file extension for your local files to figure out what kind of file it was).

Table 13.1 shows a list of the common file extensions you should be using for your files and media.

Table 13.1. File types and extensions.

Format	Extension
HTML	.html, .htm
ASCII Text	.txt
PostScript	.ps
GIF	.gif
JPEG	.jpg, .jpeg
AU Audio	.au
MPEG Video	.mpeg, .mpg

Installing Your Files

With your files in a single directory, all you have to do is put them in the appropriate spot on the server. Once the server can access your files, you're officially published on the Web. That's all there is to it.

But where is the appropriate spot on your server? Here's where you'll have to ask the person who runs your Web server. All servers are set up differently, and everyone has a different place for storing Web files. Usually your server administrator will set up a directory for you to put your files in.

The CERN and NCSA UNIX-based servers can be set up so that you can store your Web files in your home directory, rather than storing them in a central location elsewhere on the system. In this case, you'll need to create that special directory and put your files there. Again, here's where you'll have to talk to the person running your Web server to find out how they've set it up.

Some Gotchas About Moving Files Between Systems

If you're using a Web server that has been set up by someone else, you'll probably have to move your Web files from your system to theirs using FTP, Zmodem transfer, or some other method. Although the HTML markup within your files is completely portable, moving the actual files from platform to platform has its gotchas. In particular, be careful to do the following:

☐ Convert binary files as binary.

Watch out for your images and other media; make sure you send them in binary mode when you transfer them or they may not work on the other end.

Watch out for Macintosh media; in particular, that you transfer them as regular binary and not MacBinary. MacBinary files cannot be read on other platforms.

☐ Observe filename restrictions.

If you're moving your files to or from DOS systems, you'll have to watch out for the dreaded 8.3—the DOS rule that says filenames must be only 8-characters long with 3-character extensions. If your server is a PC, and you've been writing your files on some other system, you may have to rename your files and the links to them to have the right file-naming conventions. (Moving files you've created on a PC to some other system is usually not a problem.)

Also, watch out if you're moving files from a Macintosh to other systems; make sure that your filenames do not have spaces or other funny characters in them. Keep your filenames as short as possible and use only letters and numbers and you'll be fine.

☐ Be aware of carriage returns and line feeds.

Different systems use different methods for ending a line; the Macintosh uses carriage returns, UNIX uses line feeds, and DOS uses both. When you move files from one system to another, most of the time the end-of-line characters will be converted appropriately, but sometimes they are not. This can result in your file coming out double-spaced or all on one single line on the system that it was moved to.

Most of the time it does not matter, as browsers ignore spurious returns or line feeds in your HTML files. The existence or absence of either one is not terribly important. Where it may be an issue is in sections of text you've marked up with <PRE>; you may find that your well-formatted text that worked so well on one platform doesn't come out well formatted after it's been moved.

> **Note:** This is only an issue when you move files between platforms, not when you use a browser on one platform to view a file being served from another platform. The Web server and browser know enough to convert the end-of-line conventions properly.

If you do have end-of-line problems, this information may help:

☐ Many text editors allow you to save ASCII files in a format for another platform. If you know what platform you're moving to, you can prepare your files for that platform before moving them.

☐ If you're moving to a UNIX system, small filters for converting line feeds called dos2unix and unix2dos may exist on the UNIX or DOS systems.

☐ Macintosh files can be converted to UNIX-style files using the following command line on UNIX:

```
tr '\015' '\012' < oldfile.html > newfile.html
```

where `oldfile.html` is the original file with end-of-line problems, and `newfile.html` is the name of the new file.

What's My URL?

At this point you have a server, your Web pages are installed and ready to go, and all that is left is to tell people that your presentation exists. All you need now is a URL.

If you're using a commercial Web server, or a server that someone else administers, you may be able to easily find out what your URL is by asking the administrator. Otherwise, you'll have to figure it out yourself. Luckily, this isn't that hard.

As I noted in Chapter 4, URLs are made of three parts: the protocol, the host name, and the path to the file. To determine each of these parts, use the following questions:

☐ What are you using to serve the files?

If you're using a real Web server, your protocol is http. If you're using FTP or Gopher, the protocol is ftp and gopher, respectively. (Isn't this easy?)

☐ What's the name of your server?

This is the network name of the machine your Web server is located on, typically beginning with www; for example, www.mysite.com or www.netcom.com. If it doesn't start with www, don't worry about it; that doesn't affect whether or not people can

get to your files. Note that the name you'll use is the fully qualified host name—that is, the name that people elsewhere on the Web would use to get to your Web server, which may not be the same name you use to get to your Web server. That name will usually have several parts and end with `.com`, `.edu`, or the code for your country (for example, `.uk`, `.fr`, and so on).

With some SLIP or PPP connections, you may not even have a network name, just a number—something like 192.123.45.67. You can use that as the network name.

If the server has been installed on a port other than 80, you'll need to know that number, too.

☐ What's the path to my home page?

The path to your home page most often begins at the root of the directory Web pages are stored in (part of your server configuration), which may or may not be the top level of your file system. For example, if you've put files into the directory `/home/www/files/myfiles`, your path name in the URL might just be `/myfiles`. This is a server-configuration question, so if you can't figure it out, you may have to ask your server administrator.

If your Web server has been set up so that you can use your home directory to store Web pages, you can use the UNIX convention of the tilde (~) to refer to the Web pages in your home directory. You don't have to include the name of the directory you created in the URL itself. So, for example, if I had the Web page `home.html` in a directory called `public_html` in my home directory (`lemay`), the path to that file in the URL would be:

`/~lemay/home.html`

Once you know these three things, you can construct a URL. You'll probably remember from Chapter 4 that a URL looks like this:

`protocol://machinename.com:port/path`

You should be able to plug your values for each of those elements into the appropriate places in the URL structure. For example:

```
http://www.mymachine.com/www/tutorials/index.html
ftp://ftp.netcom.com/pub/lemay/index.html
http://www.commercialweb.com:8080/~lemay/index.html
```

Note: Many HTTP servers are set up to use `index.html` as the default document to load for a directory (which is why I suggested you use that name for your home page). If your server has been configured to do this, you can leave off the name of the file in your URL, making it slightly shorter to type:

`http://www.mymachine.com/www/tutorials/`

The Web server will append the name of the file to the end of the URL.

Test, Test, and Test Again

Now that your Web pages are available on the Net, you can take the opportunity to test them on as many platforms using as many browsers as you possibly can. It is only when you've seen how your documents look on different platforms that you'll realize how important it is to design documents that can look good on as many platforms and browsers as possible.

Try it and see...you might be surprised at the results.

Registering and Advertising Your Web Pages

There is no central repository of Web pages or authority to register with when you create a new Web page; most Web pages become popular through word of mouth or through other sites linking to your site. There are several common ways you can publicize your new Web page once it's up on the Net and working:

- [ ] Use the form at `http://www.yahoo.com/bin/add` to add your Web site to the Yahoo index of web pages. Yahoo is one of the most popular indexes of Web pages.

- [ ] Use the form at `http://www.ncsa.uiuc.edu/SDG/Software/Mosaic/Docs/Docs/whats-new-form.html` to add your page to the NCSA Mosaic What's New page. Note that the NCSA What's New page does not publish personal Web pages.

- [ ] If you have published your Web presentation on a commercial Web site or one provided by your Internet provider, there may be a local "What's New" page to which you can add your presentation. Check with your administrator.

- [ ] Post an announcement to the `comp.infosystems.www.announce` newsgroup on Usenet. Note that this group is moderated, so it may take some time for your posting to show up.

- [ ] Register with the W3 Consortium's Virtual Library at `http://www.w3.org/hypertext/DataSources/WWW/Geographical_generation/new-servers.html`

Tips for Good Server Administration

If you've set up your own Web server, there are several simple things you can do to make that server useful on the Web and to your readers.

Alias Your Hostname to *www.yoursystem.com*

A common convention on the Web is that the system that serves Web pages to the network has the name that begins with www. Typically, your network administrator or your network provider will create a host name alias, called a CNAME, that points to the actual machine on the network serving Web files. You don't have to follow this convention, of course, but it is helpful for several reasons:

- [ ] It's easier to remember than some other host name, and is a common convention for finding the Web server for any given site. So, if your primary system is mysystem.com and I want to get to your Web pages, www.mysystem.com would be the appropriate place for me to look first.

- [ ] If you change the machine on your network that is serving Web pages, you can simply reassign the alias. If you don't use an alias, all the links that point to your server will break.

Create a Webmaster Mail Alias

If the system you're using has the ability to send and receive mail, create a globally available mail alias for "webmaster" which points to your e-mail address, so that if someone sends mail to webmaster@yoursite.com, that mail is sent to you. Like other administrative mail aliases such as root (for general problems), postmaster (for e-mail problems), and Usenet (for news), the webmaster alias provides a standard contact address for problems or complaints about your Web server. (You may not want to hear about problems or complaints, but it is the polite thing to do.)

Create a Server Home Page

Your server may be home to several different Web presentations, especially if you are serving many different users (for example, if you've set up a Web "storefront"). In cases such as this, you should provide a site-wide home page, typically http://www.yoursite.com/index.html, that provides some general information about your site, legal notices, and perhaps an overview of the contents of your site—with links to the home pages for each presentation, of course.

The configuration file for your server software should have an entry for a site-specific home page.

Create Site-Wide Administrative and Design Guidelines

If you are the webmaster for a large organization, it may be helpful for you and for your organization to define who is responsible for the Web server: who is the contact for day-to-day complaints or problems, who is the person to set up access control for users, and who can answer questions about policy concerning what can appear in a public Web page on this site.

In addition, your organization may want to have some kind of creative control over the Web pages it publishes on the Web. You can use many of the hints and guidelines in this book to create suggestions for Web page style and create sample pages that your users can use as a basis for their own Web pages.

Summary

In this chapter, you've reached the final point in creating a Web presentation: releasing your work to the World Wide Web at large through the use of a Web server, either installed by you or available from a network provider.

From here on, everything you learn is icing on an already-substantial cake. You'll simply be adding more features (interactivity, forms) to the presentation you already have available on the Web.

Q&A

Q I really don't understand all this network stuff. CNAMEs? protocols? ports? host names? Help!!

A You don't have to know any of this if you can get access to a Web server through the people who provide your usual Net access, or if you rent space on a commercial Web site. You can let someone else do all the network stuff; all you'll have to do is make sure your documents have relative path names and can be moved as a group onto the server. And once they're there, you're done.

Q How can I set up a server to do access control (to only let certain sites in), or to run as a proxy across a firewall?

A If this were a book all about setting up Web servers, I'd have written whole chapters on these subjects. As it is, the documentation for your server should tell you how to do each of these things (and the documentation for all four servers I've mentioned in this chapter is excellent, so with a little poking around you should be able to find what you need).

Q **I'd really like to run a UNIX Web server, since I'm familiar with UNIX and those servers seem to have the most features and the most flexibility. But UNIX workstations are so incredibly expensive. What can I do?**

A You can get a cheap PC (a high-end 486 or low-end Pentium) and run UNIX on it, and then use many of the UNIX-based Web servers. Several versions of UNIX for PCs exist, including Linux, BSDI, and NetBSD. I like the freeware Linux, which you can usually pick up on CD for under $20, and both CERNs and NCSAs HTTPD run seamlessly under it (in fact, my own Web server runs on Linux, and all the scripts you'll learn about the next couple of chapters were written on Linux).

Or, simply run a server on your existing PC or Macintosh system. Although UNIX servers have the advantage of new technology appearing there first and do tend to be the most flexible, PC- and Macintosh-based servers are catching up and have been proven to be just as robust as UNIX-based servers. There is nothing on the Web that says you have to use UNIX.

Q **I created my files on a DOS system, using the .htm extension, like you told me to earlier in the book. Now I've published my files on a UNIX system provided by my job. The problem now is that when I try to get to my pages using my browser, I get the HTML code for those pages—not the formatted result! It all worked on my system at home...what went wrong?**

A Some older servers will have this problem. Your server has not been set up to believe that files with a .htm extension are actually HTML files, so they send them as text instead. Then, when your browser reads one of your files from a server, it uses the information the server sends it about the content of the file, not the file extension. So your server is messing everything up.

There are several ways you can fix this. The first is to change all the names of your files after you upload them to the UNIX system, and all the links within those files. Less hideous, but still not very useful is to create symbolic links from the .html files to the same names with an .html extension.

But by far the best way to fix this is to tell the administrator of your Web site to change their server configuration so that .htm files are sent as HTML—usually a very simple step that will magically cause all your files to work properly from then on. The documentation for the server will tell them how to do this.

14

An Introduction To CGI Scripts

CGI stands for Common Gateway Interface, a method for running programs on the Web server based on input from a Web browser anywhere on the Net. CGI scripts are an extremely powerful feature of Web browser and server interaction that can completely change how you think of a Web presentation. CGI scripts enable your reader to interact with your Web pages—to search for an item in a database, to offer comments on what you've written, or to select several items from a form and get a customized reply in return. If you've ever come across a fill-in form or a search dialog on the Web, you've used a CGI script. You may not have realized it at the time because most of the work happens on the Web server, behind the scenes. You only see the result.

As a Web author, you create all the sides of the CGI script: the side the reader sees, the programming on the server side to deal with the reader's input, and the result given back to the reader.

This chapter describes:

- ☐ What a CGI script is and how it works
- ☐ When you should use a CGI script
- ☐ What the output of a CGI script looks like
- ☐ How to create simple scripts that execute programs
- ☐ How to create scripts that prompt the reader for a small reply
- ☐ How to create scripts that return special responses
- ☐ Troubleshooting problems with your CGI scripts

Once you have learned the basics of creating CGI scripts, you can use them to create all kinds of customized Web pages. CGI scripts are the starting point from which you can create fill-in forms and clickable image maps, which you'll learn about tomorrow.

> **Note:** This chapter and the next focus primarily on Web servers running on UNIX systems, and most of the examples and instructions will only apply to UNIX. If you run your Web server on a system other than UNIX, the procedures you'll learn in this section for creating CGI scripts may not apply. But this chapter will at least give you an idea of how CGI works, and then you can combine that with the documentation of CGI on your specific server.

What Is a CGI Script?

A CGI script, most simply, is a program that is run on a Web server, triggered by input from a browser. The script is usually a link between the server and some other program running on the system; for example, a database.

CGI scripts do not have to be actual scripts—depending on what your Web server supports, they can be compiled programs or batch files or any other executable entity. For the sake of a simple term for this chapter, however, I'll call them scripts.

CGI itself is the method the CERN and NCSA Web servers on UNIX use to allow interaction between servers and programs (and specifically, between forms and programs). Other servers on other platforms may provide similar gateway capabilities, but they don't necessarily use the Common Gateway Interface to do so. However, the term CGI script has come to mean any script or program that is run on the server side, so I'll use that term here.

How Do CGI Scripts Work?

CGI scripts are called by the server, based on information from the browser. Figure 14.1 shows the path of how things work between the browser, the server, and the script.

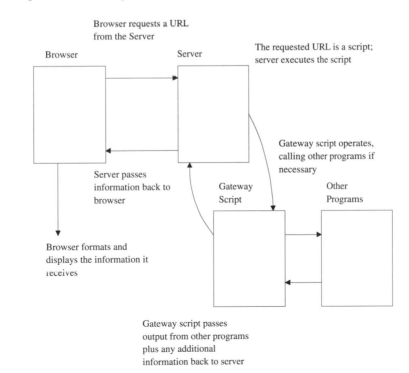

Figure 14.1. *Browser to server to script to program and back again.*

Here's a short version of what's actually going on:

1. A URL points to a CGI script the same way that it points to any other document on a server. The browser requests that URL from a server just as it would any other document.

2. The server receives the request, notes that the URL points to a script (based on the location of the file or based on its extension, depending on the server), and executes that script.

3. The script performs some action based on the input, if any, from the browser. The action may include querying a database, calculating a value, or simply calling some other program on the system.

4. The script formats its result in a manner that the Web server can understand.

5. The Web server receives the result from the script and passes it back to the browser, which formats and displays it for the reader.

Got it? No? Don't be worried; it can be a confusing process. Read on, it'll become clearer with a couple of examples.

A Simple Example

Here's a simple example, with a step-by-step explanation of what's happening on all sides of the process. In your browser, you encounter a page that looks like the page shown in Figure 14.2.

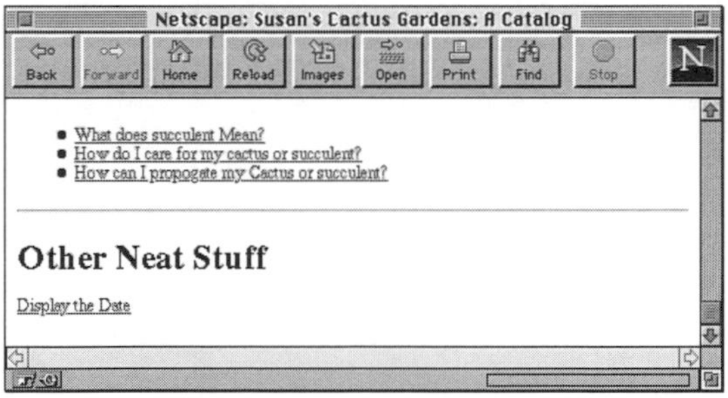

Figure 14.2. *A page with a script link.*

The link to Display the Date is a link to a CGI script. It is embedded in the HTML code for the page just like any other link. If you were to look at the HTML code for that page, that link might look like this:

```
<A HREF="http://www.somesite.com/cgi-bin/getdate">Display the Date</A>
```

The fact that there's a `cgi-bin` in the path name is a strong hint that this is a CGI script. In many servers (the CERN and NCSA servers, in particular) `cgi-bin` is the only place that CGI scripts can be kept.

When you select the link, your browser requests that URL from the server at the site www.somesite.com. The server receives the request and figures out from its configuration that the URL it's been given is a script called `getdate`. It executes that script.

The `getdate` script, in this case a shell script to be executed on a UNIX system, looks something like this:

```
#!/bin/sh

echo Content-type: text/plain
echo

/bin/date
```

This script does two things. First, it outputs the line `Content-type: text/plain`, followed by a blank line. Second, it calls the standard UNIX date program, which prints out the date and time. So the complete output of the script looks something like this:

```
Content-type: text/plain

Tue Oct 25 16:15:57 EDT 1994
```

What's that `Content-type` thing? That's a special code that the Web server passes on to the browser to tell it what kind of document this is. The browser then uses that code to figure out if it can display the document or not, or if it needs to load an external viewer. You'll learn specifics about this line later in this chapter.

So, after the script is finished executing, the server gets the result and passes it back to the browser over the Net. The browser has been waiting patiently all this time for some kind of response. When the browser gets the input from the server, it simply displays it in a new window (Figure 14.3).

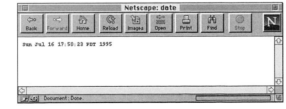

Figure 14.3. *The result of the date script.*

That's the basic idea. Although things can get much more complicated, it's this interaction between browser, server, and script that is at the heart of how CGI scripts work.

Can I Use CGI Scripts?

Before you can use CGI scripts in your Web presentations, there are several basic conditions that must be met by both you and your server. CGI scripting is an advanced Web feature, and requires knowledge on your part as well as the cooperation of your Web server provider.

Make sure you can answer all the questions in this section before going on.

Is Your Server Configured To Allow CGI Scripts?

In order to write and run CGI scripts, you will need a server. Unlike with regular HTML files, you cannot write and test CGI scripts on your local system; you have to go through a Web server to do so.

But even if you have a Web server, that server has to be specially configured to run CGI scripts. That usually means that all your scripts will be kept in a special directory called cgi-bin. And your server provider may not let you have access to that directory for security or other reasons. Before trying out CGI scripts, ask your server administrator if you are allowed to install and run CGI scripts, and if so, where to put them when you're done writing them. Also, you must have a real Web server to run CGI scripts — if you publish your Web pages on an FTP or gopher server, you cannot use CGI.

If you run your own server, you'll have to specially create a `cgi-bin` directly and configure your server to recognize that directory as a script directory (part of your server configuration, which of course varies from server to server). The next section, "Setting up CGI Capabilities on Your Server," describes how to do this. But also keep in mind the following issues that CGI scripts bring up:

- ☐ Each script is a program, and it runs on your system when the browser requests it, using CPU time and memory during its execution. What happens to the system if dozens or hundreds or thousands of these scripts are running at the same time? Your system may not be able to handle the load, making it crash or unusable for normal work.

- ☐ Unless you are very careful with the CGI scripts you write, you can potentially open yourself up to someone breaking into or damaging your system by passing arguments to your CGI script that are different from those it expects.

Can You Program?

Beginner beware! In order to do CGI, process forms, or do any sort of interactivity on the World Wide Web, you must have a basic grasp of programming concepts and methods, and you should have some familiarity with the system on which you are working. If you don't have this background, I strongly suggest that you consult with someone who does, pick up a book in programming basics (and work through it), or take a class in programming at your local college. This book is far too short for me to explain both introductory programming and CGI programming at the same time; in this chapter in particular, I am going to assume that you can read and understand the code in these examples.

What Programming Language Should You Use?

You can use just about any programming language you are familiar with to write CGI scripts, as long as your script follows the rules in the next section, and as long as that language can run on the system your Web server runs on. Some servers, however, may only support programs written in a particular language. For example, MacHTTP uses AppleScript for its CGI scripts and WinHTTPD uses Visual Basic. To write CGI scripts for your server, you must program in the language that server accepts.

In this chapter and throughout this book, I'm going to be writing these CGI scripts in two languages: the UNIX Bourne shell and the Perl language. The Bourne shell is available on nearly any UNIX system and is reasonably easy to learn, but doing anything complicated with it can be difficult. Perl, on the other hand, is freely available, but you'll have to download and compile it on your system. The language itself is extremely flexible and powerful (nearly as powerful as a programming language such as C), but it is also very difficult to learn.

Setting Up CGI Capabilities on Your Server

To run any CGI scripts, whether they are simple scripts or scripts to process forms, your server needs to be set up explicitly to run them. This might mean your scripts must be kept in a special directory or they must have a special file extension, depending on which server you're using and how it's set up.

If you are renting space on a Web server, or if someone else is in charge of administering your Web server, you have to ask the person in charge whether CGI scripts are allowed and, if so, where to put them.

If you run your own server, read on for information about configuring and using CGI scripts.

CGI on the CERN HTTPD

To enable the use of CGI scripts in the CERN HTTPD, edit your configuration file (usually `/etc/httpd.conf`), and add a line similar to the following one:

```
Exec /cgi-bin/*   /home/www/cgi-bin/*
```

The `Exec` command indicates that a directory (conventionally, the directory `cgi-bin`) contains executable scripts and not regular files, and the command tries to execute those files rather than just display their text.

The first argument indicates how that directory name will appear in the URL. Here, that directory name is `cgi-bin` and will be the first directory name after the host name in the URL (for example, `http://myhost.com/cgi-bin/`).

The second argument is the actual pathname of the CGI directory on your system. CGI directories are usually stored in the same directory as the rest of your Web files (in this example, in the `/home/www` directory), but they can be anywhere on the system. Once again, `cgi-bin` is the conventional directory name. Make sure that you also create that directory on your system.

Note: You can have as many script directories on your system as you want. Simply include multiple `Exec` lines in your configuration file.

Finally, after you've made the appropriate changes to your configuration file, restart the server using the following command:

```
httpd -restart
```

Note: If you are running your HTTPD server through `inetd`, you don't have to restart it.

CGI on the NCSA HTTPD

The NCSA version of HTTPD has two methods to indicate CGI scripts: using a special directory (as with CERN), or using a special extension, `.cgi`, which indicates that a file is a script and will be treated as a script regardless of where it is actually stored.

Note: Allowing a file extension for scripts enables you to put your scripts anywhere on the system. As long as they have a `.cgi` extension, they will be treated as executable scripts. However, keep in mind that allowing this is an enormous security hole for your system, because you might not be able to keep track of what scripts are being used and what they are doing.

To set up a script directory using NCSA, edit your `srm.conf` file (usually in the `conf` directory) and add a line similar to the following one:

```
ScriptAlias /cgi-bin/ cgi-bin/
```

The `ScriptAlias` command indicates that a directory contains executable scripts and not regular files, and tries to execute those files rather than just displaying their text.

The first argument indicates how the directory name will appear in the URL. Here, that directory name is `cgi-bin` and will be the first directory name after the host name in the URL (for example, `http://myhost.com/cgi-bin/`). By convention, this directory name is `cgi-bin`.

The second argument to `ScriptAlias` points to the actual pathname of the CGI directory as it appears on your file system. CGI directories are usually stored in the same directory as the rest of your Web files (in this example, in the `/home/www` directory), but you can put them anywhere you want to. Once again, `cgi-bin` is the conventional directory name for CGI directories. Make sure that you also create that directory on your system.

Note: You can have as many script directories on your system as you want. Simply include multiple `ScriptAlias` lines in your configuration file.

To allow the use of script files with a `.cgi` extension, edit your `srm.conf` file and add this line. (It might already be there, and you just have to uncomment it.)

```
AddType application/x-httpd-cgi .cgi
```

This line uses the `AddType` directive to add a new kind of file that the server understands. You'll find out more about these types in Chapter 18, "Web Server Hints, Tricks, and Tips." The first argument is the MIME type of CGI scripts (here `x-httpd-cgi`), and the second argument is the filename extension that indicates a file is a script.

Finally, after you've made the appropriate changes to your configuration file, you'll need to restart the server. First, find out the process ID of the server by using the `ps` command. For example, the command

```
ps aux ¦ grep httpd
```

might return the following line, in which the process number is 51:

```
root 51  0.0 2.4 420 372 con S 15:28 0:00 /usr/local/bin/httpd
```

When you know the process ID, you can restart the server using the following command, in which the last argument is the process ID of the server:

```
kill -1 51
```

Note: If you are running your HTTPD server through `inetd`, you don't have to restart it after editing the configuration files.

What If You're Not on UNIX?

If you're not on UNIX, stick around. There's still lots of general information about CGI that might apply to your server. But just for general background, here's some information about CGI on other common Web servers.

WinHTTPD for Windows includes CGI capabilities in which you manage form and CGI input through Visual Basic programs, and it includes a Visual Basic module to decode form input. Also included is a DOS CGI interface, which can be configured to handle scripts using Perl or tcl (or any other language).

WebSite, also written by Robert Denny, is a 32-bit Web server that runs on Windows NT. The CGI capabilities are very similar to those of WinHTTPD.

MacHTTP has CGI capabilities in the form of AppleScript scripts. (The new version of MacHTTP will be called WebStar and is available from StarNine.) Jon Wiederspan has written an excellent tutorial on using AppleScript CGI, which is included as part of the MacHTTP documentation in the `Tutorials:Extending_MacHTTP` folder.

CGI Script Behavior

If you've made it this far, past all the warnings and configuration, congratulations! You can write CGI scripts and create forms and imagemaps for your presentations. In this section you'll learn about how your scripts should behave so your server can talk to them and get the correct response back.

The Output Header

Your CGI scripts will generally get some sort of input from the browser by way of the server: search keys, form input, x and y coordinates for imagemaps. You can do anything you want with that information in the body of your script, but the output of that script has to follow a special form.

> **Note:** By "script output," I'm referring to the data your script sends back to the server. On UNIX, the output is sent to the standard output. On other systems and other servers, your script output may go somewhere else, for example, you may write to a file on the disk or send the output explicitly to another program. Again, this is a case where you should carefully examine the documentation for your server to see how CGI scripts have been implemented in that server.

The first thing your script should output is a special header that gives the server, and eventually the browser, information about the rest of the data your script is going to create. The header isn't actually part of the document; it's never displayed anywhere. Web servers and browsers actually send information like this back and forth all the time; you just never see it.

There are three types of headers that you can output from scripts: Content-type, Location, and Status. Content-type is the most popular, so I'll explain it here; you'll learn about Location and Status later in this chapter.

A Content-type header has the words Content-type, a special code for describing the kind of file you're sending, and a blank line, like this:

```
Content-type: text/html
```

In this example, the contents of the data to follow are of the type text/html; in other words, it's an HTML file. Each file format you work with when you're creating Web presentations has a corresponding content-type, so you should match the format of the output of your script to the appropriate one. Table 14.1 shows some common formats and their equivalent content-types.

Table 14.1. Common formats and content-types.

Format	Content-Type
HTML	text/html
Text	text/plain
GIF	image/gif
JPEG	image/jpeg
PostScript	application/postscript
MPEG	video/mpeg

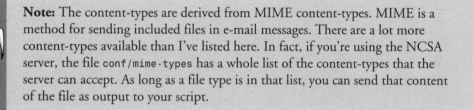

Note: The content-types are derived from MIME content-types. MIME is a method for sending included files in e-mail messages. There are a lot more content-types available than I've listed here. In fact, if you're using the NCSA server, the file conf/mime-types has a whole list of the content-types that the server can accept. As long as a file type is in that list, you can send that content of the file as output to your script.

Note that the content-type line MUST be followed by a blank line. The server will not be able to figure out where the header ends if you don't include the blank line.

The Output Data

The remainder of your script is the actual data that you want to send back to the browser. The content you output in this part should match the content type you told the server you were giving it; that is, if you use a content-type of text/html then the rest of the output should be in HTML. If you use a content-type of image/gif, the remainder of the output should be a binary GIF file, and so on for all the content-types.

Exercise 14.1: Try it.

This exercise is similar to the simple example from earlier in this chapter, the one that printed out the date, except this time, let's modify the script so that it outputs an HTML document, which will then be parsed and formatted by the browser.

First, determine the content-type you'll be outputting. Since this will be an HTML document, the content-type is text/html. So the first part of your script simply prints out a line containing the content-type, and a blank line after that:

```
#!/bin/sh

echo Content-type: text/html
echo
```

Now, add the remainder of the script: the body of the HTML document, which you had to construct yourself from inside the script. Basically what you're going to do here is

- ☐ Print out the tags that make up the first part of the HTML document
- ☐ Call the date program to add the text
- ☐ Print out the last bit of HTML tags to finish up the document

Start with the first bit of the HTML. The following commands will do this in the UNIX shell:

```
cat << EOF
<HTML><HEAD>
<TITLE>Date</TITLE>
</HEAD><BODY>
<P>The current date is: <B>
EOF
```

> **Note:** Just to explain; the cat << EOF part is essentially saying, "echo everything up to the EOF." I could have done this with individual "echo" statements, but brackets (<>) are special characters to the UNIX shell and that was more work and less easy to explain. So I did it this way. You get the idea.

So now you've printed the HTML structuring commands, a nice sentence explaining the output, and you've turned on boldface. Now call the UNIX date program to output the date itself:

```
/bin/date
```

And, finally, print out another block of HTML to finish up the page:

```
cat << EOF
</B></BODY></HTML>
EOF
```

And that's it. If you run the program by itself from a command line, you'll get a result something like this:

```
Content-type: text/html

<HTML><HEAD>
<TITLE>Date</TITLE>
</HEAD><BODY>
<P>The current date is: <B>
Tue Oct 25 17:11:12 EDT 1994
</B></P></BODY></HTML>
```

14

Looks like your basic HTML document, doesn't it?

Now, install this script in the proper place for your server. This step will vary depending on the platform you're on and the server you're using. Most of the time, on UNIX servers, there will be a special `cgi-bin` directory for scripts. Copy the script there and make sure its executable.

> **Note:** If you don't have access to the `cgi-bin` directory, you must ask your Web server administrator for access.

Now that you've got a script ready to go, you can call it from a browser. Let's assume, for the purposes of this example, that you've installed the script into a `cgi-bin` directory on a machine called www.ostrich.com. The URL to the script would then be

```
http://www.ostrich.com/cgi-bin/prettydate
```

Figure 14.4 shows the result of running the script.

Figure 14.4. *The result of the* `prettydate` *script.*

Just for reference, here's what the final script looks like:

```
#!/bin/sh

echo Content-type: text/html
echo

cat << EOF
<HTML><HEAD>
<TITLE>Date</TITLE>
</HEAD><BODY>
<P>The current date is: <B>
EOF
/bin/date
cat << EOF
</B></BODY></HTML>
EOF
```

Creating an Interactive Search

Writing a CGI script is easy if you just want to do one thing on the server and get a single result back. But what if you want to do something more complicated, like prompt your reader for a string, search for that string in a file, and then return that result as a nice formatted page?

In this case, things get considerably more complicated, as you have to somehow get input from your reader into your CGI script.

There are two primary ways of doing this: through a document-based query (sometimes called an ISINDEX query) or by using a form. You'll learn more about forms tomorrow; this section explains more about the document-based query.

14

> **Note:** Document-based queries, as you'll learn about in this section, are the old ways of getting information back to servers and to CGI scripts. Few pages use document-based queries any more, as forms have made queries much more flexible and easier to work with. If you're impatient to get on with forms, you may want to skip this section and move onto "Creating Special Script Output," later in this chapter. That section will give you more information about the sorts of things you can do with CGI scripts, and finish up the background you need to work with forms tomorrow.

Document-based queries were designed to get search keys from a browser and use them to make queries to databases or to search files. For this reason, document queries are good for getting small bits of information (like single words or phrases) back from the reader.

Document-based queries work through the interaction of three things: the use of an HTML tag called <ISINDEX>, a special form of URL a browser generates, and a set of arguments to your script.

Here's what's going on at each step of the query:

1. When a reader first requests your CGI script through a URL, your script is called with no arguments. In your script, you test for the existence of arguments, and since there are none, you output a default page that prompts for the search.

    In the HTML code for the default page, you include the special <ISINDEX> HTML tag (this tag is why document-based queries are called ISINDEX queries). The <ISINDEX> tag turns on searching in the browser.

2. The reader enters a string to search for prompt, and hits return or selects a button (depending on how searching has been implemented in the browser).

3. The browser then requests the same URL to the CGI script, except this time the URL includes the string the user specified in the search, tacked onto the end of the URL after a question mark, like this:

`http://musite.com/cgi-bin/dosearch?ostriches`

For this example, `dosearch` is the script, and `ostriches` was the string the reader typed at the search prompt.

4. The server receives the URL and passes control on to the CGI script, using the part of the URL after the question mark as the argument (or arguments) to the script itself.

5. Your script is called a second time, but this time, since it was called with arguments, it performs a different operation. In this example, it searches for the argument in a file and returns an HTML page indicating whether or not the argument was found.

Each part of the document-based query relies on the other parts. The script provides activation of the <ISINDEX> tag, which allows the query. The browser attaches the query itself to the URL, which is then passed back to the script. The script uses it to perform the appropriate action, and then output a result back to the browser.

Each part of the document-based query is described in more detail in the following sections.

The Script

In document-based queries, you base what your script does on whether or not the script was called with arguments, and (often) on the arguments you receive. The script will have two main results.

☐ If the script was called with no arguments, the result will be to output the HTML for a default page that prompts the user for a search string.

Keep in mind that the default page is generated by a script; it's not a plain HTML file. You cannot trigger searches in this way using a plain HTML document.

☐ If the script was called with any arguments, your script will use the arguments to perform the search, make a test, or perform the operation it was intended to do, and then output an appropriate result.

The *<ISINDEX>* Tag

The <ISINDEX> tag is a special HTML tag used specially for document-based queries. <ISINDEX> doesn't enclose any text, nor does it have a closing tag.

So what does <ISINDEX> do? It "turns on" searching in the browser that is reading this document. Depending on the browser, this may involve enabling a search button in the browser itself (Figure 14.5) For newer browsers, it may involve including an input field on the page itself (Figure 14.6). The reader can then enter a string to search for, and then press Return or click on the button to submit the query to the server.

The Search Prompt

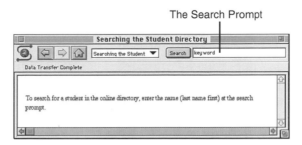

Figure 14.5. *A search prompt in the Browser Window.*

Figure 14.6. *A search prompt on the page itself.*

According to the HTML 2.0 specification, The <ISINDEX> tag should go inside the <HEAD> part of the HTML document (its one of the few tags that goes into <HEAD>, <TITLE> being the other obvious example). In older browsers, where there was a single location for the search prompt, this made sense, as neither the search prompt nor the <ISINDEX> tag was actually part of the data of the document. However, because more recent browsers display the input field on the HTML page itself, it is useful to be able to put <ISINDEX> in the body of the document so that you can control where on the page the input field appears (if it's in the <HEAD>, it'll always be the first thing on the page). Most browsers will now accept an <ISINDEX> tag anywhere in the body of an HTML document, and will draw the input box wherever that tag appears.

Finally, there is a Netscape extension to the <ISINDEX> tag that allows you to define the search prompt. Again, in older browsers, the search prompt was fixed (it was usually something confusing like "This is a Seachable index. Enter keywords"). The Netscape-only PROMPT attribute to `<ISINDEX>` allows you to define the string that will be used to indicate the input field, for example:

```
<P> To search for a student in the online directory, enter the name (last name first):
<ISINDEX PROMPT="Student's name:  ">
```

Figure 14.7 shows the result of this tag in Netscape:

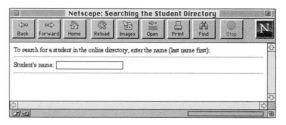

Figure 14.7. *A Netscape search prompt.*

In other browsers, as with all Netscape extensions, the prompt will be ignored and the default search prompt used instead, so you may want to use only a few words in PROMPT, and explain the purpose of the search field elsewhere.

The Search String and the Script's URL

When the reader presses return or clicks a button after entering the search string, the browser calls the URL for the same CGI script again. This time, it appends the value the reader typed into the search prompt to the end of the URL, with a question mark separating the name of the script and the argument. Because spaces and other special characters have a special meaning to URLs, if there are spaces in the search string, the browser converts them to the + character before the URL is called. Other special characters are similarly encoded.

On the server side, the server calls the script again and replaces the + in the argument list with spaces. This has the effect of calling the script with multiple arguments.

An example will make the interaction between all these parts clearer.

Exercise 14.2: Say Hello.

Although document-based queries were originally intended to perform searches on databases and other documents stored on the server, you don't have to use document-based queries to actually search anything. In your CGI script, you can use the arguments passed back from the browser for any purpose you want. For example, you could use it to create a talkative browser. In this exercise you'll do just that. In this example, the main page prompts you to say "hello" to it via the search prompt. Figure 14.8 shows that main page.

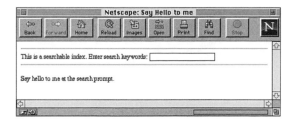

Figure 14.8. *Hello, the first page.*

From this page, you can type in a hello and choose search. If you tried typing *bonjour*, Figure 14.9 shows the response you would get from the CGI script.

Figure 14.9. *The first response.*

Our script is obviously not multilingual. If you gave in and tried saying hello, you'd get the response shown in Figure 14.10.

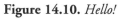

Figure 14.10. *Hello!*

Implementing this sort of script simply involves writing the script so that it tests the argument it gets from your reader and returns the appropriate page depending on what that argument was. Next, we'll go through all the steps of writing the script so that it behaves like this.

Create the Default Page

First, you need to create the case where the script is called with no arguments; that is, the first default page. But even before you do that, you should create the basic structure of this script. First, print out the script header and the first bits of the HTML page:

```
#!/bin/sh

echo Content-type: text/html
echo

cat << EOF
<HTML><HEAD><TITLE>
EOF
```

Now you need to test whether the script was called with arguments or not. In Bourne shell scripts, the test looks like this:

```
if [ $# = 0 ]; then
...
fi
```

Put the rest of the HTML needed to create the default page inside the if...fi lines, like this:

```
if [ $# = 0 ]; then
cat << EOF
Say Hello to me</TITLE><ISINDEX></HEAD><BODY>
<P>Say hello to me at the search prompt.
EOF
fi
```

And the end of the script finishes up the HTML file:

```
cat << EOF
</P></BODY></HTML>
EOF
```

So, if you saved this script and ran it without arguments, you'd get the following result:

```
Content-type: text/html

<HTML><HEAD><TITLE>
Say Hello to me</TITLE><ISINDEX></HEAD><BODY>
<P>Say hello to me at the search prompt.
</P></BODY></HTML>
```

The formatting is a little funny but HTML doesn't care about that. It'll get displayed as usual.

Note the <ISINDEX> tag. Once again, this is what activates the search feature in the browser reading this document.

Test the Arguments and Return the Appropriate Result

Now you have a basic script that works fine if there are no arguments. But when your reader types something into the search field and hits return (or presses the appropriate button), the script will be called again with whatever they typed as an argument. You'll have to add to your script to handle that argument.

Modifying the script to react differently if there are arguments is not that difficult; all you have to do is add an else to your if. However, note that in this example there can be two different results, depending on what your reader types into the search field (either the correct result, "hello," or anything else), so just adding a single else isn't going to be enough. You're going to have to add another test to make sure the response is "hello." In the Bourne shell, the structure of ifs and elses in this case would look like this:

```
if [ $# = 0 ]; then
   #the default page
else if [ $1 != "hello" ]; then
   #the not hello response
else
   #the hello response
fi
fi
```

All I've included here is the structure to create the appropriate branches, and the comments (the parts starting with #) to explain what parts go where. Now, finish up the script by adding the HTML codes in the right slots.

With the structure in place, you can add the rest of the HTML code within each section. For example, for the first section (the response to anything other than "hello"), you'd use the following:

```
else if [ $1 != "hello" ]; then
cat << EOF
Not Hello</TITLE><ISINDEX></HEAD><BODY>
<P>That's not a hello. Say hello to me at the search prompt.
EOF
```

Note that the <ISINDEX> tag is there again, since you're still expecting a response (and you want the right one this time!)

Finally, fill in the last slot with code to produce the "correct" page:

```
else
cat << EOF
How Friendly!</TITLE></HEAD><BODY>
<P>Hello to you too!
EOF
```

And here, in the final branch, you don't need an `<ISINDEX>` tag, since you're done prompting for a response. All you're producing here is the congratulatory page, which is just plain old HTML.

To test it, you can call the script from the command line with the appropriate arguments. The sayhello script with an argument of goodbye results in this output:

```
Content-type: text/html

<HTML><HEAD><TITLE>
Not Hello</TITLE><ISINDEX></HEAD><BODY>
<P>That's not a hello. Say hello to me at the search prompt.
</P></BODY></HTML>
```

And an argument of hello prints this output:

```
Content-type: text/html

<HTML><HEAD><TITLE>
How Friendly!</TITLE></HEAD><BODY>
<P>Hello to you too!
</P></BODY></HTML>
```

For each possible response the reader gives you, there is an appropriate HTML output. You've covered all the options in separate branches.

The Complete Script

Just for reference, here's the full sayhello script:

```
#!/bin/sh

echo Content-type: text/html
echo

cat << EOF
<HTML><HEAD><TITLE>
EOF

if [ $# = 0 ]; then
cat << EOF
Say Hello to me</TITLE><ISINDEX></HEAD><BODY>
<P>Say hello to me at the search prompt.
EOF
else if [ $1 != "hello" ]; then
cat << EOF
Not Hello</TITLE><ISINDEX></HEAD><BODY>
<P>That's not a hello. Say hello to me at the search prompt.
EOF
else
cat << EOF
How Friendly!</TITLE></HEAD><BODY>
<P>Hello to you too!
```

```
   EOF
   fi
   fi

   cat << EOF
   </P></BODY></HTML>
   EOF
```

Creating Special Script Output

For the majority of this chapter you've written scripts that output data, usually HTML data, that is sent to the browser for interpretation and display. But what if you don't want to send a stream of data as a result of a script's actions? What if you want to load an existing document instead? What if you just want the script to do something and not give any response back to the browser?

Fear not, you can do those things. This section explains how.

Responding by Loading Another Document

In the sayhello example in the previous section, you may have noticed that the last page you created through the script, the one that congratulated the user for saying hello, had nothing special in it that would imply it needed to be constructed in the script. The other two branches had to be constructed by the script so that they could include the <ISINDEX> tag, but the last one was just an ordinary page.

Wouldn't it have been easier, rather than constructing the content of a regular page in the script (and having to go through all that cat << EOF stuff), to simply output a file that was stored on the system? Or, even better, to redirect the server to load that existing file?

What I've just described is possible with CGI scripts. To load an existing document as the output of a script, you use a line similar to the following:

```
Location: ../docs/final.html
```

The Location line is used in place of the normal output; that is, if you use Location, you do not need to use Content-type or include any other data in the output (and, in fact, you can't include any other data in the output). Like Content-type, however, you must also include a blank line after the Location line.

The path name to the file can either be a full URL, or a relative path name. All relative path names will be relative to the location of the script itself. This one looks for the document final.html in a directory called docs one level up from the current directory:

```
else
echo Location: ../docs/final.html
echo
fi
```

If the server can find the document you've specified in the Location line, it retrieves it and
sends it back to the browser just as the output to Content-type would have been sent.

> **Note:** You cannot combine Content-type and Location output. For example, if
> you want to output a standard page and then add custom content to the bottom
> of that same page, you'll have to use Content-type and construct both parts
> yourself. Note that you could use script commands to open up a local file and
> print it directly to the output; for example, `cat filename` instead of the `cat <<`
> `EOF` the scripts in this chapter used.

So if you were using a Location line to output the last branch of the `sayhello` script, how
would you modify the script to do so?

The script was originally written such that each branch of the `if` statement printed much the
same thing. Therefore, the Content-type lines and the beginning and end of the HTML file
were specified outside the `if` statement. Because the final branch doesn't use these, you'll have
to copy them inside the branch instead. The final modified script would look like this:

```
#!/bin/sh


if [ $# = 0 ]; then
echo Content-type: text/html
echo
cat << EOF
<HTML><HEAD><TITLE>
Say Hello to me</TITLE><ISINDEX></HEAD><BODY>
<P>Say hello to me at the search prompt.
</P></BODY></HTML>
EOF
else if [ $1 != "hello" ]; then
echo Content-type: text/html
echo
cat << EOF
<HTML><HEAD><TITLE>
Not Hello</TITLE><ISINDEX></HEAD><BODY>
<P>Thats not a hello. Say hello to me at the search prompt.
</P></BODY></HTML>
EOF
else
echo Location: ../docs/sayhellofinal.html
echo
fi
fi
```

No Response

Sometimes it may be appropriate for a CGI script to have no output at all. Sometimes you just want to take the information you get from the reader. You may not want to load a new document, neither by outputting the result nor by opening an existing file. The document that was on the browser's screen before should just stay there.

Fortunately, doing this is quite easy. Instead of outputting a Content-type or Location header, use the following line (with a blank line after it, as always):

```
Status: 204 No Response
```

The Status header provides status codes to the server (and to the browser). The particular status of 204 is passed on to the browser, and the browser, if it can figure out what to do with it, should do nothing.

You'll need no other output from your script, since you don't want the browser to do anything with it—just the one Status line with the blank line. Of course, your script should do something; otherwise, why bother calling the script at all?

> **Note:** Although No Response is part of the official HTTP specification, it may not be supported in all browsers or may produce strange results. Before using a No Response header you might want to experiment with several different browsers to see what the result will be.

Troubleshooting

Here are some of the most common problems with CGI scripts and how to fix them:

- [ ] The content of the script is being displayed, not executed.

  Have you configured your server to accept CGI scripts? Are your scripts contained in the appropriate CGI directory (usually `cgi-bin`)? If your server allows CGI files with `.cgi` extensions, does your script have that extension?

- [ ] `Error 500: Server doesn't support POST`.

  You'll get this error from forms that use the POST method. This error most often means that you either haven't set up CGI scripts in your server, or you're trying to access a script that isn't contained in a CGI directory (see the previous bullet).

  It can also mean, however, that you've misspelled the path to the script itself. Check the path name in your form, and if it's correct, make sure that your script is in the appropriate CGI directory (usually `cgi-bin`) and that it has a `.cgi` extension (if your server allows this).

☐ Document contains no data

Make sure you included a blank line between your headers and the data in your script.

☐ Error 500: Bad Script Request

Make sure your script is executable (on UNIX, make sure you've done chmod +x to the script). You should be able to run your scripts from a command line before you try to call them from a browser.

Summary

CGI scripts, sometimes called server-side scripts or gateway scripts, make it possible for programs to be run on the server, and HTML or other files to be generated on-the-fly.

This chapter covers the basics of how to deal with CGI scripts, knowledge that you'll use tomorrow when you create forms and image maps. In particular, you've created simple scripts that run as links and worked with document queries using the <ISINDEX> tag.

You've also learned the three headers you can pass back to the server from your script:

☐ Content-type: The output following this header is a file of the type specified in this header. Content-types are MIME-based forms that include things like text/html or image/gif.

☐ Location: Opens and sends the specified file back to the browser; either a full URL or a relative path name.

☐ Status: An HTTP status code. Status is most generally used with 204 No Response, to produce no visible output from a script.

Q&A

Q What if I don't know how to program? Can I still use CGI scripts?

A If you have your access to a Web server through a commercial provider, you may be able to get help from the provider with your CGI scripts (for a fee, of course). Also, if you know even a little programming, but you're unsure of what you're doing, there are many examples available for the platform and server you're working with. Usually these examples are part of the server distribution, or at the same FTP location. See the documentation that came with your server; it often has pointers to further help. In fact, for the operation you want to accomplish, there may already be a script you can use with only some slight modification. But be careful; if you don't know what you're doing, you can rapidly get in over your head.

Q My Web server has a `cgi-bin` directory, but I don't have access to it. So I created by own `cgi-bin` directory and put my script there, but calling it from my Web pages didn't work. What did I do wrong?

A Web servers must be specially configured to run CGI scripts, and that means indicating specific directories or files that are meant to be scripts. You cannot just create a directory or a file with a special extension; your server administrator has to be involved. Ask him or her for help in installing your scripts.

Q Can I put the `<ISINDEX>` tag in any HTML document?

A Well, it's legal HTML, so yes, you can put it in any HTML document. And it will turn on the searching interface in the browser when that document is read. But nothing will happen if your readers type something into the search box; they'll get an error when they try to send the results of the search, or nothing at all.

The `<ISINDEX>` tag only makes sense in documents that are generated by CGI scripts that can handle the results of the query.

Q Can I call my CGI script with command-line options?

A It depends on what you actually want to do with the command-line options. But keep in mind that the only arguments your script is ever called with are those appended to the URL as part of the search query. There's no way to intercept the call to your script to add in command-line options.

You can hardcode the results of a search query in the call to your script, however. Remember, the browser sends the contents of the search input field to the server through the use of the URL, with the arguments appended to the end of the URL after a question mark. So you could, for example, set up a link to your script that included arguments in the URL itself and bypass the search input altogether. Experiment with it to see what works.

Q What if I want to do something more complicated in my search? What if I want to include a list of ten items in the search box and have the script do something with those ten items? That's an awful lot to include in a search box.

A Yes, that is an awful lot to include in a single string, and that's precisely the reason why forms were created: to allow more extensive kinds of input back from the browser. If you can wait until tomorrow, you'll learn all about forms in Chapter 15, "Forms and Image Maps."

BONUS DAY

DAY

BONUS

15

Forms and
Image Maps

With the knowledge you gained at the end of yesterday's lesson about CGI scripts, you now have the background you need to use the most powerful features of Web publishing: forms and image maps (and if you've skipped to this chapter, shame on you! Go back and read Chapter 14). Forms and Image maps make it possible for you to transform your Web pages from primarily text and graphics that your readers passively browse to interactive "toys," surveys, and presentations that can provide different options based on the reader's input.

In this chapter, you learn the last of the HTML tags and do more with CGI scripts. In particular, you learn

☐ How form-based queries are different from document-based queries, including how to handle the input you get from a form

☐ The basic form input elements: text fields, radio buttons, and check boxes, as well as buttons for submitting and resetting the form

☐ Other form elements: text areas, menus of options, hidden fields

☐ All about imagemaps: how to create map files and link the image to the file to the server

Anatomy of a Form

Yesterday you learned how to create simple interactivity in your forms using ISINDEX and documents that were generated exclusively from CGI scripts. Creating interactive presentations using forms is very similar (particularly on the server side), except it's even easier.

When you created a document-based query using ISINDEX, the CGI script did most of the work. It generated the original HTML document, and then generated a result based on the input to that same script. This made the script you had to write quite complex as you had to deal with several different branches and with generating many different HTML pages as you went along.

When you create form-based queries, you'll actually create two separate things: the HTML document that contains the form, and the CGI script to process the input from that form.

In the HTML code for the form, which you'll learn about further on in this chapter, you do two special things to link up the form with the script. First, you'll include a pointer to the script, so that the browser knows where to send the form input. Second, each element in your form will have a special name attached to it. That name is used with the value your reader enters so that you can tell which data goes with what part of the form.

Form Input: *GET* and *POST*

The third thing you'll include in the HTML code for your form is how the form input should be sent to the server. There are two choices: GET and POST, which are named after the HTTP commands that your browser uses to communicate with your server.

GET is actually the method that ISINDEX searches use to pass input back to the server. The encoded input is appended onto the end of the URL and sent back to the server. In forms, however, that input is then put into an environment variable called QUERY_STRING. Note that unlike ISINDEX searches, you don't necessarily get the input as arguments to your script.

POST passes the input back to the server on a separate stream, which is then passed directly to the standard input of your CGI script. No variables or argument is assigned.

> **Note:** As I mentioned in the last chapter, my discussion of CGI scripting in this book is going to be quite UNIX-specific. Your server may have a different way of managing form input, although GET and POST will still exist in some form. Check your server documentation to see how they handle forms.

When you create your HTML form, you'll have a choice which method to use, GET or POST. So which should you use? There are advantages and disadvantages to each. The problem with GET is that since it assigns an environment variable to the input of your form, there may be system-defined limits on the number of characters that variable can hold. So if you have a form with a lot of input to process, some of that input may be cut off. With POST, there are no such limits. So, for most forms, it makes sense to use POST most of the time. I'll be using POST in all the examples throughout this section.

The CGI Script To Process the Form

CGI scripts to process forms are almost identical to other CGI scripts. Everything you learned yesterday about gating special headers (such as Content-type) and generating your own HTML documents still applies.

There are a few things you have to watch out for with CGI scripts to process forms. For example, the first problem is that you don't get your input as arguments; instead, you get it either from the QUERY_STRING environment variable (for form input sent using GET), or from the standard input (input using POST).

The second problem is that when the browser packages the form input for delivery to the server, it puts it in a special format called URL encoding. URL encoding tacks all the names and values together, replacing space and special characters where necessary. Form input that has been URL-encoded can end up looking kind of bizarre—here's an example:

```
vitamin=on&svga=on&fish=on&theSex=female&theName=My%20Name
```

Because form input is passed to your script in this URL-encoded form, you'll have to decode it before you can use it. However, because decoding this information is a common task, there are lots of tools for doing just that. There's no reason for you to write your own decoding program unless you want to do something very unusual. The decoding programs that are out there can do a fine job, and they might consider things that you haven't, such as how to avoid having your script break because someone gave your form funny input.

I've noted a few programs for decoding form input in Appendix A, but the program I'm going to use for the examples in this book is called uncgi. Uncgi decodes the input from a form submission for you and creates a set of environment variables. These environment variables include one for each name in the name/value pairs, with the prefix WWW_ prepended to each name. Each value in the name/value pair is then assigned to its respective environment variable. So, for example, if you had a name in a form called "username," the resulting environment variable uncgi created would be WWW_username. Once you've got the environment variables, you can test them just as you would any other variable.

You can get the source for uncgi from `http://www.hyperion.com/~koreth/uncgi.html`. You'll need to know the location of your cgi-bin directory (and you'll need access to it). Compile uncgi using the instructions that come with the source, install it in your cgi-bin directory, and you're ready to go.

Exercise 15.1: Tell me your name.

Let's try a simple example for a form and the script to process it. You'll find that it's easier than you think.

In this example, you'll create the form shown in Figure 15.1. This form prompts you for your name.

In this form, you would enter your name and press the Submit button (or select the Submit link, in nongraphical browsers).

Tip: Most browsers provide a shortcut: If there is only one text field on the page (besides Submit), you can just press Return to activate the form.

Figure 15.1. *The Tell Me Your Name form.*

The input is sent to the script, which sends back an HTML document that displays a hello message with your name in it (Figure 15.2).

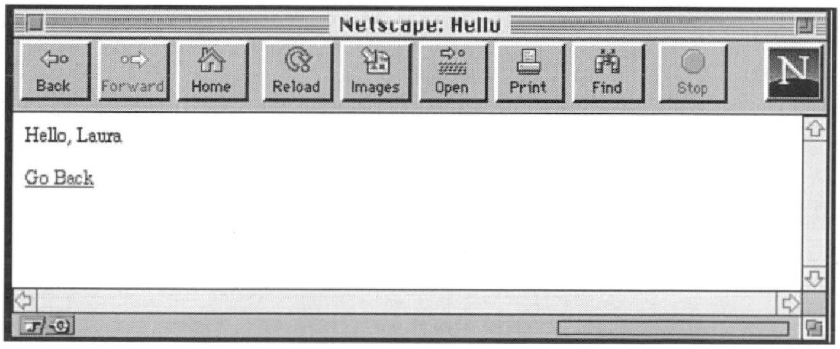

Figure 15.2. *The result of the name form.*

What if you didn't type anything at the Enter your Name prompt? The script would send you the response shown in Figure 15.3.

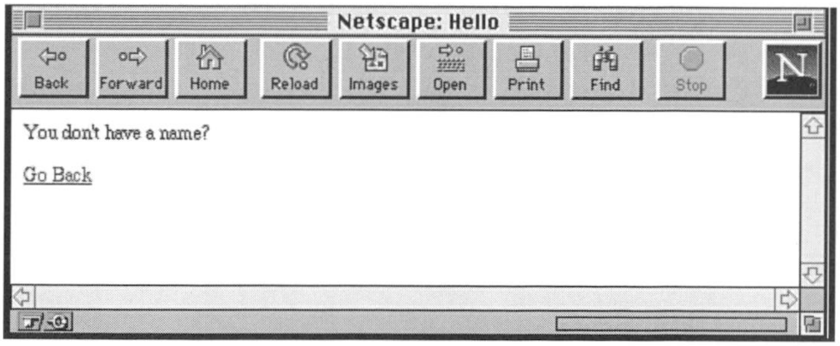

Figure 15.3. *Another result.*

The Layout

First, let's create the HTML page for this form. As with all HTML documents, start with a basic framework, with just a single level-two heading that says "Who are you?"

```
<HTML><HEAD>
<TITLE>Tell Me Your Name</TITLE>
</HEAD><BODY>
<H2>Who are you?</H2>
</BODY>
</HTML>
```

Now, add the form.

To create a form, you use the <FORM> tag to indicate that the following content is a form. <FORM> is a two-sided tag, and all the elements of the form should be included inside the opening and closing tags. You can include multiple different forms in one document, but you can't nest forms—that is, you can't include a <FORM> tag inside another FORM.

The opening tag of the FORM element usually includes two attributes: the METHOD and the ACTION. The METHOD attribute can be either GET or POST, as I described earlier in this section. The default is GET, so if you want to use POST, be sure and include METHOD=POST in your <FORM> tag.

The ACTION attribute indicates the script that will be called to process the form when it's submitted. The ACTION can be indicated by a relative path or by a full URL on your server or somewhere else. For example, the following <FORM> tag would call a script called form-name in a cgi-bin directory one level up from the current directory.

```
<FORM METHOD="POST" ACTION="../cgi-bin/form-name">
</FORM>
```

If you're using uncgi to decode form input, as I am in these examples, things are slightly different. To make uncgi work properly, you call uncgi first, and then append the name of the actual script as if uncgi were a directory, like this:

```
<FORM METHOD="POST" ACTION="../cgi-bin/uncgi/form-name">
</FORM>
```

And now with the form framework in place, we can add the elements of the form. Note that the <FORM> doesn't specify the appearance and layout of the form; you'll have to use other HTML tags for that.

The first element inside the form is the text-entry area for the name. First, include the prompt, just as you would any other line of text in HTML:

```
<P>Enter your Name:
```

And then add the HTML code that indicates a text input field:

```
<P>Enter your Name: <INPUT NAME="theName"></P>
```

The <INPUT> tag indicates a simple form element. (There are also several other form elements that use tags other than <INPUT>, but <INPUT> is the most common one.) <INPUT> usually takes at least two attributes: TYPE and NAME.

The TYPE is the kind of form element this is. There are several choices, including "text" for text-entry fields, "radio" for radio buttons, and "check" for check boxes. If you leave the TYPE attribute out, as we've done here, the element will be a text entry field.

The NAME element indicates the name of this element. As I noted before, your CGI script receives the input from the form as a series of name and value pairs. The value is the actual value your reader enters; the name is the value of this attribute. You can put anything you want here, but as with all good programming conventions, it's most useful if you use a descriptive name. Here we've picked the name theName. (Descriptive, yes?) You'll want to note down the names you use for each element, because you'll need them when you create the script to process the form.

Now add the final form element: the submit button (or link). Most forms require the use of a submit button; however, if you only have one text field in the form, you can leave it off. The form will be submitted when the reader presses Return.

```
<P><INPUT TYPE="submit"></P>
```

You'll use the <INPUT> tag for this element as well. The TYPE attribute is set to the special type of "submit," which creates a submit button for the form. The submit button doesn't require a name because there's no value attached to it.

It's a good practice to always include a submit button on your form, even if there's only one text field. The submit button is so common your readers may become confused if it's not there.

Note that each element includes tags for formatting, just as if this were text; form elements follow the same rules as text in terms of how your browser formats them. Without the <P> tags, you'd end up with all the elements in the form on the same line.

So now you have a simple form with two elements. The final HTML code to create this form looks like this:

```
<HTML><HEAD>
<TITLE>Tell Me Your Name</TITLE>
</HEAD><BODY>
<H2>Who are you?</H2>
<FORM METHOD="POST" ACTION="../cgi-bin/uncgi/form-name">
<P>Enter your Name: <INPUT NAME="theName"></P>
<P><INPUT TYPE="submit"></P>
</FORM>
</BODY></HTML>
```

15

The Script

Once you have a form in an HTML document, you need a CGI script on the server side to process the form input. Like the CGI scripts you learned about in the last chapter, the output from your script will be passed back to the server, so everything you learned about the Content-type headers and generating HTML output applies to form scripts as well.

The first step in a form script is usually to decode the information that was passed to your script through the POST method. In this example, however, because we're using uncgi to decode form input, the form decoding has already been done for you. Remember how you put uncgi in the ACTION attribute to the form, followed by the name of your script? What happens there is that when the form input is submitted, the server passes that input to the uncgi program, which decodes the form input for you, and then calls your script with everything already decoded. Now, at the start of your script, all the name/value pairs are there for you to use.

Moving on, print out the usual CGI headers and HTML code to begin the page:

```
echo Content-type: text/html
echo
cat << EOF
    <HTML><HEAD>
    <TITLE>Hello</TITLE>
    <BODY>
    <P>
EOF
```

Now comes the meat of the script. You have two branches to deal with: one to accuse the reader of not entering a name, and one to say hello when they do.

The value of the theName element, as you named the text field in your form, is contained in the WWW_theName environment variable. Using a simple Bourne shell test (-z), you can see whether this environment variable is empty and include the appropriate response in the output:

```
if [ ! -z "$WWW_theName" ]; then
    echo "Hello, "
    echo $WWW_theName
else
    echo "You don't have a name?"
fi
```

Finally, add the last bit of HTML code to include the "go back" link. This link points back to the original form.

```
cat << EOF
</P>
<P><A HREF="../lemay/name1.html">Go Back</A><P>
</BODY></HTML>
EOF
```

Like all CGI scripts, the script to process your form must be executable and installed in your cgi-bin directory. And that's it! You have both parts, and they've been linked together so that your form input gets processed and you get a response back. You now know just about all you need to know to handle forms and their interaction with CGI scripts. That wasn't bad at all, was it?

Simple Form Layout

So now that you've got the basics down, I'm sure you want to know exactly what kind of nifty interface elements you can put in a form.

In this section, you'll learn about the <INPUT> tag and the simple form elements you can create with it. There are a few other elements you can use for complex form input; you'll learn about those later on in the chapter.

Each of the elements described in this section goes inside a <FORM>...</FORM> tag, which you learned about in the previous exercise. In these examples, the form calls a script called test-cgi, which does nothing except return the values it is given.

The Submit Button

Each form can have one, and only one, submit button (or link in nongraphical browsers; for the sake of simplicity, let's just call them buttons). To create a submit button, use "submit" as the TYPE attribute in an <INPUT> tag:

```
<INPUT TYPE="SUBMIT">
```

You can change the label text of the button by using the VALUE attribute:

```
<INPUT TYPE="SUBMIT" VALUE="Submit Query">
```

This input and output example shows two simple forms with submit buttons; one with a default button and one with a custom label. Figure 15.4 shows the output in Netscape, and Figure 15.5 shows the output in Lynx.

Input

```
<FORM METHOD=POST ACTION="../cgi-bin/uncgi/test-cgi">
<INPUT TYPE="SUBMIT">
</FORM>
<UL>
<FORM METHOD=POST ACTION="../cgi-bin/uncgi/test-cgi">
<INPUT TYPE="SUBMIT" VALUE="Press Here">
</FORM>
```

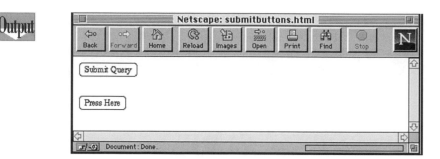

Figure 15.4. *The output in Netscape.*

```
                                                          Submit
                                                   Press Here




















<Form submit button>   Use right-arrow or <return> to submit form.
```

Figure 15.5. *The output in Lynx.*

Text Input Fields

Text fields enable your reader to type text into a single-line field. For multiple-line fields, use the `<TEXTAREA>` element, described later in this chapter.

To create a text-entry field, you can either use `TYPE="text"` in the `<INPUT>` tag, or leave off the `TYPE` specification altogether. The default `TYPE` for the `<INPUT>` tag is text. You must also include a `NAME` attribute. `NAME` indicates the name of this field as passed to the script processing the form.

```
<INPUT TYPE="text" NAME="myText">
```

You can also include the attributes `SIZE` and `MAXLENGTH` in the `<INPUT>` tag. `SIZE` indicates the length of the text-entry field, in characters; the field is 20 characters by default. Your readers can enter as many characters as they want. The field will scroll horizontally as your reader types. Try to keep the `SIZE` under 50 characters so that it will fit on most screens.

```
<INPUT TYPE="text" NAME="longText" SIZE="50">
```

MAXLENGTH enables you to limit the number of characters that your reader can type into a text field (refusing any further characters). If MAXLENGTH is less than SIZE, browsers will sometimes draw a text field as large as MAXLENGTH.

In addition to regular text fields, there are also password fields, indicated by TYPE=password. Password text fields are identical to ordinary text fields, except that all the characters typed are echoed back in the browser (masked) as asterisks or bullets. (See Figure 15.6.)

```
<INPUT TYPE="PASSWORD" NAME="passwd">
```

Figure 15.6. *Password fields.*

> **Note:** Despite the masking of characters in the browser, password fields are not secure. The password is sent to the server in clear text; that is, anyone could intercept the password and be able to read it. The masking is simply a convenience.

This input and output example shows several text fields, and their result in Netscape (Figure 15.7) and Lynx (Figure 15.8).

Input
```
<FORM METHOD=POST ACTION="../cgi-bin/uncgi/test-cgi">
<P>Enter your Name: <INPUT TYPE="TEXT" NAME="theName"><BR>
Enter your Age:
<INPUT TYPE="TEXT" NAME="theAge" SIZE="3" MAXLENGTH="3"><BR>
Enter your Address:
<INPUT TYPE="TEXT" NAME="theAddress" SIZE="80" ></P>
</FORM>
```

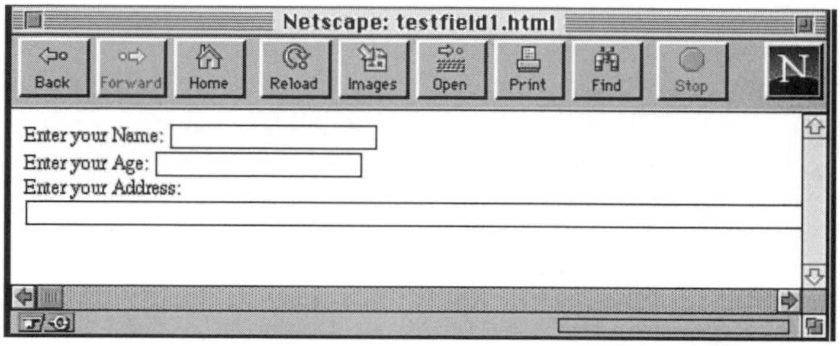

Figure 15.7. *The output in Netscape.*

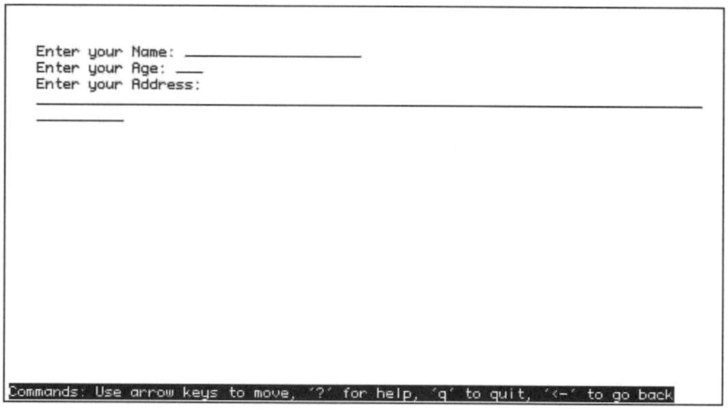

Figure 15.8. *The output in Lynx.*

Radio Buttons

Radio buttons indicate a list of items, of which only one can be chosen. If one radio button in a list is selected, all the other radio buttons in the same list are deselected.

Radio buttons use "radio" for their TYPE attribute. You indicate groups of radio buttons using the same NAME for each button in the group. In addition, each radio button in the group must each have a unique VALUE attribute, indicating the selection's value.

```
<OL>
<INPUT TYPE="radio" NAME="theType" VALUE="animal">Animal<BR>
<INPUT TYPE="radio" NAME="theType" VALUE="vegetable">Vegetable<BR>
<INPUT TYPE="radio" NAME="theType" VALUE="mineral">Mineral<BR>
</OL>
```

You can use multiple, independent groups of radio buttons by using different names for each group:

```
<OL>
<INPUT TYPE="radio" NAME="theType" VALUE="animal">Animal<BR>
<OL>
<LI><INPUT TYPE="radio" NAME="theAnimal" VALUE="cat">Cat
<LI><INPUT TYPE="radio" NAME="theAnimal" VALUE="dog">Dog
<LI><INPUT TYPE="radio" NAME="theAnimal" VALUE="fish">fish
</OL>
<INPUT TYPE="radio" NAME="theType" VALUE="vegetable">Vegetable<BR>
<INPUT TYPE="radio" NAME="theType" VALUE="mineral">Mineral<BR>
</OL>
```

When the form is submitted, a single name/value pair for the group of buttons is passed to the script. That pair includes the NAME attribute for each group of radio buttons and the VALUE attribute of the button that is currently selected.

Here's an input and output example that shows two groups of radio buttons, and how they look in Netscape (Figure 15.9) and Lynx (Figure 15.10).

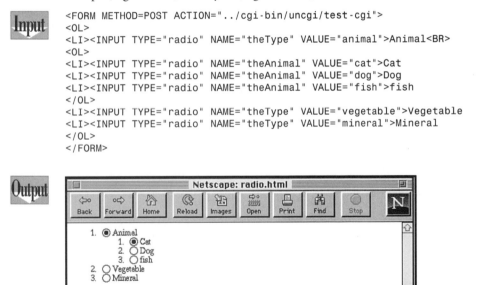

Input
```
<FORM METHOD=POST ACTION="../cgi-bin/uncgi/test-cgi">
<OL>
<LI><INPUT TYPE="radio" NAME="theType" VALUE="animal">Animal<BR>
<OL>
<LI><INPUT TYPE="radio" NAME="theAnimal" VALUE="cat">Cat
<LI><INPUT TYPE="radio" NAME="theAnimal" VALUE="dog">Dog
<LI><INPUT TYPE="radio" NAME="theAnimal" VALUE="fish">fish
</OL>
<LI><INPUT TYPE="radio" NAME="theType" VALUE="vegetable">Vegetable
<LI><INPUT TYPE="radio" NAME="theType" VALUE="mineral">Mineral
</OL>
</FORM>
```

Figure 15.9. *The output in Netscape.*

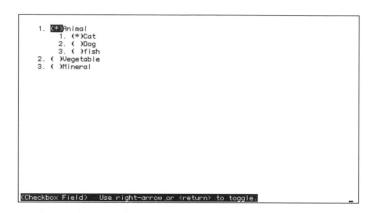

Figure 15.10. *The output in Lynx.*

Check Boxes

Check boxes make it possible to choose multiple items in a list. Each check box can either be on or off. Check boxes use `"checkbox"` as their TYPE attribute:

```
<UL>
<LI><INPUT TYPE="checkbox" NAME="red">Red
<LI><INPUT TYPE="checkbox" NAME="green">Green
<LI><INPUT TYPE="checkbox" NAME="blue">Blue
</UL>
```

When the form is submitted, only the name/value pairs for each selected check box are submitted (unchecked check boxes are ignored). By default, each name/value pair for a check box has a value of ON. You can also use the VALUE attribute to indicate the value you would rather see in your script:

```
<UL>
<LI><INPUT TYPE="checkbox" NAME="red" VALUE="checked">Red
<LI><INPUT TYPE="checkbox" NAME="green" VALUE="checked">Green
<LI><INPUT TYPE="checkbox" NAME="blue" VALUE="checked">Blue
</UL>
```

You can also implement check box lists such that elements have the same NAME attribute, similar to radio buttons. Notice, however, that this means that your script will end up with several name/value pairs with the same name (each check box that is selected will be submitted to the script), and you'll have to take that into account when you process the input in your script.

Here's another one of those input and output examples, with a series of check boxes and how they look in Netscape (Figure 15.11) and Lynx (Figure 15.12).

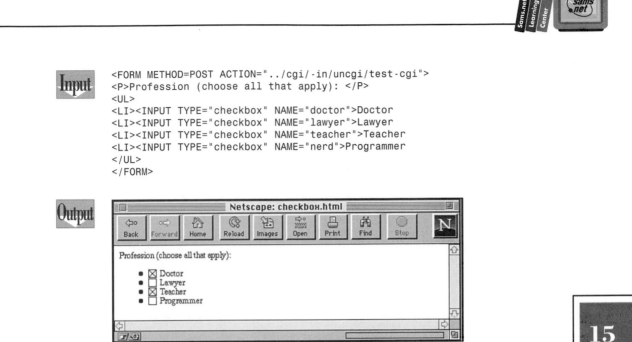

```
<FORM METHOD=POST ACTION="../cgi-in/uncgi/test-cgi">
<P>Profession (choose all that apply): </P>
<UL>
<LI><INPUT TYPE="checkbox" NAME="doctor">Doctor
<LI><INPUT TYPE="checkbox" NAME="lawyer">Lawyer
<LI><INPUT TYPE="checkbox" NAME="teacher">Teacher
<LI><INPUT TYPE="checkbox" NAME="nerd">Programmer
</UL>
</FORM>
```

Figure 15.11. *The output in Netscape.*

Figure 15.12. *The output in Lynx.*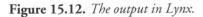

Setting and Resetting Default Values

Each form element can have a default value that is entered or selected when the form is viewed:

☐ For text fields, use the VALUE attribute with a string for the default value. The VALUE is entered in the box automatically when the form is displayed.

☐ For check boxes and radio buttons, the attribute CHECKED selects that element by default.

393

In addition to the default values for each element, you can include a reset button, similar to the submit button, on your form. The reset button clears all selections or entries your reader has made and resets them to their default values. Also like submit, a VALUE attribute indicates the label for the button.

```
<INPUT TYPE="RESET" VALUE="Reset Defaults">
```

▼ Exercise 15.2: The Surrealist Census.

Now, let's create a more complicated example. In this example, The Surrealist Society of America has created a small census, via an interactive form on the World Wide Web. Figure 15.13 shows that census.

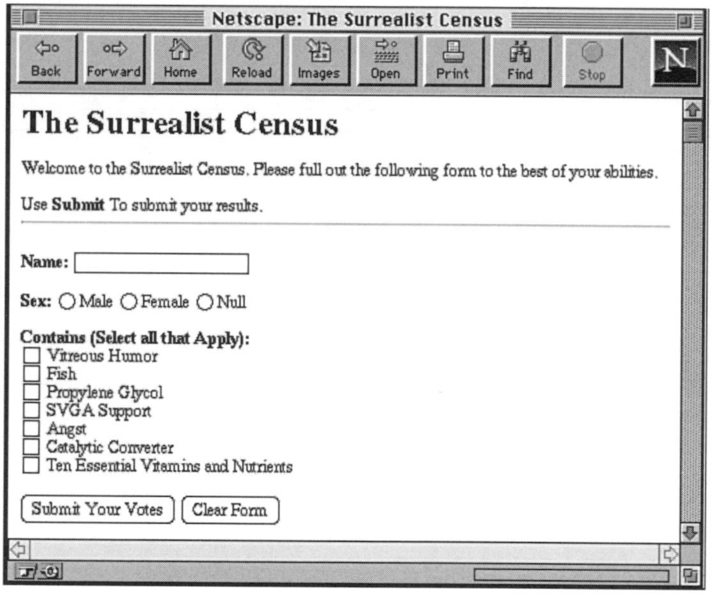

Figure 15.13. *The Surrealist Society's census form.*

After the reader fills out the form and presses Submit Your Votes, the CGI script for the form processes the input and returns a formatted report of the votes the reader has made, as shown in Figure 15.14.

Netscape: The Surrealist Census: Thank You

Thank you for voting!

Your responses were:

- Your name is Laura
- Your Sex is female
- You contain:
  - Vitreous Humor
  - SVGA Support
  - Angst
  - Ten Essential Vitamins and Minerals

Go Back

Figure 15.14. *The result of the census.*

The Form

The form to create the census falls roughly into three parts: the name field, the radio buttons for sex, and the check boxes for the things your reader contains.

Start with the basic structure, as with all HTML documents. Remember, we'll call uncgi in the action as we did in the last example:

```
<HTML><HEAD>
<TITLE>The Surrealist Census</TITLE>
</HEAD><BODY>
<H1>The Surrealist Census</H1>
<P>Welcome to the Surrealist Census. Please fill out the following
form to the best of your abilities.</P>
<P>Use <STRONG>Submit</STRONG> To submit your results.
<HR>
<FORM METHOD="POST" ACTION="../cgi-bin/uncgi/census">

</FORM>
<HH>
</BODY></HTML>
```

15

Notice that I've included rule lines before and after the form. Because the form is a discrete element on the page, it makes sense to visually separate it from the other parts of the page. This is especially important if you have multiple forms on the same page; separating them with rule lines visually divides them.

Now, let's add the first element for the reader's name. This is essentially the same element that we used in the previous example, with the name of the element theName:

```
<P><STRONG>Name: </STRONG><INPUT TYPE="TEXT" NAME="theName"></P>
```

The second part of the form is a series of radio buttons for "Sex." There are three: Male, Female, and Null (remember, this is the Surrealist Census). Since radio buttons are exclusive (only one can be selected at a time), we'll give all three buttons the same value for NAME (theSex).

```
<P><STRONG>Sex: </STRONG>
<INPUT TYPE="radio" NAME="theSex" VALUE="male">Male
<INPUT TYPE="radio" NAME="theSex" VALUE="female">Female
<INPUT TYPE="radio" NAME="theSex" VALUE="null">Null
</P>
```

Even though each <INPUT> tag is arranged on a separate line, the radio button elements are formatted on a single line. Always remember that form elements do not imply formatting; you have to include other HTML tags to arrange them in the right spots.

Now, let's add the last part of the form: the list of "Contains" check boxes:

```
<P><STRONG>Contains (Select all that Apply): </STRONG><BR>
<INPUT TYPE="checkbox" NAME="humor">Vitreous Humor<BR>
<INPUT TYPE="checkbox" NAME="fish">Fish<BR>
<INPUT TYPE="checkbox" NAME="glycol">Propylene Glycol<BR>
<INPUT TYPE="checkbox" NAME="svga">SVGA Support<BR>
<INPUT TYPE="checkbox" NAME="angst">Angst<BR>
<INPUT TYPE="checkbox" NAME="catcon">Catalytic Converter<BR>
<INPUT TYPE="checkbox" NAME="vitamin">Ten Essential Vitamins and Nutrients<BR>
</P>
```

Unlike radio buttons, any number of check boxes can be selected, so each value of NAME is unique. This will be important later when you write the script to process the form.

Finally, add the submit button so that the form can be submitted to the server. A nice touch is to also include a "Reset Form" button. Both buttons have special labels specific to this form:

```
<P><INPUT TYPE="SUBMIT" VALUE="Submit Your Votes">
<INPUT TYPE="RESET" VALUE="Clear Form"></P>
```

Whew! With all the elements in place, here's what the entire HTML file for the form looks like:

```
<HTML><HEAD>
<TITLE>The Surrealist Census</TITLE>
</HEAD><BODY>
```

```
<H1>The Surrealist Census</H1>
<P>Welcome to the Surrealist Census. Please fill out the following
form to the best of your abilities.</P>
<P>Use <STRONG>Submit</STRONG> To submit your results.</P>
<HR>
<FORM METHOD="POST" ACTION="../cgi-bin/census">
<P><STRONG>Name: </STRONG><INPUT TYPE="TEXT" NAME="theName"></P>
<P><STRONG>Sex: </STRONG>
<INPUT TYPE="radio" NAME="theSex" VALUE="male">Male
<INPUT TYPE="radio" NAME="theSex" VALUE="female">Female
<INPUT TYPE="radio" NAME="theSex" VALUE="null">Null
</P>
<P><STRONG>Contains (Select all that Apply): </STRONG><BR>
<INPUT TYPE="checkbox" NAME="humor">Vitreous Humor<BR>
<INPUT TYPE="checkbox" NAME="fish">Fish<BR>
<INPUT TYPE="checkbox" NAME="glycol">Propylene Glycol<BR>
<INPUT TYPE="checkbox" NAME="svga">SVGA Support<BR>
<INPUT TYPE="checkbox" NAME="angst">Angst<BR>
<INPUT TYPE="checkbox" NAME="catcon">Catalytic Converter<BR>
<INPUT TYPE="checkbox" NAME="vitamin">Ten Essential Vitamins and Nutrients<BR>
</P>
<P><INPUT TYPE="SUBMIT" VALUE="Submit Your Votes">
<INPUT TYPE="RESET" VALUE="Clear Form"></P>
</FORM>
<HR>
</BODY></HTML>
```

The Script

And now, let's write the script to process the form you've just created. The output of the script
essentially just prints the values from the form in a nice bulleted list. This script will look very
similar to the script you created in the last example, so we'll start with a copy of that script,
modified slightly to fit the output we want to create from this form:

```
#!/bin/sh

echo Content-type: text/html
echo

cat << EOF
    <HTML><HEAD>
    <TITLE>The Surrealist Census: Thank You</TITLE>
    </HEAD><BODY>
    <H1>Thank you for voting!</H1>
    <P>Your responses were:</P>
    <UL>
EOF

if [ ! -z "$WWW_theName" ]; then
    echo "<LI>Your name is "
    echo $WWW_theName
else
    echo "<LI>You don't have a name."
fi
```

That `if` statement should look real familiar. For the most part it's the same thing we did in the last exercise. Now, let's add a bullet for the sex the reader chose. Remember, each value of `NAME` in the original form is turned into an enviornment variable with `WWW_` prepended, so the value of these radio buttons (which were named `theSex`) will be contained in the `WWW_theSex` variable. All the names in the form will match the variables in the script.

For the `theSex` name/value pair, you don't have to test to see if `theSex` is empty; the radio button structure means at least one value must be submitted with the form, so all you really have to do for the Sex element is print the value:

```
echo "<LI>Your Sex is "
echo $WWW_theSex
```

And now, we'll add the Contains elements as a nested list. Because you don't know which of the check boxes were submitted, you'll have to test all of those variables—their values will be "on" if they were selected, and create output for the ones that were submitted, like this:

```
echo "<LI>You contain:"
echo "<UL>"

if [ "$WWW_humor" = "on" ]; then
echo "<LI>Vitreous Humor"
fi
if [ "$WWW_fish" = "on" ]; then
echo "<LI>Fish"
fi
```

I've only included the `if` statements for the first two tests here; the other five look exactly the same. You can check the script at the end of this section if you're really interested.

Finally, finish up the script by printing the rest of the HTML for the page. As part of this last bit of HTML, let's include a link back to the form. You should always provide some way out of the HTML files you generate from forms. Although going back to some known spot (such as the home page) would make the most sense, even going back to the form is better than nothing.

```
cat << EOF
    </UL></UL>
    <P><A HREF="../lemay/census.html">Go Back</A><P>
    </BODY></HTML>
EOF
```

Here's the full script for processing the census form:

```
#!/bin/sh

echo Content-type: text/html
echo

cat << EOF
    <HTML><HEAD>
```

```
    <TITLE>The Surrealist Census: Thank You</TITLE>
    </HEAD><BODY>
    <H1>Thank you for voting!</H1>
    <P>Your responses were:</P>
    <UL>
EOF

if [ ! -z "$WWW_theName" ]; then
echo "<LI>Your name is "
echo $WWW_theName
else
echo "<LI>You don't have a name."
fi

echo "<LI>Your Sex is "
echo $WW_theSex
echo "<LI>You contain:"
echo "<UL>"

if [ "$WWW_humor" = "on" ]; then
echo "<LI>Vitreous Humor"
fi
if [ "$WWW_fish" = "on" ]; then
echo "<LI>Fish"
fi
if [ "$WWW_glycol" = "on" ]; then
echo "<LI>Propylene Glycol"
fi
if [ "$WWW_svga" = "on" ]; then
echo "<LI>SVGA Support"
fi
if [ "$WWW_angst" = "on" ]; then
echo "<LI>Angst"
fi
if [ "$WWW_catcon" = "on" ]; then
echo "<LI>Catalytic Converter"
fi
if [ "$WWW_vitamin" = "on" ]; then
echo "<LI>Ten Essential Vitamins and Minerals"
fi

cat << EOF
    </UL></UL>
    <P><A HREF="../lemay/name1.html">Go Back</A><P>
    </BODY></HTML>
EOF
```

More Forms Layout

In addition to the <INPUT> tag with its many options, there are also two other tags that create
form elements: SELECT, which has the ability to create pull-down menus and scrolling lists,
and TEXTAREA, for allowing the reader to enter long blocks of text.

This section describes these other two tags. It also explains how to create "hidden" elements—form elements that don't actually show up on the page, but exist in the form nonetheless.

Selections

Selections enable the reader of a form to select one or more items from a menu or a scrolling list. They're similar to radio buttons or check boxes, in a different form.

Selections are indicated by the <SELECT> tag, and individual options within the selection by the <OPTION> tag. The <SELECT> tag also contains a NAME attribute to hold its value when the form is submitted.

<SELECT> and <OPTION> work much like lists do, with the entire selection surrounded by the opening and closing <SELECT> tags. Each option begins with a single-sided <OPTION>, like this:

```
<P>Select a hair color:
<SELECT NAME="hcolor">
<OPTION>Black
<OPTION>Blonde
<OPTION>Brown
<OPTION>Red
<OPTION>Blue
</SELECT></P>
```

When the form is submitted, the value of the entire selection is the text that follows the selected <OPTION> tag—in this case, Brown, Red, Blue, and so on. You can also use the VALUE attribute with each <OPTION> tag to indicate a different value.

Selections of this sort are generally formatted in graphical browsers as pop-up menus, as shown in Figure 15.15.

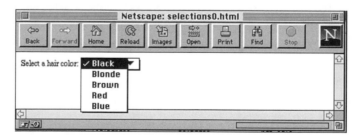

Figure 15.15. *Selections.*

You can set the default item to be initially selected by using the SELECTED attribute, part of the <OPTION> tag:

```
<P>Select a hair color:
<SELECT NAME="hcolor">
<OPTION>Black
<OPTION>Blonde
<OPTION SELECTED>Brown
<OPTION>Red
<OPTION>Blue
</SELECT></P>
```

By default, selections act like radio buttons; that is, only one item can be selected at a time. You can change the behavior of selections to allow multiple options to be selected by using the MULTIPLE attribute, part of the <SELECT> tag:

```
<P>Shopping List:
<SELECT NAME="shopping" MULTIPLE>
<OPTION>Butter
<OPTION>Milk
<OPTION>Flour
<OPTION>Eggs
<OPTION>Cheese
<OPTION>Beer
<OPTION>Pasta
<OPTION>Mushrooms
</SELECT></P>
```

Be careful when you use MULTIPLE in the script that will process this form. Remember that each selection list only has one possible NAME. This means that if you have multiple values in a selection list all of those values will be submitted to your script, and the program you use to decode the input might store those in some special way. For example, uncgi stores them in the same environment variable separated by hash signs.

Note: Each browser determines how the reader makes multiple choices. Usually, the reader must hold down a key while making multiple selections, but that particular key may vary from browser to browser.

The optional <SELECT> attribute usually displays the selection as a scrolling list in graphical browsers, with the number of elements in the SIZE attribute visible on the form itself. (Figure 15.16 shows an example.)

```
<P>Shopping List:
<SELECT NAME="shopping" MULTIPLE SIZE="5">
<OPTION>Butter
<OPTION>Milk
<OPTION>Flour
<OPTION>Eggs
<OPTION>Cheese
<OPTION>Beer
<OPTION>Pasta
<OPTION>Mushrooms
</SELECT></P>
```

Figure 15.16. *Selections with* SIZE.

Here's an input and output example that shows a simple selection list and how it appears in Netscape (Figure 15.17).

```
<P>Select a hair color:
<SELECT NAME="hcolor">
<OPTION>Black
<OPTION>Blonde
<OPTION SELECTED>Brown
<OPTION>Red
<OPTION>Blue
</SELECT></P>
```

Figure 15.17. *The output in Netscape.*

Text Areas

Text areas are input fields in which the reader can type. Unlike regular text input fields (`<INPUT TYPE="text">`), text areas can contain many lines of text, making them extremely useful for forms that require extensive input. For example, if you wanted to create a form that enabled readers to compose electronic mail, you might use a text area for the body of the message.

To include a text area element in a form, use the `<TEXTAREA>` tag. `<TEXTAREA>` includes three attributes:

□ NAME: The name to be sent to the CGI script when the form is submitted.

□ ROWS: The height of the text area element, in rows of text.

□ COLS: The width of the text area element in columns (characters).

The <TEXTAREA> tag is a two-sided tag, and both sides must be used. If you have any default text you want to include in the text area, include it between the opening and closing tags. For example:

```
<TEXTAREA NAME="theBody" ROWS="14" COLS="50">Enter your message here.</TEXTAREA>
```

The text in a text area is generally formatted in a fixed-width font such as Courier, but it is up to the browser to decide how to format it beyond that. Some browsers will allow text wrapping in text areas, others will scroll to the right. Some will allow scrolling if the text area fills up while some others will just stop accepting input.

This input/output example shows a simple text area in Netscape (Figure 15.18) and Lynx (Figure 15.19).

```
<P>Enter any Comments you have about this Web page here:
<TEXTAREA NAME="comment" ROWS="30" COLS="60">
</TEXTAREA>
</P>
```

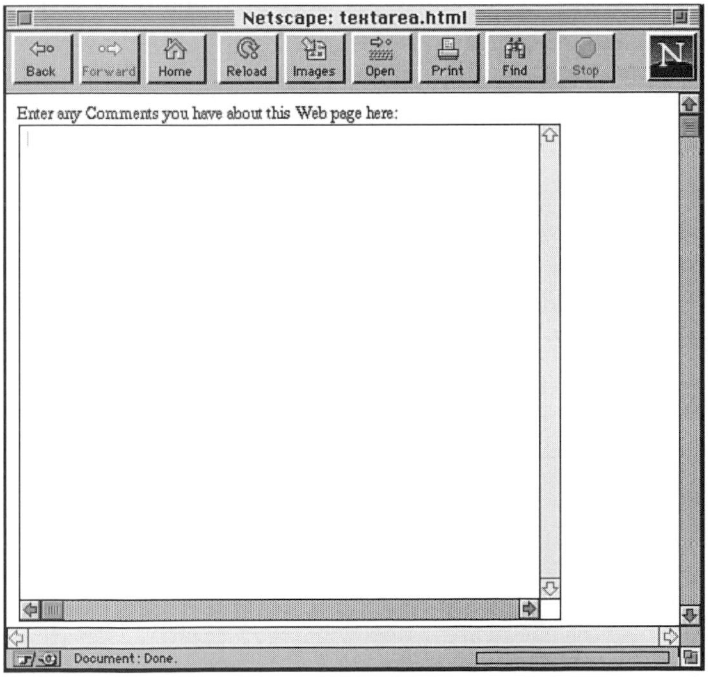

Figure 15.18. *The output in Netscape.*

Figure 15.19. *The output in Lynx.*

Hidden Fields

One value for the TYPE attribute to the <INPUT> tag is "hidden." Hidden fields do not appear on the actual form; they are invisible in the browser display. They will still appear in your HTML code if someone decides to look at the HTML source for your page.

Hidden input elements look like this:

```
<INPUT TYPE="HIDDEN" NAME="theName" VALUE="TheValue">
```

Why would you want to create a hidden form element? If it doesn't appear on the screen and the reader can't do anything with it, what's the point?

Let's take a hypothetical example. You create a simple form. In the script that processes the first form, you create a second form based on the input from the first form. The script to process the second form takes the information from both the first and second forms and creates a reply based on that information. Figure 15.20 shows how all this flows:

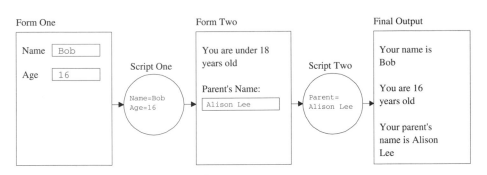

Figure 15.20. *Form to Form to Reply.*

How would you pass the information from the first form to the script that processes the second form? You can do one of two things:

- [ ] Write the information from the first form to a temporary file and then read that file back in again when the second form starts up.

- [ ] In the first script that constructs the second form, create hidden fields in the form with the appropriate information in NAME and VALUE fields. Then those names and values will be passed automatically to the second script when the reader submits the second form.

See? Hidden elements do make sense, particularly when you get involved in generating forms from forms.

What Is an Image Map?

In Chapter 9, "Using Images," you learned how to create an image that doubles as a link, simply by including the <IMG> tag inside a link (<A>) tag. By doing this, the entire image becomes a link. You could click on the image, the background, or the border, and you'd get the same effect.

In image maps, different parts of the image activate different links (Figure 15.21). Using image maps, you can create a visual hyperlinked map that links you to pages describing the regions you click. Or you could create visual metaphors for the information you're presenting: a set of books on a shelf or a photograph in which each person in the picture is individually described.

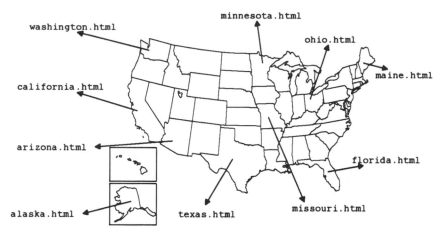

Figure 15.21. *Image maps: different places, different links.*

Image maps are a special form of CGI script. When a browser activates a link on an image map, it calls a special imagemap program as it would any other CGI script, but it also includes the x and y coordinates of where on the image the mouse was clicked. The special imagemap program then looks up a special map file that matches regions in the image to files, does some calculations to figure out which page to load, and then loads that page.

Image Maps and Text-Only Browsers

Because of the inherently graphical nature of image maps, they can only work on graphical browsers. In fact, if you try to view a document with an image map in a text-only browser such as Lynx, you don't even get an indication that the image exists. Even so, you won't be able to navigate the presentation without it.

If you decide to create a Web page with an image map on it, it is doubly important that you also create a text-only equivalent so that readers with text-only browsers can use your page. The use of image maps can very effectively lock out readers with text-only browsers; have sympathy and allow them at least some method for viewing your content.

Creating Image Maps

As with CGI scripts in general, each server has a different method of implementing image maps. The methods even vary between servers on the same platform (CERN and NCSA both have different methods of implementing image files). All servers, however, use the same basic ingredients for image maps:

- ☐ Special HTML code to indicate an image is a map
- ☐ A map file on the server that indicates regions on the image and the Web pages they point to
- ☐ An imagemapping CGI script that links it all together

This section explains how to construct clickable images in general, but will focus particular examples on the NCSA and CERN servers. If you need more information for your particular server, see the documentation that comes with that server or get help from your Web administrator.

Getting an Image

To create an image map, you'll need an image (of course). The image that serves as the map is most useful if it has several discrete visual areas that can be individually selected—for example, images with several symbolic elements, or images that can be easily broken down into polygons. Photographs make difficult image maps because their various "elements" tend to blend together or are of unusual shapes. Figures 15.22 and 15.23 show examples of good and bad images for image maps.

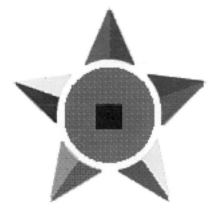

Figure 15.22. *A good image map.*

Figure 15.23. *A not-so-good image map.*

Creating a Map File

The heart of the image-map structure is a map file. Creating a map file involves sketching out the regions in your image that are clickable, finding out the coordinates that define those regions, and deciding on the HTML pages where they should point.

Note: The format of the map file depends on the imagemapping CGI script you're using on your server. In this section, I'll talk about imagemapping on the CERN and NCSA servers, and the map files that they use. If you're using a different server, you may have several different imagemapping programs to choose from with several different map formats. Check with your Web administrator or read your server documentation carefully if you're in this situation.

You can create a map file either by sketching regions and noting the coordinates or by using an imagemap-making program. The latter is easier, as the program will automatically generate a map file based on the images you draw with the mouse. The mapedit program for Windows and X, HotSpots for Windows, and WebMap for the Macintosh can all help you create map files in CERN or NCSA format.

If you need your map file in a different format, you can always write a map file yourself. Do this by first making a sketch of the regions you want to make active on your image (for example, as in Figure 15.24).

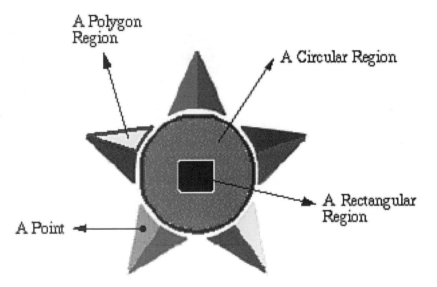

Figure 15.24. *Sketching mappable regions.*

Then, you'll need to figure out the coordinates for the endpoints of those regions. (See Figure 15.25.) Most image-editing programs have an option that will display the coordinates of the current mouse position. Use this feature to write down the appropriate coordinates.

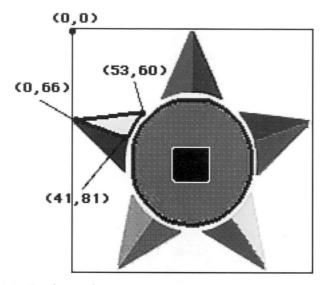

Figure 15.25. *Get the coordinates.*

For circles, note the coordinates of the center point and the radius, in pixels.

For rectangles, note the top left and bottom right corners.

For polygons, note the coordinates of each corner.

For points, note the coordinates of the point.

Note: The 0,0 origin is in the top left-hand corner of the image, and positive Y is down.

You're more than halfway there. The next step is to come up with a set of URLs to link for each region or point that is selected. You can have multiple regions pointing to the same URL, but each region must have only one link.

With all your regions, coordinates, and URLs noted, you can now write a map file for your particular server. Map files for the CERN HTTPD look something like this:

```
default URL
circle (x,y) r URL
rectangle (x,y) (x,y) URL
polygon (x1,y1) (x2,y2) ... (xN,yN) URL
```

NCSA image map files are roughly the same as CERN's, but the elements are in a different order. NCSA map files look like this:

```
default URL
circle URL x,y r
rect URL x,y x,y
poly URL x1,y1 x2,y2 ... xN,yN
point URL x,y
```

The map files for your particular imagemap program for your server may look different from this, but the essential parts are there. Substitute the values for the coordinates you noted in the previous section in each of the x or y positions (or x1, y1, and so on). You must include the parentheses in the CERN file, and the r (in the circle line) is the radius for the circle region.

The URLs you specify for either format must be either full URLs (starting with http or ftp or some other protocol), or the full path names to the files you are linking—that is, everything that you could include after the host name in a URL. You cannot specify relative path names in the image map file.

Here's a sample of a CERN map file:

```
circle (10,15) 20 /lemay/mapping.html
circle (346,23) 59 /lemay/mapping.html
polygon (192,3) (192,170) (115,217) /lemay/test/orange.html
rectangle (57,57) (100,210) /lemay/pencil.html
default /lemay/nopage.html
```

Note: CERN's map files do not include individual points.

Here's a sample of an NCSA map file:

```
circle /lemay/mapping.html 10,15 20
circle /lemay/mapping.html 346,23 59
poly /lemay/test/orange.html 192,3 192,170 115,217
rect /lemay/pencil.html 57,57 100,210
point /lemay/pencil.html 100,100
point /lemay/orange.html 200,200
```

Points, in NCSA maps, allow you to specify that a given mouse click, if it doesn't land directly on a region, will activate the nearest point. Points are useful for photographs or other images with nondiscrete elements, or for a finer granularity than just "everything not in a region."

The order of regions in the map file is relevant; the further up a region is in the file, the higher precedence it has for mouse clicks. If a part of the region is selected that occurs on overlapping regions, the first region listed in the map file is the one that is activated.

Finally, both map files include a "default" region, with no coordinates, just a URL. Default is used when a mouse click that is not inside a region is selected; it provides a "catchall" for the parts of the image that do not point to a specific link. Note that if you use an NCSA map file and you include default you shouldn't include any points. The existence of point elements precludes that of default.

Installing the Map File and the Imagemap CGI Program

Creating the imagemap file is the hardest part of making an image map. The only thing left to do is to store the map file in a central location on your server. After that, just hook up the image on your Web page to the imagemapping CGI program and to the map file.

Save your map file with a descriptive name (say, `myimage.map`). Where you store the map file isn't important, but I like to put my map files in a directory called `maps` at the top level of my Web files (the same level as the cgi-bin directory).

Finally, you'll need your imagemap program installed in your cgi-bin directory. In CERN, that program is called htimage, in NCSA it's called imagemap.

> **Note:** Be careful with the NCSA server and the imagemap program. Older versions of imagemap were more difficult to work with and required an extra configuration file; the program that comes with the 1.4 version of the server works much better. If you aren't running the most recent version of NCSA's server, you can get it from `http://hoohoo.ncsa.uiuc.edu/docs/setup/admin/imagemap.txt`.

Linking it All Together

So now you have an image, a map file, and an imagemap CGI program. All that's left is to hook it all up. In your HTML document that contains the image map, you'll use both the `<A>` and `<IMG>` tags together to create the effect of the clickable image. Here's one for the CERN Imagemap program:

```
<A HREF="../cgi-bin/htimage/maps/myimage.map">
<IMG SRC="image.gif" ISMAP>
</A>
```

Notice several things about this link. First of all, the link to the imagemap script (`htimage`) is indicated the way you would expect, but then the path to the map file is appended onto the end of it. The path to the map file should be a full path name from the root of your Web directory (everything after the hostname in your URL), in this case, `/maps/myimage.map`.

The second part of the map is the ISMAP attribute to the `<IMG>` tag. This is a simple attribute that indicates to the browser and the server to send individual mouse-click coordinates to the CGI script for processing.

Here's one for NCSA's server. It's identical to the previous example, except the name of the imagemap program is different.

```
<A HREF="../cgi-bin/imagemap/maps/myimage.map">
<IMG SRC="image.gif" ISMAP>
</A>
```

And now, try it out! Load your HTML file in the browser (it'll have to be installed on your server), and try clicking on the image map. You should be able to select various bits of the image using the mouse and have the coordinates sent as part of the URL to the imagemapping script, which in turn uses the map file to find an appropriate action for each region.

Note: If you're running the NCSA server and you don't have the newest version of imagemap you will get errors that imagemap "Cannot Open Configuration File," when you try to select portions of your image. If you get these errors, check with your Web administrator.

Exercise 15.3: A clickable bookshelf.

Image maps can get pretty hairy. The map files are prone to error if you don't have your areas clearly outlined and everything installed in the right place. In this exercise, we'll take a simple image and create an entry for both the CERN and NCSA map files for an area of an image so you can get a feel for what the map files look like and how to create them.

The image we'll use here is a simple color rendering of a bunch of books (Figure 15.26). You can't see the colors here, but from left to right, they are red, blue, yellow, and green.

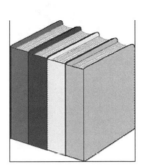

Figure 15.26. *The bookshelf image.*

First, let's define the regions that will be clickable on this image. Because of the angular nature of the books, it's most appropriate to create polygon-shaped regions. Figure 15.27 shows an example of the sort of region it makes sense to create on the image, this one is for the leftmost (red) book. You can define similar regions for each of the books in the stack. (Go ahead and draw on the figure here in the book, if you want to. I won't mind.)

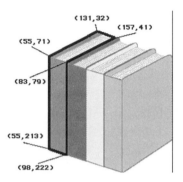

Figure 15.27. *The bookshelf with an area defined.*

With an idea of the areas for each region, now let's find the coordinates of the corners. You can use a mapping program for such as mapedit or WebMap, or you can do it by hand. I used Adobe Photoshop to find the coordinates using the "Info" window, and came up with the coordinates shown in Figure 15.28. If you had the file, you could also find coordinates for each of the polygon regions on each of the books as well.

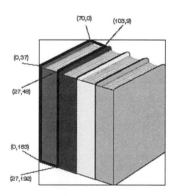

Figure 15.28. *The bookshelf with coordinates.*

With regions and a list of coordinates, all you need now are Web pages to jump to when the appropriate book is selected. These can be any documents, or they can be scripts; anything you can call from a browser you can use as a jump destination. For this example, I've created

a document called `redbook.html` in my Web directory (`/lemay` from the top of the Web root). This is the page that we'll define as the endpoint of the jump when the red book is selected.

All that's left is to create the entry in the map file for this area with the coordinates and the file to link. In the CERN map file, it would look like this:

```
polygon (78,0) (0,37) (0,183) (27,192) (27,48) (103,9) /lemay/redbook.html
```

And in NCSA's map file, the same information looks like this:

```
poly /lemay/redbook.html 78,0 0,37 0,183 27,192 27,48 103,9
```

Note that the URLs in the map file have to be absolute path names from the top of the Web root (not from the top of the file system). They cannot be relative URLs from the map file; image maps don't work like that. In this case, my `lemay` directory is at the Web root, and the `redbook.html` file is in that directory, so the URL for the purposes of the map file is `/lemay/redbook.html`

Now that you've done it for the red book, you can create identical entries for the other books in the image (blue, yellow, green). Don't forget to include a default line in the map file to map mouse clicks that don't hit any books (here, a file called notabook.html):

```
default /lemay/notabook.html
```

Now, save your map file to your map directory (or wherever you keep your maps) and create a Web page with the books on it, with the ISMAP attribute to imagemap and the link to the imagemapping CGI program. Here I've used NCSA's server with its `imagemap` script:

```
<A HREF="../cgi-bin/imagemap/maps/books.map">
<IMG SRC="image.gif" ISMAP>
</A>
```

And that's it—with everything connected, clicking on the image on each book should load the page for that part of the image.

Summary

Forms and image maps are two of the most interesting innovations that have been added to Web publishing in recent times. With the advent of these features, the Web changed from being a publishing medium with hypertext links to a fully interactive environment with the potential for being something entirely new.

In this chapter, you've learned how to lay out form elements in HTML as well as how to process the results on the server when that form is submitted. You should now know the difference between GET and POST and be able to explain why one is better. And you know the difference between a CERN and NCSA image map, how to create both of them, and how to connect clickable images, map files, and CGI scripts on the appropriate servers.

In addition, you've learned about the remaining tags defined by the current version of HTML—those that define the elements of a form. Table 15.1 presents a quick summary of all the tags and attributes you've learned about in this chapter.

Table 15.1. HTML tags from Chapter 15.

Tag	Use
`<FORM>...</FORM>`	A form. You can have multiple forms within a document, but forms cannot be nested.
`METHOD`	An attribute of the `<FORM>` tag, indicating the method with which the form input is given to the script that processes the form. Possible values are `GET` and `POST`.
`ACTION`	An attribute of the `<FORM>` tag indicating the script to process the form input. Contains a relative path or URL to the script.
`<INPUT>`	A form element.
`TYPE`	An attribute of the `<INPUT>` tag indicating the type of form element. Possible values are `SUBMIT`, `RESET`, `TEXT`, `RADIO`, `CHECKBOX` and `HIDDEN`.
	`SUBMIT` creates a button to submit the form to the script which processes the input.
	`RESET` creates a button that resets the default values of the form, if any.
	`TEXT` creates a single-line text field.
	`RADIO` creates a radio button.
	`CHECKBOX` creates a check box
	`HIDDEN` creates a form element that is not presented but has a name and a value that can then be passed onto the script that processes the form input.
`NAME`	An attribute of the `<INPUT>`, `<SELECT>`, and `<TEXTAREA>` tags. Indicates the name of the variable that holds the eventual value of this element, as submitted to the script.
`VALUE`	An attribute of the `<INPUT>` tag, indicating the default value for the form element, if any, or the value submitted with the `NAME` to the script. For `SUBMIT` and `RESET` buttons, `VALUE` indicates the label of the button.
`SIZE`	An attribute of the `<INPUT>` tag used only when `TYPE` is `TEXT`. Indicates the size of the text field, in characters.

MAXLENGTH	An attribute of the <INPUT> tag used only when TYPE is TEXT. Indicates the maximum number of characters this text field will accept.
CHECKED	An attribute of the <INPUT> tag used only when TYPE is CHECKBOX or RADIO. Indicates that this element is selected by default.
<SELECT>	A menu or scrolling list of items. Individual items are indicated by the <OPTION> tag.
MULTIPLE	An attribute of the <SELECT> tag indicating that multiple items in the list can be selected.
SIZE	An attribute of the <SELECT> tag that causes the list of items to be displayed as a scrolling list with the number of items indicated by SIZE visible.
<OPTION>	Individual items within a <SELECT> element.
SELECTED	An attribute of the <OPTION> tag indicating that this item is selected by default.
<TEXTAREA>	A text-entry field with multiple lines.
ROWS	An attribute of the <TEXTAREA> tag indicating the height of the text field, in rows.
COLS	An attribute of the <TEXTAREA> tag indicating the width of the text field, in characters.

15

Q&A

Q Is there any reason to use the GET method in my forms?

A As I noted earlier in this chapter, it's a better idea to use POST, since processing the input from POST isn't much more complicated and allows you to create forms of any length. If you use GET, however, the input to your form will be encoded into the URL where you can see it, or, more usefully, where you can save it to regular link or put it in your hotlist. The next time you call that URL with the form input appended to it, you can bypass filling out the form and go back to that same place. You may find a use for this in your presentations.

Q Do I need a server to create image maps? I want to create and test all this offline, the same way I did for regular HTML files.

A Because image maps require a CGI script on the server to interpret your mouse clicks and read from the map file, the answer is no. You must have a server for all this to work.

HTML 3.0 defines several ways of creating imagemaps that do not require a server. Much work is being done in this area, so expect it to be easier in the future.

Q   **My image maps aren't working.**

A   Here are a few things you can look for:

- ☐   Make sure that the URLs in your map file are absolute path names from the top of your root Web directory to the location of the file where you want to link. You cannot use relative path names in the map file. If absolute paths aren't working, try full URLs (starting with http).

- ☐   Make sure that when you append the path of the map file to the imagemap script (`htimage` or `imagemap`) you also use an absolute path name (as it appears in your URL).

- ☐   If you're using NCSA HTTPD, make sure you're using the newest version of `imagemap`. Requests to the new `imagemap` script should not look for configuration files.

Q   **I saw an example of a form that used an `<INPUT>` with `TYPE="IMAGE"`. It looked like another way to do image maps.**

A   You're right; it is precisely another way to do image maps. Using this form, instead of using ISMAP in your image with a link, you would create a form with the ACTION pointing to your imagemapping script and use an input tag similar to the following:

```
<INPUT TYPE="image" NAME="point" SRC="myimage.gif">
```

In that form, you wouldn't need a submit button. Clicking on the image would submit the form.

So why didn't I describe this in this chapter? Not as many browsers support it as do the standard ISMAP form of image maps. The other form is much more widely supported and requires fewer tags as well.

DAY

16

BONUS

HTML 3.0

What is HTML 3.0? HTML 3.0, which used to be called HTML+, is the next big step in the evolution of HTML as a language. It solves many of the limitations and frustrating parts of HTML 2.0, including alignment and better control over layout. It includes advanced features such as tables and math. HTML 3.0 includes an abundance of useful features and is enormously exciting in its potential.

In this chapter, I'll introduce you to HTML 3.0 and the features it provides, including the following topics:

- An overview of HTML 3.0's history, its status, and who supports it
- HTML 3.0's philosophy and its relationship to SGML
- What style sheets are and why they're cool
- HTML 3.0 additions and enhancements to the 2.0 tags, including alignment, text flow next to images, greater control over heading and list numbering, new character styles, and various other new features that give your old HTML 2 tags more flexibility
- A short note on proposed table features you didn't see in Chapter 8, "Tables"
- Figures: a better form of <IMG>
- Mathematical equations
- Other additions: tabs, footnotes, banners, divisions, notes, plus informational tags for the document HEAD

After this chapter, you'll have a good idea of what HTML 3.0 is and where it's going, which will make you well prepared to use its features in your own HTML documents when it actually arrives.

History and Status

The original HTML+ specification was proposed by Dave Raggett in late 1993 as a superset of the original HTML. HTML+ included advanced features such as forms, tables, and mathematical equations. The Web became more popular and HTML itself began to become a standard (with HTML 1 including the main text, link, and image elements and HTML 2 including forms). The ideas that were in HTML+, plus everyone else's ideas for what the "Next Generation" of HTML should be, were eventually folded into what is now called HTML 3.0.

As of this writing, HTML 3.0 is an *Internet draft*, which means that a preliminary specification has been released for comment but the contents of that specification are by no means settled. Sections or the entire contents of Internet drafts can be changed or thrown out altogether, and new features can be added in their place. HTML 3.0 is still in the discussion process, with the features and capabilities to which it refers changing weekly and sometimes even daily.

The HTML 3.0 Specification

The full HTML 3.0 specification is available on the Web at `http://www.hpl.hp.co.uk/people/dsr/html/CoverPage.html`. The description of HTML 3.0 that I use in this chapter is based on the draft that is current as of April 25, 1995. Be forewarned that because HTML is changing so quickly, the information I'm going to describe here and the information contained in the specification itself could change at any time. Do not rely on any of the proposed tags in your own documents (although it will be difficult to rely on them given that few browsers support HTML 3.0 to begin with).

Browsers That Support HTML 3.0

Although features of HTML 3.0 such as centering and tables are leaking into standard browsers, there are only two browsers that support HTML 3.0 in its current state (and their authors are to be commended for keeping up with its current state given how quickly it changes).

Arena is the W3 Consortium's *test bed* browser for HTML 3.0 (see Figure 16.1). It only runs under UNIX and X11, but it includes many of the major HTML 3.0 tags and an experimental style sheet mechanism, and it is updated reasonably frequently. If you really want to get HTML 3.0 fever, check out this browser and what it can do. It's wonderful. You can get more information about Arena from `http://www.w3.org/hypertext/WWW/Arena/`.

Emacs-w3 is a mode for the emacs text editor that allows World Wide Web browsing and support for just about every HTML tag you could ever want. Emacs-w3 is primarily a text-based browser, but it allows highlighting and font changes in versions of emacs that support them. You can get more information about emacs-w3 from `http://www.cs.indiana.edu/elisp/w3/docs.html`.

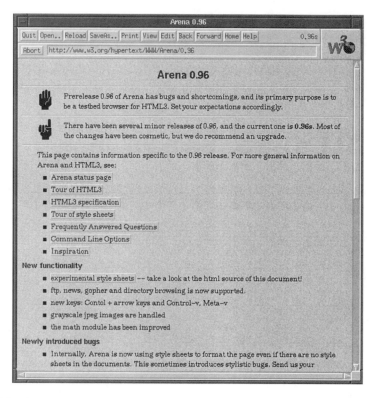

Figure 16.1. *Arena.*

How Are HTML 2.0 and 3.0 Different?

The most significant difference between HTML 3.0 and HTML 2.0 is that HTML 3.0 has more tags and features. However, it is designed to be backwards-compatible with HTML 2.0, which means that documents written in HTML 2.0 can still be read by HTML 3.0 browsers with a minimal amount of fixing. (Most of the fixing is to HTML that was questionable to begin with.)

However, this means that browsers that read HTML 2.0 documents will have problems with HTML 3.0 code. Remember what the table in Chapter 8 (Figure 8.2) looked like when viewed in a browser that didn't support tables? For this reason, the HTML specification recommends that you name your HTML 3.0 files .html3 (.ht3 for PCs) and set up your server (if you need to) to send them as the Content-type text/html; version=3.0. This way, browsers that can't understand HTML 3.0 documents will download them to a file rather than trying to display them.

Of course, in practice this doesn't always work. Tables, for example, are an HTML 3.0 feature, but their existence in pages doesn't make those pages 3.0 documents. If you're simply experimenting with HTML 3.0, you might want to follow these guidelines. If you're using new HTML 3.0 features such as tables in browsers, you should probably just isolate them on separate pages the way I've suggested throughout this book.

HTML and SGML

HTML is an SGML language, meaning that HTML was originally written in SGML. Although HTML up to HTML 2.0 has diverged somewhat from the SGML standards, HTML 3.0 will fix that. HTML 3.0 will be fully SGML compliant.

So what does this actually mean? Just what is SGML, and why is it important to HTML?

SGML stands for *Standard Generalized Markup Language.* A markup language, as you know from HTML itself, is a language that uses tags to indicate changes within a document, changes in presentation style, or changes in content type. HTML, troff, and LaTeX are all markup languages. *Generalized* means that the markup used to describe a document is based on the content of that document, not on its appearance. (Again, you've seen this in HTML with the heading and paragraph tags.) *Standard* means that the language has gone through the international standards process and is now accepted throughout the world.

SGML is actually a language that is used to define other markup languages. When you create a new markup language in SGML, you write what is called a Document Type Definition (DTD), which defines what your markup language looks like and how to handle documents that have been written in that markup language. HTML, because it was written in SGML, has a DTD.

So what does SGML compliance mean for HTML? It depends on whom you ask. On one hand, if HTML is a conforming SGML language, you can use an SGML editor to write HTML code, and there are SGML editors available right now. All you need is an SGML editor and the HTML DTD, and you're all set. Also, support for SGML makes it easier for the HTML to handle international character sets and character encodings, allowing HTML documents to be written and converted to non-Western character sets and languages. (This was a serious limitation for HTML 2.0, which up until very recently supported only one character set, ISO Latin-1.)

On the other hand, it can be (and has been) argued that SGML is big and bloated, that it is hard to write documents in by hand, and that part of HTML's beauty is that it's small and simple. Also, because the core SGML philosophy is that documents should be defined based on their content and not on their appearance, there has been a large amount of conflict in the discussions over the future of HTML between the SGML content-only purists and those who want more control over presentation in their HTML documents. (The last sentence is a polite way of saying that there have been an awful lot of flame wars.)

HTML 3.0 tries to strike a balance between all these things: keeping the language small and easy to understand while still retaining SGML compliance, and providing presentation hints in the language while still retaining the central content-based focus of SGML.

Style Sheets

Probably the most significant step toward solving the conflict over whether HTML should describe a document by its content or by its appearance was the decision to allow HTML to use style sheets.

Style sheets provide a mapping between HTML's content-based tags and specific hints for how those tags should be displayed, such as defining the color of the text, defining the space above and below the element, or indicating a numbering style for the element. Using style sheets, the author of the document can provide specific layout and presentation hints for how the page should look.

Style sheets are also hierarchical. For example, you can have a style sheet item that defines the font size for the overall document, a style sheet item that changes the font size for headings, and another that specifies the style sheet for a particular kind of heading; each item defines the differences between it and the item above it and gets more specific on the way down. One of the features of HTML that allows this kind of granularity is the CLASS attribute, which is defined on most of the elements and provides a *hook* for the style sheet to operate on.

One other important thing to note about style sheets is that they provide only hints for layout. Many of those hints can be overridden by the reader. For example, changes can be made if the reader doesn't really want to see white text on a black background, or if her favorite font is Avant Garde bold and she wants to read everything in Avant Garde bold. But style sheets can go a long way toward providing a basic framework for presentation control that doesn't involve adding a slew of new tags and features to the HTML language itself.

At least that's the theory. Currently, style sheets are even more in discussion than HTML 3.0 is, and a standard style sheet format will not be defined until HTML 3.1. Several specifications for style sheets are available and competing for attention among HTML authors and developers. I'll discuss some of the more popular proposals in the next chapter.

Now, on to HTML 3.0!

Global Changes

HTML 3.0 includes several new attributes that have been added to large groups of HTML tags, such as all the body tags or all the text element tags. Because most of the tags will contain these attributes, I've collected them here so that I only have to mention them once.

ID

The new ID attribute is available in most of the body tags (including <BODY> itself), in all of the text elements, and in other tags such as links and images. ID is used to replace the <A NAME> tag and attribute for linking to specific places within documents. By specifying that an element has an ID and a name (for example, <H1 ID="section4">), you can then link to that specific position in the same way that you linked to named anchors in HTML 2.0:

```
<P ID="theAnchor">This is a paragraph with a named anchor in it.>
...
This is a link to <A HREF="#theAnchor">the paragraph</A> with
the link in it.
```

In HTML 3.0, <A NAME> is no longer recommended as the method of linking to sections within documents; use ID instead.

LANG

The LANG attribute is also available in most of the body tags and is used to indicate the language of the element it refers to. The value of LANG is a standard ISO language abbreviation made up of a language and a country code, for example en.uk for English as spoken in the UK. The HTML browser can use this to choose a style of quotation marks, ligatures, hyphenation, and other country-specific variations on a given language.

CLASS

The CLASS attribute, which is available in most body tags, indicates the type of element this is and is used in particular by style sheets and other tools. Using CLASS specifies that this element is somehow different from the standard element. For example, with style sheets, a paragraph that was indicated by <P CLASS=QUESTION> might be rendered differently from a plain <P> paragraph. In this way, HTML tags can be extended for different purposes without having to change the language itself.

You can specify multiple classes for a single element by separating them with a period. Classes are read from left to right, with the leftmost being the most general class and the rightmost being the most specific; for example, CLASS=QUESTION.RHETORICAL is more specific than CLASS=QUESTION.

ALIGN

One of the most requested (and earliest added) new features in HTML 3.0 was the capability to specify the alignment of a text element such as a paragraph or heading. For this reason, the ALIGN attribute is now included in each of these elements, as well as in the new tags for divisions and tabs (which you'll learn about later in this chapter). ALIGN can have one of four values:

- ☐ ALIGN=LEFT renders the text flush left (the default).
- ☐ ALIGN=CENTER centers the text.
- ☐ ALIGN=RIGHT renders the text flush right.
- ☐ ALIGN=JUSTIFY adjusts the word and character spacing of the text so that both margins of the text are aligned when it is practical (usually for multiple lines of text).

NOWRAP

The NOWRAP attribute is defined on the text elements that can contain multiple lines, such as headings, paragraphs, block quotes, and addresses. NOWRAP indicates that the text in this element should not be wrapped automatically by the browser. The text will be rendered as one single line stretching out to the right, although you can put your own line breaks in as necessary:

```
<P NOWRAP>This is a paragraph that would go on for ever and
ever if there wasn't a line break right here.<BR> Now it
will continue onto the next line.</P>
```

CLEAR (For Text Flow Next to Images)

HTML 3.0 provides the general capability for text to be flowed around an image, which is specified using the <IMG> tag with the ALIGN=LEFT or ALIGN=RIGHT attributes, or by using HTML 3.0's preferred figure tag (<FIG>). You'll learn about figures and aligning text and images later in this chapter.

When text flows around an image, each new text element continues to fill in the space between the margin and the image. If you don't want to continue to fill in the space, you can use the CLEAR attribute on the first tag that breaks out of the space. CLEAR is defined for all of the text element tags (headings, paragraphs, lists, addresses, and so on) as well as for the line break (
 tag).

> **Note:** This is different from Netscape's CLEAR, which is only defined on the <BR> tag. HTML 3.0's <BR> also defines CLEAR, but including the attribute in the text instead saves on typing (you don't have to include an extra break) and makes more sense.

The CLEAR attribute has three specific values:

- ☐ CLEAR=LEFT starts the text at the next clear left margin.
- ☐ CLEAR=RIGHT starts the text at the next clear right margin.
- ☐ CLEAR=ALL starts the text at the next clear margin on both sides.

In addition, you can use the CLEAR attribute to specify that the element can only be placed alongside the figure if there is enough space for it to fit. For example, you might have a wide figure with a heading alongside it. If the margin between the figure and the heading is smaller than 100 pixels or so, the heading might look silly next to the figure (see Figure 16.2), and you'll want to force the header to appear beneath the figure instead.

Figure 16.2. *An example of too little space between the figure and the margin.*

16

To do this, use the CLEAR attribute with a measurement such as 40 pixels or 150 en, in which an en is half the point size of the current font.

Changes and Additions to HTML 2.0 Tags

This section describes specific changes that have been made in HTML 3.0 to the tags you're used to working with in HTML 2.0.

Headings

Headings act in much the same way they did in HTML 2.0. There are still six levels of headings, from 1 to 6. In addition to the global attributes I mentioned in the previous section for ID, LANG, CLASS, ALIGN, NOWRAP, and CLEAR, there are several new attributes for numbering or marking headings with bullets or icons.

Whether or not your headings are numbered is determined by the style sheet for the document, and each level of heading has its own numbering sequence. If you are using numbered headings, the SEQNUM attribute indicates the number that this heading will use, and all subsequent headings of the same level will increment from this value.

The SKIP attribute also works with numbered headings and increments the numbering value the given number of times before displaying the heading. For example, if you have a heading whose number is 4 and the next heading has the attribute SKIP=2, the second heading will display with the number 7 (it skipped 5 and 6).

The SRC attribute indicates the filename of an image to use just before the heading (for example, those little colored bullets that are so enamored of on the Web). You can also use the MD attribute to indicate the checksum of that image to make sure it's the same image that was originally intended. (You'll learn more about MD in "Images," later in this chapter.)

The DINGBAT attribute indicates a special symbol or picture to use to mark the heading. The dingbats are supplied by the browser (and therefore don't need to be downloaded over the net as a SRC image would). There is a set of default dingbat names to correspond to default images that include folder, disk.drive, text, audio, form, next, previous, home, and so on.

```
<H3 DINGBAT="folder">The SRC Directory</H3>
<P>This directory contains a listing of all the source files
available in the repository.
```

The full list of dingbats is part of the HTML 3.0 specification and is contained at http://www.hpl.hp.co.uk/people/dsr/html/icons.txt.

Paragraphs

In HTML 3.0, the paragraph tag is used in the same way as other tags; that is, the opening <P> tag should appear at the start of the paragraph, and </P> should close the end of the paragraph. The closing tag </P> is optional.

Paragraphs also now include the ID, LANG, CLASS, ALIGN, NOWRAP, and CLEAR attributes that I discussed in the previous section.

Links

Links have remained essentially the same from HTML 2.0, with the one exception of the NAME attribute, which has been replaced by ID. You can still use NAME, but ID is more flexible for creating named anchors. The <A> tag also includes the ID, LANG, and CLASS attributes.

The one new attribute to note is the MD attribute. MD stands for Message Digest and is a cryptographic checksum of the file to which this link points. If you specify the checksum of the document you're linking to, the browser will compare the value in MD with the actual checksum of the linked-to document. If these are the same, your readers can be certain that the document they are reading is the one you intended them to see. Most of the time it won't matter if the document you've linked to changes, so you won't need to use the MD attribute, but for certain secure documents this might be important.

> **Note:** The HTML specification doesn't specify what a browser should do if the checksums do not match. I assume that the browser will at least warn the reader that the document has changed.

Three other attributes of the <A> tag indicate information about the document you're linking to and its relationship to the current document. The optional TITLE attribute indicates the title of the document you're linking to (it can be displayed along with the URL in some browsers); the REL and REV attributes indicate the relationship and reverse relationship defined by this link.

Extensions to REL include a series of values for defining browser toolbars or other buttons:

```
REL=home
REL=ToC
REL=Index
REL=Glossary
REL=Copyright
REL=Up
REL=Next
REL=Previous
REL=Help
REL=Bookmark
REL=StyleSheet
```

Note: The last three attributes were actually part of the HTML 2.0 specification but are rarely used. I mention them here for completeness and because HTML 3.0 browsers and tools might begin to use them.

Finally, there is the SHAPE attribute, which enables you to specify areas within an image and the documents to which they link (to create image maps entirely in HTML). I'll discuss the use of SHAPE more in the "Figures" section, later in this chapter (where the SHAPE attribute is used).

Lists

In HTML 3.0, the three standard lists still exist as in HTML 2.0: unordered (bulleted), ordered (numbered), and definition lists. All three now have an optional list header (the new <LH> tag) and a COMPACT attribute.

Note: The MENU and DIR lists are now considered obsolete and will usually be rendered in similar ways to UL and DL.

The list header tag <LH> is used to indicate a label for the list, in the same way that the <CAPTION> tag indicates a caption for a table. Also, some browsers provide the capability to hide and unhide full lists, in which case the list header serves as the marker for the list.

List headers are used in the same way that list items (<LI>) are used. They are optional and are placed just after the list tab and just before the items in the list, like this:

```
<UL>
<LH>Spices Available
<LI>Parsley
<LI>Oregano
<LI>Basil
<LI>Rosemary
</UL>
```

The COMPACT attribute is new for all the list tags. It indicates that the browser should render the list in a more compact form, by tightening up the spacing between the list items, by shrinking the font size, or in some other way. It is used like this:

```
<UL COMPACT>
<LH>Spices Available
<LI>Parsley
<LI>Oregano
</UL>
```

Additions to Unordered Lists

In HTML 3.0, you have much greater control over unordered lists, with the following additional attributes available:

☐ The PLAIN attribute tells the browser not to display the bullets at all, creating a list of plain list elements.

☐ The SRC attribute indicates the filename of an image to use in place of the bullet you've just suppressed with PLAIN. You can also use the MD attribute to indicate the checksum of that image to make sure it is the same image that was originally intended.

☐ The DINGBAT attribute indicates a special bullet to use in the list, just like in headings.

☐ The WRAP attribute with a value of horiz can be used to display list items horizontally across the page, the way the now-obsolete <DIR> list was supposed to work. It's useful for very small list items that can fit in a columnar form, such as numbers or directory listings. The default WRAP is vert.

Additions to Ordered Lists

There are two new attributes for ordered lists that affect the numbering of those lists: CONTINUE, which continues the ordering of this list where the previous ordered list left off; and SEQNUM, which indicates the value that the list should start with (the same as Netscape's START attribute). For example, the following list would start at the number 4:

```
<OL SEQNUM=4>
<LI>Orange
<LI>Apple
<LI>Kumquat
</OL>
```

Additions to List Items

The LI (list item) tag also has some new attributes, which match the new attributes for the UL and OL lists.

The SRC attribute indicates the filename of an image to use in place of the bullet in UL lists that have the PLAIN attribute specified, as in the following example:

```
<UL PLAIN>
<LI SRC="red.gif">Annie
<LI SRC="green.gif">Alison
<LI SRC="blue.gif">Amanada
</UL>
```

You can also use the MD attribute to indicate the checksum of that image to make sure it's the same image that was originally intended.

The DINGBAT attribute is used in the same way it is used with the UL and heading tags: the names of the dingbats are defined as part of the HTML 3.0 specification, and the browser substitutes the appropriate image as necessary.

The SKIP attribute is used in ordered lists, and indicates that this list item is to be incremented by the given number before being displayed. For example, if the previous list item was numbered 10 and this one has the SKIP=5 attribute, this list item would be numbered 16.

Rule Lines

In HTML 3.0, you will be able to specify a custom image for the rule line by using the SRC attribute just as you would with <IMG SRC>, as in this example:

```
<HR SRC="rainbowline.gif">
```

In text-only browsers, the image is ignored and the HR is treated as usual.

You can also use the MD attribute to indicate the checksum of that image to make sure it's the same image that was originally intended.

Block Quotes

The block quote tag, which was called <BLOCKQUOTE> in HTML 2.0, is now called <BQ>. The old tag should still be supported for backwards-compatibility. Unlike paragraphs and headings, block quotes do not include the ALIGN attribute.

In addition, the new <CREDIT> tag can be used to indicate the author of the quotation. The <CREDIT> tag follows the text of the quote, coming just before the closing </BQ>, as in this example:

```
<BQ NOWRAP>
Life's but a walking shadow, a poor player,<BR>
And then is heard no more. It is a tale <BR>
Told by an idiot, full of sound and fury,<BR>
Signifying nothing.<BR>
<CREDIT>William Shakespeare</CREDIT>
</BQ>
```

Images

In HTML 3.0, the <IMG> tag has been scaled back in favor of the much more flexible <FIG> tag. <IMG> can still be used for small images and dingbats that are intended to be placed within a single line of text or used as icons for navigation. For larger images, images with clickable maps defined, or images that will have text flowed around them, you should use <FIG> instead.

For compatibility with the Netscape extensions, the <IMG> tag in HTML 3.0 includes the ALIGN=RIGHT and ALIGN=LEFT attributes, which behave as they do in Netscape with the text following the image flowing to the left or to the right.

The HTML 3.0 <IMG> tag also includes the WIDTH and HEIGHT attributes, which specify the width and height of the image. The UNITS attribute indicates the units of WIDTH and HEIGHT, which can be specified as UNITS=PIXELS or UNITS=EN (an EN is half the point size of the current text).

Finally, there is the MD attribute, which is also used in the <A> tag for links, and is used for icons and dingbats in several of the other tags. The MD attribute provides a checksum to make sure that the image you're indicating by name or URL is the same image you had intended to include. If the image has changed, the checksums will be different. How the difference is noted to the reader will probably be handled by the browser reading the document.

New Character Style Tags

HTML 3.0 adds several new tags for character styles, both logical and physical. The new logical tags are as follows:

- ☐ <DFN>: The first definition of a term. This tag was proposed for HTML 2 but ended up in HTML 3.0 instead. Many browsers already support it.
- ☐ <Q>: A short quotation within a paragraph (as opposed to block quotes, which create their own paragraphs). The quotation format (whether it is in italics or quotation marks) is determined by the browser and by the LANG attribute of the enclosing text block.
- ☐ <LANG>: The language of the enclosed text, if it is different from that of the LANG attribute in the enclosing text block.
- ☐ <AU>: The name of an author.
- ☐ <PERSON>: The name of a person (so that it can be extracted using indexing programs, or perhaps automatically linked to that person's home page).
- ☐ <ACRONYM>: An acronym.
- ☐ <ABBREV>: An abbreviation.
- ☐ <INS>: Inserted text (used, for example, in legal documents where showing what text has been inserted is important).
- ☐ <DEL>: Deleted text (again, used in legal documents).

The new physical tags are as follows:

- ☐ <UL>: Underlined text. This is another proposed 2.0 feature that ended up here.
- ☐ <S>: Strikethrough.

☐ `<BIG>`: The text is rendered in a larger font.

☐ `<SMALL>`: The text is rendered in a smaller font than the surrounding text. Both `<BIG>` and `<SMALL>` are similar to Netscape's font change tags.

☐ `<SUB>`: Subscript.

☐ `<SUP>`: Superscript.

New Special Characters

HTML 3.0 defines five new special character entities for use in your HTML documents: three special spaces and two special dashes. Table 16.1 shows these new special characters. Remember that, as with all the character entities, you need both the opening ampersand (&) and the closing semicolon (;).

Table 16.1. New character entities.

Entity	Meaning
	An en space, with an en being half the point size of the current font (or a single space in a monospaced font).
	An em space, with an em being the same size as the point size of the current font (or two spaces in a monospaced font).
	A nonbreaking space. Words separated by a nonbreaking space will not be split across two lines by the browser.
&endash;	An en dash (a dash the size of an en).
&emdash;	An em dash (a dash the size of an em).

Forms

Because forms are defined in HTML 2.0, I probably should have included the changes to forms in the last section. But, because there are lots of changes, I've split them off here. HTML 3.0 forms include some new input types, graphical selection menus, and client-side form scripts.

Form Scripts

Probably the most interesting change to forms is the proposed capability for forms to include scripts that tell the browser how to manage the form elements and the contents of those elements (for example, to dynamically define a form element from the values of other

elements, or to constrain the possible values of a field). Form scripts can examine and change the properties of form elements, and scripts can include events such as mouse clicks and keyboard events. Form scripts are limited to this small set of behaviors; they can't read or write from the browser's system, nor can they send messages to the server.

Details on script support in HTML 3.0 are sketchy. The current specification says nothing about the language that these scripts might be written in or how the browser is going to interpret these scripts. This functionality will probably be better defined as the specification is further developed.

General Additions

The majority of the changes to forms have occurred in the individual form element tags: INPUT, TEXTAREA, and SELECTION. The standard ID, LANG, and CLASS attributes can be used. In addition, two attributes, ERROR and DISABLED, have been added to all three form element tags.

If DISABLED is included in the element tag, the form element is drawn as usual but is not active. So, for text input fields, you can't enter any text, selection menus cannot be selected, and so on. The browser might choose to render these in a grayed out format or in some other way to indicate that the form field is not available. You might want to use this to create general forms that have certain elements enabled or disabled based on the user's previous input or some other state.

ERROR indicates an error message explaining why a value for a form element is incorrect. The HTML 3.0 specification isn't overly clear about what that means. I am assuming it can be used to indicate errors after the reader fills out your form and submits it. In your form script you could check the input for errors and then return the same form back with the elements that have the wrong input marked with the ERROR attribute. For example, if your reader entered a 20 in a field that can only have values between 1 and 10, you could include the ERROR attribute in that tag with the value Please include a value less than ten. The browser is expected to provide a method for marking fields that contain errors and then to display the error message in some way.

New Input Types

Three new input field types have been added to the <INPUT> tag: ranges, file attachments, and image *scribble*.

Ranges are specified using the RANGE attribute to <INPUT>, and they allow the user to choose a numeric value between an upper and a lower bound (for example, using a slider). The MIN and MAX attributes indicate the lower and upper bounds of the range, respectively. VALUE can be used to indicate the initial value of the range. For example, the following line of HTML creates a slider that allows the user to choose a value between 0 and 255.

16

```
<INPUT NAME="red" TYPE=RANGE MIN=0 MAX=255>
```

If either the upper or lower values of the range are floating-point numbers, the reader can select any floating point value between the upper and lower bounds. Otherwise, the possible values are all integers.

File attachments, specified by the FILE attribute, are used to allow the reader of the form to attach a file to a form submission, which could allow the reader to submit changed HTML pages to a Web server. The ACCEPT attribute restricts the types of files that can be accepted; for example, to allow only HTML files to be included, ACCEPT might contain text/html. Wildcards are allowed and multiple file types can be separated by commas. For example, the following HTML creates a file attachment widget (it's up to the browser to decide how to render this), which can accept both HTML and any kind of image files:

```
<INPUT NAME="include" TYPE=FILE ACCEPT="text/html, image/*">
```

Finally, image scribble allows the form to contain an image, on which the reader can then draw. For browsers that can't display images, a text field is substituted for the image. Image scribble is indicated by the SCRIBBLE attribute, and the SRC attribute indicates the image to use. You can also use the MD attribute to indicate the checksum of the image, as with other images. Here's an example of how to use image scribble fields:

```
<INPUT TYPE=SCRIBBLE SRC="map.gif" NAME="map">
```

You can also use the MD attribute to indicate the checksum of the image, as with other images. How the form submits the scribble data or how the CGI script is supposed to handle that data is not yet specified in the HTML 3.0 specification.

Changes to Existing Input Types

Both the submit and reset buttons can now have images, specified using the SRC attribute and displayed instead of the default button appearance. The images you use for submit and reset buttons should look like buttons, although they can contain any image. Also, the MD attribute allows the same MD checksum for the image.

If the submit input field contains a NAME attribute, you can use multiple submit buttons on the same form. The NAME and VALUE of the submit button that was pressed to submit the form are sent along with the form input to the CGI script, enabling you to perform different actions depending on which button was pressed.

Both the HTML 2.0 and 3.0 specifications define the IMAGE attribute to <INPUT>, which allows an image to be used in a form. When the image is selected with the mouse, the form is submitted and the coordinates of the mouse click are sent to the server as the VALUE, acting as sort of an alternative way of specifying an image map. Although this feature was part of the HTML 2.0 specification, it was not widely supported or used, and a note in the HTML 3.0

specification asks whether it can be phased out in favor of the images in SUBMIT and RESET. The future of this attribute is in question.

Text Areas

In addition to the DISABLED and ERROR attributes I mentioned earlier in this chapter, the TEXTAREA tag also has a new ALIGN attribute. This attribute indicates the alignment of the text area with the surrounding text, similar to the way inline images are aligned.

If the ALIGN attribute has values of TOP, MIDDLE, or BOTTOM, the appropriate edge of the text area is aligned with the baseline of the surrounding text (the default is TOP). If ALIGN is LEFT or RIGHT, the text that follows it will flow into the space between the text area and the margin the same way it does for images.

Graphical Selection Menus

Selection menus in HTML 3.0 have been extended to allow the selection menu to be specified as a clickable image. The overall selection menu is an image (and behaves like a regular image in terms of alignment and text flow); the individual options are specified as zones on the image that map to VALUEs. Because the selection menu is defined as both a graphical image map and a text menu, both graphical and text-only browsers can use it. Graphical selection menus can work especially well for things such as button bars, for which you have a list of possible locations. By using a graphical selection menu, you can create a button bar that works equally well in both graphical and text-only browsers.

To accomplish this, you use the SRC attribute to the <SELECT> tag to indicate an image. The following new attributes to SELECT also refer to that image:

- ☐ The MD attribute contains the checksum of the image, if necessary.
- ☐ WIDTH and HEIGHT act as they do for regular images, specifying the width and height of the given image.
- ☐ The UNITS attribute specifies the units for WIDTH and HEIGHT. Possible values are PIXELS or EM. (Yes, EM and not EN. I don't know why.)
- ☐ The ALIGN attribute works as it does with regular images. TOP, MIDDLE, and BOTTOM indicate the alignment of the image within a line of text, and LEFT and RIGHT align the image to the left or right margin, flowing all subsequent text to the left or the right of that image.

With the graphical SELECT in place, now you have to define each of the OPTIONs for the menu. These are defined as they would be for the text-only menu. (Remember, the menu is available in both graphical and text-only browsers.) An addition is the new SHAPE attribute to specify which zones of the image point to which OPTION values.

The SHAPE attribute takes one of four string values that indicate the shape of the zone:

☐ SHAPE="default" is used for a selection that is not in any other zone.

☐ SHAPE="circle x, y, r" is used when the zone is a circle centered at the point specified by x,y and with the radius r.

☐ SHAPE="rect x,y,w,h" is used when the zone is a rectangle with x,y as its upper left corner and w,h as its width and height in pixels.

☐ SHAPE="polygon x1,y1,x2,y2,..." is used when the zone is a polygon that starts at the point x1,y1 and continues on to the point x2,y2, and so on until the last point. The polygon is completed using a line drawn between the starting and ending points.

As with image maps, image coordinates have their origin at the top left corner, with x extending to the right and y extending down. If x and y are integers, the coordinates are interpreted as pixel values. Otherwise, they are interpreted as values from 0.0 to 1.0, which indicate percentages across the image.

If two shapes overlap and the mouse is clicked in the overlapping space, the center of both shapes is calculated and the center closest to the mouse point wins.

Here's an example. The following HTML 3.0 code shows a graphical selection menu with four rectangular zones, such as you might see in a button bar:

```
<SELECT NAME="buttonbar" SRC="buttons.gif" WIDTH=400 HEIGHT=100>
<OPTION VALUE="home" SHAPE="rect 0,0,100,100">Home
<OPTION VALUE="search" SHAPE="rect 100,0,100,100">Search
<OPTION VALUE="mail" SHAPE="rect 200,0,100,100">Feedback
<OPTION VALUE="index" SHAPE="rect 300,0,100,100">Index
</SELECT>
```

Tables

I explain much of the current HTML 3.0 table definition in Chapter 8, so I won't repeat it here. I will, however, note the attributes and features that are proposed in HTML 3.0 but not yet implemented in either Netscape's or Mosaic's implementations.

Common Attributes

The <TABLE> tag, like most HTML body elements in HTML 3.0, includes the ID, LANG, and CLASS attributes. It also includes the NOWRAP attribute, which refers to the contents of the table. To prevent strange looking tables using NOWRAP, make sure that you break lines by hand using <BR>.

Tables and Text Alignment

You can flow text around tables as you can with images. By default, tables are centered on the page, but by using the ALIGN attribute, you align the table to the left or the right and subsequent text flows around the table. The ALIGN attribute, when used with tables, can have six values (two extra from the normal ALIGN):

☐ ALIGN=LEFT aligns the table with the left text margin. Subsequent text, if it fits, will flow to the right of the table.

☐ ALIGN=CENTER (the default) centers the table within the page. Text will not flow to either side of the image.

☐ ALIGN=RIGHT aligns the table with the right margin. Subsequent text, if it fits, will flow to the right of the table.

☐ ALIGN=JUSTIFY sizes the table to fit into the width of the page. No text will flow to either side of the table.

☐ ALIGN=BLEEDLEFT aligns the table with the left window margin. BLEEDLEFT differs from plain LEFT in that the table can be part of text flowing next to an image or another table. LEFT continues to flow the text with the current left text margin; BLEEDLEFT moves down until a clear left margin is reached.

☐ ALIGN=BLEEDRIGHT aligns the table with the right window margin in the same way that BLEEDLEFT works.

You can also turn off text flow around tables by using the NOFLOW attribute in the <TABLE> tag. If the current table is part of a text flow around an image or another table, you can use the CLEAR attribute as you would with any other text tag to break out of the current flow to a left or right clear margin.

16

Table Widths, Column Widths, and Column Alignment

The WIDTH and COLSPEC attributes indicate the width of the table and the width of its columns, respectively. The units you use to measure the table and column widths are specified by the UNITS attribute, which can have three values:

☐ UNITS=EN (the default): The widths are measured in en units, with an en being half the point size of the current text. By specifying the table widths in en, the table can be drawn a row at a time without having to wait for all the content to arrive over the Net.

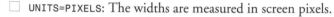

- [ ] `UNITS=PIXELS`: The widths are measured in screen pixels.
- [ ] `UNITS=RELATIVE`: The widths are measured as percentages. For example, a table width of `50` with relative units will space 50 percent of the current text column (which might not be 50 percent of the page, depending on whether the text is flowing around an image or another table).

To indicate the width of the entire table, use the `WIDTH` attribute. To specify the widths of individual columns within the table and the column alignments, use the `COLSPEC` attribute, in which the value for `COLSPEC` is a list of the columns in the table with their alignments and widths both specified. Here's an example:

```
<TABLE UNITS=RELATIVE COLSPEC="L40C30R30">
```

In this example, there are three columns whose widths are measured by percentages. The contents of the first column are left-aligned and the column takes up 40 percent of the total table width. The contents of the second column are centered and the column takes up 30 percent of the table width. The third column is also 30 percent wide but is right-aligned.

The alignment values must be capital letters and can include `L` for left-alignment, `C` for center-alignment, `R` for right-alignment, `J` for justified, and `D` for decimal alignment (which is particularly useful for columns of numbers).

For that last alignment value, the `DP` attribute is used to indicate what the decimal point is (the default is a period). The decimal point can also be changed by the `LANG` attribute.

Table Rows

Table rows are specified using `<TR>`, as you learned in Chapter 8. Table rows can contain the `ID`, `LANG`, `CLASS`, and `NOWRAP` attributes, just as with most body tags.

`ALIGN` and `VALIGN`, which you learned about in Chapter 8, are part of HTML 3.0. `ALIGN` has two additional values, `JUSTIFY` and `DECIMAL`. The `DP` attribute to indicate the decimal point can be used here as well. The alignment options in the `<TR>` tag can only be used to override the default alignments. They can't override any alignment in the table's `COLSPEC` attribute.

Heading and Data Cells

Table and data cells appear in the same way that you learned about in Chapter 8, with the following additions:

- [ ] `ID`, `LANG`, `CLASS`, and `NOWRAP` (again).
- [ ] `ALIGN` can have the values `JUSTIFY` and `DECIMAL` in addition to `LEFT`, `RIGHT`, and `CENTER`. Note that `COLSPEC` takes precedence over cell alignments the same way it does for row alignments.

- [ ] DP indicates the value of the decimal point.

- [ ] AXIS is the abbreviated name for a header cell, which can be used if the contents of the table are being read aloud by a text-to-speech processor. The axis defaults to the contents of the cell.

- [ ] AXES is a comma-separated list of short axis names, which identify the row and column headers that refer to this cell. It is also used in text-to-speech generators to indicate the position of a cell within a table.

Figures

Figures and images are very similar: both display an image on the screen and both can wrap text alongside an image. Figures, however, allow image maps without a CGI program on the server side, they can have associated captions and credits, and they can have formatted alt text substituted on text-only browsers. In HTML 3.0, using figures is the preferred way of placing large images on the page, whereas the use of images should be restricted to small images that are placed inline with the text, such as small bullets and dingbats.

Using *<FIG>*

To include a figure in your HTML page, use the <FIG> tag. The SRC attribute is used to indicate the name of the image. Inside the opening and closing text, indicate the text that will be used in text-only browsers to substitute for the image, as in this example:

```
<FIG SRC="map.gif">
      [a map of the united states]
</FIG>
```

The text inside the <FIG> tags serves the same purpose as the ALT attribute in the IMG tag. However, because the text content that replaces the image isn't an attribute, you can include any text or HTML tags you want to as alternate text in a figure tag: formatted text, lists, tables, equations, links, anything.

The <FIG> tag includes most of the same attributes that <IMG> does, including ID, LANG, CLASS, MD, WIDTH, HEIGHT, UNITS, and CLEAR.

Figure Alignment

You can align the figure and allow text flow around it using (surprise!) the ALIGN attribute. By default, figures are centered in the current text column and flow around the figure is disabled, but by using the ALIGN attribute, you can align the table to the left or to the right

16

and subsequent text will flow around it. The ALIGN attribute can have six possible values (which should all look familiar from tables):

☐ ALIGN=LEFT aligns the figure with the left text margin. Subsequent text, if it fits, flows to the right of the figure.

☐ ALIGN=CENTER (the default) centers the figure. Text will not flow to either side.

☐ ALIGN=RIGHT aligns the figure with the right margin. Subsequent text, if it fits, flows to the right of the figure.

☐ ALIGN=JUSTIFY scales the figure to fit into the width of the page. No text will flow to either side of the figure.

☐ ALIGN=BLEEDLEFT aligns the figure with the left window margin. BLEEDLEFT differs from plain LEFT in that the figure can be part of text flowing next to another figure or table. LEFT continues to flow the text with the current left text margin; BLEEDLEFT moves down until a clear left margin is reached.

☐ ALIGN=BLEEDRIGHT aligns the figure with the right window margin in the same way that BLEEDLEFT works.

You can also entirely turn off text flow around figures by using the NOFLOW attribute in the <FIGURE> tag.

Figure Overlays

Figure overlays are used to layer a second image over the primary image as you would overlay a transparency over a page. Overlays are best for when you want to use the same image multiple times in the same presentation with only small changes. Using overlays, you can specify the main image as the SRC attribute, and then use different overlays for the changes in each one. By indicating images in this way, the primary image only needs to be downloaded once, and then the overlays (which are usually smaller files) can be downloaded as needed. This can significantly speed up the time it takes to load some pages, because multiple large images with only small differences do not need to be individually retrieved from the server.

To specify an overlay on a figure, use the <OVERLAY> tag inside a <FIG> tag, like this:

```
<FIG SRC="map.gif">
<OVERLAY SRC="arkansas.gif">
<H3>Arkansas</H3>
</FIG>
```

In this example, the map of the United States had an overlay that highlighted the state of Arkansas. Theoretically, the majority of the overlay here would have a transparent background so that the primary image can show through.

The <OVERLAY> tag has several attributes similar to most of the image tags, including SRC to indicate the name of the image, plus MD, WIDTH, HEIGHT, and UNITS. In addition, the X and Y attributes indicate the offset of the overlay from the top left corner of the base image, with X to the right and Y downwards. The units of X and Y are specified by the UNITS attribute in pixels or en.

You can have as many overlay images in a figure as you want, and overlays can overlap. The order in which the overlays are displayed is determined by the order in which they appear in the <FIG> element.

Creating Image Maps in Figures

Figures provide two methods for creating clickable image maps. The first is the IMAPMAP attribute, which contains a CGI script to process mouse clicks, much in the same way that the ISMAP attribute worked with images. Both the <FIG> and the <OVERLAY> tags can have an IMAGEMAP attribute. Image maps in the overlay have precedence over those in the primary image, and if a mouse click occurs on overlapping overlays, the first overlay specified in <FIG> takes precedence over any others.

The second method of managing clickable image maps is by creating special links in the figure text that define the zones in the image that are clickable and the files they point to. This method is not only far faster to process than a server-side program, but it also allows image maps to be used in text-only browsers, because the figure description text is what defines the image map itself.

The easiest way to create an image map using a figure is to first pretend that you don't have an image map at all and define the links you're creating in a text-only fashion. For example, if you are implementing a button bar image map, you might want to define a link menu first that has each of the locations the button bar points to with links to the appropriate files, as in the following example:

16

```
<UL>
<LI><A HREF="home.html">Home</A>
<LI><A HREF="search.html">Search</A>
<LI><A HREF="products.html">Products</A>
<LI>A HREF="mail.html">Feedback</A>
</UL>
```

Then, when the links and the text are in place, surround it with a figure:

```
<FIG SRC="buttonbar.gif">
<UL>
<LI><A HREF="home.html">Home</A>
<LI><A HREF="search.html">Search</A>
<LI><A HREF="products.html">Products</A>
<LI><A HREF="mail.html">Feedback</A>
</UL>
</FIG>
```

To make the image actually clickable, you have to add the SHAPE attribute to each <A> tag in the text. The SHAPE attribute defines the zones in the image that point to the appropriate file,

in the same way that the SHAPE attribute in graphical menus worked. As with SHAPE in the <OPTION> tag, SHAPE attribute in the <A> tag takes one of four string values that indicate the shape of the zone:

☐ SHAPE="default" is used for a selection that is not in any other zone.

☐ SHAPE="circle x, y, r" is used when the zone is a circle centered at the point specified by x,y and with the radius r.

☐ SHAPE="rect x,y,w,h" is used when the zone is a rectangle with x,y as its upper left corner and w,h as its width and height in pixels.

☐ SHAPE="polygon x1,y1,x2,y2,..." is used when the zone is a polygon that starts at the point x1,y1 and continues to the point x2,y2, and so on until the last point. The polygon is completed using a line drawn between the starting and ending points.

As with image maps, image coordinates have their origin at the top left corner, with x extending to the right and y extending down. If x and y are integers, the coordinates are interpreted as pixel values. Otherwise, they are interpreted as values from 0.0 to 1.0, which indicate percentages across the image. If two shapes overlap and the mouse is clicked in the overlapping space, the center of both shapes is calculated and the center closest to the mouse point wins.

To finish up that example, if the image for the button bar is 40 by 100 pixels wide with four buttons that are 100 pixels square, here's what the final HTML 3.0 code for the figure would look like:

```
<FIG SRC="buttonbar.gif">
<UL>
<LI><A HREF="home.html" SHAPE="rect 0,0,100,100">Home</A>
<LI><A HREF="search.html" SHAPE="rect 100,0,100,100">Search</A>
<LI><A HREF="products.html" SHAPE="rect 200,0,100,100">
      Products</A>
<LI><A HREF="mail.html"SHAPE="rect 300,0,100,100">Feedback</A>
</UL>
</FIG>
```

Figure Captions and Credits

As with tables, figures can have a <CAPTION> tag that indicates a caption for the figure itself. Figure captions are usually placed below the figure, although you can use the ALIGN attribute to place the caption to any side of the figure. The possible values of ALIGN are TOP, BOTTOM, LEFT, or RIGHT. The <CAPTION> tag follows any overlays in the figure.

As with the <BQ> tag (block quotes), you can use the <CREDIT> tag within a figure to refer to the author or artist of the figure itself. The <CREDIT> tag appears at the end of the figure, after any alternate text and just before the closing </FIG>.

Math

One of HTML 3.0's more ambitious features is the capability to display inline mathematical equations such as the one shown in Figure 16.3.

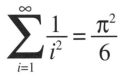

$$\sum_{i=1}^{\infty} \frac{1}{i^2} = \frac{\pi^2}{6}$$

Figure 16.3. *An equation.*

Math in HTML 3.0 has been heavily influenced by the math in the LaTeX package, although because of restrictions in SGML, many LaTeX constructions are slightly different in HTML, such as the use of brackets {} and the ^ and _ characters. However, if you are familiar with LaTeX math, HTML 3.0 math will seem familiar and easy to construct.

To create an HTML equation, you use the $...$ tags. Within those tags, you can have constants, functions, numbers, and so on, plus additional special tags for indicating the arrangement of smaller expressions within the equation (described later in this section).

The MATH tag supports the ID and CLASS attributes for creating named anchors and subclassing equations. For the latter in particular, the HTML 3.0 specification suggests CLASS=CHEM, which is used for chemical formulas (because variables tend to be rendered in a different font than in regular math expressions). Also, the BOX attribute causes the equation to be displayed with a border around it.

You can only create single-line equations in HTML. If you need a multiline equation, you can use tables to align multiple sets of equations.

16

Note: My apologies if this section seems overly vague. I have not done extensive work with equations in HTML or otherwise, and my background knowledge of the subject is sketchy. Most of the content in this section is directly from the HTML 3.0 specification. If you have further questions or need more examples, look at the HTML 3.0 specification, where there is much more information available.

<BOX>

The `<BOX>` tag is used to indicate invisible brackets, for placing numerators over denominators with or without dividing lines, and for creating "stretchy" integrals and other signs that match the height of the expression. You can use brackets (`{}`) to substitute for the `<BOX>` tag, as in the following example:

```
<MATH>{1 <over> x * y}</MATH>
```

> **Note:** If you actually want to use brackets inside an expression, you have to use the `&lcub;` and `&rcub;` entities for the opening and closing brackets.

The `<BOX>` tag allows several tags within it. In this example, the `<OVER>` tag inside a box (as in the previous example) indicates that a line is to be drawn between the numerator and the denominator. You can use the `<ATOP>` tag instead, which has the same effect but without the dividing line, and use the `<CHOOSE>` tag to enclose the expressions within parentheses.

Also, the `SIZE` attribute in `<BOX>` (which can only be used if you use the tag instead of using curly brackets) is used to achieve oversized delimiters. The possible values are `NORMAL`, `MEDIUM`, `LARGE`, and `HUGE`.

<SUB> and *<SUP>*

The `<SUB>` and `<SUP>` tags are used to indicate subscripts and superscripts, respectively, or to indicate limits for integrals and related signs. For example, the following code results in $x^2 + y$:

```
<MATH>x<SUP>2 + y</SUP></MATH>
```

The underscore character (`_`) can be used as a replacement for `<SUB>` and `</SUB>`, and the caret (`^`) character can replace `<SUP>` and `</SUP>`. Note that, unlike in LaTeX, you need underscores or carets on *both sides* of the subscripted or superscripted characters. For example, to create a sum with limits from n= 0 to infinity, you use the following equation (with the `&sum;` and `&inf;` entities denoting the sum and infinity characters):

```
&sum;_n = 0_^&inf;^
```

Normally, superscripts and subscripts are placed to the right of the term to which they refer. You can change how the superscripts and subscripts are aligned using the `ALIGN` attribute to the `<SUP>` and `<SUB>` tags. (You can't use it with the underscore and caret forms.) `ALIGN` can have three values:

☐   `ALIGN=LEFT` places the script or limit to the left of the term.

- ☐ `ALIGN=CENTER` places the script centered on the term and above or below it (depending on whether it's a superscript or a subscript, of course).
- ☐ `ALIGN=RIGHT` places the script or limit to the right of the term.

> **Note:** Although `<SUP>` and `<SUB>` are also entities for affecting normal characters, the capabilities I mentioned here are only available when you use them inside equations.

*<ABOVE>*and *<BELOW>*

`<ABOVE>` is used to draw a line, arrow, bracket, or other symbol above the expression it encloses. The `<BELOW>` tag does the same thing below the expression, as in the following example:

```
<ABOVE>x + y + z</ABOVE>
```

This example draws a line above the expression x + y + z.

Both `<ABOVE>` and `<BELOW>` have one attribute, `SYM`, which indicates the symbol to draw. Possible values are `CUB`, `LINE`, `LARR` (left arrow), `RARR` (right arrow), `HAT`, and `TILDE`.

Instead of using `<ABOVE>` and `<BELOW>`, HTML 3.0 defines shorthand tags for simple vectors, bars, dots, double-dots, hats, and tildes by using the `<VEC>`, `<BAR>`, `<DOT>`, `<DDOT>`, `<HAT>`, and `<TILDE>` tags, respectively. Here's an example:

```
<BAR>x / y</BAR>
```

This example draws a bar over the expression x / y.

<SQRT> and *<ROOT>*

`<SQRT>` and `<ROOT>` enable you to create root expressions, as in the following example:

```
<SQRT>x^2^ + y^2^</SQRT>
```

This would display the root sign over the expression $x^2 + y^2$.

The `<ROOT>` tag requires the `<OF>` tag to indicate the radix and the radicand, like this:

```
<ROOT>3<OF>x^2^ + y^2^</ROOT>
```

This would result in the cube root of the same expression as in the previous example.

16

447

<ARRAY>

The <ARRAY> tag creates matrices and other array-like expressions. An array, like a table, is made up of several rows, with each row containing multiple items. Rows are indicated by <ROW> and items by <ITEM>, like this:

```
<array>
      <row><item>a_11_<item>a_12_<item>&cdots;<item>a_1n_
      <row><item>&vdots;<item>&vdots;<item>&cdots;<item>&vdots;
      <row><item>a_n1_<item>a_n2_<item>&cdots;<item>a_nn_
</array>
```

This example, which is shown in Figure 16.4, uses the &cdots; and &vdots; entities to represent the dots.

$$a_{11} \quad a_{12} \quad \cdots \quad a_{1n}$$

$$\vdots \qquad \vdots \qquad \cdots \qquad \vdots$$

$$a_{n1} \quad a_{n2} \quad \cdots \quad a_{nn}$$

Figure 16.4. *Arrays.*

Arrays have several attributes:

☐ ALIGN indicates the alignment of the array with the expressions before and after it. The possible values are TOP, MIDDLE, and BOTTOM, which work in the same way as image alignment options.

☐ COLDEF defines how the individual items within columns are to be aligned; the possible values are L for left, C for center, and R for right. Column alignments are specified as a string, such as CCRL for a four-column array.

☐ LDELIM and RDELIM indicate the entity or character to be used for the left and right delimiters, respectively. The default is no delimiter.

☐ The LABELS attribute can be used to label the rows and columns, similar to LaTeX's bordermatrix command. If LABELS is used, the first row and the first item of each successive row are used as the labels. Note that there must be an item in the first position of the first row (for the top left corner), although its contents will be ignored.

<TEXT>

The <TEXT> tag is used to include text within a MATH element. Text is rendered literally.

\<B\>, \<T\>, and \<BT\>

The `<B>`, `<T>`, and `<BT>` tags are used to change the character formatting of variables and constants. By default, functions, numbers, and constants are rendered in an upright font, while variables are in italic. The `<B>` tag is used for boldface, `<T>` is used for an upright font, and `<BT>` is used for a combination of the two.

Math Entities

HTML math defines an extensive set of special entities for use in equations, including entities for functions, operators, dots, Greek letters and symbols, accents, arrows, and pointers. I don't have the space to list them all here, so check the HTML 3.0 specification at `http://www.hpl.hp.co.uk/people/dsr/html/maths.html` for more information.

Other Additions

In this section, I've collected the other extra features in HTML 3.0 that didn't fit anywhere else, which include backgrounds, tabs, divisions, banners, and notes, as well as a suite of informational tags that can be put into the `<HEAD>` element of your document.

Backgrounds

HTML 3.0 includes the capability for you to set a tiled background image for your pages using the `BACKGROUND` attribute in the `<BODY>` tag, like this:

```
<BODY BACKGROUND="tiles.gif">
```

> **Note:** It looks as though background color and tiled images will be moved into style sheets instead of remaining in HTML 3.0 itself, in which case this tag might go away. However, given Netscape's support of it, `BACKGROUND`, as well as `BGCOLOR`, might end up in the language anyway.

Tabs

HTML 3.0 has tabs! Use the `<TAB>` tag to set tab stops in a document and then indent bits of text to those tab stops.

16

The easiest way to use tabs is to simply use the INDENT attribute, which indicates how far in en units to tab, like this:

```
<P><TAB INDENT=6>This line is indented 6 en units.
```

It only works for that one line, and you can't use the same tab positions again, but if all you want to do is create a simple indent, this is the way to do it.

You can also create named tab stops, and then tab to those stops in any text that follows the definition of the tab stops. To do this, use the ID attribute to create a tab stop and assign a name to it, like this:

```
<P>On the first day<TAB ID="tabOne">, I shaved my cat.
```

In subsequent text, you can tab to a named tab stop, like this:

```
<P><TAB TO="tabOne">On the Second day, I frosted my car.
```

You can create left, right, centered, and decimal tabs just like in most word processors by using the ALIGN attribute in the tab itself, not in the tab stop definition (which is slightly different than in most word processors). To create an aligned tab, use the ALIGN attribute. The possible values for ALIGN are as follows:

- ALIGN=LEFT (the default) causes the text following the tab to be aligned to the right of the tab stop.

- ALIGN=RIGHT causes the text following the tab, up to the next line break or tab, to be aligned to the left of the tab stop. If TO is not specified, the text is aligned against the right margin.

- ALIGN=CENTER causes the text following the tab, up to the next line break or tab, to be centered at the tab stop. If TO is not specified, the text is aligned between the left and right margins.

- ALIGN=DECIMAL causes the text following the tab, up to the next line break or tab, to be aligned around its decimal point at the tab stop. If TO isn't specified, the tab is considered a single space character. The DP attribute can be used to indicate the character to be used as the decimal point (the default is .).

Footnotes

The <FN> tag is used to indicate a footnote or *pop-up* note. To define a footnote, use the ID attribute to give it a named anchor, and then create a link to that anchor in the text. Here's an example:

```
<P><A HREF="#fn1>85% of those surveyed</A> said that eggplant is amongst their
least favorite foods.
...
<FN ID="fn1">Lemay, 1994</FN>
```

Banners

A banner is a section of an HTML document that is considered separate from, but part of, that document. Banners are usually displayed in a separate part of the window, such as a toolbar, and can be used for button bars, corporate logos, copyright statements, or other information. Banners remain on-screen at all times (they are not scrolled with the rest of the document), so the features they contain are available at all times.

To create a banner, simply enclose the HTML code you want to include in the banner inside a <BANNER> tag, like this:

```
<BANNER>
   <P><A HREF="index.html">
      <IMG SRC="h.gif" ALT="[HOME]"> </A>
   <A HREF="new.html">
      <IMG SRC="n.gif" ALT="[NEWS]"> </A>
   <A HREF="search.html">
      <IMG SRC="s.gif" ALT="[SEARCH]"> </A>
   <A HREF="mailto:beanpole@lne.com">
      <IMG SRC="m.gif" ALT="[MAIL]"> </A>
   <A HREF="warez.html">
      <IMG SRC="f.gif" ALT="[WAREZ]"> </A>
</BANNER>
```

Divisions

Divisions are used to break up a page into independent chunks, in which each chunk can have its own style sheet or can be managed separately from other elements in the document. Divisions create document parts that are smaller than the page in its entirety but larger than the individual document elements. For example, you might have a page that has three semantic sections: a header, a body, and a footer. Using divisions, you can actually create these sections and refer to them by name (by CLASS, actually) and format them differently in the style sheet based on that name.

16

To create a division, surround the HTML code that makes up that division with <DIV>...</DIV> tags, as in the following example:

```
<DIV CLASS=SUMMARY>
<H1>Beanpole Software Incorporated<BR>
<H1>Company Profile</H1>
<P>Beanpole Software was founded in 1993 by...
</DIV>
```

Divisions can also be aligned and wrapped around figures and tables just like other text-based elements. Aligning a division is particularly useful when you have a lot of centered text and don't want to include ALIGN=CENTER in every single paragraph type. Just use a division instead.

```
<DIV ALIGN=CENTER>
<H1>Dave and Susan Black are Pleased to Announce</H1>
<H2>The wedding of their Daughter Alice</H2>
```

```
<H2>To Tom White of Utah</H2>
<P>On September 14, 1995
</DIV>
```

The ALIGN attribute in DIV has all the same values as the usual ALIGN attribute: LEFT, RIGHT, CENTER, and JUSTIFY. In addition, the ID, LANG, CLASS, CLEAR, and NOWRAP attributes are also available for divisions.

Notes

Notes, cautions, and warnings are called *admonishments* in the HTML 3.0 specification. Notes, cautions, and warnings are used to advise the reader of some point or draw attention to a particular paragraph because it says something important.

The <NOTE> tag is used to indicate a note, and the specification says that the appropriate CLASS values are NOTE, CAUTION, and WARNING. Theoretically, other types of notes could also be specified using CLASS if you chose to include them. The CLASS is usually used in the style sheet to indicate an icon or special dingbat for the note, caution, or warning; or, you can use your own graphic, using the SRC attribute (and you can specify a checksum for the image using the MD attribute). Without a style sheet or an associated graphic, the note is usually rendered as slightly indented. You might want to surround a note with rule lines to set it off from the text, like this:

```
<HR>
<NOTE CLASS=WARNING SRC="warning.gif" >
Do not drink the leftover solvent!
</NOTE>
<HR>
```

This example should appear something like the note shown in Figure 16.5.

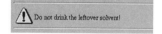

Figure 16.5. *A warning.*

<HEAD> Tags

Several tags can be used in the <HEAD> part of an HTML document to indicate various information about the HTML document itself—extra information that doesn't appear in the body of the HTML document but can be used by browsers, servers, or other tools to index or keep track of that document.

You've already seen a couple of the <HEAD> tags in the previous book: <TITLE>, <ISINDEX>, and <BASE> are used to indicate the document title, that the document is searchable, and the base URL for the document, respectively. In this section, you'll learn about <LINK>, <META>, <RANGE>, and <STYLE>.

> **Note:** Many of these tags were actually a part of HTML 2.0 but were not commonly used. I'm including them here for completeness and because I expect that more browsers will start to take advantage of them.

<LINK>

The <LINK> tag is used to indicate the relationship between this document and another document. Link has three attributes:

- ☐ REL defines the relationship between this document and another.
- ☐ REV defines a reverse relationship between another document and this one.
- ☐ HREF indicates the URL of another document (as in the <A> tag).

The values of the REL and REV attributes are up to you and up to the tools that use them. The most common use of <LINK> currently is the following line, which indicates the author of the document:

```
<LINK REV="made" HREF="mailto:lemay@lne.com">
```

Some browsers (notably, Lynx) can use this line to send comments to the author of the file.

Another use of <LINK> is to create tool bars for common elements of documents, such as REL values of home, next, previous, TOC, index, glossary, and so on. By using <LINK> elements to refer to these, the browser or authoring tool can automatically generate tool bars or button bars in the window header or elsewhere that link to those documents.

A third method of using <LINK> is for a banner, such as with the <BANNER> element. In this case, REL=BANNER and HREF point to the banner file. Using LINK for the banner has the advantage of not needing to include the banner content in every file. By keeping it separate, you only have to edit it once.

Finally, there are style sheets. A proposed method of including style sheets with a document is to use <LINK REL=StyleSheet> to point to the style sheet for the current document. Alternatively, the <STYLE> element (which you'll also learn about in this chapter) is used for style sheet information as well.

<META>

The `<META>` tag is used to describe metainformation about the document—information about the document itself, for use by indexing or cataloguing programs, web robots, or other programs. To define metainformation, use the NAME attribute to indicate the type of information and the CONTENT attribute for its specifics, as in the following example:

```
<META NAME="Author" CONTENT="Laura Lemay">
<META NAME="Keys" CONTENT="plans, global, eggplant, explosives">
```

> **Note:** Don't use META to describe the parts of an HTML document that could better be described by other tags. For example, don't use META to give the document a title; that's what TITLE is for.

`<META>` can also be used to generate special HTTPD headers, to be sent by the server, that can activate special features in the client. In this instance, the attribute HTTP-EQUIV indicates the name of the header, and CONTENT indicates its contents. Here's an example:

```
<META HTTP-EQUIV="Expires"
      CONTENT="Wed, 31 May 1995 12:00:00 PST">
```

This line in an HTML document will generate the following header:

```
Expires: Wed, 31 May 1995 12:00:00 PST
```

Don't use META to replace headers that the server already generates (such as Content-type or Date) or you might confuse the server, the client, or both (most servers should ignore such headers in a META tag anyway).

<RANGE>

Range is used to mark a range of content within the document—for example, to tell a search program to search only a specific portion of the whole page. The `<RANGE>` tag has four attributes:

- ☐ ID identifies the range.
- ☐ CLASS indicates the type of range.
- ☐ FROM indicates the start of the range.
- ☐ TO indicates the end of the range.

The values of both FROM and TO are anchors as defined by ID attributes in the body of the document. You can also use the `<SPOT>` tag to create an anchor anywhere in the document, like this:

```
<SPOT ID="spot1">
```

With the spot defined, you can then use it to refer to the beginning or end of the range.

<STYLE>

The style tag is used to indicate style characteristics of the current document that override the global style sheet and any other styles mentioned in <LINK>. As I mentioned in the section on style sheets at the beginning of this chapter, style sheets are not a part of HTML 3.0, and as such are even less defined than is HTML 3.0, so this might change in the future. For now, the STYLE tag encloses various style definitions and has one attribute, NOTATION, to describe the kind of style format it uses (for example, dsssl-lite).

Summary

You have seen the future. This is HTML 3.0, which is what HTML will very soon become. After struggling with the limitations of HTML 2.0 in your Web design career, 3.0 should seem like a feast of features: text alignment, text flow alongside images and tables, figures, math, client-side image maps, support for style sheets for enhanced control over layout, as well as a wealth of other technical features such as the capability to use different languages and non-Western character sets (it is, after all, the *World* Wide Web).

But HTML 3.0 isn't here yet. Only a few features have leaked into existing browsers, with the rest still in discussion by the standards groups. But that will undoubtedly change, perhaps more rapidly now that work on HTML 2.0 is winding down. Stay tuned. There's more yet to come.

16

Q&A

Q **A lot of the language you're using to describe some of these elements is really vague. How can I get specifics on how to use the new elements?**

A A lot of my language is vague because the language in the specification is vague, and it's very likely that the specification is vague because extensive discussion has not yet happened for that specific part. Remember, this is a work in progress. Many parts of this chapter, or all of this chapter, could change extensively before HTML 3.0 is adopted as a standard. This is cutting-edge stuff. Stay tuned.

Q **How can I join in the discussions on HTML 3.0?**

A You can join the www-html mailing list by sending mail to listserv@w3.org. In the body of your message, include the line subscribe www-html yourname. Or you can use the form at http://www.w3.org/hypertext/WWW/Mailing/Form.html to subscribe. Note that www-html is a discussion group about the design of HTML, not a group for basic user questions.

A

Sources for Further Information

Haven't had enough yet? In this appendix you'll find the URLs for all kinds of information about the World Wide Web, HTML, developing Web presentations, and locations of tools to help you write HTML documents. With this list you should be able to find just about anything you need on the Web.

Note: Some of the URLs in this section refer to FTP sites. Some of these sites may be very busy during business hours, and you may not be able to immediately access the files. Try again during non-prime hours.

Also, some of these sites, for mysterious reasons, may be accessible through an FTP program, but not through Web browsers. If you are consistently getting refused from these sites using a browser, and you have access to an FTP program, try that program instead.

Collections of HTML and WWW Development Information

Yahoo's WWW Section
http://www.yahoo.com/Computers/World_Wide_Web/

The Virtual Library
http://WWW.Stars.com/

The HTML FAQ
http://www.umcc.umich.edu/~ec/www/html_faq.html

The Developer's JumpStation
http://oneworld.wa.com/htmldev/devpage/dev-page.html

The Repository
http://cbl.leeds.ac.uk/nikos/doc/repository.html

The Home of the WWW Consortium
http://www.w3.org/

Netscape's HTML Assistance Pages
http://home.mcom.com/assist/net_sites/index.html

The Spider's Web Pages on the Web

http://gagme.wwa.com/~boba/web.html

The HTML Writer's Guild

http://www.mindspring.com/guild/

WWW Indexes

Web Crawler

http://webcrawler.cs.washington.edu/WebCrawler/

Yahoo (my favorite index)

http://www.yahoo.com/

ALIWEB, a great Web index

http://web.nexor.co.uk/public/aliweb/aliweb.html

Lycos

http://lycos.cs.cmu.edu/

An Index of Indexes

http://www.biotech.washington.edu/WebCrawler/WebIndexes.html

Browsers

A general list

http://www.w3.org/hypertext/WWW/Clients.html

Netscape (X, Windows, Mac)

http://home.netscape.com/comprod/netscape_nav.html

NCSA Mosaic (X, Windows, Mac)

http://www.ncsa.uiuc.edu/SDG/Software/Mosaic/NCSAMosaicHome.html

Lynx (UNIX and DOS)

http://www.cc.ukans.edu/about_lynx/

WinWeb (Windows)

http://www.einet.net/EINet/WinWeb/WinWebHome.html

MacWeb (Macintosh)

http://www.einet.net/EINet/MacWeb/MacWebHome.html

Internet Explorer (Windows 95)

http://www.microsoft.com/Windows/ie/iexplorer.htm

Arena (X)

http://info.cern.ch/hypertext/WWW/Arena/

Emacs-W3 (for Emacs)

http://www.cs.indiana.edu/elisp/w3/docs.html

NetCruiser

http://www.netcom.com/netcom/cruiser.html

Web Explorer (OS/2 Warp)

ftp://ftp.ibm.net/pub/WebExplorer/

Cello (Windows)

http://www.law.cornell.edu/cello/cellofaq.html

Specifications for HTML, HTTP, and URLs

The HTML Level 2 specification

http://www.w3.org/hypertext/WWW/MarkUp/html-spec/index.html

The HTML+ 3.0 draft specification

http://www.hpl.hp.co.uk/people/dsr/html/CoverPage.html

The HTTP specification

http://info.cern.ch/hypertext/WWW/Protocols/HTTP/HTTP2.html

Netscape's Extensions (plus tables and backgrounds)

http://home.netscape.com/assist/net_sites/html_extensions.html

Mosaic Tables

http://www.ncsa.uiuc.edu/SDG/Software/XMosaic/table-spec.html

Pointers to URL, URN, and URI information and specifications

http://www.w3.org/hypertext/WWW/Addressing/Addressing.html

Tools and Information for Images

Frequently Asked Questions About JPEG

http://www.cis.ohio-state.edu/hypertext/faq/usenet/
jpeg-faq/faq.html

Yahoo's GIF List

`http://www.yahoo.com/Computers/Software/Data_Formats/GIF/`

A Good Summary about the GIF/CompuServe/Unisys Problem

`http://www.xmission.com/~mgm/gif/`

Frequently Asked Questions from `comp.graphics`

`http://www.primenet.com/~grieggs/cg_faq.html`

The Colorspace FAQ

`ftp://turing.imag.fr/pub/compression/colorspace-faq`

Very Technical Information About Gamma Levels and Color

`http://www.inforamp.net/~poynton/Poynton-colour.html`

Some Good Information about Transparent GIFs

`http://melmac.harris-atd.com/transparent_images.html`

giftrans

`ftp://ftp.rz.uni-karlsruhe.de/pub/net/www/tools/giftrans.c`

LView Pro for Windows (at the OAK Simtel Mirror)

`ftp://oak.oakland.edu/SimTel/win3/graphics/lviewp1a.zip`

Graphic Converter for Macintosh (at the HyperArchive sumex-aim Mirror)

`http://hyperarchive.lcs.mit.edu/HyperArchive/Archive/`
`grf/util/graphic-converter-212.hqx`

GIF Converter for Macintosh (at the HyperArchive sumex-aim Mirror)

`http://hyperarchive.lcs.mit.edu/HyperArchive/Archive/grf/`
`util/gif-converter-237.hqx`

Transparency (Macintosh)

`ftp:// med.cornell.edu/pub/aarong/transparency`
`http://hyperarchive.lcs.mit.edu/HyperArchive/Archive/grf/`
`util/transparency-10b4.hqx`

GIFTool (UNIX)

`http://www.homepages.com/tools/`

Sandra's Clip Art Server

`http://www.cs.yale.edu/IITML/YALE/CS/HyPlans/`
`loosemore-sandra/clipart.html`

Anthony's Icon Library

`http://www.galcit.caltech.edu/~ta/tgif/tgif.html`

Yahoo's Clip Art List

`http://www.yahoo.com/Computers/Multimedia/Pictures/Clip_Art/`

Yahoo's Icons List

http://www.yahoo.com/Computers/World_Wide_Web/Programming/Icons/

PNG (Portable Network Graphics) Specification

http://sunsite.unc.edu/boutell/png.html

Sound and Video

Audio Formats FAQ

http://www.cis.ohio-state.edu/hypertext/faq/usenet/
audio-fmts/top.html

Yahoo's Sound Information

http://akebono.stanford.edu/yahoo/Computers/Multimedia/Sound/

Alison Zhang's Multimedia File Formats on the Internet: Sound and Music

http://ac.dal.ca/~dong/music.htm

The Internet Underground Music Archive (IUMA)

http://www.iuma.com/

SOX (UNIX and DOS sound converter)

Http://www.spies.com/Sox/

WAVany (Windows sound converter)

ftp://oak.oakland.edu/SimTel/win3/sound/wvany10.zip

WHAM (Windows sound converter)

ftp://gatekeeper.dec.com/pub/micro/msdos/win3/
sounds/wham133.zip

CoolEdit, a Sound Editor for Windows

http://www.ep.se/cool/

Audio Applications (commercial, bundled, shareware) for SGI Systems

http://reality.sgi.com/employees/cook/audio.apps/

SoundHack (sound editor for Macintosh)

http://hyperarchive.lcs.mit.edu/HyperArchive/Archive/
snd/util/sound-hack-0743.hqx

Sound Machine (sound capture/converter/editor for Macintosh)

http://hyperarchive.lcs.mit.edu/HyperArchive/Archive/
snd/util/sound-machine-21.hqx

SoundAPP (Macintosh sound converter)

http://hyperarchive.lcs.mit.edu/HyperArchive/Archive/snd/util/sound-app-
151.hqx

Alison Zhang's Multimedia File Formats on the Internet: Movies

http://ac.dal.ca/~dong/movies.htm

FastPlayer (Macintosh QuickTime player and "flattener")

ftp://ftp.ncsa.uiuc.edu/Mosaic/Mac/Helpers/fast-player-110.hqx

QFlat (Windows QuickTime "flattener")

ftp://venice.tcp.com/pub/anime-manga/software/viewers/qtflat.zip

Sparkle (MPEG player and converter for Macintosh)

http://hyperarchive.lcs.mit.edu/HyperArchive/Archive/gst/
mov/sparkle-243a.hqx

XingCD (AVI to MPEG converter)

Send mail to xing@xingtech.com or call 805/473-0145

AVI-Quick (Macintosh converter for AVI to QuickTime)

http://hyperarchive.lcs.mit.edu/HyperArchive/Archive/gst/mov/avi-to-qt-
converter.hqx

SmartCap (Windows QuickTime and AVI Converter)

ftp://ftp.intel.com/pub/IAL/Indeo_video/smartc.exe

http://www.intel.com/product/tech-briefs/indeo.html

The MPEG FAQ

http://www.crs4.it/~luigi/MPEG/mpegfaq.html

QuickTime Information

http://quicktime.apple.com/

Yahoo's Movies Information

http://akebono.stanford.edu/yahoo/Computers/Multimedia/Movies/

Servers and Server Administration

CERN HTTPD

http://www.w3.org/httpd_3.0/

NCSA HTTPD

http://hoohoo.ncsa.uiuc.edu/docs/Overview.html

NCSA HTTPD for Windows

http://www.city.net/win-httpd/

MacHTTP

http://www.biap.com/

NCSA Server Includes

http://hoohoo.ncsa.uiuc.edu/docs/tutorials/includes.html

Current List of Official MIME Types

ftp://ftp.isi.edu/in-notes/iana/assignments/
media-types/media-types

Access Control in NCSA HTTPD

http://hoohoo.ncsa.uiuc.edu/docs/setup/access/Overview.html

http://hoohoo.ncsa.uiuc.edu/docs/tutorials/user.html

http://hoohoo.ncsa.uiuc.edu/docs/setup/admin/UserManagement.html

Access Control in CERN HTTPD

http://www.w3.org/hypertext/WWW/AccessAuthorization/
Overview.html

http://www.w3.org/hypertext/WWW/AccessAuthorization/
CERNServerNutShell.html

Avoiding Robots

http://web.nexor.co.uk/mak/doc/robots/norobots.html

Web Providers

An index from HyperNews

http://union.ncsa.uiuc.edu/HyperNews/get/www/leasing.html

The Common Gateway Interface (CGI) and CGI Scripting

Yahoo's CGI List

http://www.yahoo.com/Computers_and_Internet/Internet/World_Wide_Web/
CGI___Common_Gateway_Interface/

The original NCSA CGI documentation

http://hoohoo.ncsa.uiuc.edu/cgi/

The CGI Specification

http://hoohoo.ncsa.uiuc.edu/cgi/interface.html

Information about CGI in CERN HTTPD
`http://www.w3.org/hypertext/WWW/Daemon/User/CGI/Overview.html`

A library of C programs to help with CGI development
`http://wsk.eit.com/wsk/dist/doc/libcgi/libcgi.html`

An index to HTML-related programs written in Perl
`http://www.seas.upenn.edu/~mengwong/perlhtml.html`

An archive of CGI Programs at NCSA
`ftp://ftp.ncsa.uiuc.edu/Web/httpd/Unix/ncsa_httpd/cgi`

Un-CGI, a program to decode form input
`http://www.hyperion.com/~koreth/uncgi.html`

`cgi-lib.pl`, a Perl Library to Manage CGI and Forms
`http://www.bio.cam.ao.uk/wob/form.html`

Forms and Image Maps

The original NCSA forms documentation
`http://hoohoo.ncsa.uiuc.edu/cgi/forms.html`

Mosaic form support documenation
`http://www.ncsa.uiuc.edu/SDG/Software/Mosaic/Docs/fill-out-forms/`
`overview.html`

Image maps in CERN HTTPD
`http://www.w3.org/hypertext/WWW/Daemon/User/CGI/HTImageDoc.html`

Image maps in NCSA
`http://wintermute.ncsa.uiuc.edu:8080/map-tutorial/image-maps.html`

Some Perl scripts to manage forms
`http://www.bio.cam.ac.uk/web/form.html`

Mapedit: A tool for Windows and X11 for creating Imagemap map files
`http://sunsite.unc.edu/boutell/mapedit/mapedit.html`

WebMap (Macintosh map creator)
`http://hyperarchive.lcs.mit.edu/HyperArchive/Archive/text/html/web-map-`
`101.hqx`

HotSpots (a Windows image map tool)
`http://www.hooked.net/users/1auto`

HTML Validators, Link Checkers, and Simple Spiders

Yahoo's List of HTML Validation and HTML Checkers

http://www.yahoo.com/Computers/World_Wide_Web/HTML/
Validation_Checkers/

The Hal HTML Validator

http://www.halsoft.com/html-val-svc/

Weblint

http://www.unipress.com/weblint/

htmlchek

http://uts.cc.utexas.edu/~churchh/htmlchek.html

EIT's Verify Links

http://wsk.eit.com/wsk/dist/doc/admin/webtest/verify_links.html

lvrfy (link checker)

http://www.cs.dartmouth.edu/~crow/lvrfy.html

MOMSpider

http://www.ics.uci.edu/WebSoft/MOMspider/)

Yahoo's List of Web Spiders and Robots

http://www.yahoo.com/Reference/Searching_the_Web/Robots__Spiders__etc_/

Access Counters

Yahoo's List of Access Counters

http://www.yahoo.com/Computers/World_Wide_Web/Programming/
Access_Counts/

Access Counters Without Server Includes

ftp://128.172.69.103/Q800/Pub/WWW/cgis/counter.tar.Z

A Good Access Counters Tutorial

http://melmac.harris-atd.com/access_counts.html

Log File Parsers

Yahoo's List

http://www.yahoo.com/Computers/World_Wide_Web/HTTP/Servers/
Log_Analysis_Tools/

wusage

http://siva.cshl.org/wusage.html

getstats

http://www.eit.com/software/getstats/getstats.html

HTML Editors and Converters

A list of converters and editors, updated regularly

http://www.w3.org/hypertext/WWW/Tools/

A better list of converters

http://www.yahoo.com/Computers/World_Wide_Web/HTML_Converters/

A great list of editors

http://www.yahoo.com/Computers/World_Wide_Web/HTML_Editors/

The Future of HTML and the Web

Information About Arena (HTML 3.0 Browser)

http://www.w3.org/hypertext/WWW/Arena/

Style Sheets Overview

http://www.w3.org/hypertext/WWW/Style/

DSSL Specification (PostScript)

ftp://ftp.jclark.com/pub/dsssl/dsssl.ps.gz

DSSL-Lite Home Page (including the specification and archives of the discussion list)

http://www.falch.no/~pepper/DSSSL-Lite/

Jim Clark's DSSL Home Page

http://www.jclark.com/dsssl/

CSS Specification

http://www.w3.org/hypertext/WWW/Style/css/draft.html

Adobe Acrobat

http://www.adobe.com/Acrobat/Acrobat0.html

General Information About PDF

http://www.ep.cs.nott.ac.uk/~pns/pdfcorner/pdf.html

Netscape's Dynamic Documents (Client Pull and Server Push)

http://home.netscape.com/assist/net_sites/dynamic_docs.html

http://home.netscape.com/assist/net_sites/pushpull.html

Animate (tools for server push)

http://www.homepages.com/tools/

Java and HotJava

http://java.sun.com/

http://java.sun.com/documentation.html

VRML FAQ

http://www.oki.com/vrml/VRML_FAQ.html

VRML Home Site

http://vrml.wired.com/

Other VRML Information and Examples

http://www.well.com/user/caferace/vrml.html

http://www.utirc.utoronto.ca/AdTech/VRML/links.html

http://www.arc.org/vrml/

Web Security Overview

http://www.w3.org/hypertext/WWW/Security/Overview.html

Yahoo's List on Security, Encryption, and Authentication

http://www.yahoo.com/Science/Mathematics/
Security_and_Encryption/

SHTTP Information

http://www.eit.com/projects/s-http/

SSL Information

http://www.netscape.com/info/security-doc.html

Terisa

http://www.terisa.com/

Other

Tim Berners-Lee's style guide

http://www.w3.org/hypertext/WWW/Provider/Style/Overview.html

The Yale HyperText Style Guide

http://info.med.yale.edu/caim/StyleManual_Top.HTML

Some good information on registering and publicizing your Web page

http://www.cl.cam.ac.uk/users/gdr11/publish.html

B

An HTML Reference

This appendix is a reference to the HTML tags you can use in your documents, according to the HTML 2.0 Specification. Tags in common use that are either HTML 3.0 or Netscape extensions are noted as such. Note that some browsers other than Netscape may support the Netscape extensions.

 **Note:** A few of the tags in this section have not been described in the body of the book. If a tag is mentioned here that you haven't seen before, don't worry about it; that means that the tag is not in active use or is for use by HTML-generating and -reading tools, and not for general use in HTML documents.

HTML Tags

These tags are used to create a basic HTML page with text, headings, and lists.

Comments

<! ... >
Creates a comment.

Structure Tags

<HTML>...</HTML>
Encloses the entire HTML document.

Can Include: <HEAD> <BODY>

<HEAD>...</HEAD>
Encloses the head of the HTML document.

Can Include: <TITLE> <ISINDEX> <BASE> <NEXTID> <LINK> <META>

Allowed Inside: <HTML>

<BODY>...</BODY>

Encloses the body (text and tags) of the HTML document.

Attributes:

BACKGROUND="..." (HTML 3.0 only) The name or URL for an image to tile on the page background.

BGCOLOR="..." (Netscape 1.1) The color of the page background.

TEXT="..." (Netscape 1.1) The color of the page's text.

LINK="..." (Netscape 1.1) The color of unfollowed links.

ALINK="..." (Netscape 1.1) The color of activated links.

VLINK="..." (Netscape 1.1) The color of followed links.

Can Include: <H1> <H2> <H3> <H4> <H5> <H6> <P> <OL> <UL> <DIR> <MENU> <DL> <PRE> <BLOCKQUOTE> <FORM> <ISINDEX> <HR> <ADDRESS>

Allowed Inside: <HTML>

<BASE>

Indicates the full URL of the current document.

Attributes: HREF="..."; The full URL of this document.

Allowed Inside: <HEAD>

<ISINDEX>

Indicates that this document is a gateway script that allows searches.

Attributes:

PROMPT="..." (HTML 3.0) The prompt for the search field.

Allowed Inside: <BLOCKQUOTE> <BODY> <DD> <FORM> <HEAD> <LI>

<LINK>

Indicates a link between this document and some other document. Generally used only by HTML-generating tools. <LINK> represents document links to this one as a whole, as opposed to <A> which can create multiple links in the document. Not commonly used.

Attributes:

HREF="..." The URL of the document to be linked to this one.

NAME=... If the document is to be considered an anchor, the name of that anchor.

REL="..." The relationship between the linked-to document and the current document, for example, "TOC" or "Glossary."

REV="..." A reverse relationship between the current document and the linked-to document.

URN="..." A Uniform Resource Number (URN), a unique identifier different from the URL in HREF.

TITLE="..." The title of the linked-to document.

METHODS="..." The method with which the document is to be retrieved; for example, FTP, Gopher, and so on.

Allowed Inside: <HEAD>

<META>

Indicates metainformation about this document (information about the document itself); for example, keywords for search engines, special HTTP headers to be used for retrieveing this document, expiration date, and so on. Metainformation is usually in a key/value pair form.

Attributes:

HTTP-EQUIV="..." Creates a new HTTP header field with the same name as the attributes value, for example HTTP-EQUIV=Expires. The value of that header is specified by CONTENT.

NAME=... If meta data is usually in the form of key/value pairs, NAME indicates the key, for example, Author or ID.

CONTENT=... The content of the key/vaue pair (or of the HTTP header indicated by HTTP-EQUIV).

Allowed Inside: <HEAD>

<NEXTID>

Indicates the "next" document to this one (as might be defined by a tool to manage HTML documents in series). <NEXTID> is considered obsolete.

Headings and Title

All heading tags have the following characteristics:

Attributes:

`ALIGN=CENTER`: (HTML 3.0 only) Centers the heading.

Can Include: `<A>` `<IMG>` `<BR>` `<EM>` `<STRONG>` `<CODE>` `<SAMP>` `<KBD>` `<VAR>` `<CITE>` `<TT>` `<B>` `<I>`

Allowed Inside: `<BLOCKQUOTE>` `<BODY>` `<PRE>` `<ADDRESS>` `<FORM>` `<TH>` `<TD>`

<H1>...</H1>

A first-level heading.

<H2>...</H2>

A second-level heading.

<H3>...</H3>

A third-level heading.

<H4>...</H4>

A fourth-level heading.

<H5>...</H5>

A fifth-level heading.

<H6>...</H6>

A sixth-level heading.

<TITLE>...</TITLE>

Indicates the title of the document.

Allowed Inside: `<HEAD>`

Paragraphs

<P>...</P>

A plain paragraph. The closing tag (</P>) is optional.

Attributes:

ALIGN=CENTER (HTML 3.0 only) Centers the paragraph.

Can Include: <A> <IMG>
 <EM> <STRONG> <CODE> <SAMP> <KBD> <VAR> <CITE> <TT> <B> <I>

Allowed Inside: <BLOCKQUOTE> <BODY> <DD> <FORM> <LI>

Links

<A>...</A>

With the HREF attribute, creates a link to another document or anchor; with the NAME attribute, creates an anchor which can be linked to.

Attributes:

HREF="..." The URL of the document to be linked to this one.

NAME=... The name of the anchor.

REL="..." The relationship between the linked-to document and the current document, for example, "TOC" or "Glossary." Not commonly used.

REV="..." A reverse relationship between the current document and the linked-to document. Not commonly used.

URN="..." A Uniform Resource Number (URN), a unique identifier different from the URL in HREF. Not commonly used.

TITLE="..." The title of the linked-to document. Not commonly used.

METHODS="..." The method with which the document is to be retrieved; for example, FTP, Gopher, and so on. Not commonly used.

Can Include: <IMG>
 <EM> <STRONG> <CODE> <SAMP> <KBD> <VAR> <CITE> <TT> <B> <I>

Allowed Inside: <ADDRESS> <B> <CITE> <CODE> <DD> <DT> <EM> <H1> <H2> <H3> <H4> <H5> <H6> <I> <KBD> <LI> <P> <PRE> <SAMP> <STRONG> <TT> <VAR> <TH> TD>

Lists

<OL>...</OL>

An ordered (numbered) list.

Attributes:

TYPE="..." (Netscape only) The type of numerals to label the list with. Possible values are A, a, I, i, 1.

START="..." (Netscape) The value to start this list with.

Can Include: <LI>

Allowed Inside: <BLOCKQUOTE> <BODY> <DD> <FORM> <LI> <TH> TD>

<UL>...</UL>

An unordered (bulleted) list.

Attributes:

TYPE="..." (Netscape) The bullet dingbat to use to mark list items. Possible values are DISC, CIRCLE, SQUARE.

Can Include: <LI>

Allowed Inside: <BLOCKQUOTE> <BODY> <DD> <FORM> <LI> <TH> TD>

<MENU>...</MENU>

A menu list of items.

Can Include: <LI>

Allowed Inside: <BLOCKQUOTE> <BODY> <DD> <FORM> <LI> <TH> TD>

<DIR>...</DIR>

A directory listing; items are generally smaller than 20 characters.

Can Include: <LI>

Allowed Inside: <BLOCKQUOTE> <BODY> <DD> <FORM> <LI> <TH> TD>

<LI>

A list item for use with <OL>, <UL>, <MENU>, or <DIR>

Attributes:

TYPE="..." (Netscape) The type of bullet or number to label this item with. Possible values are DISC, CIRCLE, SQUARE, A, a, I, i, 1.

VALUE="..." (Netscape) The numeric value this list item should have (affects this item and all below it in <OL> lists).

Can Include: <A> <IMG>
 <EM> <STRONG> <CODE> <SAMP> <KBD> <VAR> <CITE> <TT> <B> <I> <P> <OL> <UL> <DIR> <MENU> <DL> <PRE> <BLOCKQUOTE>

Allowed Inside: <DIR> <MENU> <OL> <UL>

<DL>...</DL>

A definition or glossary list. The COMPACT attribute specifies a formatting that takes less whitespace to present.

Attributes: COMPACT

Can Include: <DT> <DD>

Allowed Inside: <BLOCKQUOTE> <BODY> <DD> <FORM> <LI> <TH> TD>

<DT>

A definition term, as part of a definition list.

Can Include: <A> <IMG>
 <EM> <STRONG> <CODE> <SAMP> <KBD> <VAR> <CITE> <TT> <B> <I>

Allowed Inside: <DL>

<DD>

The corresponding definition to a definition term, as part of a definition list.

Can Include: <A> <IMG>
 <EM> <STRONG> <CODE> <SAMP> <KBD> <VAR> <CITE> <TT> <B> <I> <P> <OL> <UL> <DIR> <MENU> <DL> <PRE> <BLOCKQUOTE> <FORM> <ISINDEX> <TABLE>

Allowed Inside: <DL>

Character Formatting

All the character formatting tags have these features:

Can Include: <A> <IMG>
 <EM> <STRONG> <CODE> <SAMP> <KBD> <VAR> <CITE> <TT> <B> <I>

Allowed Inside: <A> <ADDRESS> <B> <CITE> <CODE> <DD> <DT> <EM> <H1> <H2> <H3> <H4> <H5> <H6> <I> <KBD> <LI> <P> <PRE> <SAMP> <STRONG> <TT> <VAR> <TH> TD>

<EM>...</EM>

Emphasis (usually italic).

<STRONG>...</STRONG>

Stronger emphasis (usually bold).

<CODE>...</CODE>

Code sample (usually Courier).

<KBD>...</KBD>

Text to be typed (usually Courier).

<VAR>...</VAR>

A variable or placeholder for some other value.

<SAMP>...</SAMP>

Sample text.

<DFN>...<DFN>

(Proposed) A definition of a term.

<CITE>...</CITE>

A citation.

<B>...</B>

Boldface text.

<I>...</I>

Italic text.

<TT>...</TT>

Typewriter font.

Other Elements

<HR>

A horizontal rule line.

Attributes:

SIZE="..." (Netscape) The thickness of the rule, in pixels.

WIDTH="..." (Netscape) The width of the rule, in pixels.

ALIGN="..." (Netscape) How the rule line will be aligned on the page. Possible values are LEFT, RIGHT, CENTER.

NOSHADE="..." (Netscape) Causes the rule line to be drawn as a solid black.

Allowed Inside: <BLOCKQUOTE> <BODY> <FORM> <PRE>

*
*

A line break.

Attributes:

CLEAR="..." (HTML 3.0) Causes the text to stop flowing around any images. Possible values are RIGHT, LEFT, ALL.

Allowed Inside: <A> <ADDRESS> <B> <CITE> <CODE> <DD> <DT> <EM> <H1> <H2> <H3> <H4> <H5> <H6> <I> <KBD> <LI> <P> <PRE> <SAMP> <STRONG> <TT> <VAR>

<NOBR>...</NOBR> (Netscape)

Causes the enclosed text not to wrap at the edge of the page.

Allowed Inside: <A> <ADDRESS> <B> <CITE> <CODE> <DD> <DT> <EM> <H1> <H2> <H3> <H4> <H5> <H6> <I> <KBD> <LI> <P> <PRE> <SAMP> <STRONG> <TT> <VAR>

<WBR> (Netscape)

Wrap the text at this point only if necessary.

Allowed Inside: <A> <ADDRESS> <B> <CITE> <CODE> <DD> <DT> <EM> <H1> <H2> <H3> <H4> <H5> <H6> <I> <KBD> <LI> <P> <PRE> <SAMP> <STRONG> <TT> <VAR>

<BLOCKQUOTE>... </BLOCKQUOTE>

Used for long quotes or citations.

Can Include: <H1> <H2> <H3> <H4> <H5> <H6> <P> <OL> <UL> <DIR> <MENU> <DL> <PRE> <BLOCKQUOTE> <FORM> <ISINDEX> <HR> <ADDRESS> <TABLE>

Allowed Inside: <BLOCKQUOTE> <BODY> <DD> <FORM> <LI> <TH> TD>

<CENTER>...</CENTER>

All the content enclosed within these tags is centered.

Can Include: <A> <IMG>
 <EM> <STRONG> <CODE> <SAMP> <KBD> <VAR> <CITE> <TT> <B> <I>

Allowed Inside: <BLOCKQUOTE> <BODY> <DD> <FORM> <LI> <TH> TD>

<ADDRESS>...</ADDRESS>

Used for signatures or general information about a document's author.

Can Include: <A> <IMG>
 <EM> <STRONG> <CODE> <SAMP> <KBD> <VAR> <CITE> <TT> <B> <I>

Allowed Inside: <BLOCKQUOTE> <BODY> <FORM>

<BLINK>...</BLINK> (Netscape)

Causes the enclosed text to blink irritatingly.

Font Sizes (Netscape)

<FONT>...</FONT>

Changes the size of the font for the enclosed text.

Attributes:

SIZE="..." The size of the font, from 1 to 7. Default is 3. Can also be specified as a value relative to the current size, for example, +2.

Can Include: <A> <IMG>
 <EM> <STRONG> <CODE> <SAMP> <KBD> <VAR> <CITE> <TT> <B> <I>

Allowed Inside: <A> <ADDRESS> <B> <CITE> <CODE> <DD> <DT> <EM> <H1> <H2> <H3> <H4> <H5> <H6> <I> <KBD> <LI> <P> <PRE> <SAMP> <STRONG> <TT> <VAR>

<BASEFONT>

Sets the default size of the font for the current page.

Attributes:

SIZE="..." The default size of the font, from 1 to 7. Default is 3.

Allowed Inside: <A> <ADDRESS> <B> <CITE> <CODE> <DD> <DT> <EM> <H1> <H2> <H3> <H4> <H5> <H6> <I> <KBD> <LI> <P> <PRE> <SAMP> <STRONG> <TT> <VAR>

Images

<IMG>

Insert an inline image into the document.

Attributes:

ISMAP This image is a clickable image map.

SRC="..." The URL of the image.

ALT="..." A text string that will be displayed in browsers that cannot support images.

ALIGN="..." Determines the alignment of the given image. If LEFT or RIGHT (HTML 3.0, Netscape), the image is aligned to the left or right column, and all following text flows beside that image. All other values such as TOP, MIDDLE, BOTTOM, or the Netscape only

(TEXTTOP, ABSMIDDLE, BASELINE, ABSBOTTOM), determine the vertical alignment of this image with other items in the same line.

VSPACE="..." The space between the image and the text above or below it.

HSPACE="..." The space between the image and the text to its left or right.

WIDTH="..." (HTML 3.0) The width, in pixels, of the image. If WIDTH is not the actual width, the image is scaled to fit.

HEIGHT="..." (HTML 3.0) The width, in pixels, of the image. If HEIGHT is not the actual height, the image is scaled to fit.

BORDER="..." (Netscape only) Draws a border of the specified value in pixels to be drawn around the image. In the case of images that are also links, BORDER changes the size of the default link border.

LOW3RC-"..." (Netscape only) The path or URL of an image that will be loaded first, before the image specified in SRC. The value of LOWSRC is usually a smaller or lower resolution version of the actual image.

Allowed Inside: <A> <ADDRESS> <B> <CITE> <CODE> <DD> <DT> <EM> <H1> <H2> <H3> <H4> <H5> <H6> <I> <KBD> <LI> <P> <SAMP> <STRONG> <TT> <VAR>

Forms

<FORM>...</FORM>

Indicates a form.

Attributes:

ACTION="..." The URL of the script to process this form input.

METHOD="..." How the form input will be sent to the gateway on the server side. Possible values are GET and POST.

ENCTYPE="..." Only one value right now: application/x-www-form-urlencoded.

Can Include: <H1> <H2> <H3> <H4> <H5> <H6> <P> <OL> <UL> <DIR> <MENU> <DL> <PRE> <BLOCKQUOTE> <ISINDEX> <TABLE> <HR> <ADDRESS> <INPUT> <SELECT> <TEXTAREA>

Allowed Inside: <BLOCKQUOTE> <BODY> <DD> <LI> <TH> <TD>

<INPUT>
An input widget for a form.

Attributes:

TYPE="..." The type for this input widget. Possible values are CHECKBOX, HIDDEN, RADIO, RESET, SUBMIT, TEXT, or IMAGE.

NAME="..." The name of this item, as passed to the gateway script as part of a name/value pair.

VALUE="..." For a text or hidden widget, the default value; for a check box or radio button, the value to be submitted with the form; for Reset or Submit buttons, the label for the button itself.

SRC="..." The source file for an image.

CHECKED For checkboxes and radio buttons, indicates that the widget is checked.

SIZE="..." The size, in characters, of a text widget.

MAXLENGTH="..." The maximum number of characters that can be entered into a text widget.

ALIGN="..." For images in forms, determines how the text and image will align (same as with the <IMG> tag).

Allowed Inside: <FORM>

<TEXTAREA>...</TEXTAREA>
Indicates a multiline text entry widget.

Attributes:

NAME="..." The name to be passed to the gateway script as part of the name/value pair.

ROWS="..." The number of rows this text area displays.

COLS="..." The number of columns (characters) this text area displays.

Allowed inside: <FORM>

<SELECT>...</SELECT>
Creates a menu or scrolling list of possible items.

Attributes:

NAME="..." The name that is passed to the gateway script as part of the name/value pair.

SIZE="..." The number of elements to display. If SIZE is indicated, the selection becomes a scrolling list. If no SIZE is given, the selection is a pop-up menu.

MULTIPLE Allows multiple selections from the list.

Can Include: <OPTION>

Allowed Inside: <FORM>

<OPTION>

Indicates a possible item within a <SELECT> widget.

Attributes:

SELECTED With this attribute included, the <OPTION> will be selected by default in the list.

VALUE="..." The value to submit if this <OPTION> is selected when the form is submitted.

Allowed Inside: <SELECT>

<FRAMESET>...<FRAMESET> (Netscape 2.0 and up)

The main container for a frame document.

Attributes:

COLS="column_width_list" The size of the frame's columns in pixels, percentages, or relative scale.

ROWS="row_height_list" The size of the frame's rows in pixels, percentages, or relative scale.

<FRAMES> (Netscape 2.0 and up)

Attributes:

MARGINHEIGHT="value" The height of the frame, in pixels.

MARGINWIDTH="value" The width of the frame, in pixels.

NAME="window_name" Naming the frame enables it for targeting by link in other documents. (Optional)

NORESIZE A flag to denote the frame cannot be resized.

SCROLLING="yes¦no¦auto" Indicates (*yes/no/auto*) whether a frame has scrollbars.

SRC The URL of the document displayed in the frame.

<NOFRAMES>...<NOFRAMES> (Netscape 2.0 and up)

Creates frames that can be viewed by non-frame browsers only. A frames-capable browser ignores the data between the start and end <NOFRAMES> tags.

Tables (HTML 3.0)

<TABLE>...</TABLE>

Creates a table, which can contain a caption (<CAPTION>) and any number of rows (<TR>).

Attributes:

BORDER="..." Indicates whether the table should be drawn with or without a border. In Netscape, BORDER can also have a value indicating the width of the border.

CELLSPACING="..." (Netscape only) The amount of space between the cells in the table.

CELLPADDING="..." (Netscape only) The amount of space between the edges of the cell and its contents.

WIDTH="..." (Netscape only) The width of the table on the page, in either exact pixel values or as a percentage of page width.

Can Include: <CAPTION> <TR>

Allowed Inside: <BLOCKQUOTE> <BODY> <DD> <LI> <FORM>

<CAPTION>...</CAPTION>

The caption for the table.

Attributes:

ALIGN="..." The position of the caption. Possible values are TOP and BOTTOM.

<TR>...</TR>

Defines a table row, containing headings and data (<TR> and <TH> tags).

Attributes:

ALIGN="..." The horizontal alignment of the contents of the cells within this row. Possible values are LEFT, RIGHT, CENTER.

VALIGN="..." The vertical alignment of the contents of the cells within this row. Possible values are TOP, MIDDLE, BOTTOM, and BASELINE (Netscape only).

Can Include: <TH> <TD>

Allowed Inside: <TABLE>

<TH>...</TH>

Defines a table heading cell.

Attributes:

ALIGN="..." The horizontal alignment of the contents of the cell. Possible values are LEFT, RIGHT, CENTER.

VALIGN="..." The vertical alignment of the contents of the cell. Possible values are TOP, MIDDLE, BOTTOM, and BASELINE (Netscape only).

ROWSPAN="..." The number of rows this cell will span.

COLSPAN="..." The number of columns this cell will span.

NOWRAP Do not automatically wrap the contents of this cell.

WIDTH="..." (Netscape only) The width of this column of cells, in exact pixel values or as a percentage of the table width.

Can Include: <H1> <H2> <H3> <H4> <H5> <H6> <P> <OL> <UL> <DIR> <MENU> <DL> <PRE> <BLOCKQUOTE> <FORM> <ISINDEX> <HR> <ADDRESS> <TABLE>

Allowed Inside: <TR>

<TD>...</TD>

Defines a table data cell.

Attributes:

ALIGN="..." The horizontal alignment of the contents of the cell. Possible values are LEFT, RIGHT, CENTER.

VALIGN="..." The vertical alignment of the contents of the cell. Possible values are TOP, MIDDLE, BOTTOM, and BASELINE (Netscape only).

ROWSPAN="..." The number of rows this cell will span.

COLSPAN="..." The number of columns this cell will span.

NOWRAP Do not automatically wrap the contents of this cell.

WIDTH="..." (Netscape only) The width of this column of cells, in exact pixel values or as a percentage of the table width.

Can Include: <H1> <H2> <H3> <H4> <H5> <H6> <P> <OL> <UL> <DIR> <MENU> <DL> <PRE> <BLOCKQUOTE> <FORM> <ISINDEX> <HR> <ADDRESS> <TABLE>

Allowed Inside: <TR>

Internet Explorer 2.0 Tags

<BODY>

You can add BGPROPERTIES=FIXED to the <BODY> tag to get a nonscrolling background. <BODY BACKGROUND="*mybackground.gif*" BGPROPERTIES=FIXED>

<TABLE>

Internet Explorer 2.0 fully supports tables as specified in the HTML 3.0 draft standard. Using the ALIGN=RIGHT or ALIGN=LEFT attributes, you can set the alignment of your tables. Using the BGCOLOR=#*nnnnnn* attribute, you can specify a different color for each cell in a table.

<IMG>

You can add video clips (.AVI files) to your pages with a string of new attributes to the <IMG> tag, most notably the dynamic source feature, DYNSRC=*URL*. You can integrate video clips in such a way as to not exclude viewers without video-enabled browsers. If your browser supports inline clips, you see the video; if not, you see a still image.<IMG SRC="earth.gif" DYNSRC="spinearht.avi">

You can use START=FILEOPEN or START=MOUSEOVER and a variety of LOOP commands to gauge when and for how long the clip is played.

<BGSOUND>

You can now use soundtracks for your web pages. Samples or MIDI formats are accepted.

`<BGSOUND SRC="whistle.wav">`

You can use LOOP features to specify the repetition of the background sound.

<MARQUEE>

As you might guess, this new tag offers your pages a scrolling text marquee. Your text can appear using different attributes, such as ALIGN=RIGHT and can have behaviors of SLIDE, SCROLL (the default), and ALTERNATE.`<MARQUEE ALIGN=MIDDLE>Buy Low, Sell High!<MARQUEE>`

Character Entities

Table B.1 contains the possible numeric and character entities for the ISO-Latin-1 (ISO8859-1) character set. Where possible, the character is shown.

Note: Not all browsers can display all characters, and some browsers may even display different characters from those that appear in the table. Newer browsers seem to have a better track record for handling character entities, but be sure and test your HTML files extensively with multiple browsers if you intend to use these entities.

Table B.1. ISO-Latin-1 character set.

Character	Numeric Entity	Character Entity (if any)	Description
	&#00;–&#08;		Unused
	&#09;		Horizontal tab
	&#10;		Line feed
	&#11;–&#31;		Unused
	&#32;		Space
!	&#33;		Exclamation mark

continues

Table B.1. continued

Character	Numeric Entity	Character Entity (if any)	Description
"	&#34;	&quot;	Quotation mark
#	&#35;		Number sign
$	&#36;		Dollar sign
%	&#37;		Percent sign
&	&#38;	&amp;	Ampersand
'	&#39;		Apostrophe
(	&#40;		Left parenthesis
)	&#41;		Right parenthesis
*	&#42;		Asterisk
+	&#43;		Plus sign
,	&#44;		Comma
-	&#45;		Hyphen
.	&#46;		Period (fullstop)
/	&#47;		Solidus (slash)
0–9	0–9		Digits 0–9
:	&#58;		Colon
;	&#59;		Semi-colon
<	&#60;	&lt;	Less than
=	&#61;		Equals sign
>	&#62;	&gt;	Greater than
?	&#63;		Question mark
@	&#64;		Commercial at
A–Z	A–Z		Letters A–Z
[	&#91;		Left square bracket
\	&#92;		Reverse solidus (backslash)
]	&#93;		Right square bracket
^	&#94;		Caret
—	&#95;		Horizontal bar

Character	Numeric Entity	Character Entity (if any)	Description
`	&#96;		Grave accent
a–z	a–z		Letters a–z
{	&#123;		Left curly brace
|	&#124		Vertical bar
}	&#125;		Right curly brace
~	&#126;		Tilde
	&#127;–		Unused
¡	&#161;		Inverted exclamation
¢	&#162;		Cent sign
£	&#163;		Pound sterling
¤	&#164;		General currency sign
¥	&#165;		Yen sign
¦	&#166;		Broken vertical bar
§	&#167;		Section sign
¨	&#168;		Umlaut (dieresis)
©	&#169;		Copyright
ª	&#170;		Feminine ordinal
‹	&#171;		Left angle quote, guillemet left
¬	&#172;		Not sign
-	&#173;		Soft hyphen
®	&#174;		Registered trademark
¯	&#175;		Macron accent
°	&#176;		Degree sign
±	&#177;		Plus or minus
²	&#178;		Superscript two
³	&#179;		Superscript three
´	&#180;		Acute accent
µ	&#181;		Micro sign

B

continues

Table B.1. continued

Character	Numeric Entity	Character Entity (if any)	Description
¶	&#182;		Paragraph sign
·	&#183;		Middle dot
¸	&#184;		Cedilla
¹	&#185;		Superscript one
º	&#186;		Masculine ordinal
›	&#187;		Right angle quote, guillemet right
1/4	&#188;		Fraction one-fourth
1/2	&#189;		Fraction one-half
3/4	&#190;		Fraction three-fourths
¿	&#191;		Inverted question mark
À	&#192;	&Agrave;	Capital A, grave accent
Á	&#193;	&Aacute;	Capital A, acute accent
Â	&#194;	&Acirc;	Capital A, circumflex accent
Ã	&#195;	&Atilde;	Capital A, tilde
Ä	&#196;	&Auml;	Capital A, dieresis or umlaut mark
Å	&#197;	&Aring;	Capital A, ring
Æ	&#198;	&AElig;	Capital AE dipthong (ligature)
Ç	&#199;	&Ccedil;	Capital C, cedilla
È	&#200;	&Egrave;	Capital E, grave accent
É	&#201;	&Eacute;	Capital E, acute accent
Ê	&#202;	&Ecirc;	Capital E, circumflex accent

Character	Numeric Entity	Character Entity (if any)	Description
Ë	&#203;	&Euml;	Capital E, dieresis or umlaut mark
Ì	&#204;	&Igrave;	Capital I, grave accent
Í	&#205;	&Iacute;	Capital I, acute accent
Î	&#206;	&Icirc;	Capital I, circumflex accent
Ï	&#207;	&Iuml;	Capital I, dieresis or umlaut mark
Ð	&#208;	&ETH;	Capital Eth, Icelandic
Ñ	&#209;	&Ntilde;	Capital N, tilde
Ò	&#210;	&Ograve;	Capital O, grave accent
Ó	&#211;	&Oacute;	Capital O, acute accent
Ô	&#212;	&Ocirc;	Capital O, circumflex accent
Õ	&#213;	&Otilde;	Capital O, tilde
Ö	&#214;	&Ouml;	Capital O, dieresis or umlaut mark
×	&#215;		Multiply sign
Ø	&#216;	&Oslash;	Capital O, slash
Ù	&#217;	&Ugrave;	Capital U, grave accent
Ú	&#218;	&Uacute;	Capital U, acute accent
Û	&#219;	&Ucirc;	Capital U, circumflex accent
Ü	&#220;	&Uuml;	Capital U, dieresis or umlaut mark
Ý	&#221;	&Yacute;	Capital Y, acute accent
Þ	&#222;	&THORN;	Capital THORN, Icelandic

Table B.1. continued

Character	Numeric Entity	Character Entity (if any)	Description
β	&#223;	&szlig;	Small sharp s, German (sz ligature)
à	&#224;	&agrave;	Small a, grave accent
á	&#225;	&aacute;	Small a, acute accent
â	&#226;	&acirc;	Small a, circumflex accent
ã	&#227;	&atilde;	Small a, tilde
ä	&#228;	&aauml;	Small a, dieresis or umlaut mark
å	&#229;	&aring;	Small a, ring
æ	&#230;	&aelig;	Small ae dipthong (ligature)
ç	&#231;	&ccedil;	Small c, cedilla
è	&#232;	&egrave;	Small e, grave accent
é	&#233;	&eacute;	Small e, acute accent
ê	&#234;	&ecirc;	Small e, circumflex accent
ë	&#235;	&euml;	Small e, dieresis or umlaut mark
ì	&#236;	&igrave;	Small i, grave accent
í	&#237;	&iacute;	Small i, acute accent
î	&#238;	&icirc;	Small i, circumflex accent
ï	&#239;	&iuml;	Small i, dieresis or umlaut mark
ð	&#240;	&eth;	Small eth, Icelandic
ñ	&#241;	&ntilde;	Small n, tilde
ò	&#242;	&ograve;	Small o, grave accent
ó	&#243;	&oacute;	Small o, acute accent
ô	&#244;	&ocirc;	Small o, circumflex

Character	Numeric Entity	Character Entity (if any)	Description
			accent
õ	&#245;	&otilde;	Small o, tilde
ö	&#246;	&ouml;	Small o, dieresis or umlaut mark
÷	&#247;		Division sign
ø	&#248;	&oslash;	Small o, slash
ù	&#249;	&ugrave;	Small u, grave accent
ú	&#250;	&uacute;	Small u, acute accent
û	&#251;	&ucirc;	Small u, circumflex accent
ü	&#252;	&uuml;	Small u, dieresis or umlaut mark
ý	&#253;	&yacute;	Small y, acute accent
þ	&#254;	&thorn;	Small thorn, Icelandic
ÿ	&#255;	&yuml;	Small y, dieresis or umlaut mark

B

C

MIME Types

MIME Types

Table C.1 lists the MIME types supported by either CERN or NCSA. If your server does not list an extension for a particular MIME type or if the MIME type you want to use is not listed at all, you will have to add support for that type to your server configuration. See Chapter 18, for more details.

Table C.1. MIME types and HTTPD support.

MIME Type	What It Is (If Noted)	File Extensions (NCSA)	File Extensions (CERN)
application/acad	AutoCAD Drawing files		dwg, DWG
application/clariscad	ClarisCAD files		CCAD
application/drafting	MATRA Prelude drafting		DRW
application/dxf	DXF (AutoCAD)		dxf, DXF
application/i-deas	SDRC I-DEAS files		unv, UNV
application/iges	IGES graphics format		igs, iges, IGS, IGES
application/octet-stream	Uninterpreted binary	bin	bin
application/oda		oda	oda
application/pdf	PDF (Adobe Acrobat)	pdf	pdf
application/postscript	PostScript, Encapsulated PostScript, Adobe Illustrator		ai, PS, ps, eps
application/pro_eng	PTC Pro/ENGINEER part		prt, PRT
application/rtf	Rich Text Format	rtf	rtf
application/set	SET (French CAD standard)		set, SET
application/sla	Stereolithography		stl, STL
application/solids	MATRA Prelude Solids		SOL
application/STEP	ISO-10303 STEP data files		stp, STP, step, STEP
application/vda	VDA-FS Surface data		vda, VDA
application/x-mif	FrameMaker MIF Format	mif	

MIME Type	What It Is (If Noted)	File Extensions (NCSA)	File Extensions (CERN)
application/x-csh	C-shell script	csh	csh
application/x-dvi	TeX dvi	dvi	dvi
application/x-hdf	NCSA HDF Data File	hdf	hdf
application/x-latex	LaTeX source	latex	latex
application/x-netcdf	Unidata netCDF	nc, cdf	nc,cdf
application/x-sh	Bourne shell script	sh	sh
application/x-tcl	TCL script	tcl	tcl
application/x-tex	TeX source	tex	tex
application/x-texinfo	Texinfo (emacs)	texinfo, texi	texinfo, texi
application/x-troff	troff	t, tr, roff	t, tr, roff
application/x-troff-man	troff with MAN macros	man	man
application/x-troff-me	troff with ME macros	me	me
application/x-troff-ms	troff with MS macros	ms	ms
application/x-wais-source	WAIS source	src	src
application/zip	ZIP archive	zip	
application/x-bcpio	Old binary CPIO	bcpio	bcpio
application/x-cpio	POSIX CPIO	cpio	cpio
application/x-gtar	GNU tar	gtar	gtar
application/x-shar	Shell archive	shar	shar
application/x-sv4cpio	SVR4 CPIO	sv4cpio	sv4cpio
application/x-sv4crc	SVR4 CPIO with CRC	sv4crc	sv4crc
application/x-tar	4.3BSD tar format	tar	tar
application/x-ustar	POSIX tar format	ustar	ustar
audio/basic	Basic audio (usually μ-law)	au, snd	au, snd
audio/x-aiff	AIFF audio	aif, aiff, aifc	aif, aiff, aifc
audio/x-wav	Windows WAVE audio	wav	wav
image/gif	GIF image	gif	gif

continues

C

Table C.1. continued

MIME Type	What It Is (If Noted)	File Extensions (NCSA)	File Extensions (CERN)
`image/ief`	Image Exchange Format	`ief`	`ief`
`image/jpeg`	JPEG image	`jpeg, jpg, jpe`	`jpg, JPG, JPE, jpe, JPEG, jpeg`
`image/tiff`	TIFF image	`tiff, tif`	`tiff, tif`
`image/x-cmu-raster`	CMU raster	`ras`	`ras`
`image/x-portable-anymap`	PBM Anymap format	`pnm`	`pnm`
`image/x-portable-bitmap`	PBM Bitmap format	`pbm`	`pbm`
`image/x-portable-graymap`	PBM Graymap format	`pgm`	`pgm`
`image/x-portable-pixmap`	PBM Pixmap format	`ppm`	`ppm`
`image/x-rgb`	RGB Image	`rgb`	`rgb`
`image/x-xbitmap`	X Bitmap	`xbm`	`xbm`
`image/x-xpixmap`	X Pixmap	`xpm`	`xpm`
`image/x-xwindowdump`	X Windows dump (xwd) format	`xwd`	`xwd`
`multipart/x-zip`	PKZIP Archive		`zip`
`multipart/x-gzip`	GNU ZIP Archive		`gzip`
`text/html`	HTML	`html`	`html, htm`
`text/plain`	Plain text	`txt`	`txt, g, h, C, cc, hh, m, f90`
`text/richtext`	MIME Richtext	`rtx`	`rtx`
`text/tab-separated-values`	Text with tab separated values	`tsv`	`tsv`
`text/x-setext`	Struct enhanced text	`etx`	`etx`
`video/mpeg`	MPEG video	`mpeg, mpg, mpe`	`MPG, mpg, MPE, mpe, MPEG, mpeg`
`video/quicktime`	QuickTime Video	`qt, mov`	`qt, mov`
`video/x-msvideo`	Microsoft Windows Video	`avi`	`avi`
`video/x-sgi-movie`	SGI movieplayer format	`movie`	`movie`

INDEX

home pages

Sams
Learning
Center

SAMS
PUBLISHING

HTML 3

Sams
Learning
Center

SAMS
PUBLISHING

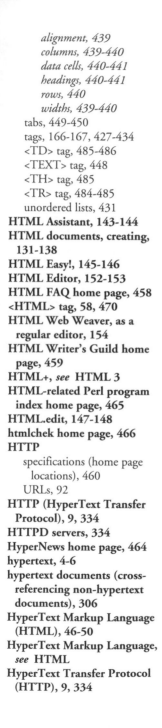

WinHTTPD for Windows (CGI scripts)

Add to Your Sams.net Library Today with the Best Books About the Internet and its New Technologies

ISBN	Quantity	Description of Item	Unit Cost	Total Cost
1-57521-040-1		World Wide Web Unleashed 1996	$49.99	
1-57521-041-X		The Internet Unleashed 1996	$49.99	
0-672-30745-6		HTML and CGI Unleashed	$39.99	
1-57521-039-8		Presenting Java	$19.99	
0-672-30735-9		Teach Yourself the Internet in a Week, Second Edition	$25.00	
1-57521-004-5		The Internet Business Guide, Second Edition	$25.00	
0-672-30595-X		Education on the Internet	$25.00	
0-672-30718-9		Navigating the Internet, Third Edition	$22.50	
1-57521-005-3		Teach Yourself More Web Publishing with HTML in a Week	$29.99	
0-672-30764-2		Teach Yourself Web Publishing with Microsoft Word in a Week	$29.99	
0-672-30669-7		Plug-n-Play Internet for Windows	$35.00	
1-57521-010-X		Plug-n-Play Netscape for Windows	$29.99	
0-672-30723-5		Secrets of the MUD Wizards	$25.00	
		Shipping and Handling: See information below.		
		TOTAL		

Shipping and Handling: $4.00 for the first book, and $1.75 for each additional book. Floppy disk: add $1.75 for shipping and handling. If you need to have it NOW, we can ship product to you in 24 hours for an additional charge of approximately $18.00, and you will receive your item overnight or in two days. Overseas shipping and handling adds $2.00 per book and $8.00 for up to three disks. Prices subject to change. Call for availability and pricing information on latest editions.

201 W. 103rd Street, Indianapolis, Indiana 46290

1-800-428-5331 — Orders   1-800-835-3202 — FAX   1-800-858-7674 — Customer Service

Book ISBN 1-57521-064-9